SIMPLY PUT

The Plain English Grammar Guide

GIACOMO GIAMMATTEO

Inferno Publishing Company

Inferno Publishing Company

Houston, TX

For more information about this book visit my website.

Edition ISBNs

Trade Paperback 978-1-949074-91-8

E-book 978-1-949074-90-1

Cover design by Natasha Brown

Book design by Giacomo Giammatteo

This edition was prepared by Giacomo Giammatteo gg@giacomog.com

❀ Created with Vellum

INTRODUCTION

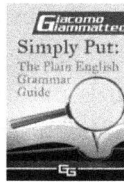

Does the world need another grammar book? *I* think so. And it needs one because existing books are filled with explanations using grammatical terms that many people don't understand, and the people who do understand don't need the book.

The way most grammar books are written, the only people who can understand them, don't need them, and the people who need them can't understand them.

Grammar has its own language, so to speak, but so do most specialties. Consider a couple of made-up paragraphs relating to a bricklayer and a blackjack dealer.

Anyone in these professions would have no problem understanding what's being said, but unless someone is familiar with the terminology, I'm betting they would have a problem.

Bricklaying

The bricklayer grabbed his trowel and slapped some mud on the next course. He was halfway through when the twig snapped and the line pin fell out of the joint, taking the line down with it.

As he reached to pick up the line, he felt a few drops of rain. *Shit! Guess I'm gonna have to strike-up and quit.*

And that's just what he did. He reached into the tool bag, yanked out a runner and a striker, then quickly struck the joints.

"Better hurry," the foreman said. "We've still got to parge the back wall."

Blackjack

The dealer took his hand off the shoe and slid some chips to player four—he'd made a call bet for $5,000, but as big a whale as player four was, the dealer knew he'd have that back before long, probably with a few tokes to boot. Besides, the dealer knew the guy had a marker of $25,000.

The dealer slid the first cards out of the shoe but kept a careful watch on the anchorman. He'd been sending odd signals to the first baseman, and the dealer didn't like it.

Like all my grammar books, I have done everything possible to explain things clearly *without* resorting to grammatical terms or complex explanations.

In this book, things are explained using examples and plain English. The book covers a lot of ground, including misused words, capitalization, acronyms and initializations, plurals, redundancies, dialogue, and punctuation. It also includes several sections geared toward professional writers.

You'll also find a chapter dealing with common grammar myths —the ones people love to correct even though they're not wrong.

Note: Throughout the book, I have cited definitions and explanations regarding usage based on the *Chicago Manual of Style* (CMOS), *AP Stylebook* (Associated Press), and an assortment of dictionaries. Often, for whatever reason, the citations are missing punctuation, such as a missing space or missing terminal punctuation: period, question mark, etc.

In all cases, I have left the citation as in the original and did not address these issues.

By the way, throughout the book I use "different than" as opposed to "different from." I do this because I like it.

When citing a comparative, I think *than* works better. Besides, most dictionaries and style guides have acknowledged that using *than* following *different* is not such a grievous sin.

Also, as in all my nonfiction books, I use 🐗 as a symbol for a tip or a way to remember how to tell the difference between words.

🐗 (Dennis) is my pet wild boar. We rescued him when he was only a few days old, and he's been with us for ten years. Of course, he's a little bigger, weighing in at four hundred pounds.

When we first got him, he was twelve pounds. In any case, I use an image of a wild boar to draw attention to a particular section/tip. I hope it helps you remember things.

Style Guides

Before we get into the details, let's discuss one thing: style guides. I'll talk many times about CMOS (*Chicago Manual of Style*) or *AP Stylebook* (Associated Press), and though they are both well-established and influential, they differ in many areas.

CMOS is used primarily by writers of books (especially novels), and AP is the recommended source for journalists. They agree on most topics, but differ on some of the finer points: how to abbreviate states, whether to use periods with D.C. and others, the use of serial commas, the use of apostrophes with words ending in *s,* how to hyphenate many words, whether to put spaces before and after dashes, and whether to use italics or quotations for some works of art.

That may sound as if it encompasses a lot of differences, but when you consider the number of items those style guides cover, it's not much.

But as you'll hear me say numerous times, select a style guide and a dictionary and stick with it.

PARTS OF SPEECH AND HOW TO USE THEM

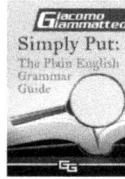

There are eight parts of speech, and I'm guessing you're familiar with most of them. Some people claim there are nine while others claim there are more (or less), but CMOS (*The Chicago Manual of Style*) recognizes eight, so for the purposes of this book, we'll stick with that.

Parts of Speech		
adjectives	adverbs	articles and determiners*
conjunctions	interjections	nouns
prepositions	pronouns	verbs

In the image above (or on the previous page), the asterisk following "articles and determiners" is used because "articles and determiners" is not one of the parts of speech recognized by CMOS. Technically, *articles* are adjectives with a specific purpose.

We'll cover them separately because they are important for good communicating.

Now let's look at each part of speech in more detail.

Chapter One

ARTICLES AND DETERMINERS

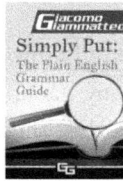

*A*rticles and Determiners

There are three articles: *a, an,* and *the.* You can read more on usage practices in the chapter entitled "Misused Words." That entry is the first in the list.

Articles are the simplest determiners, and they are broken down into two groups: indefinite (*a, an*) and definite (*the*). *A* and *an* are used with count nouns, while *the* can be used with either count nouns or uncountable nouns. Examples follow:

- *An* apple *a* day is good for you.
- *The* wine hasn't been opened.
- *A* basket of fruit is on *the* porch.
- *The* butter is on *the* shelf.

I said *a* and *an* are used with count nouns, but I can think of one scenario where they could be used with uncountable nouns. When referring to something you might consume, like ordering wine at a restaurant or asking for a beer or glass of water, you might refer to it in the following manner:

- I'll have a beer (meaning "bottle, can, or glass of beer").
- I'll have what he ordered: a red wine (meaning "glass of wine").
- May I please have a Coke?

As far as determiners go, let's look at what *Merriam-Webster's* has to say:

---

a word belonging to a group of limiting noun modifiers that in English consists of a, an, any, each, either, every, neither, no, one, some, the, that, those, this, these, what, whatever, which, whichever, possessive adjectives (as my), and possessive-case forms (as Joe's) and is characterized by occurrence before descriptive adjectives modifying the same noun (as that in "that big yellow house" or his in "his new car")

— MERRIAM-WEBSTER'S

Below is a table showing the primary determiners. In the text that follows the table, the determiners are in italics.

a	An	any
each	either	every
neither	many	no
one	some	that
the	these	this
those	what	whatever
which	whichever	

- I want *the* apple on *the* counter.
- No, not *that* one, *the* other one.
- *Those* are *the* grapes I want.

You'll notice in *Merriam-Webster's* definition, they list "possessive adjectives" (and others) as belonging to this group. Let's look at how they function.

A possessive determiner, according to *OED* (*Oxford English Dictionary*) is:

Possessive determiners [adjectives]

Words like *my, our, your, his, her, its,* and *their* are known as possessive determiners [or possessive adjectives]. They come before nouns and indicate ownership of the noun in question, as their name suggests:

— OED

- *My* car was stolen.
- *Her* leg broke while climbing rocks.
- The party is for everyone; bring *your* kids.
- *Our* kids love to swim.

Don't confuse these with possessive pronouns. Although some sites will list them as "possessive pronouns," most will call them "possessive adjectives" or "possessive determiners." The difference is that possessive determiners *precede* the noun (they own it), while possessive pronouns *replace* the noun.

In the following sentences, the possessive determiners are in *italics*, and the possessive pronouns in **bold**.

- It's not *his* green car; it's **mine**.
- *Your* brain is addled if you think that car is **yours**.
- When *my* lawyer gets here, it won't be *my* ass on the line, it'll be **theirs**.

I'll state it once again:

Possessive determiners come *before* a noun and indicate possession; possessive pronouns *replace* the noun.

Possessive Determiners

- *His* house
- *My* car

- *Her* jewelry
- *Our* cabin
- *Their* assets

Possessive Pronouns

- The house is **his.**
- The car is **mine.**
- The jewelry is **hers.**
- The cabin is **ours.**
- The assets are **theirs.**

According to Yourdictionary:

There are four different types of determiners in English: quantifiers, articles, demonstratives, and possessives.

Demonstrative pronouns are also used as determiners in English. Four of them are the same as demonstrative determiners: *this, that, these, and those.* Demonstratives are used in a situation in which the speaker can point to the item they mean, making them even more specific than a definite article.

— YOURDICTIONARY.COM

Below you'll find a few examples of demonstrative determiners. (I know that sounds scary, but it just means words that are used to point things out.)

- Do you want *this* wine, or not?
- I don't want *that* wine; I want the other one.
- Are *these* the drapes you ordered?
- *Those* are the ones I ordered.

Demonstrative determiners and demonstrative pronouns consist of the same four words, but usage is a little different. It's covered in the "Demonstrative Pronouns" chapter.

Quantifiers

Quantifiers are just like they sound; they indicate a number (how many or how few). Quantifying determiners are words such as *all, few,* and *many* as well as numbers (one, two, five, nine, etc.), which are specific.

- Sure, I'll take a *few* beers.
- He only wants *three* cannoli.
- She went shopping and got *some* new clothes.

Possessive Determiners

This category of determiners is both easy—and not. Let's get rid of the *not* first. People refer to these determiners in a variety of way: possessive determiners, possessive adjectives, and possessive pronouns are a few.

This was mentioned earlier in this chapter, but I'll repeat some of it here:

Don't confuse these (possessive determiners) with possessive pronouns. Although some sites will list them as "possessive pronouns," most call them "possessive adjectives" or "possessive determiners." The difference is that possessive determiners *precede* the noun (they own it), while possessive pronouns *replace* the noun.

Refer back to the examples as needed.

That covers it for determiners: articles, demonstratives, quantifiers, and possessives.

ADJECTIVES

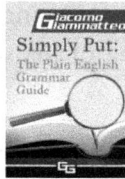

*a*djectives

Adjectives are words that modify (usually describe) a noun or pronoun. The sentences below have the adjectives in italics. (I haven't counted determiners as adjectives in this exercise.)

- The *big, brown* dog bit me.
- When I went to the beach, I met a *gorgeous, blonde-haired* girl.
- That house—the *big, expensive* one—is where my boss lives.

Adjectives tell you things like the color, number, size, etc., of the nouns that follow them.

I need to rephrase that because not all adjectives precede the noun they describe. In some cases, especially with linking verbs, the adjectives follow the noun and verb.

In the sentences below, the *italicized* word is a linking verb, and the adjective that modifies the subject follows the verb. It is in **bold.**

- That lasagna *smells* **delicious**.
- The brownie *tastes* **good**.
- She *seems* **healthy**.

Now switch the sentence around a little.

- The **delicious-smelling** lasagna *tastes* **good**.

Mark Twain was a stickler for using the right word and only the right word. I'll paraphrase one of his sayings dealing with just that issue:

The difference between the almost right word and the right word is the difference between the lightning-bug and lightning.

— MARK TWAIN (SAMUEL CLEMENS)

Mark Twain, like Hemingway, was intent on cutting unnecessary words, which is one of the many reasons why his (and Hemingway's) work shines. Many writers use adjectives piled upon adjectives in an attempt to create a better visual image, but all a writer needs to do is use the right one.

Forming Adjectives

Adjectives can be formed from nouns, and even from words that function as verbs. Let's look at a few.

The following sentences show the nouns underlined, the verbs in *italics*, and the adjectives in **bold.**

- She *had torn* the **critical** documents into **tiny** shreds before any of us *could stop* her.
- He *was playing* tennis and *got* a **torn** ligament.

NOTE THAT IN THE FIRST EXAMPLE, *TORN*, ALONG WITH THE helping verb *had*, is functioning as a verb, but in the next sentence *torn* is an adjective describing *ligament.*

Now we'll look at how nouns can be turned into adjectives.

- He *frequented* the **corner** bookstore on the weekends.
- The coffee shop on the corner *was* his favorite.
- My wife *loves* **corner** cabinets.
- While hunting, he *cornered* the prey.

In these examples, *corner*, or a form of it, is used as a noun, verb, and adjective. The last example doesn't show a noun being turned into an adjective; it shows a form of the same word being used as a verb.

Compound Adjectives

Nouns are frequently combined to make compound adjectives and are usually connected by hyphens when they precede a noun.

- A **hands-on** manager
- A **world-class** engineer
- A **top-notch** gamer
- A **two-hundred-year-old** tree

Some compound adjectives have become so engrained in the language, no hyphens are necessary.

- He wants an **ice cream** cone.
- She's a **high school** student.
- Have you completed your **income tax** forms.

There is more on compound adjectives in the next chapter, which deals with *adverbs.*

Chapter Three

ADVERBS

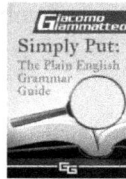

*A*dverbs can modify or describe a verb, adjective, another adverb, or a word group. Adverbs provide information relating to time, place, manner, cause, degree, or circumstance.

Below are a few examples with the adverbs in **bold.**

- Those spiders are **everywhere**.
- I'll go dancing with her **anytime.**
- She woke up feeling **badly.**
- He was **only partly** to blame.
- She was **justifiably** let go; the shooting was self-defense.

In the examples above, the adverbs modify verbs. Below are a few examples where adverbs modify adjectives, other adverbs, and even entire sentences.

- She will be *unusually late* for the performance.
- Shawna is an *extremely tall* woman.
- Tony finished *very quickly* for a man with no experience.
- *Fortunately,* an escort will not be necessary.

Many adverbs end in *ly* but nowhere near all of them. As you can see, the adverbs in the first two examples did not end in *ly*. And some adjectives and even nouns end in *ly*, so don't think that if a word ends in *ly* it's an adverb. At the end of this chapter you'll find two small charts: one is a short list of adjectives that end in *ly*, and it's followed by a list of adverbs that do *not* end in *ly*.

Adjectives That End in *ly*

The list at the end of this chapter is by no means comprehensive. For a much larger list, visit my website.

SOME WORDS CAN BE USED AS ADJECTIVES AND ALSO AS ADVERBS. The trick to identifying them is to analyze the sentence for which word is being modified. I'll give a few examples below using some of the words on the list.

- He caught the *early* flight to Houston.

This is an adjective because *early* is modifying *flight* and it's answering *what* flight—the *early* one.

On the other hand, we've got the following:

- "He got up *early* to catch the flight."

In this case, *early* is an adverb because it's modifying "got up." It's answering the question *when* did he get up—*early*.

The most common question that adverbs answer is *how*. Along with *how*, they also answer the questions *when, where,* and *why*. These questions are asked of the *verb* in the sentence, not the noun. It shows that in the example above. We ask *when* the person *got up. Got up when.*

Let's look at a few verbs modified by adverbs and determine which questions the adverbs answer. Verbs will be in *italics* and adverbs in **bold.**

- He *ran* **quickly**.
- She *performed* **poorly**.
- After *going* to bed **late**, he *woke up* **lazily**.
- Although *feeling* better, he **still** *felt* **badly**.

Now let's look at the relationships.

- He *ran* quickly. (Ran *how?*)
- She *performed* poorly. (Performed *how?*)
- After *going* to bed **late**, he *woke up* **lazily**. (Going *when?* and Woke up *how?*)
- Although *feeling* better, he **still** *felt* **badly**. (*Still* answers the question of *when* related to *felt* (ongoing, *still*), and *badly* answers *how* he felt.)

One of the reasons you may need to properly identify the part of speech is so that the word can be correctly hyphenated when it is used as a compound modifier. Adverbs that end in *ly* (and *very*) are *not* hyphenated whereas other adverbs are.

Many people question whether to hyphenate the term "finely tuned engine," and they may be tempted to leave the hyphen out because you don't hyphenate adverbs that end in *ly*; however, *finely* is an adjective and, as such, needs the hyphen. The phrase should be punctuated as follows: "finely-tuned engine."

The same would apply to the following adjectives:

- It was a *family-owned* restaurant
- He was an *elderly-looking* gentleman
- That is a *gnarly-looking* tree root

But the following adverbs are not hyphenated.

- He was a *smartly dressed* gentleman.
- She was a *very friendly* dog.

beastly	brotherly	burly	cleanly
cowardly	deadly	family	friendly
gnarly	grizzly	heavenly	hilly
nightly	scary	shapely	Smelly

The above list of adjectives is only a small percentage of them; there are hundreds.

The list below is of adverbs that *do not* end in *ly*. Again, this list is only a portion of the words.

afterward	already	fast	hard
long	more	never	often
quick	rather	soon	tomorrow
very	well	where	Yesterday

Along with the two above lists, there are a small number of nouns that end in *ly,* and these would also need hyphenation if used as a compound modifier.

PRONOUNS

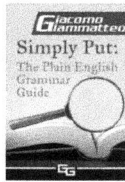

There are many different types of pronouns, and each of them are used in specific ways so that we understand their function and meaning.

In the chapters that follow, we'll look at demonstrative, indefinite, interrogative, intensive, personal, possessive, reciprocal, reflexive, and relative pronouns.

A pronoun is a word often used in place of a specific noun, and it frequently refers back to that noun (antecedent). In the following examples, the pronouns that refer back to the subjects are in *italics,* and the nouns referred to are underlined.

- The <u>detective</u> said *he* was going to solve this murder (he = detective).
- The <u>kidnapper</u> demanded *he* be paid the ransom in twenty-dollar bills (he = kidnapper).
- As much as my <u>mom</u> wanted me to attend the prom, *she* knew I wasn't going to go (she = mom).

That last sentence is full of pronouns: *my, me, she, I, it*. The one we want, though, is *she*; it refers back to mom.

There are many types of pronouns:

- Demonstrative pronouns take the place of the nouns they refer to.

- Indefinite pronouns are like the word implies; they refer to people or things, but not definite ones.

- Intensive pronouns are almost identical to reflexive pronouns, but with one significant difference: intensive pronouns are nonessential.

- Interrogative pronouns are used to begin questions.

- Personal pronouns refer to specific persons or things.

- Possessive pronouns show ownership.

- Reciprocal pronouns (there are only two) are used to show actions or feelings that are shared by more than one person.

- Reflexive pronouns *reflect* back to the subject (usually) and always end with *-self* or *-selves*.

- Relative pronouns refer to previously mentioned nouns. They also connect clauses or phrases to nouns or other pronouns.

Chapter One

DEMONSTRATIVE PRONOUNS

*D*emonstrative **Pronouns**
(These were mentioned briefly in the "Articles and Determiners" chapter.)

A demonstrative pronoun and a demonstrative adjective (determiner) are similar; however, the pronoun takes the place of the noun or noun phrase, while the adjective modifies the noun and is always followed by the noun. Here are a few examples with the adjectives (determiners) in *italics* and the pronouns in **bold.**

- *The* lasagna smells delicious.
- *That* lasagna smells delicious.
- **That** smells delicious.
- What is *that* snake?
- What is **that**?

In the second sentence ("that lasagna smells delicious"), *that* is an adjective (determiner) modifying lasagna. In the third sentence (**that** smells delicious), *that* is a pronoun taking the place of lasagna. In the fourth sentence, *that* is once again functioning as an adjective (determiner), modifying snake. Imagine someone pointing to the snake and saying "That one." In the last sentence, *that* is taking the place of *snake* as a pronoun.

DEMONSTRATIVE PRONOUNS

Demonstrative pronouns			
neither		none	such
that		these	this
Those			

Demonstrative pronouns aren't used as much in writing as they are in everyday conversation because demonstratives are often used to point things out. For that reason, the way to use them depends on how close or far you are from what is being discussed.

For things that are near, use *this* and *these*. For things that are farther away, use *that* and *those*.

RELATIVE PRONOUNS

*R*elative pronouns are placed immediately after the nouns they modify.

The most common relative pronouns are *who, whom, whose, which, whoever, whomever* and *that*. *What, when* and *where* can be used as relative pronouns as well. A few examples follow the chart below:

Relative Pronouns		
that	what	when
which	where	who
whoever	whom	whomever
whose		

- The dog *that* bit me was brown.

- The car *that* hit me, which was a black van, didn't even stop.
- Max, *whom* we love dearly, needs to be put to sleep.
- A plumber *who* has a leaky pipe is not very good.
- A gardener *whose* gardens are bare makes me wonder.
- The new CEO, *whomever* he may be, has a tough challenge waiting.

I used two examples with *whom* (one was *whomever*); however, *whom* is seldom used in everyday speech. It is still seen in writing (especially formal writing) but even that is experiencing a downward trend. Most people use *who* in its place. The use of *whom* is more common with British English, but it's fading. My suggestion is if you're not sure how to use it, or if you don't want to sound too formal, rewrite the sentence to avoid it.

Back to relative pronouns:

Remember we said *what, when,* and *where* could also be used as relative pronouns. Here are a few examples:

- My Aunt Rose lived in a time *when* walking was the primary means of transportation.
- She lived in the city *where* walking simplified things.
- A vacation is *what* I was talking about.

Notice in each example how the relative pronoun (the italicized word) refers to the noun it modifies. The relative pronouns act as a bridge, connecting the phrases.

Some purists insist that *whose* should not be used with things, but it has been used that way for hundreds of years.

Chapter Three

RECIPROCAL PRONOUNS

Reciprocal Pronouns

There are only two reciprocal pronouns: "each other" and "one another."

Remember how we said reciprocal pronouns were used to show actions or feelings to more than one person? Let's look at a few examples:

- Jimmy and Missy gave *each other* matching sweaters for Christmas.
- Adalina and Carmine took turns watching *each other* swim.
- The first grade kids exchanged goodbye presents with *one another*.
- During recess, the kids played with *one another*.

"Each other" is used when there are only two people or things, and "one another" is used when there are more than two.

Using reciprocal pronouns allows you to make your writing clear without having to clumsily repeat names, so instead of saying

"Jimmy gave Missy a sweater, and she gave him a sweater" we say "Jimmy and Missy gave each other sweaters."

When you're speaking of a larger group, the use of "one another" makes it much simpler; in fact, it's easy to modify what you're saying by using exclusion.

- All twenty students (except Bobby and Shelby) gave *one another* parting gifts.

Remember that "each other" is used for when you're referring to two people, and "one another" for more than that.

✖ Six of us went to dinner, and we tasted *each other's* food.

✔ Six of us went to dinner, and we tasted *one another's* food.

Now, on to reality. In everyday writing and speech, the phrases "each other" and "one another" are used interchangeably. There may be a few purists who insist on the so-called rule of "each other" for two only, but those few are dwindling and, I think, will soon be gone.

The truth is that using "each other" or "one another" in either of the sentences above is fine.

One more thing to note. When "each other" and "one another" are used to indicate possession, the way to show that is with an apostrophe *s,* not by adding the *s,* and then the apostrophe.

✔ They respected *each other's* honesty.

✖ They respected *each others'* honesty.

✔ The U.S. Marines admire *one another's* courage.

✖ The U.S. Marines admire *one anothers'* courage.

Chapter Four

INTERROGATIVE PRONOUNS

*I*nterrogative **Pronouns**
This may be the simplest of all the pronouns. An interrogative pronoun begins a question. Examples follow the chart:

For use with people	For use with things
who	what
whom	which
Whose	

- *Who* caused the accident?
- *Whom* did you say was calling? (*Whom* is seldom used.)
- *Whose* car keys are these?
- *Which* dog bit you?
- *What* restaurant do you like best?

That's it. Use *who, whom,* and *whose* for people, and *what* and *which* for things.

Animals that haven't been given a name or had the gender identified use *which*, but if a gender has been established or a name given, *who* (or *whose*) would be used.

Chapter Five

INDEFINITE PRONOUNS

For use with things

*I*ndefinite Pronouns

If interrogative pronouns were the easiest, indefinite pronouns aren't far behind. Indefinite pronouns are used in much the same way as others, but they don't refer to specific things.

The rules dealing with indefinite pronouns may seem daunting, but they aren't. One thing to be aware of is whether an indefinite pronoun is singular, plural, or both. The chart below breaks them down.

INDEFINITE PRONOUNS

Singular	Plural	Singular or Plural
another	both	all
anybody	few, fewer	any
anyone	many	more
anything	others	most
each	several	none
either		some
everybody		such
everyone		
everything		
little		
much		
neither		
nobody		
no one		
nothing		
one		
other		
somebody		
someone		
something		

One thing to remember is the verb used may change depending on whether you use a singular or plural pronoun. Pronouns that end with —*one,* —*body,* or —*thing* are always singular regardless of words that may come between the pronoun and verb.

Singular—an

- If *anybody* wants to go to the zoo, they should raise their hand.
- *Anyone* who has an objection needs to state it now.
- *Everybody* I know enjoys spaghetti.
- *Nobody* I know likes cabbage.
- *One* of my wife's friends spent the summer in Spain.

Note that the pronoun *none* is not considered to be a word ending with —*one*.

Plural

- *Both* are going to the movies.
- *Few* ever achieve stardom.
- *Many* make valiant attempts at heroics.

Singular or Plural

- *All* of us are going, or *none* of us are.
- *All* of us are going, or *no one* is.
- *Some* people never learn from their mistakes.
- *Any* who miss the exam will receive a failing grade.
- *Some* of the butter is salted (uncountable noun).
- *Some* of the raindrops (countable) are splashing in the bucket.
- Here's your tea, but *most* of the sugar is gone.
- *Most* of the rooms in our house were destroyed by fire.

Chapter Six

REFLEXIVE PRONOUNS

R **eflexive Pronouns**
Reflexive pronouns always end in either *self* or *selves*.
Below is a chart showing them.

Reflexive Pronouns		
herself	himself	itself
myself	oneself	ourselves
themselves	yourself	yourselves

You can add *themself* to the list because *The Chicago Manual of Style* gave its nod of approval last year.

Some people use *theirselves*, but it is considered nonstandard, and if you look at the Google Ngram below, you'll see it lags far behind in usage, although not as far as the recently accepted *themself*.

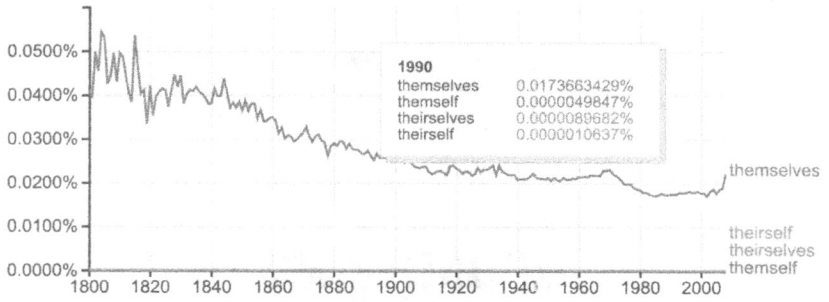

1990	
themselves	0.0173663429%
themself	0.0000049847%
theirselves	0.0000089682%
theirself	0.0000010637%

Chapter Seven

INTENSIVE PRONOUN

*I*ntensive **Pronouns**
It's actually easy to tell a reflexive pronoun from an intensive pronoun despite their being almost identical. The key word in that statement is *almost*.

Intensive pronouns are *not* an essential part of the sentence's structure. To test this, simply write (or say) the sentence without the pronoun. If it still makes sense, it is an intensive pronoun. If it doesn't, it is a reflexive pronoun and needs to be included. Consider the following. The intensive pronouns are in *italics*, the reflexive in **bold.**

- I made the cake *myself*, Mommy.
- The president *himself* shook my hand.
- She appeared to be in control of **herself**.

Now test it out by removing the pronouns from each sentence.

- I made the cake, Mommy.
- The president shook my hand.
- She appeared to be in control of.

As you can see, the last one doesn't work. The word *of* is hanging out there by **itself**.

The pronoun you choose depends on a lot of things, and one of them is whether that pronoun functions as the subject or object of the sentence. Look at the chart below to compare:

Subject	Object
he	him
I	me
it	it
she	her
they	them
we	us
you	you

SUBJECT: OBJECT

In the following examples, the subject pronoun is in *italics* and the object pronoun is in **bold.**

- *He* went to the store.
- *We* went with **him.**
- *They* wanted to go to the beach, but *we* didn't want to go with **them.**

Chapter Eight

POSSESSIVE PRONOUNS

These were covered to some extent in the "Articles and Determiners" chapter, but we'll add a little more information here.

The following words—depending on who you listen to—may be referred to as *possessive adjectives, possessive determiners,* or *possessive pronouns*, and even though they refer to similar things, there are differences. In the "Articles and Determiners" chapter, we mentioned the primary difference between the two, but let's go more in-depth. First, here's a chart that lists the possessive pronouns and shows how they differ from determiners and regular personal pronouns.

Regular Pronoun	Used as a Determiner	Used as a Possessive Pronoun
I	my	mine
you	your	yours
he	his	his
she	her	hers
it	its	
we	our	ours
they	their	theirs

I'll include a short explanation from Yourdictionary.com:

The strong (or absolute) possessive pronouns are **mine, yours, his, hers, its, ours, yours**, and **theirs**. They refer back to a noun or noun phrase already used, replacing it to avoid repetition: "I said that phone was **mine**."

The weak possessive pronouns (also called possessive adjectives) are **my, your, his, her, its, our, your**, and **their**. They function as determiners in front of a noun to describe who something belongs to: "I said that's **my** phone."

For further clarification, we'll use a few examples. Regular pronouns will be in *italics*, determiners <u>underlined</u>, and (absolute) possessive pronouns in **bold.**

- *I* went to the zoo with <u>my</u> niece, and *we* lost <u>our</u> umbrella. Later in the day, *she* saw someone with *it* and yelled, "Hey, that's **ours**."

In the sentences below, see how the determiner precedes the noun, and how the possessive pronoun replaces the noun. The charts (below or on the following page) show it also. Once again, the determiner will be underlined and the absolute possessive pronoun in **bold.**

- <u>This</u> car has given me nothing but trouble.
- **This** has given me nothing but trouble.
- <u>That</u> actor's performance may win an Oscar.
- **His** performance may win an Oscar.
- <u>That</u> book is my favorite.
- **That** is my favorite.

Determiner (being replaced by the noun)	Pronoun (being replaced by the noun)
The *black van* car has given me nothing but trouble.	The *black van* has given me nothing but trouble.
The *Godfather* film was fantastic.	The *Godfather* was fantastic.
The *Count of Monte Cristo* book is my favorite.	The *Count of Monte Cristo* is my favorite.

Determiner	Possessive Pronoun
This car has given me nothing but trouble.	*This* has given me nothing but trouble.
That actor's performance may win an Oscar.	*His* performance win an Oscar.
That film was fantastic.	*That* was fantastic.
That book is my favorite.	*That* is my favorite.

We'll end this with a chart that shows possessive determiners and (absolute) possessive pronouns according to singular and plural classification.

Singular or Plural	determiner	pronoun
First person (singular)	my	mine
Second person (singular)	your	yours
Third person (singular)	his/her/its	his/hers/its
First person (plural)	our	ours
Second person (plural)	your	yours
Third person (plural)	their	theirs

Possessive determiners and (absolute) possessive pronouns

Chapter Nine

PERSONAL PRONOUNS

*P*ronouns are meant to make communicating easier. They are used to refer to people, places, things, or animals. Without pronouns, communicating with others could be awkward. Consider the following two sentences. The first is written without using pronouns, and the second is written normally.

- Sandy felt bad so Sandy went to the doctor. Sandy had to sit in the waiting room for two hours before the doctor saw Sandy. After the doctor treated Sandy, Sandy felt better.
- Sandy felt bad, so she went to the doctor. She had to sit in the waiting room for two hours before he saw her. After he treated her, she felt better.

Although that piece of writing isn't great prose, it shows how pronouns make it easier and less awkward to communicate using everyday speech.

Subject and Object Pronouns

Some people differentiate between what are often referred to as subject pronouns and object pronouns, though they are both regular old pronouns, just used differently. Below is a chart showing the relationship.

Person	Subject	Object
First (singular)	I	me
Second (singular)	you	You
Third (singular)	he/she/it	him/her/it
First (plural)	we	us
Second (plural)	You	you
Third (plural)	they	them

Pronouns have many subcategories for dealing with specific issues, but that doesn't mean the "regular old pronoun" isn't without its problems. There has always been an issue regarding second-person references being the same in singular as in plural. Look at the sentence below and tell me how many people are invited to the party.

• We're having a party on Friday. You can come if you like.

In that example, we don't know if the person is addressing one friend or a roomful of people. Even where people use dialect to express themselves, it isn't clear, and in some cases it has become a controversy in its own right. Look at *y'all*, which is frequently used in the South.

It may have originally been used to establish number, as in "*You all* can come with me," but many diehard Southerners claim that *y'all* can mean one or one hundred.

And then there is the gender issue, which has been going on for what seems like ages. For the longest time, *they* was used to refer to plural things only, but then sensitivities to gender equality rose, requiring people to construct awkward phrases such as "He/she did it" or "Either he or she is the one to go."

As a result, *they* began to be used to refer to either gender in the singular form. As a result, many years later, *themself* has been recognized in the same way.

Part Two

NOUNS

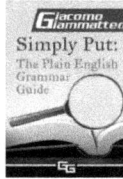

Nouns name things: people, places, and objects. Along with verbs, they are the cornerstone of sentence structure; in fact, a sentence can consist of a single noun and accompanying verb (later you'll see where even nouns aren't needed):

- I run.
- He shoots.
- Dogs bite.

All of the above are technically complete sentences even if they are simple ones.

In the sentence below, the nouns are in **bold.**

- The **dog,** a German **shepherd**, was not just a guard **dog** but one that searched for **drugs** as well.

There are many kinds of nouns: abstract, collective, common, concrete, countable (count)/uncountable (mass), gerunds, infinitives, and proper nouns.

Some sources list other nouns, such as material nouns, but they are easily placed in other categories.

In the following chapters, we'll look at a few of the different types of nouns.

Chapter Ten

ABSTRACT NOUNS

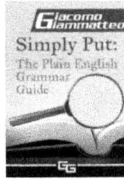

Simply Put:
The Plain English
Grammar
Guide

*a*bstract nouns refer to things we can't sense, so an abstract noun can't be heard, seen, smelled, tasted, or touched. An abstract noun can be an idea: faith; democracy; a unit of measurement, such as 3 feet, 16 meters, or 189 pounds; or a characteristic or emotion, such as love or honesty.

In the following sentences, the abstract nouns are in **bold.**
• His **love** for her was never ending.
• She wanted to marry him, but she doubted his **honesty.**
• He showed his **disapproval** by frowning.
• She had an **air** of superiority.

As you can see in the above sentences, each word in **bold** is an abstract noun. You can't touch, taste, see, hear, or smell *love* any more than you can *honesty* or *disapproval*.

In the last example (using *air*), it depends on how the word is being used. When you use *air* to refer to the invisible substance that surrounds us, it is a concrete noun because even though you can't see it with the naked eye, it can be seen at the molecular level, it can be felt if the wind is blowing, and it can be heard as it blows through the trees and such (though, technically speaking, you're not hearing the wind; you're hearing the effect it has on other things).

But that sentence doesn't use *air* in that manner. *Air* is used to mean an impression someone gives: "The deserted mansion had an air of mystery to it"; "After so many successes, she had an *air* of confidence that was undeniable."

There are other similar words. Consider the following sentences. The concrete nouns will be in **bold**, the abstract in *italics*:

• He died suddenly. Apparently he had a bad **heart.**

• Our team won, and it was all due to the quarterback, who played with a broken leg; he has a lot of *heart.*

• She cut herself on the sharp **edge** of the knife.

• I'm betting on Sam to win; he has the *edge* when it comes to experience.

In both examples showing abstract nouns, *heart* and *edge* are similar to other abstract expressions, such as *courage* and *honesty*.

There is a fairly comprehensive list of abstract nouns on my No Mistakes Publishing site, and it is easy to download.

Chapter Eleven

CONCRETE NOUNS

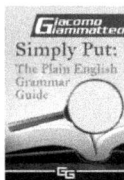

*W*e'll do concrete nouns even though it isn't in alphabetical order because we just did abstract nouns and they are closely related.

Concrete nouns are nouns that aren't abstract, so any person, place, or thing you *can* experience with one of your five senses—sight, sound, smell, taste, or touch—is a concrete noun.

There isn't much to add to this.

Chapter Twelve

COLLECTIVE NOUNS

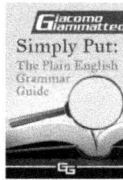

*C*ollective nouns refer to groups, whether the group is made up of people (team, committee, family), animals (herd, flock, colony), or things (bunch, bundle, set).

When a collective noun is considered as a single unit, the collective noun is used with a singular verb or singular pronoun, but if it's considered plural, a plural verb is needed.

- The jury *has* rendered its decision (considered as a group, singular).
- The jury *have* already eaten (plural, all the members already ate).
- The colony of ants *is* restless (considered as one, singular).
- The colony of ants *have* attacked (plural, all of them).
- A herd of buffalo *was seen* on the plains (a mass of buffalo, appearing as a herd).
- A herd of buffalo *have run* amok in the town (hundreds of individual buffalo).

In American English, collective nouns usually take singular verbs, but in British English, they are often treated as plurals.

This is most often seen when referring to companies. And although companies are not technically collective nouns, they are treated as such frequently.

There is also a difference in usage between American and British English when dealing with many collective nouns.

American English	British English
Amazon has raised prices.	Amazon have raised prices.
Google is very diversified.	Google are very diversified.
Apple has announced a new phone.	Apple have announced a new phone.

AMERICAN ENGLISH: BRITISH ENGLISH

And the following shows the chart in text.

- Amazon *has* raised prices (U.S.).
- Amazon *have* raised prices (U.K.).
- Google *is* very diversified (U.S.).
- Google *are* very diversified (U.K.).
- Apple *has* announced a new phone (U.S.).
- Apple *have* announced a new phone (U.K.).

Chapter Thirteen

COMMON NOUNS

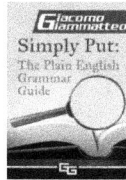

A common noun is any noun that is not a proper noun. The following sentences have common nouns in *italics* and proper nouns in **bold.**

- **Washington State** is a proper noun.
- But *state* is a common noun.
- The **University of Texas** is a proper noun.
- But a *university* in Texas is a common noun.

The majority of the tens of thousands of nouns are common; however, there are still thousands of proper nouns, and distinguishing between the two often presents problems. The best solution is to find a good dictionary as a resource, but even that may not solve all your capitalization issues. Sometimes further research is needed.

Chapter Fourteen

PROPER NOUN

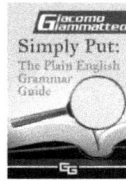

A proper noun is the opposite of a common noun; it is a noun that has been named or specified. A few examples follow.

- The monument in the nation's capital is more than five hundred feet high.
- The *Washington Monument* is more than five hundred feet high.
- There are many marathons every year.
- The *Boston Marathon* is run every year.

Proper nouns require capitalization, and while there is a lot of disagreement between dictionaries and style guides on which words should and shouldn't be capitalized, select one resource and stick with it.

Proper nouns follow a long list of rules, depending upon the category they fall into. There are rules for geographic points and directions, documents, animal names, foods, wines, honorifics, job titles, man-made structures, deities, celestial bodies, and many more; in fact, this is such a complex subject, I wrote a several-hundred-page book on capitalization alone.

Chapter Fifteen

COMPOUND NOUNS

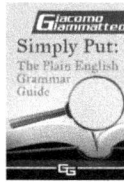

$\mathcal{A}$ compound noun is made by joining two or more words to form one word:

- backyard = back + yard
- mother-in-law = mother + in + law
- babysitter = baby + sitter

A compound noun doesn't have to be connected, though; it can consist of separate words that function as one:

- post office, as in "The post office is closed."
- upper class, as in "She thinks she's a member of the upper class, but she isn't."

Chapter Sixteen

COUNTABLE/UNCOUNTABLE NOUNS

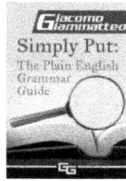

*C*ountable nouns are nouns you can count, and they can be made plural as well, or you can use quantifiers with them. As usual, examples follow with the countable nouns in italics.

- The *hawk* chased the *crow* away from its *nest*.
- The *hawks* chased the *crows* away from their *nests*.
- Three *hawks* chased five *crows* away from two *nests*.
- Several *hawks* chased a few *crows* away from their *nests*.

Remember, you can't use indefinite articles (*a* and *an*) with (most) plurals or uncountable nouns.

❌ A water is gone.
❌ A butter fell on the floor.
❌ A luggage is missing.
❌ *A* hawks chased the crows away from their nests.

And you can't pluralize uncountable nouns.

☑ The butter is gone!
❌ The *butters* is gone!
❌ *Several* butter is gone!
☑ The water is cold!

✖ The *waters* is cold!
✖ *Several* water is cold!
As you can see it doesn't work.

A NOUN THAT CAN'T BE COUNTED IS AN UNCOUNTABLE NOUN.
Uncountable nouns refer to things (or people) that are, in reality,
plural, but the nouns take singular verbs. I'll give examples.

- A pond is technically made up of millions of drops of
  water, but when referring to it, we say "water" as if it
  were a single thing.

Quite often, foods and liquids fit the bill as being uncountable
nouns. Consider the following:

- Cheese
- Milk
- Butter
- Water
- Bread
- Fruit
- Meat
- Rice
- Coffee

There are many more words that belong in the list, but I think
you get the idea.

Singular Use

As mentioned, a singular verb is required with an uncountable
noun. The following sentences are examples:

✅ The cheese *has* all been eaten.
✖ The cheese have all been eaten.
✅ Fruit *goes* rotten quickly.
✖ Fruit go rotten quickly.

☑ Meat *spoils* if left in the heat.

✖ Meat spoil if left in the heat.

Here are a few words considered uncountable that may surprise you.

- Garbage
- Furniture
- Luggage
- Equipment

You don't say "Let's move the *furnitures*" or "Don't forget the *luggages*."

On the other hand, you need to be careful because some words may be uncountable when used one way but not when used another. Let's look at a few (countable is in *italics* and uncountable is in **bold**):

Dirt

- The rain turned the **dirt** to mud.
- The archeologist said that the different *dirts* (meaning sandy, chalky, silty, rocky, clay based, etc.) have a different feel to them.

Chicken, hair, and time.

- There is plenty of **chicken** left; it's in the fridge.
- Fifteen *chickens* live in the farmer's coop.
- His **hair** has turned gray on the sides.
- He's going bald; there are barely ten *hairs* on his head.
- *Times* are changing; duels to the death are no longer legal.
- As they say, **time** is relative.

As you can see in the above sentences, the nouns in bold

(uncountable) use a singular verb, and the nouns in italics (countable) use plural verbs.

You might ask why it's important to know whether you're dealing with a countable or uncountable noun, and the exercises above show one reason: it makes you aware of agreement issues between subjects and verbs.

Below is a short list of other words that are both countable and uncountable.

- Paper
- Room
- Memory
- Coffee
- Beer
- Tea
- Truth

Chapter Seventeen

GERUNDS

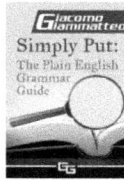

Gerunds (and gerund phrases)
A gerund is merely a noun formed by adding *-ing* to a verb. One thing to note is that because gerunds are formed from verbs (action words) they denote action as well. Gerunds always name an activity, not a place or thing. Below are a few familiar gerunds:

- swimming (action)
- eating (action)
- crying (action)
- working (action)

In the sentence "He likes swimming," *swimming* is a noun (gerund). The same would apply to "He likes eating" or "She is crying" or "She is working."

Those are all nouns (gerunds) functioning as objects, but gerunds can also function as the subjects of sentences. We'll turn the above around to see.

- *Swimming* is fun.

- *Eating* is necessary.
- *Crying* is sometimes necessary.
- *Working* is a fact of life.

Let's put the discussion of *gerunds* on hold while we peek at *infinitives* because the next parts involve both.

Chapter Eighteen

INFINITIVES

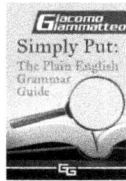

(Noun) Infinitives

Infinitives are verbs prefaced by the word *to* and which actually function as nouns (or adjectives or adverbs).

- I love *to eat* ravioli.
- *To see* is a gift for some.
- She wants nothing but *to love* and be loved.

Infinitives can also be noun phrases:

- Ever since college, he loves *to smoke weed.*
- *To be successful* was her goal in life.

Now we'll continue the discussion of gerunds and infinitives.

We're going to delve into infinitives a bit now, because it coincides with some issues affecting gerunds.

Some verbs can be followed by an infinitive or a gerund *without* causing a change in meaning:

1. Will you continue **working** after you give birth?
2. Will you continue **to work** after you give birth?

Some verbs can be followed by an infinitive or a gerund but *with* a change in meaning:

1. He stopped **drinking** coffee. (He never drank coffee again.)
2. He stopped **to drink** coffee. (He stopped what he was doing and drank some coffee.)

There are certain verbs that can be followed by either a gerund or an infinitive and no change in meaning will result. Look at the examples below.

- The healing *begins to take* effect immediately.
- The healing *begins taking* effect immediately.
- If she *continues to drink* like that, she'll be dead in five years.
- If she *continues drinking* like that, she'll be dead in five years.
- If you *intend to work*, do it now.
- If you *intend working*, do it now.

There are a few other nouns that function in this manner:

- hate
- like
- love
- prefer
- start

Here are a few more verbs that change meaning depending on whether you use a gerund or infinitive.

- You must *remember to kill* him.
- You must *remember killing* him.
- If you *stop to get* gas, you'll be late.
- If you *stop getting* gas, you'll be late.

As you can see, the meaning changes depending on whether you use a gerund or infinitive.

THERE'S BEEN A LOT OF DISCUSSION ABOUT WHETHER IT IS OKAY or taboo to split an infinitive, that is, to place a word between the word *to* and the base verb. This is covered in the chapter entitled "You Can't Split Infinitives" under "Grammar Myths."

Chapter Nineteen

POSSESSIVE NOUNS

A possessive noun is nothing more than a noun showing ownership:

- *Bob's* car.
- *Sally's* fish.
- *Apple's* refund policy.
- The *government's* diplomacy.

There are rules for how to show ownership with plural nouns, nouns ending in *s*, and compound nouns, but those rules are discussed in the "Apostrophes" chapter, under "Punctuation."

Part Three

VERBS

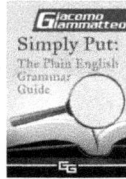

Verbs are the life of the party—where all the action is. Nouns are the drivers and verbs drive. In the following sentences, we'll use *italics* for nouns and **bold** for verbs.

For a sentence to be complete, it has to have a verb. Supposedly, it has to have a noun as well, but that isn't technically true. You can create a lot of sentences without nouns. Verbs are in bold. Check out the following.

- **Get** out, please.
- **Go**!
- The graduating *class* **went** to the *beach*.
- The *prom* **was** for *seniors* only.

Sentences can be made from verbs and adverbs only; in fact, as evidenced by the second example, a sentence may be a verb only, with the subject implied (you), as in "[You] go!"

Here are a few more sentences:

- The dog **bit** her on the leg, and she **went** to the hospital.
- He **drank** too much at the party.

In the last sentence, *he* is a pronoun taking the place of a noun (whoever it was who drank too much).

Not all verbs are considered action verbs. There are sense verbs as well.

- He said, "That lasagna **smells** delicious.
- I **feel** good.
- She **seems** to be better now.

Sense verbs are discussed in more detail in the "I Feel Good" chapter under "Usage."

Chapter Twenty

INFINITIVES

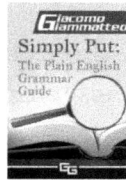

We've covered how infinitives can function as nouns, but infinitives can also function as adjectives or adverbs. Let's look at how infinitives are formed and what role a verb plays in that.

An infinitive is the base form of a verb preceded by the word *to* but, when using infinitives, *to* is functioning as part of the verb, not as a preposition.

You don't conjugate an infinitive or add an *s, -ed, -ing,* or an *-es.* Look at the examples below:

✗ She wanted *to laughs.*
✗ She wanted *to laughed.*
✗ She wanted *to laughing.*
✗ She wanted *to laughes.*

None of the above are correct. The correct form is shown below.

✅ She wanted *to laugh.*

Yourdictionary.com has a good example:

Sometimes you'll see sentences like this:

She went from kissing him to slapping him in no time.

You see "to slapping," and it's easy to think that's an infinitive verb, but it isn't. It's a preposition (to) and a gerund (slapping). You can tell it's not an infinitive because of the -ing on the end of the verb. Infinitives never have an -ing ending.

— YOURDICTIONARY.COM

I know this seems like a short chapter, but we covered a lot about infinitives in the "Gerunds" chapter as well as the "You Can't Split Infinitives" chapter.

Chapter Twenty-One

HELPING VERBS

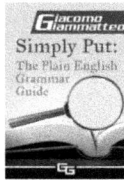

There are twenty-three helping verbs. The table below shows them, but not in the typical alphabetical order. While doing research for this book, I stumbled across a YouTube site that had a rendition of a song taught by an elementary-school teacher relating to how to remember the helping verbs. The words are in the order sung in the song.

Helping Verbs			
am	is	are	was
were	being	been	be
have	has	had	do
does	did	will	would
shall	should	may	might
must	can	Could	

Those twenty-three helping verbs break down into just three main verbs: *be, do,* and *have.*

Helping verbs (auxiliary verbs) appear before the main verb and often help to express or identify tense. They also express slight variations in the meaning. Consider the following sentences using different helping verbs.

- I *might* go to the funeral.
- I *should* go to the funeral.
- I *can* go to the funeral.
- I *must* go to the funeral.

Might implies that "maybe you'll go and maybe you won't."

Should implies that it's a slight obligation, not a life-or-death situation, but something you may be expected to do.

Can states you are able to attend if you want.

Must is the strongest implication. You *have* to go. It's mandatory.

.   .   .

THE VERB *IS* CAN FUNCTION AS BOTH A HELPING VERB AND AN action verb, so you have to learn to recognize its role in the sentence. Don't worry; it's easy.

A helping verb is just like its name says: a helper, so if *is* is functioning by itself, it isn't being used as a helping verb.

- Michele *is* beautiful (no helper).
- That dog *is* huge (no helper).
- I think she *is looking* at you (helper).

Of the twenty-three helping verbs, nine are known as *modal* verbs (*can, could, shall, should, ought to, will,* or *would*).

Modal verbs help to show ability, obligation, possibility, permission, or necessity (among others). You can see examples of that in the chart below and the sentences that follow:

Expression affected	Verbs	Examples
ability/request	can	Can you go to the dance? I can swim like a fish.
past ability/future possibility/suggestion	could	Could you have shot him if necessary? You could turn her in if you have to. You could do it if you had to.
permission/future possibility	may	May I have your daughter's hand? I may go to Ireland someday.
present/future possibility	might	If he buys enough tickets, he might win the lottery. If I win the lottery, I might go to Ireland.
necessity/obligation	must	He promised. Now he must go. It was your uncle; you must go to the funeral!
obligation	ought to	She's not feeling well; you ought to visit.
offer/suggestion	shall	Shall I come over?
advice/uncertain prediction	should	He should go to Atlanta if he gets the job.
willingness/certainty/promise	will	If you want I will go with you. I will be making the journey, regardless of what happens. I will kill him.
request/arrangement	would	Would you accompany my daughter to the opera?

- Bella *can* play soccer well. (ability)

- If his luck holds out, he *should* go to Las Vegas. (suggestion/advice)
- She got her wish, now she *ought to* keep her promise. (obligation)

"Ought to" is considered a semi-modal verb. What does that mean? I'll let Cambridge English Dictionary explain:

Ought to is a semi-modal verb because it is in some ways like a modal verb and in some ways like a main verb. For example, unlike modal verbs, it is followed by to, but like modal verbs, it does not change form for person:

I ought to phone my parents.

It ought to be easy now.

The negative is formed by adding 'not' after ought (ought not to). It can be contracted to oughtn't to. We don't use don't, doesn't, didn't with ought to:

We ought not to have ordered so much food.

Not: We don't ought to have ordered so much food.

— CAMBRIDGE ENGLISH DICTIONARY

The chart on the next page, from Wikipedia, shows some of the ways these verbs help with clarification:

Helping Verb	Function	Examples
be	Express tense (the tense depends on the conjugation of *to be*; *is* is present, *was* is past, *will be* is future, etc.) and a sense of continuity.	He **is** sleeping.
Express tense (the tense depends on the conjugation of *to be*; *are* is present, *were* is past, *will be* is future, etc.) and indicate the passive voice		They **were** seen.
can	Express ability	I **can** swim. Such things **can** help.
could	Express possibility	That **could** help.
do	Express negation (requires the word *not*)	You **do** not understand.
Ask a question	**Do** you want to go?	
have	Express tense (the tense depends on the conjugation of *to be*; *are* is present, *were* is past, *will be* is future, etc.) and indicate a sense of completion	They **have** understood.
might	Express possibility	We **might** give it a try.
must	Express confidence in a fact	It **must** have rained.
should	Express a request	You **should** listen.
Express likelihood	That **should** help.	
will	Express future tense	We **will** eat pie. The sun **will** rise tomorrow at 6:03.
would	Express future likelihood	Nothing **would** accomplish that.

Chapter Twenty-Two

VERB TENSES

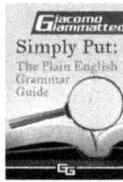

Now we're getting into an area where additional grammatical terms are necessary. If your job consists of writing, I recommend reading on. If you have no interest in verb tenses, feel free to skip this section.

Depending on who you listen to, there are anywhere from three to twelve verb tenses. I know it sounds like quite a variation, but it's a matter of how they define what constitutes a tense. Let's take a look.

English has only two ways to form a tense from the basic verb alone: past and present.

If we start out with a basic verb, such as *swim*, we can only form two tenses with it:

- I/you/he/we, etc., swim. (present)
- I/you/he/we, etc., swam. (past)

That's it.

If we want to form any other tense, we need a helping verb.

- We're going to the pool on Sunday, and I *will be* swimming all day.
- She loves water so much, she *will swim* from morning to night.
- I *would have swum* all day if I *had*n't *been* stung.
- There *have been* days when I*'ve* (I have) *swum* all day.

Notice that in every example (other than the two preceding these four) a helping verb was needed.

You've already seen how helping verbs affect the subtleties of a sentence's meaning; now you can see how they affect tense. If you want to express yourself in any tense other than present and past, a helping verb is required.

The tenses can be broken down into four basic categories:

Verb	Verb Tense	Simple Tense	Progressive/continuous Tense	Perfect Tense	Perfecet Progressive Tense
eat	past	Ate	I was eating	I had eaten	I had been eating
eat	present	I eat | he eats	I am eating | he is eating	I have eaten	I have been eating | he has been eating
eat	future	I will eat	I will be eating	I will have eaten	I will have been eating
drink	past	I drank	I was drinking	I had drunk	I had been drinking
drink	present	I drink	I am drinking | he is drinking	I have drunk | he has drunk	I have been drinking
drink	future	I will drink	I will be drinking	I will have drunk	I will have been drinking

Along with the above, there are also conditional tenses. There are four main types of conditional sentences:

- Zero-conditional statement: expressing a real condition that always happens.
- First-conditional: unreal, but likely to happen.
- Second-conditional: probably won't happen.
- Third-conditional: didn't happen but might have.

Before we start, know that most conditional statements will contain a clause introduced by the word *if*. *When* can sometimes be used, and occasionally *unless*. (Unless is used in place of "if not".)

Now let's look at when and how to use conditional sentences.

Zero-conditional sentences are used to state that if one thing is done, then something else will happen. Look at the examples below.

- If you drink enough alcohol, you get drunk.

You're making a statement or telling a truth. If you do X, Y happens. You're not saying "You might get drunk" or "You could get drunk." You're saying "You get drunk."

With Zero-conditional Sentences, you use the simple present tense with the *if* clause and the main clause.

✖ If you drink enough alcohol, you will get drunk.

✔ If you drink enough alcohol, you get drunk.

✖ If you jump into the ocean, you will get wet.

✔ If you jump into the ocean, you get wet.

First-conditional Sentences are used to make statements that will probably happen sometime in the future but not definitely.

- If you're persistent enough, you will reach your goal.
- If you drink too much coffee, it will keep you awake.

Note that these statements indicate that something will probably happen but not necessarily. Sometimes, no matter how persistent a person is, they don't achieve their goals. And some people can drink coffee all day and have no trouble sleeping.

Also note that the *if* clause takes the simple present tense and the main clause takes the simple future tense. The sentences below are incorrect because they use the simple present tense for the main clause.

✖ If you're persistent enough, you reach your goal.

✗ If you drink too much coffee, it keeps you awake.

Second-conditional Sentences are used when what is stated probably won't happen. It *could*, but it probably won't.

- If I became president, I'd provide free healthcare for everyone.
- If I won the Oscar for best performance in a leading role, I'd keep my acceptance speech short.

A few things to note. First, I used italics on "I'd provide" and "I'd keep," but the word I is contained in there. It's being used as a contraction for "I would." So "would provide" and "would keep" are the verbs of interest.

Note that with the second conditional sentence, we use the simple past tense for the *if* clause, and we use an auxiliary (helping) modal verb with the main clause. In the examples, I used *would*, but I could have used *might*, or *should*, or *could*.

✓ If I became president, I *might* abolish the death sentence.

✓ If I won the Oscar, I *could* retire early.

Third-conditional Sentences are used when stating that things (the current situation) may be different if something different had happened in the past.

- If you *had called* earlier, I *would have been* there on time.
- If I *had spent* more time with her, she *might* not *have left*.

In each of these sentences, it's easy to see how things could have turned out differently: if you had called earlier, and if I had spent more time with her.

Both of those scenarios are well within the realms of possibility, but the fact is, they didn't happen. They were both conditions that could have happened, but didn't.

Notice when using the third-conditional sentence we use a past-perfect verb (*had* + past tense) with the *if* clause, and a modal auxiliary plus *have* plus past tense with the main clause. In the following sentences, the wrong tense is used with the *if* clause.

✕ If you *called* earlier, I would have been there on time.

✕ If I *spent* more time with her, she might not have left.

Punctuating Conditional Sentences

Since we're on the subject, we may as well discuss how to punctuate a conditional sentence. It's not as difficult as you think. As complex as conditional sentences might be, the punctuation is straightforward.

Place a comma following the *if* clause when it starts a sentence, but not when the *if* clause follows the main clause.

- If you drink enough alcohol, you will get drunk (comma needed).
- You will get drunk if you drink enough alcohol (no comma needed).

Let's look at a couple sentences using *when* and *unless*.

- When you touch a hot stovetop, you get burned.
- Smoking kills you, unless you don't inhale.

Chapter Four

PREPOSITIONS

*P*repositions

There are hundreds of prepositions, and they function to make communicating smoother and to make sense of what would be gibberish without them. Consider the following two paragraphs.

The first example is a random paragraph I took from one of my books; the second is that same paragraph with the prepositions removed.

From behind her ear she pulled a yellow pencil, tucked into a tight bun of red hair, then opened the receipt book clipped to the pocket of her apron. Cigarette smoke lingered on her breath, almost hidden by the gum she chewed.

---

her ear she pulled a yellow pencil, tucked a tight bun red hair, then opened the receipt book clipped to the pocket her apron. Cigarette smoke lingered her breath, almost hidden the gum she chewed.

I'm guessing if you read the second paragraph, you mentally filled in the blanks where a few of the prepositions were missing, but even if you did, I'm sure the reading wasn't nearly as smooth as the first example.

And while we're at it, let's look at that again. The first example begins with "From behind," which is nothing more than what's known as a complex preposition—or two or more prepositions or words turned into a preposition. There are lots of them. Consider the following:

- ahead of . . .
- according to . . .
- along with . . .
- because of . . .

There are plenty more to choose from. The point is that they're not that unusual.

Preposition Rules

There are a few rules to adhere to regarding prepositions:

- Be careful what follows a preposition. A preposition is usually followed by a noun or pronoun (whichever one it is, is called the object of the preposition). It is what the preposition is referring to. Look at the noun in the following sentence. "Look at the *wall*."
- Verbs do not immediately follow prepositions, so when you see a word that appears to be a verb, it is likely a gerund or an infinitive.
- Tissues were made for crying (gerund, a noun).
- Airplanes were made to fly (infinitive, functioning as noun).

Prepositions can function as adjectives (modifying a noun) or as adverbs (modifying a verb), and they can also function as nouns (when used with "to be" verbs).

- Look at that rainbow *with all the bright colors.*
- Here are the keys. Make sure he gets the van *with the wheelchair ramp.*

In both sentences above, the prepositional phrase (in italics) is modifying (describing) the nouns that precede it (rainbow and van).

In the following examples, the prepositional phrases modify the verbs.

- The pack of wolves ran *after the elk.*
- The snake got away; it went *under the leaves.*

And lastly, prepositions can function as a noun when following a form of the verb "to be." In the following sentences, the prepositional phrase is in *italics* and the "to be" form of the verb is in **bold.**

- Our swimming pool **is** *in the neighborhood.*
- The killer **is** standing *between numbers three and four.*
- I **am** *before him* in the queue.

You need to be careful with verbs containing a word that looks like a preposition.

- The robbers *held up* the bank.
- We drank all night and *ran up* the tab.

In both of the above cases, the italicized words are functioning as verbs. A way to check this is to move what appears to be the prepositional phrase to the beginning of the sentence and see if it still sounds right.

- *Up the bank,* the robbers held.
- *Up the tab* we drank all night and ran.

Compare that to the following sentences using real prepositional phrases.

- The cat hid *under the bed.*
- *Under the bed,* the cat hid.
- We'll stay dry *beneath the tree.*
- *Beneath the tree,* we'll stay dry.

These constructions may not sound ideal, but they *do* work.

Part Four

CONJUNCTIONS

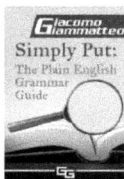

Conjunctions

If you think of a conjunction as merely a connecting word, it may make it easier.

There are three basic conjunctions (coordinating, subordinating, and correlative), and they're used to join (connect) the different parts of a sentence (words, phrases, clauses). And that's their only job; they're don't multitask.

Let's look at each one.

Chapter Twenty-Three

COORDINATING CONJUNCTIONS

Coordinating conjunctions are the most common of the three. There are seven coordinating conjunctions, and they are easily identified by the well-known acronym: FANBOYS.

- for
- and
- nor
- but
- or
- yet
- so

A coordinating conjunction connects words, phrases, or clauses that are considered equally important:

- Bob went to the store, *and* then he went to the bank.
- Kristen drove the kids to school *and* stopped to buy groceries on her way home.
- Sean wanted to go to Ireland, *but* he had no money.

- Dana didn't accept Nick's proposal, *nor* did she accept Tom's.

For how to punctuate with conjunctions, see the appropriate section under "Punctuation."

Chapter Twenty-Four

SUBORDINATING CONJUNCTIONS

Subordinating Conjunctions

A subordinating conjunction connects a dependent clause to an independent clause for support.

Subordinating conjunctions exist for a reason. Aside from being used to connect two clauses, they imply that the clause that follows has something to add to the main clause. Consider the sentences below.

- We decided not to travel to Europe *because* of the recent terrorist attacks.
- She got sick at work, *so* she went home.
- The house burned down *as a result* of careless smoking.
- Kaitlin was able to drive *once* the snow stopped.

In each of the sentences above, the subordinating conjunction introduces a clause which provides additional information showing cause and effect or addressing time relationships, such as in the last example. It answers when Kaitlin was able to drive.

Note that the clause introduced by the conjunctions cannot function on its own.

- . . . because of the recent terrorist attacks.
- . . . so she went home.
- . . . as a result of careless smoking.
- . . . once the snow stopped.

Subordinate conjunction list

after	although	as	as if
as long as	as much as	As soon as	as though
because	before	even	even if
even though	if	if only	if when
If then	inasmuch	in order that	just as
lest	now	now that	once
provided	provided that	rather than	since
so that	supposing	than	that
though	till	unless	until
when	whenever	where	whereas
wherever	whether	which	while
who	whoever	why	

The above chart shows a list of subordinating conjunctions. You can go to my website to download it if for reference.

PUNCTUATING SUBORDINATING CONJUNCTIONS:

Subordinating conjunctions usually do not require a preceding comma when they end the sentence; however, a comma follows a subordinating conjunction when the dependent (subordinating) clause begins the sentence. Note how, in the sentences below, the comma follows the *clause*, not the conjunction itself.

- *As long as you're sick,* you should stay in bed (comma after dependent clause).
- He put gas in the car *even though the tank was half full* (no comma preceding dependent clause).
- She built a huge fire *so she could keep warm* (no comma preceding dependent clause).

The above sentences are punctuated correctly, with a comma following the leading dependent clause, but no comma preceding a dependent clause when it occurs at the end of the sentence. See the chapter on "When to Use a Comma with So" for more information on punctuating that construction.

Subordinate Conjunction List (next page)

This is not a comprehensive list, but it covers the vast majority of them.

Subordinate conjunction list

after	although	as	as if
as long as	as much as	As soon as	as though
because	before	even	even if
even though	if	if only	if when
If then	inasmuch	in order that	just as
lest	now	now that	once
provided	provided that	rather than	since
so that	supposing	than	that
though	till	unless	until
when	whenever	where	whereas
wherever	whether	which	while
who	whoever	why	

Chapter Twenty-Five

CORRELATIVE CONJUNCTIONS

*C*orrelative conjunctions are found in pairs, and they are used to connect words, phrases, and clauses. It is easier to show how they work with examples.

- At the wedding reception, they served *both* shrimp *and* lobster.
- She drank *neither* coffee *nor* tea.
- Lions are fast but not nearly *as* fast *as* cheetahs.
- I would *rather* face a firing squad *than* my wife's wrath.
- *Not only* did he eat a lot of shrimp, *but also* a lot of lobster.
- I *not only* went to Italy, *but also* saw Pavarotti while I was there.
- *The more* I see that dog, *the more* I want to keep her.

Remember that correlative conjunctions come in pairs, one on each side of the word or phrase you're connecting.

One thing to note is the "not only/but also" construction is frequently written and spoken without the "but also" part. A couple of examples are below.

- He *not only* fell off the bike, [*but also*] he broke his leg.
- She *not only* quit smoking, [*but also*] she quit drinking.

In each of the sentences above, we omitted the "but also" part of the conjunction, although we could have used it.

Also, when using "not only" to start a clause, the verb and subject immediately following it are inverted (turned around).

- *Not only* **did I** tell off my boss, [*but also*] I quit.

When you use *no sooner* or *hardly*, the subject and verb are also inverted.

- *No sooner* **had I** gotten to work, than the boss began yelling.
- *Hardly* **had he** lifted the weight, when his hamstring popped.

as/as	as many as	both/and	either/or
hardly/when	if/then	Just as/so	neither/nor
not only/but also	no sooner/than	not/but	rather/than
scarcely/when	such/that	the more/the more	what with/and
whether/or			

Chapter Twenty-Six

CONJUNCTIVE ADVERBS

$\mathcal{A}$ lot of people think conjunctive adverbs are the same as subordinating conjunctions, but they're not. There are similarities, but there are differences as well.

As previously noted, subordinating conjunctions can either introduce a dependent clause at the beginning of a sentence or a dependent clause following an independent one. Examples of subordinating conjunctions follow:

- He was intent on going to the show *although* the admission was high.
- *Although* the admission was high, he was intent on going to the show.

Some people consider conjunctive adverbs as a fourth type of conjunction, but they're not true conjunctions. They can sometimes function as connecting words, but they don't follow all the rules required for conjunctions. That said, let's look at a few examples of conjunctive adverbs versus subordinating conjunctions. Subordinating conjunctions are in *italics*, adverbial conjunctions in **bold.**

- He went to the opera *since* the admission was reasonable.
- The cost of admission is inexpensive *unless* it's a weekend.
- *When* they set the price for admission, they did a good job.
- They set him free after three years; **however**, he wasn't happy.
- She suggested going to England; **instead**, he booked a flight to France.
- He knew the guilty party; **yet**, he wouldn't say who it was.

Notice in the first three examples how the italicized words (subordinating conjunctions) connect an independent clause with a dependent one. In the last three sentences, however, the words in bold connect two independent clauses with a semicolon preceding them and a comma following them.

Some conjunctive adverbs act as connecting words, but sometimes they function as mere adverbs. If a conjunctive adverb is used to connect independent clauses, a semicolon precedes the conjunctive adverb, and a comma follows it. The conjunctive adverbs are *italicized,* and the plain adverbs are in **bold.**

- I witnessed the crime; *however*, it was dark. (conjunctive adverb)
- I think; *therefore*, I am. (conjunctive adverb)
- She told him not to go; *nevertheless*, he went. (conjunctive adverb)
- I want a new car; *besides*, I need one. (conjunctive adverb)
- She was a gambler; *consequently*, she went broke. (conjunctive adverb)
- She gambled and, **consequently**, went broke. (adverb)

- He was tall but **still** not tall enough. (adverb)
- He was tall; *still*, he wasn't tall enough. (conjunctive adverb)

A comprehensive list of conjunctive adverbs is found below (or on the next page).

accordingly	additionally	also	anyway
besides	certainly	comparitively	consequently
conversely	elsewhere	equally	finally
further	furthermore	hence	henceforth
however	in addition	in comparison	in contrast
incidentally	indeed	instead	Likewise
meanwhile	moreover	namely	nevertheless
next	nonetheless	now	otherwise
rather	similarly	still	subsequently
then	thereafter	therefore	thus
undoubtedly	yet		

Chapter Five

INTERJECTIONS

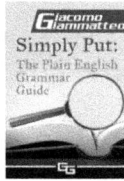

As a part of speech, interjections are easy to grasp; they're words used to show emotion. They are also usually short and used for effect, especially with dialogue. Below are a few examples:

- "*Oh my!* I didn't expect that."
- "*Dear me*," she said. "I should have been there."
- "*Hey!* Enough's enough."

Interjections are often followed by an exclamation point (especially when found in dialogue), but not always.

Part Two

PUNCTUATION

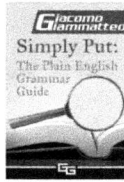

It's been said before, but it's worth repeating: punctuation is like a traffic system. Each punctuation mark tells the reader what to do: stop as if it were a red light (period); slow down similar to a yellow light (comma); or pause like a yield sign (semicolon). Other marks carry different messages. (Depending on how you drive, the comma and semicolon signals may be reversed.)

The thing to remember is that without punctuation, readers have no way of knowing what the writer intends.

Without further ado, let's dig into the sometimes-confusing world of punctuation.

I always say my books will not venture into using grammatical terms, but punctuation requires a little more than most. Still, it won't get too technical. I promise.

One more thing before we move on.

Many of the online grammar sites and even the style guides and dictionaries I checked refer to a lot of rules using the terms *always* or *never,* when what they should say is *usually* or *seldom.*

Always means "on every occasion" or "all the time."

Never means "not at any time" or "at no time."

If a rule has exceptions (and most do), then you shouldn't use *always* or *never*.

A couple of examples of what I'm speaking of are below, and they deal with the use of punctuation used with quotation marks.

More than one site said, "Periods and commas *never* go outside quotation marks" and "All other punctuation *always* goes outside quotation marks." As you'll see in the "Quotation Marks" chapter, that isn't *always* the case.

Chapter Six

COMMA RULES

A couple of these examples were taken from a *Business Insider* article and a couple were taken from the Grammarly site; the rest are mine.

Commas are one of the worst offenders when it comes to misuse. Many writers think they can do whatever they want with a comma and no one will be the wiser, nor will the reader question them. A mistake or misplaced comma can be chalked up to a writer's style, they say.

But nothing is further from the truth. When it comes to commas, there are strict guidelines on when to use them and when not to use them. It's true that you can get away with a few misuses and attribute it to a stylistic choice, but too many mistakes will draw the critics out in droves.

I break one of the comma rules when writing dialogue in my novels, but it's a subtle misuse, and most people probably don't even notice. I do it because I think the book reads better that way. But the remainder of rules regarding punctuation I adhere to, or at least I try to.

One note about commas before we begin. Commas are meant to indicate a pause or a break between the different parts of a sentence. Above all else, they are meant to clarify or make the meaning more clear. They do this in various ways: to separate items in a list, to offset the nonessential parts of a sentence, to mark a pause following an introductory clause or word, and to note who is being spoken to when using dialogue.

The main thing to understand is that commas are not there because of some arbitrary rule; the rules regarding when and how to use commas exist to enhance clarity—no other reason.

With that said, let's delve into the rules on commas.

Rule 1

- Use a comma after a dependent clause that starts a sentence.

I told you I wouldn't resort to grammatical terms, so let's dumb it down. A "dependent clause" is no different than a dependent child; they both rely on something else for support. A dependent child relies on their parents or guardians, and a dependent clause relies on the rest of the sentence for support; in other words, it doesn't make sense by itself. Let's look at a few examples:

- When I went to the bank, (dependent clause).
- When I took a walk, (dependent clause).
- After driving to the city, (dependent clause).

All the above are dependent clauses and require more substance to complete the sentence. Examples are below:

- When I went to the bank, I made a deposit (complete sentence).
- When I took a walk, I got robbed (complete sentence).
- After driving to the city, I lay down and napped (complete sentence).

If you switch the order of the sentence, the comma is no longer needed. Let's take a look.

- I made a deposit when I went to the bank.
- I got robbed when I took a walk.
- I lay down for a nap after driving to the city.

That took a lot of explaining for one simple rule, but I like to use examples because I think people understand them better.

Rule 2

- Use a comma before a coordinating conjunction that connects two independent clauses.

That rule is rife with grammatical terms, so let's break it down in plain English.

A "coordinating conjunction" is a word that *connects*. In this case, it connects two "independent clauses," which means they could be stand-alone sentences. Let's look at a few examples.

PS: from now on, when I refer to a "connecting word," it means a conjunction of some sort; after all, a *conjunction connects*.

☑ I went to the bank, and I made a deposit.

☑ I took a walk, and I got robbed.

In both of the sentences above, each part of the sentence on either side of the connecting word *and* could be its own sentence.

- I went to the bank.
- I made a deposit.

If you remove the subject (I) from the second part, though, it changes everything because that sentence can no longer stand on its own, which means you no longer need a comma to separate them.

☑ I went to the bank and made a deposit.

☑ I took a walk and got robbed.

The coordinating conjunctions (connecting words) are easy to remember if you use the acronym, FANBOYS. It stands for: *for, and, nor, but, or, yet,* and *so.*

There are other types of conjunctions (or connecting words), but we'll get to them at another time.

Rule 3

- Use a comma to separate items in a list of three or more.

This rule applies when you have three or more items. In the following sentence only two items are mentioned, so you don't need a comma to separate them.

✖ I went to the bank to make a deposit, and get a withdrawal (two items).

☑ I went to the bank to make a deposit, get a withdrawal, and open a new account (three items).

✖ The sandwiches I like are turkey, and peanut butter.

☑ The sandwiches I like are turkey, peanut butter, and tomato with cheese.

You need to be careful when using commas with lists. There is still a controversy regarding the use of the final comma, which is referred to as the Oxford comma. Some people swear by it, while others claim it is not needed.

The Oxford comma is suggested for a reason: to clear up ambiguity. Take the last sentence and look at it both ways.

☑ The sandwiches I like are turkey, peanut butter, and tomato with cheese.

✖ The sandwiches I like are turkey, peanut butter and tomato with cheese.

Although I doubt this would confuse anyone, it could. Taken at face value, the sentence could mean that you like turkey sandwiches as well as peanut-butter-and-tomato sandwiches with cheese.

I am a proponent of the Oxford comma, and if you want to be understood clearly, I suggest you follow suit.

I'll give one more example. One of my favorite movies is an

older western featuring Clint Eastwood. The title is: *The Good, the Bad and the Ugly*. And it's punctuated exactly that way, with no comma after *bad*.

However, when I say it, and when I hear others pronounce the name, there is a definite pause after *bad* as if a comma belongs there. In fact, the Italian name for the movie (it was made in Italy) is *Il Buono, il Brutto, il Cattivo*.

As you can see, there are commas after all the nouns. I think it sounds better that way.

Besides, if you don't use a comma, it could be interpreted as being about two people: the good, and the bad and ugly. With the comma, it leaves no doubt: the good, the bad, and the ugly.

Rule 4

• Use a comma to offset nonessential information.

I'll simplify this. If you have a phrase or part of a sentence that is merely there to provide additional information, use a comma to offset it.

Use a comma before it if it completes the sentence, and on each side of it if it comes in the middle of the sentence. Examples follow:

☑ I went to the bank and saw Jane, one of the tellers.

☑ I went to the bank and saw Jane, one of the tellers, as she got out of the cab.

In each case, the phrase offset by the comma was not needed.

☑ I went to the bank and saw Jane.

☑ I went to the bank and saw Jane as she got out of the cab.

As you can see, when we removed "one of the tellers" from each sentence, it was still a complete sentence and the meaning didn't change. "One of the tellers" was simply additional information about Jane.

If the word or phrase is necessary though, *do not* use a comma. Here are a couple of sentences showing the difference.

☑ My niece Bella calls me almost every night.

☑ My wife, Mikki, fixes my coffee every day.

In the first sentence, we didn't use a comma because *Bella* is a necessary part of the sentence. I needed to mention her name to distinguish her from the other nieces I have. If I had just said, "My niece calls me almost every night" you wouldn't know which niece calls.

In the second sentence, however, *Mikki* is not needed because I only have one wife (thank God). There is no need to mention her name.

Rule 5

Use a comma to offset a negative comment in opposition to the sentence. And use it whether it occurs mid-sentence or at the end.

- I went to the bank, not the restaurant.
- I stopped at the restaurant, not the bank, so I have no money.

Rule 6

Place a comma between adjectives that modify the same noun. It will be easier to show this with examples.

- Mollie was a pretty mean dog.
- The bear that attacked was a big, furry bear.
- She lived in a big, expensive house.

Sometimes several adjectives are used before a noun but don't modify the noun the same way. If they modify the noun independently, put a comma between them.

There are several ways you can tell whether to use a comma or not. The first is to place the word *and* between the adjectives and see if the sentence still makes sense. Let's take the sentences above and check.

- Mollie was a pretty and mean dog.
- The bear that attacked was a big *and* furry bear.

- She lived in a big *and* expensive house.

Sentence number one changes meaning. Mollie goes from being considered "pretty mean" (somewhat mean) to being thought of as *pretty* and *mean.*

Sentences two and three sound fine. "It was a big and furry bear" and "She lived in a big and expensive house." Neither of those sentences are ideal as far as I'm concerned, but they work.

The second way to determine what and how the adjectives modify is to rearrange them.

- Mollie was a mean pretty dog.
- The bear that attacked was a furry, big bear.
- She lived in an expensive, big house.

Now look at each sentence, and how rearranging the adjectives affected the meaning. In sentence one, it now reads "Mollie was a mean pretty dog," meaning Mollie was a pretty dog that was mean. That's different than the original. In the original, it said Mollie was mean, but it didn't imply she was pretty.

Sentences two and three don't change in meaning.

Rule 7

- When a title follows a name, use commas to separate it from the rest of the sentence.

Again, examples show it best.

- Donald Trump, the president, is disliked by many people.
- Sean McGonnigle, the chief of police, was reappointed by the mayor.

Rule 8

- Use commas to separate the month and day from the year in a date, and to separate the street address, city, and state in an address.

As usual, examples follow:

- He was born on April 21, 2015.
- He lives at 555 Orange Street, Austin, TX 78617.

If only the month and year are used, no comma is necessary.

- He was born in April 2015

Rule 9

- Use commas to separate numbers of four digits or more.

Most everyone knows this, but we'll give examples just in case.

- 36,577
- 1,998
- 124,222
- 2,467,655

One more note about commas with numbers:

If you are writing about metric measurements, use spaces instead of commas. This will avoid confusion for European readers who are accustomed to seeing commas used as decimal points. The examples below will show it better.

- He bought a farm in Tuscany, a 16,7 hectare one (European way).
- He bought a farm in Tuscany, a 16.7 hectare one (U.S. way).

- For the resort, they needed a minimum of 2 449 hectares. (A space was used instead of a comma.)

If we had used a comma and not a space in the last example, a person used to seeing commas used as decimal points would have read that as "2.449" hectares (quite a difference).

Rule 10

- Use a comma after an adverb that introduces a clause.

Here are a few example sentences:

- Inadvertently, I spilled the wine.
- Finally, he caught the killer.
- Mistakenly, he locked her up.

Many guides make exceptions for one-word introductions where clarity is not affected. The words *now, nowadays, today,* and *yesterday* are some of the words allowed exceptions.

- Yesterday we went to the zoo.

You *could* use a comma after *yesterday*, but you don't have to. Either way is fine. The following sentences are more examples:

- Now is the time to go.
- Nowadays everyone has a cell phone.

Rule 11

- Use a comma *after* a conjunctive (connecting) adverb that links/connects two independent clauses.

Below are examples:

- My sister got carded at the store; therefore, we got no wine.
- My dog isn't very big; however, he scared off the intruder.
- She studied hard for the test; consequently, she got an *A*.

If the situation does not call for a semicolon, use commas on either side of the conjunctive adverb (connecting word).

- He didn't believe, however, that money was a factor.

Below is a list to use as a reference.

LIST OF CONJUNCTIVE ADVERBS

- accordingly
- additionally
- also
- besides
- comparatively
- consequently
- conversely
- elsewhere
- equally
- finally
- further
- furthermore
- hence
- henceforth
- however
- in addition
- in comparison
- in contrast
- indeed

- instead
- likewise
- meanwhile
- moreover
- namely
- nevertheless
- next
- nonetheless
- now
- otherwise
- rather
- similarly
- still
- subsequently
- then
- thereafter
- therefore
- thus.
- yet

Rule 12

- Use commas when attributing quotes.

Whether you're writing novels or nonfiction, you will invariably come across the need to use a direct quote, and when you do, a comma will be needed to offset that quote. The examples below show how.

- "I'm not staying," Joe said. "I'll be leaving after dinner."
- Margaret glared and said, "Why not?"

Rule 13

- Use a comma after *yes* and *no* when they occur at the beginning of a sentence.

Take a look at the two examples below:

- *Yes*, I'm going to the bank.
- *No*, I won't be making a deposit while I'm there.

Rule 14
Use a comma when directly addressing someone.

- It's time for us to go, Captain.
- You'll go, Detective, when I say you can go.
- Captain, it's not right to hold us back.

This doesn't cover every instance where you may need a comma, but it covers most of them. Even a professional writer may go years without encountering a circumstance not mentioned here.

In a later chapter, we cover many examples of how and when to use commas with specific words and phrases.

Part Five

MORE COMMA RULES

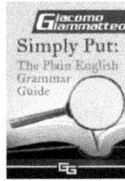

Like everything else, there are rules that govern punctuation with dialogue tags. It just so happens that one of them I don't agree with.

There aren't many times when I don't listen to my editors, but there are a few. I don't mean the odd occurrence when an editor may make a call on whether to capitalize a word or something like that. I'm talking about repeated usage that is contrary to the *rules* of writing.

I'm going to discuss one of those rules now. It deals with the use of commas. But before we do that, let's take a look at some other rules governing comma usage.

I know we just spent a lot of time learning about commas, but they're tricky to understand, so it may be worthwhile to review some of the rules. If you don't think you need to go over them, skip this part.

What Are Commas Used For?

According to the *Oxford English Dictionary*:

A comma marks a slight break between different parts of a sentence. Used properly, commas make the meaning of sentences clear by grouping and separating words, phrases, and clauses. Many people are uncertain about the use of commas and often sprinkle them throughout their writing without knowing the basic rules.

Here are the main cases when you need to use a comma:
• in lists of three or more items
• in direct speech
• to separate clauses
• to set off certain parts of a sentence
• with *however* and other conjunctions (connecting words)

There are a lot of rules governing the use of commas, and some of them can be confusing. The rules dealing with lists and dialogue are fairly rigid, but they are also simple to understand. The separation of clauses is more complex. I've tried to list the more confusing ones below, and I explain them in plain language instead of using grammatical terms so that anyone can understand how it's done.

I sometimes think that dictionaries and grammarians are associated with the legal and insurance professions; they continually try to complicate things with obscure language.

WHEN NOT TO USE COMMAS

There are a few hard-and-fast rules, and there's one I see broken frequently. I'm guilty of it myself. What rule?

Do *not* use commas *after such as, like,* or *although*—unless what follows is a nonessential clause (unnecessary).

Examples follow:

✗ I love Italian foods such as, ravioli, lasagna, and gnocchi.

✓ I love Italian foods, such as ravioli, lasagna, and gnocchi.

✓ I love Italian foods, such as ravioli, lasagna, and gnocchi, but not dishes that include seafood.

Commas are required when the clause is not needed for the sentence to be true. Take the clause out and see: "I love Italian foods but not dishes that include seafood."

The next few examples deal with using commas with the word *although* and *like*.

❌ I like Italian food although, I eat steaks every week (no comma *after although*).

✅ I like Italian food, although I eat steaks every week.

❌ Even though I love Italian food, I eat things like, burgers and hot dogs (no comma after *like*).

✅ Even though I love Italian food, I eat things like burgers and hot dogs.

Do not use commas in front of dependent words, like *because, when, if, until, and unless*. (For a more complete list of dependent words, see the list on my website.)

❌ The dog was panting, because it had just chased the mailman.

✅ The dog was panting because it had just chased the mailman.

❌ We'll go to the mall, when your mother gets home.

✅ We'll go to the mall when your mother gets home.

When to Use a Comma

Use a comma after a dependent clause that starts a sentence.

- "When I went to the bank, I made a deposit."

As mentioned previously, a dependent clause cannot stand on its own. It is not a complete sentence, and that's why it's called a dependent clause; it needs the rest of the sentence to support it.

Commas always follow these clauses when they're found at the start of a sentence, but when a dependent clause ends the sentence, it no longer requires a comma:

- "I went to the bank and made a deposit"
- "I made a deposit when I went to the bank."

Use commas to separate independent clauses when they are joined by any of these seven coordinating conjunctions: *and, but, for, or, nor, so, yet.*

✅ "I went to the bank *and* made a deposit." (No comma before *and* because "made a deposit" is not a complete sentence.)

✅ I went to the bank, *and* I made a deposit. A comma is necessary because "I made a deposit" is a complete sentence.

❌ I went to the bank, *and* made a deposit. (No comma is necessary.)

❌ I went to the bank *and* I made a deposit. (Comma is necessary after *bank*.)

And don't forget that the comma goes *before* the conjunction (for, and, nor, but, or, yet, so), not *after* it.

There is a case where a comma also goes after the connecting word. Look at the following, which you'll see later as well.

- A semicolon should not be used in place of a colon. It's not a good substitute, and, despite its name association, it doesn't want to be a colon.

Notice the comma after *and*. We need a comma there because the phrase that follows—despite its name association—is a nonessential clause; it's not needed. Take it out and see.

- A semicolon should not be used in place of a colon. It's not a good substitute, and it doesn't want to be a colon.

As you can see, we still need the comma preceding *and* because it joins two independent clauses.

Dependent markers are words added to the beginning of an independent clause that make it a dependent clause. The following is a list of those words:

- **after**
- **although**

- **as**
- **as if**
- **because**
- **before**
- **even if**
- **even though**
- **if**
- **in order to**
- **since**
- **though**
- **unless**
- **until**
- **whatever**
- **when**
- **whenever**
- **whether**
- **while**

An example might be:

- I made a deposit *when* I went to the bank.

Notice that "I made a deposit" and "I went to the bank" are both independent clauses, but by adding *when* to the beginning of the second clause, it becomes a dependent clause because you didn't just make a deposit, you made it *when you went to the bank*.

Another example could be shown by turning the sentence around.

- When I went to the bank, I made a deposit.

Note that we need a comma after bank in this situation because it falls under the rule mentioned earlier: use a comma after a dependent clause that starts a sentence.

Now we're about to get confusing, so put on your learner's hat.

Independent Marker Word

An independent marker word is a connecting word used at the beginning of an independent clause. These words can always begin a complete sentence.

When the second independent clause in a sentence has an independent marker word, a semicolon is needed before the independent marker word (yes, that dreaded semicolon). These words are also called *conjunctive adverbs*.

✅ I wasn't planning on going to the bank; *however*, I needed to make a deposit.

As you can see *however* joins the two independent clauses using a semicolon.

✅ I don't want to go to the bank; *nevertheless*, I need to make a deposit.

✅ "I'll be driving down Fourth Street; *therefore*, I'll stop by the bank and make a deposit.

A Partial List of Independent Marker Words/Conjunctive Adverbs

- also
- consequently
- fortunately
- furthermore
- hopefully
- however
- in addition
- in fact
- instead
- likewise
- meanwhile
- moreover
- nevertheless
- on the other hand
- otherwise
- therefore

- unfortunately

There are other words that could be added to this list, but these are the more commonly used ones.

Use commas before every sequence of three numbers when writing a number larger than 999. (Two exceptions are when writing years and house numbers.)

For example, you would write numbers this way: 4,176 or 10,000 or 1,304,687.

But you would write, "He was born in 1972," and "She lives at 2419 Canal Street."

Use commas before and after nonessential words, phrases, and clauses—that is, parts of the sentence that interrupt it without changing the essential meaning.

Below is an example of such a sentence. It's a sentence I used previously, but it's a good example.

☑ A semicolon should not be used in place of a colon. It's not a good substitute, and, despite its name association, it doesn't want to be a colon.

Note that this breaks the *rule* that says *not* to place a comma *after* a coordinating conjunction, but an analysis will show that the comma after *substitute* is required because it separates two independent clauses, and the comma after *and* is required because it precedes a nonessential phrase ("despite its name association"). That phrase is nonessential because if you remove it, the sentence still makes sense and the meaning doesn't change.

☑ A semicolon should not be used in place of a colon. It's not a good substitute, and it doesn't want to be a colon.

With the preceding sentence, you can eliminate that comma by rewording the sentence to make the second clause dependent:

✅ A semicolon should not be used in place of a colon. It's not a good substitute and doesn't want to be a colon.

Below are a few examples of combining appositives with nonessential phrases.

✅ My wife, Mikki, who loves to shop, is at the fabric store.

✅ My brother Chris, who loves to drink, is at the store getting beer.

In the first example, we used commas to offset *Mikki,* as it is nonessential. Since I only have one wife, naming Mikki is unnecessary. We also offset the nonessential phrase "who loves to shop," as it is not necessary. As you can see below, the sentence works fine without either one of these.

✅ My wife is at the fabric store.

In the second example, we don't offset *Chris* with commas as I have more than one brother, so using his name is necessary. The nonessential phrase follows the same reasoning as the first example. Now look at the essential parts of that sentence.

✅ My brother Chris is at the store getting beer.

There is a time (when using a nonessential clause) that you should opt for a different punctuation mark. I cover this later on in the chapter dealing with dashes, but it won't hurt to touch on it here.

We've gone over nonessential phrases and how you should use commas to offset them, but there is an exception. (Isn't there always?)

If that *additional* bit of information contains commas of its own, use an *em dash* on either side of it instead of a comma; it makes it easier to understand. I've included an example of that below, where the sentence is presented both ways—with and without the em dash.

- My van, the one with the wheelchair ramp, automatic doors, and wench, is black.
- My van—the one with the wheelchair ramp, automatic doors, and wench—is black.

As you can see, the use of the em dashes makes the sentence easier to read than the one without em dashes.

Use commas to separate items in a series of three or more:

- My brother Chris picked up hot dogs, hamburgers, potato chips, and Coke when he went to the store.

If he had only picked up two items, the commas would not have been necessary.

- My brother Chris picked up hot dogs and hamburgers when he went to the store.

And notice in the first example, there is no comma following *Coke* and before *went*. You only use commas to separate the items in the list.

Use a comma after introductory adverbs.

✅ Finally, he got home with the food.

✅ At last, I could breathe.

Also insert a comma when phrases like "on the other hand," *however*, and *furthermore* start a sentence.

No comma is necessary with *however* when it is used to mean "no matter how" or "to whatever extent."

- *However* you do it, get it done.
- *However* it has to be done, just do it.

Look at the sentences with those meanings substituted.

- No matter how you do it, get it done.
- Whatever has to be done, just do it.

Use a comma when attributing quotes.

The rule for where the comma goes depends on where the attribution is placed within the sentence.

If attribution comes before the quote, place the comma prior to and outside of the quotations marks:

- My brother said, "I picked up some beer."

But if the attribution comes after the quote, put the comma inside the closing quotation marks.

- "I got some beer," said my brother (or "my brother said").

Use a comma to separate each element in an address. Also use a comma after a city-state combination within a sentence.

☑ I work downtown at 1212 Milam Street, Houston, Texas 77070.

or

☑ I love to visit San Francisco, California, one of my favorite cities.

Use commas to separate full dates (weekday, month and day, and year). Separate the parts of an address from each other as well as from the rest of the sentence.

☑ August 1, 1960, was the day I was born.

Keep the commas even if you add a day's name.

☑ Friday, April 21, 2015, is a day I'll not soon forget.

You don't need to add a comma when the sentence contains only the month and year.

☑ February 2015 was a disastrous month.

☑ The meeting is set for October 2029, in Philadelphia.

I learned this because in many of my books, I'll list the date and location at the heading of each chapter. I used to use commas to separate month from year until my editor corrected me.

Use a comma when the first word of the sentence is a free-standing "yes" or "no." In other words, you could have stopped with the one-word answer.

☑ I asked my brother if he got chips, and he said, "Yes, I got chips as well as pretzels."

He could have simply said *yes*, but he added more.

Use a comma when directly addressing someone or something in a sentence.

☑ Tommy asked, "Can I go out to play, Mom?"

Use a comma to offset negation in a sentence.

☑ "I made a deposit, not a withdrawal, when I stopped at the bank."

Notice that this is similar to the use of commas with nonessential clauses. If you remove the negative part of the sentence, the meaning of the primary sentence stays the same.

- "I made a deposit when I stopped at the bank."

There are plenty of other rules regarding commas, but most of the common ones are mentioned here. The ones that aren't—like where and when to place commas between adjectives when they are used as descriptors—are easy enough to find.

Part One

WHEN TO USE A COMMA WITH . . .

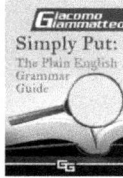

A while ago, I promised to address the issues many people have when using commas with certain words and phrases. The next few chapters don't cover them all, but they deal with a few of the more confusing ones.

Knowing when and how to use commas is one of the more challenging things to learn about punctuation.

Periods, question marks, exclamation points, and even the others are easy in comparison.

Chapter One

WHEN TO USE A COMMA WITH ...

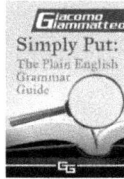

*A*s Well As

A lot of people pay no attention to commas, and it shows. Commas are critical to reading enjoyment. They instruct readers when to pause or slow down just as other punctuation helps readers know when to get excited or surprised, stop for a long pause, stop-and-go more quickly, etc.

The key to the proper use of commas is knowing when and how to use them. Many writers seem to be confused when to use a comma with "as well as."

Many of the "as" phrases present a problem: "such as," "as in," "as if," "as though," and more. But "as well as" seems to trip people up *as much,* if not more, than the others.

We'll get to those other phrases in time; for now, let's focus on "as well as."

I did a search using Google's Ngram viewer using "as well as" with and without a comma preceding it or following it. The results showed that people used a comma almost as much as they didn't.

Although the results were surprising, they were understandable. "As well as" is used in situations where it doesn't need a comma, but it is also used where it does require one.

The phrase "as well as" is often used to compare things, such as "She's beautiful *as well as* intelligent."

When it's used like this, it doesn't need a comma. But it's also used in ways that do need a comma.

Let's look at a few definitions from *Merriam-Webster's* and Dictionary.com before we go on.

Merriam-Webster's

: and in addition : AND
    brave as well as loyal
    as well as preposition
    Definition of as well as (Entry 2 of 2)
    : in addition to : BESIDES
    the coach, as well as the team, is ready

Dictionary.com

>as well ,
    in addition; also; too:
    She insisted on directing the play and on producing it as well. equally: The town grew as well because of its location as because of its superb climate. as well as, as much or as truly as; equally as: Joan is witty as well as intelligent.

Let's look at the examples provided by the dictionaries:

- He's brave *as well as* loyal.
- The coach, *as well as* the team, is ready.
- Joan is witty *as well as* intelligent

In the first example, we're saying he's brave *and* loyal. In that case, no comma is needed. The sentence flows (reads well) without a pause.

In the second example, "as well as the team" seems more like an afterthought. It's like saying "The coach is ready. Oh, yeah, the team is too." You could also read it as "The coach is ready *in addition to* the team."

When you have a similar situation—where the person or item mentioned after "as well as" seems like an *aside* or something *less important*—then you should use a comma.

In the last example: "Joan is pretty as well as intelligent," it seems obvious that "as well as" is used as a conjunction (a connecting word like *and*), and since it is not connecting two independent clauses, no comma is necessary.

Let's look at a few more examples.

- Barbara, *as well as* Tammy, is going to the party.
- Sean and Maddy, *as well as* Nora and Bruce, are going to the beach.
- He doesn't play golf *as well as* his father

In the first and second examples, "as well as" is used to offset two *asides,* so commas are necessary on both sides of the phrase.

Also note how in the first example, even though we mention Barbara and Tammy, we used a singular verb form while in the example with Sean and Maddy, we used a plural.

The reason is because "as well as" does not make the subject a compound subject which would require the plural. This only happens in cases where you combine the nouns, in effect, making more than one subject.

- Barbara and Tammy *are* going to the party.

In the above case, there is no aside simply a conjunction (connecting word) which is used to create multiple subjects: Barbara *and* Tammy.

In the third example, we state "He doesn't play golf *as well as* his father." In that sentence, we're using *as well as* to compare. We're comparing how well he plays golf to how well his father plays. No comma is necessary.

Summary

That sums it up for "as well as" and comma usage.

🖐 If you are adding a phrase or clause and using it as an *aside*, use a comma to offset it. And remember, if that phrase falls in the middle of the sentence, it needs commas on both sides (as we did above). If the phrase comes at the end of the sentence, only use a comma preceding it.

🖐 Any other time you use "as well as," no comma is necessary.

Chapter Two

WHEN TO USE A COMMA WITH BECAUSE

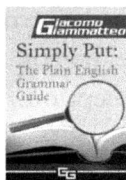

Because is most often used to connect two clauses in a sentence.

- I went to sleep early because I was tired.

You usually don't need a comma before *because*. An exception to this rule applies when the clarity of the sentence is at risk. We'll look at when that may happen later.

Regardless of where *because* falls in the sentence, it is introducing a clause that should answer the question why.

- Because it was raining, they didn't go swimming. (*Why* didn't they go swimming?)

That is a dependent clause introducing a complete sentence.

- Because it was raining . . . (dependent clause).
- They didn't go swimming (complete sentence).

In cases where *connecting words*, such as *because, though, since, etc.,* introduce a complete sentence, a comma follows. Now let's look at the reverse.

- They didn't go swimming because it was raining (no comma needed).
- She went to the party because she loved dancing (no comma). (*Why* did she go to the party?)

When a connecting word introduces a dependent clause following a complete sentence, no comma is needed.

And here comes the exception. You knew there'd be one, didn't you?

As I mentioned earlier, exceptions are made if clarity is at risk. When a sentence begins with a negative, it often muddles the clarity of what follows.

- He didn't win the race because of his ego.
- He didn't win the race, because of his ego.

In the first example (no comma), we're implying he won the race but it wasn't due to his ego. (It could have been anything else—someone tripped him, his physical ability, his determination, etc.)

In the second example (with comma), we're implying he *didn't win the race*, and it was *due to* his ego (maybe he hung back too long wanting to show an explosive finish).

- He didn't go for the touchdown because of her.
- He didn't go for the touchdown, because of her.

The same reasoning applies in the above examples.

In the first example, he went for the touchdown, but we're implying the reason he went for it had nothing to do with her. In other words, he went for the touchdown for any number of reasons, but not because of her. He may have had a bet on the game, maybe he wanted to break a record, or perhaps he simply wanted to win.

- He didn't go for the touchdown because of her; he
  wanted to break the school record.

In the second example, perhaps he didn't go for the touchdown because *she* was rooting for the other team (her school) and he didn't want to embarrass her by padding the score.

You should use commas to clarify as much as possible, but the simpler solution may be to reword the sentence.

- He didn't go for the touchdown because his fiancé was in
  the stands and rooting for the other team.

Or perhaps there is a more sinister reason why he didn't go for the touchdown.

- He didn't go for the touchdown because he was being
  paid to shave points.

Just remember, you don't use a comma before *because* with the possible exception of when a negative introduces the sentence. In cases like that, it may be simpler to reword the sentence.

We didn't cover *since*, but it is almost interchangeable with *because*, and in examples like the ones we gave, the same rules apply.

Chapter Three

WHEN TO USE A COMMA WITH SO

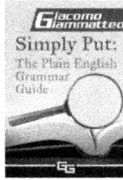

Simply Put:
The Plain English
Grammar
Guide

One of the more difficult things for me to learn regarding punctuation was when to use a comma with the word *so*.

The use of *so* didn't seem to fit with the normal instances of when to use commas with conjunctions. Sometimes it did and at other times, it didn't. I looked it up in *Garner's Modern American Usage* book and CMOS (*Chicago Manual of Style*).

As is often the case, those explanations left me more confused than when I started.

Finally, I stumbled on an explanation written on Grammarly's site. After reading the blog, I was able to grasp the subtleties of when—and when not to—use a comma with *so*.

I think one of the problems is that *so* is so versatile. It covers a lot of ground for such a little word. Let's look at how it's used.

1. *So* is used as *therefore*, to show the result or consequence of something.
2. *So* is used as *so that*, to show reason or purpose.
3. *So* is used to express *addition,* as in "and also."
4. *So* is used as an intensifier, though it's often frowned upon when used that way.

5. *So* is used to agree or acknowledge the truth of something, as in "I heard it's so."

6. *So* is often used as a substitute for something already stated, as in "She didn't like his manners, and she told him *so*."

For right now, let's look at the first two usage examples.

The Trick

When you use *so,* substitute *therefore* or "so that" in your head. Say the sentence using those words. If *therefore* works, use a comma; if "so that" works better, do not use a comma. Make sure the sentence retains the same meaning.

One scenario that may mix you up is when you have the words "so that" written in a sentence. I've provided an example below.

- I couldn't care less about Grammarly's suggestion of a dangling modifier, *so that* advice was useless.

The presence of the "so that" phrase may throw you off at first, but if you carefully follow through with the substitution, you'll see it works. Try it with both options, but remember to substitute for *so* only, not for "so that."

- I couldn't care less about Grammarly's suggestion of a dangling modifier *so that that* advice was useless.

- I couldn't care less about Grammarly's suggestion of a dangling modifier, *therefore* that advice was useless.

Therefore is the only substitution that works because you're only substituting for *so,* not for "so that." In other words, if you substituted "so that" the sentence would read as above: "I couldn't care less about Grammarly's suggestion of a dangling modifier, *so that that* advice was useless."

More Examples

- We stayed out all night, *so* we could see the meteor storm pass.

In some instances, the substitution doesn't seem to work. Look at the sentence above. I could substitute "so that" or *therefore* and have either one work.

But if you do the substitutions, and then look closely at the sentences, there is a different meaning depending on which substitution you use.

- We stayed out all night, *therefore* we could see the meteor storm pass.
- We stayed out all night *so that* we could see the meteor storm pass.

In the first sentence, they stayed out all night, and as a *result*, they could see the meteor storm.

In the second sentence, the *reason* they stayed out all night was so they could see the meteor storm.

Two more examples follow.

- We built a fire *so* we kept warm.
- We built a fire, *so* we kept warm.

If you analyze the sentences, you'll see they are similar to those above. In the first sentence, they built a fire *in order* to keep warm (reason or purpose). In the second sentence, they built a fire, and *as a result*, they kept warm.

Substituting *therefore* or "so that" doesn't clarify things enough in the above cases because either one of the substitutions will work. You have to know what message is being conveyed. Are you trying to tell the *reason* they built the fire? Or are you relating the *result*?

Bottom Line (for this part)

The bottom line is simple. If the sentence works with both

substitutions, use a comma with the one that reflects *result* (therefore) and no comma with the one that reflects *reason* (so that).

Other Uses of *So*

When *so* is used as an adverb meaning "to a great extent" or "to a degree," as in "I love you *so* much" or "That felt *so* good" there is no need for a comma before it or immediately following it.

An exception I can think of is if you said something similar to "I love you so, but I can't marry you."

In that case, however, you are adding an independent clause after *so,* and it's that clause that is requiring the comma (preceding *but*).

When *so* is used as a substitute for something already stated, as in "She didn't like his manners, and she told him *so,*" no comma is necessary preceding *so* or following it (assuming words follow it, and no other construction demands a comma). Usually, when used in this manner, *so* comes at the end of a sentence: "Have you finished packing?" "I think *so.*"

When *so* is used to mean "in the same way," no comma is needed, as in "She swam like a fish, and *so* did he."

When used to indicate a measurement (usually accompanied by a gesture), as in "That fish was *so* long" or meaning "to an extent," as in "A man can only do *so* much." In either case, no commas are necessary before or after.

When *so* is used as an introductory word (beginning a sentence), as in "So you finally got here" or "So you arrived!," no commas are needed; in fact, in most cases, *so* isn't needed. Look at the sentences without *so.* "You finally got here" and "You arrived!" Both are fine without *so.*

There are other ways to use *so,* but I can't think of any that would require using a comma immediately preceding or following it.

Chapter Four

WHEN TO USE A COMMA WITH AS

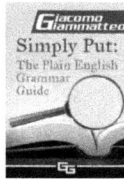

*D*etermining when to use a comma is often difficult, but with the word *as* it seems even more difficult. Consider the following examples:

- He built a fire *as* it was snowing.
- He built a fire, *as* it was snowing.

Which one is correct? Both.
It depends on the intended meaning. Let's analyze them.

- He built a fire *as* it was snowing.

Without a comma, what we're saying is "He built a fire *while* it was snowing."

- He built a fire, *as* it was snowing.

In this example (with the comma), we're saying "He built a fire *because* it was snowing." The *reason* he built a fire was due to the snow.

Let's look at a few more examples.

- He ate lunch *as* the kids were playing (while).
- He ate lunch, *as* the kids were playing (because).
- Tina yelled for us to come to dinner *as* the baby was crying (while).
- Tina yelled for us to come to dinner, *as* the baby was crying (because).

In the examples above, you can see that when *as* is used in place of *while*, there is no comma, but when it's used in place of *because*, it may need a comma if what follows *as* is nonessential.

Chapter Five

WHEN TO USE A COMMA WITH LIKE AND SUCH AS

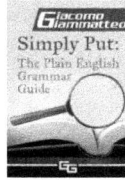

Giacomo Giammatteo
Simply Put:
The Plain English
Grammar
Guide

*T*his chapter will be slightly different. We'll be discussing *how* to use *like* and "such as" along with how to use commas with them.

Like and "such as" are often used interchangeably and for good reason—they are extremely close in meaning and usage.

I'll repeat this later, but *like* is often used in a comparative mode while "such as" is more inclusive. Let's look at a few examples.

- Dogs such as Great Danes and poodles don't bite.

You don't use a comma before "such as" because it introduces a phrase that is a necessary part of the sentence. We can tell this by removing the phrase to see if the sentence still means the same thing.

- Dogs don't bite.

We all know that's not true. Some dogs *do* bite; therefore, the phrase "such as Great Danes and poodles" is needed.

However, if you said, "Herding dogs, such as Australian shepherds and border collies, are very active," you would need commas. Remove the phrase and see.

- Herding dogs are very active.

Not only does it make sense, it means the same thing. With the phrase intact, we're only adding information, and it's information that isn't needed.

When you use *like* it tells us that what comes before it is to be used in a comparative manner to what comes after it. A few examples follow using both terms.

- She loves long-haired cats, such as the Persian and the ragdoll.
- Her husband loves short-haired dogs, such as the boxer and Dalmatian.
- Her husband loves dogs like the German and Anatolian shepherds, but he can't tolerate the long hair.

Let's look at the sentences above. In the first one, we said, "She loves long-haired cats, such as the Persian and the ragdoll." By using "such as" we indicated that what followed was to be included as examples of *long-haired cats*; in other words, they *were* long-haired cats.

Example two was the same: the Dalmatian and boxer *are* short-haired dogs.

However, in the third example, we said her husband loves dogs *like* the German and Anatolian shepherds, meaning he loves dogs that have something in common with them. Perhaps it is their size, traits, mannerisms, etc., however, he doesn't love the shepherds (they are long-haired dogs) but dogs like them.

Like Is Used for Comparison

We'll go through this again.

While *like* and "such as" are frequently interchangeable, there are differences. *Like* is used to compare what follows, and "such as" includes what follows. Sometimes it may seem like splitting hairs, but if you analyze the sentences, there is a difference. Look at the examples below:

- My grandson loves fruits like strawberries and cantaloupe.
- My grandson loves fruits, such as strawberries, blackberries, cantaloupe, and honeydew.

In the first example, we use *like* to say he loves fruits *that are similar to strawberries and cantaloupe*. It doesn't mean he likes those specific fruits; he may hate *them* but like fruits that are similar.

In the second example, we use "such as" to be specific—saying he loves strawberries, blackberries, cantaloupe, and honeydew.

 Remember to use *like* for comparisons and "such as" when you want to cite examples.

Bottom Line

I don't think anyone is going to misunderstand you if you use *like* instead of "such as" or vice versa, but it helps to know the difference.

Now that I've touted all this nonsense, let me say that *like* and "such as" are as interchangeable as any words I know. I've cited some differences that the strictest grammarians adhere to, but in everyday life, writers can, and should, use whichever word they want.

"Such as" comes across as more formal, and if that's the style a writer is aiming for, they should use it.

If you have a situation where it seems natural to use "such as," then use it. If you think *like* sounds better, use *it*.

Chapter Six

COMMAS WITH "THAT IS," "NAMELY," AND "FOR EXAMPLE"

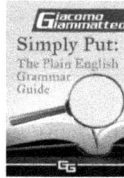

hat is, namely, and *for example* are three expressions that are usually followed by commas, however, there are recommended ways of treating them that differ from the typical practice.

Chicago Manual of Style (CMOS) has the following to say:

Expressions of the type that is are traditionally followed by a comma. They are best preceded by an em dash or a semicolon rather than a comma, or the entire phrase they introduce may be enclosed in parentheses or em dashes.

— CMOS

Let's look at a few examples:

- There are dogs that are far worse biters than pit bulls —*namely*, rat terriers and other small dogs.

- The water district (*that is*, John Moore) voted to increase rates again.
- The water district raised rates again; *that is*, the head of the committee raised them to get his wife a new car.
- Our cat's room held proof of her hunting prowess—*for example*, rat and squirrel tails, remnants of frogs and lizards, and feathers from various birds.

In this same section, CMOS goes on to say:

When *or* is used in a sense analogous to that is (to mean "in other words"), the phrase it introduces is usually set off by commas.

— CMOS

- The surveyor's tool, *or* transit, is used to align points, determine levels, and measure distances.

When *or* is used this way (as "in other words"), it places the phrase it introduces as nonessential, therefore, necessitating commas on either side of the phrase. As you can see in the example, *transit* is merely additional information and not necessary to the sentence.

Chapter Seven

PERIODS

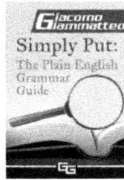

*T*he period may be the easiest of all punctuation marks to master.

The long and short of it is this: a period ends a sentence. It's similar to a traffic signal that has turned red; it means stop.

If a person has problems dealing with the period, it usually involves the use of a period with other punctuation.

The rules are short and simple. End a sentence with a period. If other punctuation such as a question mark or an exclamation point ends the sentence, then omit the period.

One potentially confusing situation is when a sentence that is not a direct question ends in a quote or when the name of an artistic work requires a question mark. An example would serve best.

- When my kids were younger, they loved the song "Who Let the Dogs Out?"

As you can see, the period was left out even though the sentence was a statement, not a question. The same applies to exclamation points.

Abbreviations are another potential sticking point. Consider the following:

- Don't forget. The meeting starts at 8:30 a.m., so be there.
- Don't forget. The meeting starts at 8:30 a.m.

As you can see, when we remove "so be there" the period following the abbreviation serves as the period that ends the sentence.

Some of the more commonly used abbreviations occur with names. Let's look.

- *Mr.* Johnson will be there; he's giving a speech.
- *Ms.* Simmons will accompany her husband to accept the award.
- And don't forget *Dr. J.* Tomkins starts the evening off at 8:00.

As you can see, periods were required after *Mr., Ms., Dr.* and the initial *J*.

THE PROPER USE OF PERIODS WITH PARENTHESES WILL BE covered in the section dealing with that punctuation mark.

It's just as important to know when *not* to use a period, which isn't often, but it does happen. Many style guides recommend omitting the period after uppercase abbreviations such as FBI, IRS, CBS, HBO, etc; in fact, most initialisms are no longer written that way. A few exceptions are U.S. (United States) or U.S.A. (United States of America). There are others, but those two may be the most recognizable.

If you were to end a sentence with either one of them, the period would be omitted as the example below shows.

✅ I have traveled all over, but I'm glad to be back home in the good old U.S.A.

❌ I have traveled all over, but I'm glad to be back home in the good old U.S.A..

Despite the many rules, the use of periods often boils down to a style choice. Many style guides differ on how words should be punctuated, and I think abbreviations fit that category more than any. Consider some of the variations in geographical terms alone:

- USA or U.S.A.
- UK or U.K.
- Washington DC or Washington D.C.
- NYC or N.Y.C.

No matter the style you choose, it should agree with the style guide you follow. If you don't have a style guide, select a style and be consistent.

Another recommendation for geographical terms is to use periods when referring to American states or Canadian provinces but not when using the two-letter postal abbreviation.

- I went to Col. and Nev. last month, and next month, I'll be going to AZ and UT, if all goes well.

WHILE WE'RE ON GEOGRAPHY, WHEN WRITING ABOUT THE U.S. or the U.K., the full name should be used when they are nouns, but the abbreviations can be used when they're used as adjectives.

- He's from the United States.
- He's a U.S. citizen.
- Her U.K. citizenship is about to be confirmed.
- Her cousins live in the United Kingdom.

Using periods with time indicators or indicators of eras is optional.

- The party starts at 8:00 pm or p.m.
- Julius Caesar died in 44 BC or B.C.
- Augustus Caesar ruled until AD 27 or A.D. 27.

If you have doubt, consult a good dictionary, but be sure to commit to one resource and stick with it as not all dictionaries agree, and you want to be consistent above all else.

Now on to a topic that remains controversial and often elicits passionate debate.

- Should you use one or two spaces following the end of a sentence?

Thirty or forty years ago, two spaces was the norm; it is no longer the case. A single space is preferred and recommended.

That wraps up periods. The one or two points that weren't covered will be dealt with in those sections.

Chapter Eight

QUIZ 1

Simply Put:
The Plain English
Grammar
Guide

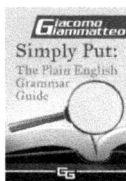

Punctuation Quiz 1—Commas

The following sentences may or may not have misplaced or omitted punctuation. See if you can spot the issues. And remember, there may be more than one thing wrong in any sentence, or there may be nothing wrong.

1. Sally went home for a nap then decided to stay awake.
2. When Sally went home, she took a nap before dinner.
3. Going home was not her first choice, but once she made the decision she took a nap.
4. Bob went to the store and bought some ice cream and cake.
5. The dog that bit me, the German shepherd, is right over there.

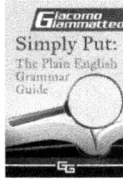

Punctuation Quiz 2—Commas

1. I went to the store and got some milk.
2. When I visited Italy I returned with limoncello.
3. We vacationed in Europe, and bought a lot of clothes.
4. I went to Italy to see the sights, but also the people.
5. I took a train from Rome to Naples and while on the train, I saw Sofia Loren.

Chapter Ten

QUESTION MARKS

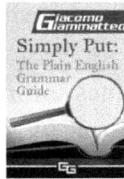

$\mathcal{I}$f the period is the easiest punctuation mark to learn, the question mark may be next in line.

Let's start off with the most common use of a question mark: direct questions.

The rule is as follows.

- Question marks follow direct questions.
- Indirect questions take a period.

Here are a few examples.

- Where are you going? (direct question).
- I wonder where he thinks he's going (indirect question).

For punctuation placement with quotation marks, see that section.

A question mark that completes a book title, song, etc., is retained even if it falls in the middle of the sentence.

- Do your kids like the song "Who Let the Dogs Out?," a one-hit wonder by Baha Men?

- "Who Let the Dogs Out?" is my grandson's favorite song.

If the question mark following the work comes at the end of a sentence, only one end punctuation mark is used.

- My grandson loves "Who Let the Dogs Out?"

If a sentence requiring a question mark is inserted into another sentence, whether it is set off by em dashes, parentheses, or enclosed in quotations, keep the required question mark.

- "He asked me to go to the prom with him. He said, and I quote 'Will you please go with me?', and of course I said *yes*."
- I wondered where to take her to eat dinner (Should we get Chinese food?), but I decided I should just ask her.
- She told me—Did I hear correctly?—that she'd go to the prom.

Use a question mark when necessary even if it isn't a complete sentence.

- "Her birthday is Monday. Or is it Tuesday? Wednesday? Hell, I don't know."

However, if multiple questions are contained within the same sentence, use only one punctuation mark at the end of the sentence.

- Her birthday is Monday, or is it Tuesday or Wednesday? Hell, I don't know.

Questions That Don't Follow the Rules.

This refers to *requests*. While they may sound like the typical direct question, they are punctuated as if they were an indirect question.

- Will you please put extra cream in that coffee.
- Would someone *please* shut that dog up.

If you're uncertain about a fact when writing, it is often shown by using a question mark within parentheses or brackets to let the reader know of your uncertainty.

- The Pyramid of Cheops was built 4500 (4600?) years ago.

A little bit more on the rule regarding requests. If you ask a favor or make a request that someone *may not* comply with, use a question mark.

When directing a request to someone where the expectation is that they *will* comply, a period should be used (like a wife asking her husband to pick up something at the store). A few examples follow:

- Do you mind telling me your ethnicity and age?
- Would everyone please give a big hand to Susie.

That does it for question marks. If we didn't cover anything here, it will be addressed in the appropriate section.

Chapter Eleven

EXCLAMATION POINTS

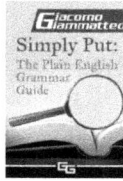

*E*xclamation points are similar to jalapeños—one or two is fine, but too many are . . . well, too many.

There was an episode of *Seinfeld* where Elaine, who worked at a publishing company, was editing a book, and there was a big argument over the use of exclamation points.

The bottom line is that exclamation points are used for *extreme* emphasis and lose all effect if used too often. The *Oxford English Dictionary* cites the following as one of the reasons to use exclamation points:

---

direct speech that represents something shouted or spoken very loudly

---

EXCLAMATION POINTS BY NATURE DENOTE SURPRISE, ANXIETY, fright, etc. Because of this, there is no need to state such when using them in dialogue. I often see examples like the following:

- "Call the police!" he yelled (or shouted or screamed).

The use of the exclamation point already tells us he uttered it excitedly. There's no need to tell us again. Some editors may disagree, but from a reader's point of view, I don't want the writer telling me the character yelled or shouted. The exclamation point is enough.

When used, the exclamation point ends the sentence. No other punctuation is necessary.

The use of exclamation points combined with quotation marks is addressed in the discussion on quotation marks.

Chapter Twelve

QUIZ 3

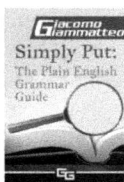

*P*unctuation **Quiz 3** (Fix the punctuation in each sentence.)

1. I love Italian pastries such as, *cannoli*, *sfogliatelle*, and *pizzelle*.

2. I love Italian food, such as ravioli, lasagna, and gnocchi.

3. I love Italian food, such as ravioli, lasagna, and gnocchi but not dishes that include seafood.

Chapter Thirteen

QUIZ 4

Giacomo Giammatteo
Simply Put:
The Plain English
Grammar
Guide

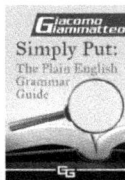

*P*unctuation **Quiz 4**

This one we'll do differently. It will be multiple choice. Choose the sentence or sentences that are punctuated correctly.

The dog was panting, because it had just chased the mailman.
The dog was panting because, it had just chased the mailman.
The dog was panting because it had just chased the mailman.

YOU'LL GO TO THE BEACH WHEN I SAY YOU CAN YOUNG MAN.

You'll go to the beach, when I say you can, young man.
You'll go to the beach when I say you can, young man.
You'll go to the beach when I say you can young man.

YOU CAN'T GO TO THE BEACH AND IT'S BECAUSE I SAID SO.

You can't go to the beach, and it's because I said so.
You can't go to the beach and it's because, I said so.
You can't go to the beach, and it's because, I said so.

. . .

CELL PHONES WHICH WERE A RARITY EVEN IN THE '90S ARE NOW everywhere.

Cell phones, which were a rarity even in the '90s are now everywhere.

Cell phones which were a rarity even in the '90s, are now everywhere.

Cell phones, which were a rarity even in the '90s, are now everywhere.

Cell phones, which were a rarity even in the '90's, are now everywhere.

BARBARA EARNED FIFTY DOLLARS FOR BABYSITTING BUT SHE SPENT it all on eyeliner and makeup.

Barbara earned fifty dollars for babysitting, but she spent it all on eyeliner, and makeup.

Barbara earned fifty dollars for babysitting but, she spent it all on eyeliner and makeup.

Barbara earned fifty dollars for babysitting but, she spent it all on eyeliner, and makeup.

Barbara earned fifty dollars for babysitting, but she spent it all on eyeliner and makeup.

Chapter Fourteen

PARENTHESES

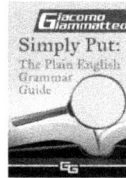

*P*arentheses—**When and How to Use Them**

I'm guessing most of you know the way to use parentheses, but you may be surprised at some of the rules regarding how to punctuate them. Let's take a look.

The spelling of the word itself is the first thing to look at. *Parentheses* (with an *es* at the end) is plural and is almost always used that way. This differs from *ellipsis* and *ellipses*.

Both words indicate the plural form when spelled with an *es* at the end, but *ellipsis* (singular) *is* the punctuation mark, while *parenthesis* (singular) is only half the punctuation mark.

Parentheses are used to indicate side remarks or to provide additional information. An example follows:

- My black van (the one with the wheelchair ramp) has a handicap license plate.

Remember that whatever is inside the parentheses must not be critical to the sentence; in other words, if you remove what is inside the parentheses, the sentence should still make sense. If you try that with the above sentence, you'll see it works.

- My black van has a handicap license plate.

As you can see, the reader doesn't get the additional information, but the sentence is still complete.

This is the same as what we discussed with *nonessential phrases*, those offset by commas.

Punctuation with Parentheses

Punctuation with parentheses is more complicated. The common practice is to place the punctuation inside the parentheses *if* you've got a complete sentence.

- I wondered where to take her to eat dinner (Should I get Chinese food?), but I decided I should just ask her.

If the parentheses information completes the sentence, place the punctuation outside.

- He went north at the fork in the road (though he could have gone south).

If the words inside the parentheses do not form a complete sentence, then place the punctuation outside the parentheses.

- He came to a fork in the road and paused to think (Which way to go?).

Notice in the sentence above, the period follows the parentheses, while the question mark is inside the parentheses. If a question mark or an exclamation point applies to what is inside the parentheses, they go inside.

Commas almost always follow the parentheses, but not always. If you want to determine whether or not to use a comma, simply take out the parenthetical information and apply the rules we talked about in the section on commas.

- He came to a fork in the road (checked his map), then decided to head north (comma needed).
- He came to a fork in the road, then decided to head north (sentence without parenthetical information).
- He came to a fork in the road (checked his map) and headed north (no comma needed).
- He came to a fork in the road and headed north.

As you can see, punctuation is determined by the structure of the sentence *without* the information within the parentheses.

One thing before we go further. Remember that whatever thought is within the parentheses should not be a primary part of the sentence; in other words, the sentence should stand alone. You should be able to remove the words inside the parentheses and have the sentence still make sense (presuming it made sense before).

Just when you thought you were done, we're going to add a few more rules. If you have a sentence, and you insert a parenthetical thought in the middle which is functioning as an aside or inside comment, you don't capitalize the thought or end it with a period.

- When Sean graduated from college, he was drafted by the Giants (he wanted the Patriots) which upset him.

On the other hand, if the sentence inside the parentheses comes at the end of the original sentence and adds information to the original, it requires an initial capital letter as well as a period at the end, inside the parentheses.

- When the Giants drafted Sean he was upset. (He hoped the Patriots would have chosen him.)

If what you're placing inside the parentheses is an extension of the original sentence or simply explaining something in the sentence, you do not capitalize the initial letter or end it with a period. I'll provide and example from this book.

- Seldom do three letters stir such confusion. And yet it's easy to spot the differences. It's (with apostrophe) is always, and only, a contraction—either for "it is" or "it has," as in "It's been raining" (it has been raining). Or "It's mine" (it is mine).

As you can see "It has been raining" is merely explaining the phrase preceding it: "It's been raining," and the same applies to "It is mine."

Other things to place inside parentheses include:

1. The numbers in numbered lists, such as "Bring these items to the interview: (1) a résumé, (2) a portfolio showing your design work, and (3) a list of references."
2. Area codes for phone numbers: (415) 624-5555. We don't think much about this now as most smartphones and contact-management lists format this automatically.
3. Time zones, which are often cited in emails and other correspondence when arranging interviews. An example follows:

- "The flight leaves at 6:00 p.m. (EST)."

To indicate a person's birth or death date, as in:

- John Lennon (10/9/1940–12/8/1980), was a British (Liverpool) citizen and member of the rock band The Beatles.

To explain the meaning of, or to clarify, an abbreviation or acronym, as in:

- John Smith, the CMO (chief marketing officer) was just promoted again.

You may also do the reverse. "John Smith, the chief marketing officer (CMO), was just promoted again."

It's only necessary to do this the first time you cite it. The rest of the time, the parentheses are not necessary.

The meaning of the acronym is not capitalized unless it's a proper noun. Note that *chief marketing officer* (above) is lowercase, but if the acronym had represented a proper noun, it would have been capitalized as in the example below.

- When we went to Houston, we visited NASA (National Aeronautics and Space Administration) and saw some interesting videos.

Though seldom used, the following rule is worth mentioning. Translations of a foreign language are often placed in parentheses.

- He claimed to know how to speak Italian, but his vocabulary was limited to *buon giorno* and *buonanotte* (good morning and good night).

A final note on punctuation and capitalization inside parentheses.

If what's inside the parentheses forms a complete sentence, and it ends with a question mark or exclamation point, keep the terminal punctuation (? !), inside the parentheses. Only capitalize the first letter if it's a proper noun or if what is contained inside the parentheses is a quoted sentence, or if it's a complete sentence coming at the end of the main sentence.

- It looked as if we were in trouble. We had good advice (her dad told us "Don't go!"), but we didn't listen.
- It seemed as if he was going to prison for what he did. (Why shouldn't he?)

If the parenthetical sentence ends in a period and occurs mid sentence, *do not* capitalize the first letter (unless it's a proper noun), but still place the period inside the parentheses. If the sentence follows the main sentence, capitalize the initial letter.

One more thing to note. As we already said, the text inside the parentheses is not essential to the sentence and that affects which verb you would use. Look at the following.

- Dana and Nick *are* going to the party.
- Dana (and Nick) is going to the party.

In the first example, we're saying both Dana and Nick are going to the party, and there is equal emphasis on each. In that case, a plural verb is necessary because there are two subjects—two people going to the party.

In the second example, the focus is on Dana. *She's* the one going to the party, and oh yeah, Nick is too. In this case, we're saying Dana is going and then adding that Nick is also.

Chapter Fifteen

ELLIPSES

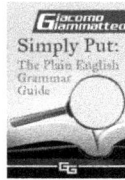

*T*o start things right, let's get this out of the way—it is *ellipsis* (singular) and *ellipses* (plural).

Ellipses are used to indicate words that have been omitted and, in most fiction writing, pauses in dialogue or narrator thought.

- He wanted to tell her what he'd done, but . . .
- I want to tell you what I've done . . . but I'm afraid you might get angry (pause in thought).
- She was going to be married, but then . . .

Some style guides suggest no spaces either before or after the ellipsis, while others suggest a space preceding and following an ellipsis. Either style works as long as you keep it consistent.

Most writing programs today have a feature that automatically converts three successive periods into an ellipsis, and some editors will accept that. Even with the automatic conversion though, many editors want to see a space between each dot. (Writing programs do the same with two consecutive hyphens—convert them into an em dash.)

An exception many writers make regarding spacing is that if the ellipsis occurs at the end of a sentence, they omit the space after the ellipsis. In the first example below, there is a space before the ellipsis but none after it. The second has a space before and after the ellipsis.

- Jane said, "He wanted to tell her what he'd done, but . . ."
- Jane said, "He wanted to tell her what he'd done, but . . .
  "

I have to admit, I like it better with no space following the ellipsis.

Note that the *Chicago Manual of Style* (CMOS) suggests spaces on either side of an ellipsis, but AP suggests no spaces. Once again, pick a style guide and be consistent.

Let's look at more of what the style guides have to say. This is from AP:

> In general, treat an ellipsis as a three-letter word, constructed with three periods and two spaces, as shown here.

— ASSOCIATED PRESS STYLEBOOK

AP's recommended formatting is:

- . . .

And not the way writing apps format three periods:

- ...

AP goes on to say:

>Use an ellipsis to indicate the deletion of one or more words in condensing quotes, texts and documents. Be especially careful to avoid deletions that would distort the meaning:

— ASSOCIATED PRESS STYLEBOOK

- I do solemnly swear that I will faithfully execute . . .

>PUNCTUATION GUIDELINES: If the words that precede an ellipsis constitute a grammatically complete sentence, either in the original or in the condensation, place a period at the end of the last word before the ellipsis. Follow it with a regular space and an ellipsis: I no longer have a strong enough political base. ... [*sic*]

— ASSOCIATED PRESS STYLEBOOK

The last part of AP's guideline is where a lot of writers go wrong; they use the ellipses only and do not place a period preceding it. If you look above at the example of the presidential oath, you'll see the ellipsis has no period preceding it, but that's because what precedes it is not a complete sentence. If it had been, you would have needed a period followed by a space and an ellipsis.

- I know she loved me. . . .

If what's written is a complete sentence that requires punctuation other than a period, use that punctuation first, followed by a space and ellipsis.

- What if he decides to come? . . .

If an ellipsis is used for deleted words (parts of a speech or quote), and it falls at the end of a paragraph, but is continued at the beginning of the next paragraph, start that paragraph with an ellipsis.

Below is an example taken from *AP Stylebook*'s online site. It cites parts of President Nixon's resignation speech.

>Good evening. ... [*sic*]

    In all the decisions I have made in my public life, I have always tried to do what was best for the nation. ... [*sic*]

    ... However, it has become evident to me that I no longer have a strong enough political base in ... [*sic*] Congress.

— AP STYLEBOOK

The use of the ellipses lets the reader know that parts of the speech have been removed.

By the way, in a couple of the above examples using AP's wording, I used [*sic*] after the ellipsis. I did that because AP had explicitly stated to "treat an ellipsis as a three-letter word, constructed with three periods and two spaces . . ." and yet they continually formatted them as ...

Another Note About Ellipses

If an ellipsis follows a complete sentence, the writer may choose to begin the next letter with a capital even if it didn't start with a capital in the original quote.

- The company announced it was going to begin a new insurance policy on Monday, but it would only be for full-time employees, and, according to Rose, assistant to the CEO, the plan would go into effect immediately.

- The company announced it was going to begin a new

insurance policy on Monday. . . . According to Rose, assistant to the CEO, the plan would go into effect immediately.

If you notice, we placed a period after *Monday* (preceding the ellipsis), and we capitalized *According* even though it hadn't been capitalized in the original.

Chapter Sixteen

QUOTATION MARKS

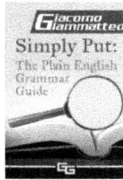

*J*t wouldn't seem as if quotation marks would be difficult to master, but getting them right takes a bit of learning. Some aspects of usage are easy—like knowing you enclose dialogue within a pair of quotation marks. The following is an example:

- "You can't go to the beach," she said.

That was easy. You put the words someone (she) said inside of the quotation marks.

The more difficult part comes when you add other punctuation. (By the way, I'm using *quote* and *quotation* interchangeably although some people may think that's wrong.)

What kind of punctuation?

Things like periods, commas, question marks, exclamation points, semicolons, colons, em dashes, etc.

Commas and Periods

We'll tackle the easiest ones first: commas and periods. Commas and periods go *inside* the quotation marks, as seen in the previous example.

- "You can't go to the beach," she said.

You could also turn the sentence around and use a period inside the quotation marks.

- She said, "You can't go to the beach."

So the first rule is:

🐗 Periods and commas go *inside* the closing quotation marks (in American English). There are, of course, exceptions, and we'll deal with those later.

By the way, you'll see the wild boar icon (🐗) often. I use it to call attention to rules and such.

Please note that everything discussed here applies to what's known as "American English"; in other words, the English used in the United States, not in countries where British English is used.

There is one exception to this rule. (Isn't there always?) You put commas and periods within quotation marks except when a parenthetical reference follows. To further explain, I'll give you an example from Purdue University's excellent online site.

- According to Foulkes's study, dreams may express
  "profound aspects of personality" (184).

And here's another one.

- Professor Karber's book on "economic crisis" almost
  caused an "economic crisis" (Karber, p. 255).

Notice that in both sentences the ending punctuation comes after the parentheses and outside the quotation marks.

Another rare exception occurs when you may be providing instructions on how to type something (like a password), and you use quotation marks to designate that. As an example:

- To access the account, type "#,!^@$".

The period has to go outside of the marks so there is no confusion. If the period were inside the quotation marks, it could be considered part of the password.

The above examples are just the type of things I mean when I say you can't say *always*. Many books and sites dedicated to grammar say, "Periods *always* go inside of quotation marks." While I agree that they *usually* go inside, they don't *always* go inside.

Question Marks, Exclamation Points, and Em Dashes

Question marks and exclamation points are the two main forms of punctuation you need to be concerned about, but you can throw em dashes in with them.

These bits of punctuation are the ones with the most flexibility. The accepted rule is that you put a question mark or exclamation point within the quotation marks *if* the punctuation applies to the quotation itself. Place the punctuation *outside* the closing quotation marks if the punctuation applies to the whole sentence. I realize that may be confusing, so I'll provide a few examples:

- His teacher asked him, "Did you do your homework?" (inside)
- Did his teacher actually say, "He did his homework"? (outside)

In the first instance, we're explaining that the teacher asked the student a question. In the second, we are asking if the teacher said what was in quotes. The first sentence is a statement containing a question listed within quotation marks, while the second is a question regarding a statement the teacher made.

Now to tackle em dashes. Em dashes are easier because there is only one easy-to-spot instance when an em dash is used *inside* a quotation mark, and that's when the em dash is used to mark an interruption in dialogue. The following is an example.

- "You better get out of here, or I'll—"
- "Or you'll what?"

That's it. There is no other time I can think of when an em dash would be *inside* the quotation marks (unless it is contained within the sentence).

And now for an example using an em dash outside the quotation marks. Em dashes are seldom used in this manner, but if they need to be, this is how.

- "You shouldn't have betrayed me"—the mob guy slammed his fist on the hood of the car—"but now you'll pay for that."

In the above case, the dialogue is interrupted by *action*. That's why an em dash is required. It could have also been a *thought* as in the following.

- "You shouldn't have betrayed me"—the mob guy thought of what to do next—"but now you'll pay for that."

Or you could have eliminated the em dashes by using a dialogue tag like "the mob guy said."

- "You shouldn't have betrayed me," the mob guy said as he slammed his fist on the hood of the car, "but now you'll pay for that."

This differs from the first example we used because in that sentence, the dialogue was interrupted by another person, so the quotation had to be closed, then reopened with a new speaker. You can see it repeated below.

- "You better get out of here, or I'll—"
- "Or you'll what?"

In the cases where we used the em dash, the dialogue was interrupted by the original speaker. In one case, he interrupted it with action; in the other, it was with thought, but both times the original speaker continued with the dialogue.

Colons and Semicolons

Note that in one of the earlier sentences, when I was explaining the rules governing commas and periods, I used a semicolon that was placed *outside* the quotation marks. I've made note of it again:

- Please note that everything discussed here will apply to what's known as "American English"; in other words, . . .

Another example:

- As Lucky Luciano said, "The mob never dies"; it does get new bosses.

In these examples, the semicolon is placed *outside* the quotation marks because that's where semicolons go. The same applies to colons. Here's an example using a colon:

- The gangster cited three things he attributed to what he called his "rise to fame": tough luck, bad timing, and knowing the right people.

Note:

While researching this, I came across several sites that included "em dashes" with semicolons and colons as punctuation marks that *always* go outside the quotation marks. But as we've seen, that isn't the case. Em dashes have a long history of being used *inside* quotation marks when it comes to interrupting dialogue.

Using Quotation Marks When Referring to Individual Letters

Some writers use quotation marks (as opposed to italics) to emphasize letters when the letters refer to themselves.

- One of the differences between U.S. and U.K. spelling is how we spell *traveling*. The preferred way to spell it in the United States is with one *l* while in the United Kingdom, it is with two *l*'s.

Note that the last example uses an apostrophe to make the *l* plural. It is one of the few times an apostrophe is used that way (more on that later).

I don't use quotation marks in that manner. I use italics for letters.

Emphasizing Words

Though you technically can use quotes for the same purpose, I like to use italics to emphasize a word and when referring to the word itself because it's less cumbersome, especially when you're setting the definition of a word in quotes.

- The sergeant ordered the men to *move* it. (emphasis)

Also when referring to the word itself.

- When used as a verb *move* means "to reposition something or someone." (referring to the word as itself)

If you notice, in the first sentence the use of italics emphasizes *move* so that as you read the sentence you almost hear the word *move* yelled.

In the second sentence, the use of italics indicates you are referring to the actual word. A good way to test this is to see if you can use "the word" just before the word in quotes:

- When used as a verb (the word) *move* means to reposition something or someone.

Now try it with the first sentence; it doesn't work.

- The sergeant ordered the men to (the word) *move* it.

I never knew this trick until my editor told me. At the time, she was tasked with editing my *No Mistakes Grammar Bites* books, and I had used quotation marks for a lot of words, the ones I wanted to emphasize as well as the ones used as words. Her suggestion made it much easier to read.

Using Scare Quotes

Scare quotes have become popular in the past few decades, and though they sometimes fall out of favor, it hasn't stopped people from using them—possibly even overusing them.

Scare quotes are almost always used to emphasize that a word or short phrase is being used sarcastically or in irony. I've included a few examples.

- She was brutally beaten and almost killed while sleeping at the city's "haven" for battered women.
- He served what he called a "diet" meal, loaded with cheese and cream.

In each case, it is obvious the writer is being sarcastic, and that sarcasm is emphasized by using quotation marks around the word or phrase.

Quotes Within Quotes

This is a tricky one, and although it's seldom used, it's worth noting.

About the only time you'll need this rule is if you're mentioning what someone else said inside a sentence already surrounded by quotation marks; in other words, a "quote within a quote."

If that confuses you, think of it this way: Suppose you're writing a book and a character is talking (which would be inside quotation marks), but what the character says contains a few words someone else said. Below is a character explaining Bill's actions and thought process.

- Sean explained, "Bill was going to tag along, but then Margaret said, 'It's dangerous,' and her words must have given him pause."

Notice that what Margaret said ('it's dangerous') is surrounded by single quotation marks while the whole sentence (what Joe explained) is surrounded by double quotation marks.

Thin Space

If you are using quotes within quotes, and you wind up with a single quotation followed by a double quotation mark, use a *thin space* to separate them.

If you can't make a thin space (half space) with your keyboard, use a whole space. (I cover how to make a thin space in the "Miscellaneous" section.) The following sentence shows when such an instance may occur. It may be difficult to see, but the first example uses a *thin space*, and the second uses a regular space.

- "Dominic's exact words were 'I'm gonna kill him.' "
- "Dominic's exact words were 'I'm gonna kill him.' "

One last thing about quotations: a quote within a quote is repeating what someone else said (but it's written out), and when done in that manner, the word *that* is implied. Here's an example:

- ✗ Jim told us, "Before she died, Mary said *that* 'Their love would last forever. ' "
- ☑ Jim told us, "Before she died, Mary said, 'Their love would last forever.' "

Several other times (that I can think of) when single quotes are used are as follows. The first is when a quote is used in a headline. The following is an example:

- The Presidential Candidate Promised 'No More Taxes.'

- Author Says 'Chapter One' of His New Book Will Shock You.

In a normal sentence, "No more taxes" would be enclosed in double quotes (in the United States), but in a headline, it requires single quotes. The same would apply to other things that ordinarily require double quotes, such as song titles or chapters of books, etc.

Please note that in the examples above, the capitalization may not conform to what is required for a headline.

The second is when discussing linguistics or phonetics. If a foreign word is italicized, and if the definition follows, that definition is enclosed in single quotation marks.

- Giorgio is fond of using *ciao*, 'goodbye,' to say hello as well.

Another instance where you should use single quotes . . .

We already discussed that if a quote is inside another quote, you use single quotes to enclose it, but there is another case where you do as well.

Imagine you have a person who has a nickname that you would ordinarily enclose in quotes, such as Nicky "The Rat" Fusco or Tony "The Brain" Sannulo. Now imagine someone mentioning their names while speaking to a third party. An example is below.

- Kate glanced over her shoulder, then looked at Frankie. "Why don't you ask your friend Tony 'The Brain' Sannulo. I'm sure he would know."

The reason for the single quotes instead of double is because it occurs within a sentence wrapped in double quotes already.

Another example would be if a word, meant to be enclosed with double quotes, is used within a quotation:

- Bob said, "When I say 'immediately,' I mean some time before December."

Notice in the example above, the comma goes inside the quotes. It would be the same if a situation like that occurred at the end of a sentence and required a period.

- Bob said, "I meant sometime before December; that's why I said, 'immediately.' "

And just to clarify, the above is correct with double quotes as well.
✅ The word he said was "immediately."
❌ The word he said was "immediately".
The above example is for those people who use quotes around single words. As I mentioned, I use italics, so for me, that sentence would have read as shown below:

- Bob said, "When I say *immediately*, I mean some time before December."

And yet another time to use them is the following.

For some writing, where the topic is not well-known, the author will use single quotes for words people may not be familiar with:

- The foreman instructed all the bricklayers to 'strike' the joints.

In bricklaying, at least in the Northeast, a commonly referred to practice is "striking," which is nothing more than polishing the mortar joints so they appear smooth.

Another example may be if someone were writing an article or even a book on blackjack (or any specialist topic). They may want to use a blackjack dealer's slang or jargon but are unsure how many people are familiar with the meaning. Most people know terms such as *bust, double-down, card-counting, push, etc.,* but not many would know what "anchorman" or "first baseman" mean.

An anchorman is the player in the last seat of the table, on the dealer's far right, who is last to act.

A first baseman is the player in the first seat of the table, on the dealer's far left, who is first to act.

Since this is the case, the author may wish to enclose these words in single quotes to distinguish them as words used in that profession.

- In blackjack, the 'first baseman' bets first, and the 'anchorman' goes last.

Quotation Marks Summary

In summary, these are the ways you combine quotation marks with other punctuation marks:

- Semicolons and colons always go *outside* the closing quotation mark.
- Periods and commas usually go *inside* the closing quotation mark (in American English).
- Question marks, exclamation points, and em dashes require you to think about the sentence a little to determine where they go.

And just for grins, here are a few sentences showing the differences between American and British English.

- American: "My love of music began with 'Hey, Jude.' It hooked me."
- British: 'My love of music began with "Hey, Jude". It hooked me'.

If you notice, the quotations are reversed, and the period for the British English is placed outside the quotation marks. Here's one more.

- **American**: The word he was looking for was "fulgent."
- **British**: The word he was looking for was 'fulgent'.

For many punctuation issues, the way it's done for British English is the reverse of what is done in the United States; however, you should look it up before finalizing. There may be differences in British English depending on whether it's formal or informal writing.

For the use of single and double quotation marks with measurements, see the chapter on numbers.

Chapter Seventeen

QUIZ 5

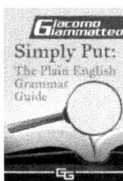

Q **uiz 5**

Bill turned to Jean. "That's what she told me. She said, "Do it, or else" and so I did it."

Bill turned to Jean. "That's what she told me. She said, "Do it, or else." and so I did it."

Bill turned to Jean. "That's what she told me. She said, 'Do it, or else,' and so I did it."

WE SHOULD STOP AND VISIT MAGGIE; SHE LIVES IN WASHINGTON D.C.

We should stop and visit Maggie. She lives in Washington D.C..

We should stop and visit Maggie; she lives in Washington D.C..

We should stop and visit Maggie, she lives in Washington D.C.

MY KIDS LOVED THE SONG, "WHO LET THE DOGS OUT?".

My kids loved the song "Who Let the Dogs Out?."

My kids loved the song "Who Let the Dogs Out?"

My kids loved the song, "Who Let the Dogs Out?."

. . .

Is the traffic bad in D.C.?
   Is the traffic bad in D.C?
   Is the traffic bad in DC?
   Traffic is bad in DC.!
   Traffic is bad in D.C.!
   Traffic is bad in DC!

Chapter Eighteen

BRACKETS

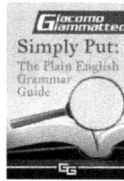

*F*irst, let's get it straight how to refer to them. Originally, [] were called *brackets* and () were referred to as *parentheses*.

Nowadays, many people are referring to them as *round brackets* () and *square brackets* [], especially in British English. Now back to learning about brackets.

You may go through life and never use brackets, but then again, you *may* find a need for them. In case you do, it would be great to know how to use them.

1. If you're quoting someone else but want to add clarification, use brackets.

Look at the example below.

- I talked to Rose after lunch, and she said, "Tom introduced us to Bob [his brother], but that's as much as I know about him."

You also use brackets to enclose the word *sic* or to make some other comment. In the following example, we're indicating the date was erroneous in the source.

- America was discovered by Columbus in 1592 [*sic*].

When a math problem has more than one level of enclosure to deal with:

- For the physics final, the class was given the following problem to solve. $9[x + 5 (2 + 4)] = 654$.

In the rare event that a third level is needed, you would use $\}$ on the outside, so the order would be: $\{ [( )] \}$.

Another use for brackets (one of the more frequent uses) is to enclose comments that explain, clarify, or add information to a sentence. It shows that those comments were by the author, and not part of the original quote.

- Steven Spielberg said, "They [the studios] finance for-sure projects only."

In that instance, *they* is clarified by the phrase "the studios," which is contained in the brackets.

Chapter Nineteen

BRACES

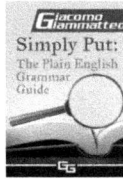

I feel safe in saying that unless you're a physicist, mathematician, chemist, or someone of that ilk, you will probably *never* use a brace unless you're playing around.

The only reason to use a brace—that I know of—is to enclose the third level of a nested equation when parentheses and brackets have already been used for the first two, so unless you're working in one of the aforementioned fields, you probably won't run into braces.

There are a few other examples of when braces might be used, although they are not that common:

Examples for Use of Braces:

- Number set: {2, 4, 6, 8, 10, 12} The set of numbers for this problem.
- To list equal choices. Order your favorite ice cream {chocolate, vanilla, or strawberry} and an appropriate cone.

Although I saw some similar things listed as examples, I have never seen braces used this way in real life.

Chapter Twenty

SEMICOLONS

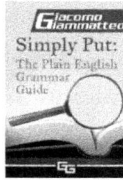

𝒶 Quick Lesson on Semicolons

There are three main circumstances when semicolons should be used.

☀ To join two closely related independent clauses. (This is the primary reason semicolons are used, and it is the way you'll likely see them used most often.)

- John rushed to the store; he had to get milk and bread, or his wife would kill him.

See how the second clause is closely tied to the first? John's life depends on that first clause. The second clause explains why John had to rush to the store.

You could have changed that sentence around a little and still used the semicolon.

- John rushed to the store to get milk and bread; he had to, or his wife would kill him.

☀ To separate lists that include commas.

- John had fifteen minutes to do three things: fill the car with gas; stop and get milk, bread, and a special treat; and get home before the new season of (take your pick) started.

This sentence was full of punctuation: a colon, several semi-colons, a couple of commas, and parentheses. Despite that, I'm hoping it was easy to read. You can thank punctuation for that.

☼ To join two clauses using a conjunctive adverb. (That's why I didn't want to go into detail. Whenever I bring up conjunctive adverbs at parties, everyone walks away.)

I said I wouldn't resort to grammatical terms in these books, so let's forget I said that. The third use of a semicolon is to join two independent thoughts using a word that happens to be an adverb. (I referred to them earlier as connecting words.)

- John had three things to do; however, he decided to take a shower before going.

SOME PEOPLE SWEAR THAT THE DREADED SEMICOLON IS A monster and has no place in the modern world. I disagree. I think the semicolon has a few specific purposes, and they benefit us all.

It's okay for writers to play with grammar. You don't have to write in complete sentences. Not all the time. Readers usually know what you mean because people often think that way.

Writers can put periods damn near anywhere. Well. Ma.ybe.

As the preceding example shows, you can't get away with putting periods after every word and certainly not in the middle of a word, but choppy sentences in a novel are fine. Really. They are.

You can even mess up with commas and em dashes or misplace the punctuation inside of parentheses. Readers will assume you are taking liberties as a writer, and they won't worry about it.

Where you run into trouble is when you start messing with

punctuation that most people don't know about, or they only know enough to be dangerous. What am I talking about?

Well, the dreaded semicolon for instance.

The semicolon is so feared that even some editors are afraid of it. I recently had a writer tell me her editors steered her clear of the use of semicolons, going so far as to suggest that one per book was too many.

And Kurt Vonnegut was no friend of the semicolon. This is what Vonnegut had to say:

Do not use semicolons. They are transvestite hermaphrodites representing absolutely nothing. All they do is show you've been to college.

I'm not sure about the transvestite hermaphrodites, but I'm pretty sure that was not a glowing endorsement.

So why all this talk about semicolons?

I'm here to defend them. I've taken out my sword and drawn a line in the sand; I've had enough. Semicolons are magnificent little creatures that get no respect. Semicolons are like snakes; people fear them, so they kill them.

I'm of a different mindset. I believe semicolons add a special flavor to a well-constructed sentence, a subtlety that a period cannot accomplish.

A well-placed semicolon is precious—like a stolen kiss between secret lovers.

When You Should Use a ;

The following is a repeat a few of the rules we've talked about, but unless you feel you have a solid grasp on the proper use of semicolons, I suggest you read on.

bay bridge

☀ The most common use for a semicolon is to connect two closely related sentences. Think of semicolons like bridges. Imagine Manhattan if there were no bridges connecting it to New Jersey, or Brooklyn, or Queens, or the Bronx. That would make New York an entirely different place. Or suppose San Francisco had no bridge across the bay to Oakland. It wouldn't be thought of as San Francisco/Oakland anymore. It would just be San Francisco. And Oakland.

That's just one of the jobs a semicolon does; it connects two closely related clauses/sentences and brings them closer. Here are some examples:

- I can't eat past midnight tonight; I have to fast for a blood test tomorrow.
- I'm not working in the garden today; I saw a copperhead there this morning.
- Bob drove ninety miles per hour on his way to the hospital; his daughter's life depended on it.

In each of the above, there is a close relationship between the clauses, a relationship that couldn't be served by a comma and wouldn't be served by a period.

☼ Another common use for semicolons is to clarify and separate a list.

- In my book *Murder Takes Time,* there are four main characters: Nicky Fusco, the hit man; Frankie Donovan, the cop; Angela Catrino, the love interest; and Tony Sannullo, the mob guy.

Let's look at that sentence if we used only commas.

- In my book *Murder Takes Time*, there are four main characters: Nicky Fusco, the hit man, Frankie Donovan, the cop, Angela Catrino, the love interest, and Tony Sannullo, the mob guy.

The second example, using all commas, is confusing. Using semicolons clarifies the meaning.

☼ The third instance where you use a semicolon is to join sentences with a conjunctive adverb. Depending on the device you're reading with, either below or on the next page you'll find a list of conjunctive adverbs. This is not a comprehensive list, but it covers many of the more common ones.

accordingly	additionally	also	anyway
besides	certainly	comparitively	consequently
conversely	elsewhere	equally	finally
further	furthermore	hence	henceforth
however	in addition	in comparison	in contrast
incidentally	indeed	instead	Likewise
meanwhile	moreover	namely	nevertheless
next	nonetheless	now	otherwise
rather	similarly	still	subsequently
then	thereafter	therefore	thus
undoubtedly	yet		

For a more robust list of conjunctive adverbs, consult your dictionary or style guide.

- He always wanted to dance; however, he had no coordination.

What You Don't Do with Semicolons

A semicolon should *not* be used in place of a colon. It's not a good substitute, and despite its name association, it doesn't want to be a colon. Semicolons are perfectly content doing the job they were meant to do.

A semicolon should *not* join two unrelated clauses.

Fear of Semicolons

I don't know why people are afraid. Look at them: ;;;;;;; They're not frightening; in fact, they're kind of cute. And it's easy to recognize not only what a semicolon is but what its function is. It is made up of a comma and a period.

The period is on top, so your first inclination is to stop—as if it were a period—but then you see the comma and continue. It couldn't be simpler. If you want to cast blame at the confusion surrounding semicolons, throw stones at the people who named it a semicolon; it would have been better with a name like *periomma*, or *commeriod*.

Chapter Twenty-One

COLONS

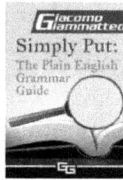

*U*se a colon to introduce a list only when following a complete sentence.

An exception may be made when a word or phrase introduces a series or a list, and the verb is *understood*. In such cases a colon is usually required.

Suppose you're making a list of the *pros* and *cons* of something. Instead of writing, "The *pros* are" and "The *cons* are," you could write:

Pros:

- Easy to do
- Inexpensive
- Fast

Cons:

- Won't be able to bill many hours
- Not as good quality
- Hazardous

Now may be the best time to talk about lists since they are often introduced by a colon. Lists are usually unordered (preceded by a bullet) or ordered (number list).

CMOS suggests as its preferred way that if a bulleted list consists of incomplete sentences, that each item can begin with a lowercase letter and does not require a period to end the punctuation (except proper nouns). It further states that if a line carries to the next line, it should be indented.

- Won't be able to bill many hours which will reduce invoicing.
- Shouldn't have to negotiate hourly rate each time.

In the two examples above, each item was capitalized and each ended with a period. Also each line that carried over was indented.

It's not necessary to keep items lowercase or to eliminate punctuation. Either way works as long as it's consistent.

Not all lists should be introduced with a colon. The general rule is that if the introductory text can stand as a grammatically complete sentence, use a colon; otherwise do not. Below are a few examples:

When Jenny comes to spend the night, please have her bring the necessary items: a blanket, a pillow, snacks, any music she wants to listen to, and something to read.

Please send Jenny with: a blanket, a pillow, snacks, any music she wants to listen to, and something to read.

Sometimes it seems as if it's a complete sentence because you're reading the entire thing. To check yourself, read only the part before the colon. In the second example, that would look like this:

- Please send Jenny with:

As you can see, that isn't a complete sentence. Now compare that with the first example.

- When Jenny comes to spend the night, please have her bring the necessary items:

☀ This rule doesn't apply to all situations, but it does to many. A colon should introduce a clause equal to the clause that introduced it. For example, in the sentence above the, "necessary items" Jenny has to bring are the items listed after the colon: a blanket, a pillow, snacks, any music she wants to listen to, and something to read. Let's look at another example.

- They have three black dogs: a poodle, an Australian shepherd, and a mutt.

Notice that what comes after the colon is simply a different way of describing what came before it. It could have been switched. Try it.

- They have a poodle, an Australian shepherd, and a mutt: all three of them black dogs.

When used in this sense, colons function similar to *i.e.,* which is explained in the chapter on Latin expressions.

☀ Colons are also used to separate times, as in 8:30 or 11:00.

☀ There are capitalization rules regarding colons as well. If the clause that follows the colon is not a complete sentence, do not use a capital letter to start it. Here are a couple of examples.

- Here's what I expect: Bring the items I asked for and nothing else.
- Here's what you should bring: gum, coke, and chips.

It's fine to capitalize *bring* in the first sentence (according to

AP), although *Chicago* style is to lowercase after a colon unless what follows consists of *two* or more complete sentences, so *Chicago* wouldn't have capitalized *bring*. If you decide to capitalize any complete sentence, make sure you capitalize all of them. Be consistent.

You do not use a colon when the items listed could be considered part of the sentence. Let's revisit the sentence we used previously:

☑ When Jenny comes to spend the night, please have her bring a blanket, a pillow, snacks, any music she wants to listen to, and something to read.

✖ When Jenny comes to spend the night, please have her bring: a blanket, a pillow, snacks, any music she wants to listen to, and something to read.

The second example had no need for a colon after *bring*. The first example did not contain one.

You may also use a colon between two independent clauses when the second clause explains the first.

- He doesn't have time to learn Italian: he's leaving in less than a month.

The colon is often used for emphasis, and often in lieu of an em dash. While em dashes are preferred by many writers, colons are an acceptable option.

- His trip to Italy could be summed up in one word: magnificent.

The colon is used for other purposes as well.

- To signify the ratio of items—2:5
- To designate passages of the Bible—Leviticus 19:28
- After a salutation—Dear John:

Colons are suggested when formally addressing someone in correspondence, whether that is a salutation or something as simple as a memo.

- Dear Rick: I was going . . .
- Note: Randy, make sure to . . .

Using Colons to Introduce Quotes

There are occasions when you may wish to use colons to introduce quotations: if the material following a colon is very long, you may use a colon to introduce it; if you are reporting on a transcript involving more than one person; if you are citing an interview; it can be used to introduce ongoing dialogue; it can be used when asking a question within the sentence. Examples follow:

Court Transcript

- Judge: "Answer the question."
- Defendant: "I was never at the scene. If someone says I was, they're lying."
- Prosecutor: "If you weren't, then tell us where you were."

Interview

- Detective Johnson: "Tell me how you found the body."
- Ms. Marson: "I came home from the grocery store and found him lying in the kitchen."

A Question Within a Sentence

- As he prepared to take his first skydive he worried: What if the chute doesn't open?

Introducing a Direct Quotation

- Have you read his latest book? I loved the part where the

killer said: "You'll do it now or you won't do anything again."

As a final note, do not use a colon after "such as," "including," and "for example." The use of those phrases are discussed elsewhere.

Chapter Twenty-Two

APOSTROPHES

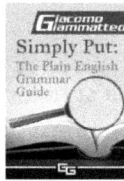

*A*postrophes are the cause of a lot of confusion when it comes to writing. People use them when they shouldn't and don't use them when they should.

It's not that difficult to master the use of the apostrophe though. Dig into the next few chapters, and you'll have proper usage committed to memory.

If all else fails, you can always come back to this section and brush up on it.

MAYBE IT'S BECAUSE APOSTROPHES ARE SO SMALL, BUT PEOPLE seem to either ignore or overuse them. Perhaps they think no one will notice.

There are several rules governing apostrophes. Let's take a look.

1. An apostrophe is used to indicate possession.

- Around the corner is Bob's house.
- That used to be Bridgette's car.

There are variations depending on the noun used to indicate possession. If a noun ends in the letter *s* some style guides suggest making it an apostrophe + *s*, while others suggest using an *s*, and then an apostrophe. The sentences below show this.

- Texas' state capital is Austin.
- Texas's state capital is Austin.
- That is the Jones's house.
- That is the Jones' house.

The main thing is to pick a style and be consistent. It should be a style that agrees with the guide you use for other grammatical rules.

Apostrophes are also used in contractions.

- Learning the difference between *it's* and *its* is easy.
- I should've gone with them.

Occasionally apostrophes are used to form plurals but only in a few circumstances.

- Plurals of *lowercase* letters (and four uppercase ones: A, I, M, U) as in: Dot your *i*'s and cross your *t*'s. (See "Italics or Quotation Marks" for details on pluralizing A, I, M, U.)
- Plurals of certain words used as words, as in: "We need to confirm the vote. How many *yes*'s and how many *no*'s did we have?" (an alternative is *yeses* and *noes*).
- Plurals of certain abbreviations, as in: "The university staff includes sixteen PhD's." (The abbreviation for MD also qualifies for this.)

Please note that depending on the style guide you follow, PhD and MD may or may not use periods in the abbreviation. Some guides recommend Ph.D. and M.D. while others suggest PhD and MD. Either one is fine as long as you remain consistent.

Another common mistake is to use an apostrophe to make a plural where a decade is concerned:

✗ He grew up in the 1960's.

✓ He grew up in the 1960s.

Some people will use 1960's or '50s, and it's accepted though not preferred. The main thing, as always, is to be consistent.

Don't make the mistake of using the apostrophe incorrectly when dealing with a noun that is already plural.

✓ The children's party was at noon.

✗ The childrens' party was at noon.

Children is already plural. It means more than one child, so the apostrophe goes after the *n*. We don't add an *s* first.

When using an apostrophe with a phrase like *brother-in-law* think of what you're describing. If you are telling someone about your *brother-in-law's* house, then the apostrophe goes after the phrase, as your brother-in-law is the person who owns the house. If it was a business owned by two brothers-in-law, then the correct way to say it would be my *brothers-in-law's* business.

If two people jointly own the same thing, use an apostrophe for the second person only.

✓ You see that Lexus? It's John and Judy's.

✗ You see that Lexus? It's John's and Judy's.

Do not use an apostrophe with personal pronouns like *hers, its, yours, theirs, whose, ours, mine,* or *his.*

A typographical point more than anything, but be careful not to use a single quotation mark in place of an apostrophe, especially when it comes before a word. I say this because many writing programs automatically correct it in the wrong way. So if you want to start a sentence with the word *because,* but the person is speaking a dialect, you may want to use 'cause. The problem is that even if you hit the right keys, the computer may correct it to 'cause.

More on Apostrophes

Using Apostrophes with Words Ending in S.

While researching the proper use of apostrophes, I came across a practice that was new—at least to me. I was looking for good explanations of when and how to use the apostrophe for words that ended in the letter *s*, and I found what I wanted on grammarbook.com.

Some people use an apostrophe + *s* for every word, and some use an apostrophe for words ending in *s*, but they don't add an extra *s*. And others differentiate depending on whether it is a proper noun. Here are a few examples of how I've seen it done.

- The shark's fin could be seen above the water. (singular)
- The rattlesnake's den was deep in the hillside. (singular)
- The rattlesnakes' den was deep in the hillside. (plural)
- Texas' policy is to prosecute to the full extent of the law. (singular)
- Tobias's beard, and all his hair, had turned white with age. (singular)

Style guides weren't much help; they disagreed with each other as much as they agreed. When I read this article on grammarbook.com, I liked it, and I thought it made sense. You can't ask for more when you're dealing with grammar. They graciously allowed me to copy the following from their site:

Another widely used technique, the one we favor, is to write the word as we would speak it. For example, since most people saying "Mr. Hastings' pen" would not pronounce an added *s*, we would write *Mr. Hastings' pen* with no added *s*. But most people would pronounce an added *s* in *Jones's*, so we'd write it as we say it: *"Mr. Jones's golf clubs."* This method explains the punctuation of for goodness' sake.

To show plural possession of a word ending in an *s* or *s* sound, form the plural first; then immediately use the apostrophe.

Examples:
the classes' hours
the Joneses' car
guys' night out
two actresses' roles

Thanks again to grammarbook.com for allowing me to use this.

Even More on Apostrophes

The little apostrophe shouldn't present so many problems, but it does. Most people understand the concept when it is used with contractions, but some people become confused when presented with issues such as "should I use an apostrophe to pluralize things." (The answer is *no* except in rare situations.) There are also a few cases where an unusual or complex form of possession needs to be expressed. We'll look at a few of these now.

Joint Possession

When people need to refer to joint ownership, there is often a question of where to put the apostrophe. Let's take a look at a few examples as that usually helps.

☑ Rose and Jim's horse.
☑ Rose's and Jim's horses.

I marked these as both correct because, depending on what you're trying to say, they may both be correct.

In the first example, you're talking about a horse jointly owned by Rose and Jim. There is one horse, and Rose and Jim share ownership.

In the second example, by adding an apostrophe to both names, you're talking about multiple horses owned by Rose and Jim separately. (Notice that horses is used in the second sentence, not horse.)

- When you mention one thing owned by more than one person, use an apostrophe with the final (closest) name.

- When you speak about separate things owned by more than one person, use an apostrophe with all the names.
- To make it clear, when two or more people own a single item, place the apostrophe on the last item only.

BEFORE WE FINISH, LET'S LOOK AT A FEW MORE EXAMPLES.

- I love Liz and Chad's kitchen (one kitchen).
- Sahrina and Steve's pool is heated (one pool).
- Nick and Dana's kids are all polite. (The kids belong to them together.)
- Bruce's and Mary's dogs are rambunctious. (Each one has separate dogs.)

However, if either of the parties mentioned is written as a pronoun, use the possessive form for both. Be careful though *not* to use possessive pronouns (mine, yours, hers, his, its, ours, theirs); instead, use possessive adjectives (my, your, her, his, its, our, their). Note that *his* and *its* are common to both groups, so you may have to use them if the situation demands.

I know this rule demands a few examples.

✗ Rose and my horse.

✗ Mine and Rose's horse.

✅ Rose's and my horse.

✅ We went for a ride on his and Rose's horse (*his* meaning Jim).

✗ He and Rose's horse was smaller than most. (*He* is not a possessive.)

✅ Yours and Rose's horse ran quickly.

✗ Rose's and your horse galloped a lot.

If you have a sentence structure that doesn't sound right to you, try rewording it to make it smoother.

Prepositions of Possession

There are three primary prepositions of possession: *of, with, to.* The typical way to use them is shown below.

- *To* is used with a pronoun, such as *it, him,* or *her* (often used with "belongs to").
- *With* is used with an adjective or a noun.
- *Of* is used with a noun or a possessive pronoun, such as *mine, yours, his,* or *hers.*

Here are a few examples:

- The colosseum is a prime example *of* ancient Roman architecture.
- A friend *of my* daughter went on a trip to Greece.
- The boar *with* the sharp tusks has long tusks as well.
- The *Mona Lisa belongs to* Italy, but it resides in France.
- The tomato and basil plants *belong to* my grandfather.

With prepositions of possession, you don't need an apostrophe.

One More Issue

All this talk about apostrophes brings up an example that is often debated. Look at the following sentences. Which is right?

✗ A friend *of* my brother's is coming to dinner.

☑ A friend *of* my brother is coming to dinner.

☑ My brother's friend is coming to dinner.

It should be easy to figure out that the third example is correct, and it is. It's simple; it's your brother's friend. But the other two examples present an issue for some people.

Based on what we just learned, we can see that the second example is the one we're looking for. It uses *of,* one of the prepositions of possession, so *brother* doesn't need an apostrophe.

Now for another example:

☑ The horse *belongs to* Rose and Jim.

☑ The cat *with* Bob is his.

Neither of these needs an apostrophe for the same reason as above.

Before abandoning *apostrophes*, let's look at one more issue. I've seen references to a person's "Achilles' tendon," but there's no need for the apostrophe in that expression. An "Achilles tendon" is a recognized part of the human anatomy, as evidenced by the screen-shot taken from *WEbMD's* site.

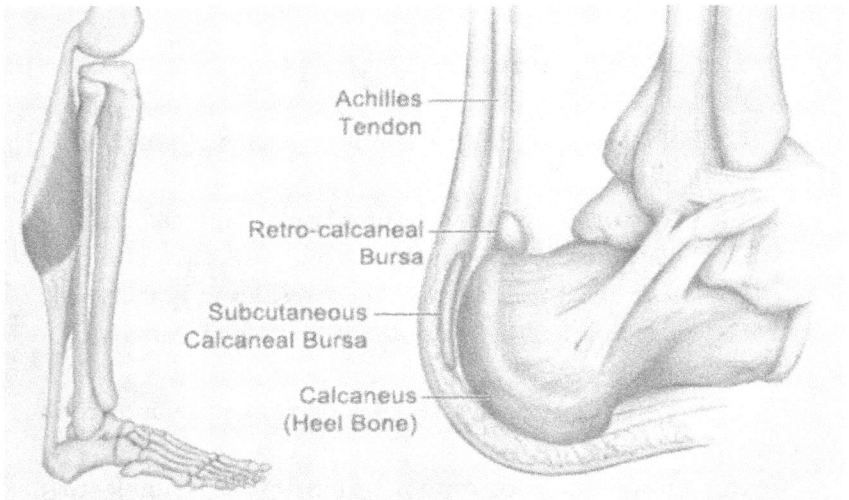

On the other hand, "Achilles' heel" would require an apostrophe because it refers to something symbolic—a seemingly invincible person's weakness (usually a simplistic one). *Merriam-Webster's* has it as an entry and lists it as shown below:

Achilles' heel noun
  Definition of *Achilles' heel*
  : a vulnerable point

— MERRIAM-WEBSTER'S

Many of the British sources I checked with, however, have abandoned the use of the apostrophe with this word. Consider the entry in the *Cambridge English Dictionary*.

---

a small problem or weakness in a person or system that can result in failure:
Math has always been my Achilles heel.

The Guardian (British newspaper) has even dropped the capitalization of *Achilles*, and lists it as "achilles heel," without the apostrophe or the capital *A*.

Chapter Twenty-Three

APOSTROPHES WITH POSSESSIVES

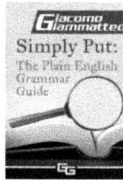

*I*f you have read much, you may have noticed the many times apostrophe use is inconsistent. A couple of words often seen differently are "farmer's market" and "farmers' market" and even "farmers market" with no apostrophe.

I've included a screenshot that shows the results of a search using Google for "farmer's market."

Notice how "Heart of the City . . ." has it listed as "Farmers Market" and in another spot we see "San Francisco Farmers' Market."

Even worse is the treatment received by (arguably) the city's most famous landmark: Fisherman's Wharf. See the screenshots below.

Welcome to San Francisco's Fisherman's Wharf

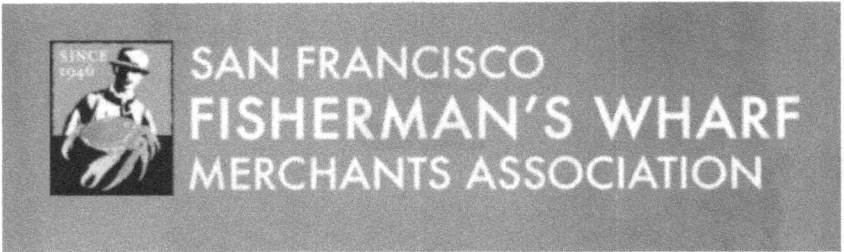

Notice how in the two screenshots above, "Fisherman's Wharf" is spelled with an apostrophe. In the top one, they have San Francisco in the possessive form also.

But in the two screenshots that follow, you'll see "Fishermans Wharf."

Fishermans Wharf

4.5 ★★★★☆ (4,484) · Tourist attraction

286-298 Jefferson St

Buzzing oceanfront tourist center

Hyatt Centric Fishermans Wharf San Francisco

4.3 ★★★★☆ (1,794) · Hotel

555 North Point St

Upscale, modern rooms, plus a pool

You have likely seen other phrases, such as "teachers college," "teachers lounge," "homeowners association," "plumbers union," and such.

In all those cases, the words are not being used in a possessive sense but as descriptors, telling what kind of college/lounge, what kind of association, and what kind of union. It's not a college *owned* by teachers but a college *for* teachers.

Different style guides treat this differently. AP says the following:

Do not add an apostrophe to a word ending in *s* when it is used primarily in a descriptive sense: citizens band radio, a Cincinnati Reds infielder, a teachers college, a teamsters request, a writers guide.

AP also recommends: farmers market, plumbers strike, etc.

Chicago doesn't agree and specifically recommends an apostrophe after *farmers*: "farmers' market."

This disagreement is one more reason why it's wise to pick a guide and stick with it.

Now we'll look at a few more examples based on AP's recommendations.

Descriptive Phrases

Do not add an apostrophe to phrases when they are in use primarily as a descriptor. It's easier to show examples.

- I think CMOS is the best *writers* style guide.
- The New York *Yankees* outfielders are all big men.
- The coal *miners* demand regarding increased wages went ignored.
- His sister is six *months* pregnant.

In the sentences above, the words are not used as possessives as much as descriptors of what follows. It's not the *writers'* style guide, as in a style guide owned by a group of writers; it's describing the kind of style guide—a writers guide as opposed to an editors guide.

The same logic applies to the Yankees. We're not speaking of outfielders owned by the Yankees, we're using *Yankees* to describe the outfielders, to distinguish them from the outfielders who play for the Red Sox or Astros or Dodgers.

And the same goes for the coal miners. We're not speaking of a demand owned by the coal miners; we're describing who made the demand.

It can sometimes be difficult to determine whether to use an apostrophe. One way to test is to see if you can substitute the words *by, for,* or *of*. (You probably have to rearrange the wording.) If *by* or *for* works better, do not use an apostrophe, but if *of* works better, use one. Look at the examples below, which use the sentences we already used.

- I think CMOS is the best *writers* style guide.
- The New York *Yankees* outfielders are all big men.
- The coal *miners* demand regarding increased wages went ignored.
- His sister is six *months* pregnant.

Now let's do some substitution.

- I think CMOS is the best style guide *for* writers.
- The outfielders *for* the New York Yankees are all big men.
- The demand *by* coal miners regarding increased wages went ignored.
- His sister has been pregnant *for* six months.

As you can see, *for* and *by* were easily substituted when the sentences were reworded.

You could have substituted *of* instead of *for* in the sentences dealing with the Yankees and the coal miners, but I don't think the substitution sounds as good.

Let's look at one more:

- The detective didn't believe the witnesses' eyesight, so he continued to question each of them.

I used an apostrophe on this one because it seemed to be more of a possessive statement. Even though the *witnesses eyesight* could be descriptive, it also sounded as if it was possessive. When you do the substitution, it bears that out.

- The detective didn't believe the eyesight *of* the witnesses, so he continued to question each of them.

As you can see, *of* works fine, but *for* and *by* don't work at all.

Plurals Not Ending in *s*

If a plural word does not end in *s* and is in the possessive form, an apostrophe *s* (*'s*) is required.

- Texas *Children's* Hospital
- Young *Men's* Christian Association

Possessive Phrases

In addition, some phrases may be difficult to determine also. One suggestion is to apply the same test we performed above with *of, for,* and *by*.

- A day's wages.
- Three weeks' vacation.
- Two months' severance package.
- Four hours' wait.

Those sayings could be reworded like this:

- A day *of* wages.
- Three weeks *of* vacation.
- Two months *of* severance pay.
- Four hours *of* waiting.

As you can see, *of* worked fine as a substitute in each example, whereas *for* or *by* would have been more difficult to make work (if at all).

Sometimes when a sentence contains both the possessive form of a noun or pronoun as well as a phrase using *of* to indicate possession, it can be confusing.

Look at the example below:

✘ We went to dinner last night with my sister and a friend of my *brother's*.

The apostrophe isn't needed after *brother*. We mentioned this earlier. It's not needed because you used *of* which indicates possession, however, in the example below, an apostrophe is needed because there is no *of*.

✅ We went to dinner last night with my sister and my *brother's* friend.

Because we're talking about *brother* in the possessive form, it needs to be possessive; in other words, it needs an apostrophe.

Some people don't worry too much about little things like apostrophes, but apostrophes are no different than other punctuation; they help people read without problems, clarifying what the author meant when they wrote it.

Chapter Twenty-Four

INANIMATE OBJECTS

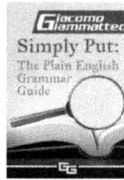

*W*hile we're speaking of *of*, let's look at a few more scenarios where you may use *of* in place of an apostrophe. (That's a lot of *ofs*, isn't it?)

- We were driving across Arizona when the car's engine overheated.

Some people claim inanimate objects shouldn't have a possessive form, as in the case above. But writing the "car's engine" is similar to writing the "engine of the car" except it sounds better. You're not claiming the engine is owned by the car, simply that the engine is part of the car.

Another example would be to say your sick grandmother is at "death's door" or "I'll meet you at heaven's gate." There's nothing wrong with any of those constructions; they're used all the time. I wouldn't go wild using such phrases, but the occasional usage sounds fine.

Chapter Twenty-Five

HYPHENS

*M*ost editors will tell you (and they're speaking from experience) that the most frequent errors in spelling occur with compound words. Many people become confused and don't know whether they should use two words, a hyphen between them, or a single word.

Questions regarding hyphenation abound when it comes to spelling, and whether to use a hyphen or one or two words.

The confusion about whether to use one word or two is understandable as the dictionaries often disagree about which version to use. Add to that the fact that many writers spell the words wrong, and it becomes easy to see how confusion sets in.

Chapter Twenty-Six

TWO WORDS OR ONE?

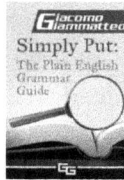

Simply Put:
The Plain English
Grammar Guide

Giacomo Giammatteo

The screenshot below shows the results of a Google Ngram search for the use of *barcode*, *bar-code*, and *bar code*.

Barcode

barcode, bar-code, bar code

As you can see from the image, the two-word version is the more commonly used version, although usage is slipping in favor of the one-word version. The hyphenated version is used far less often.

Barcode, Bar Code, or Bar-code?

When you're writing, you might ask yourself—is it *barcode, bar code,* or *bar-code?*

The *OED* (*Oxford English Dictionary*) lists *barcode* as one word. Dictionary.com and Collins Dictionary also list it as one word.

Merriam-Webster's lists it as *bar code,* spelled as two words (as did most of the dictionaries I checked with).

I think most people are familiar with the word *barcode,* so my vote goes for the one-word variation. I don't think there would be any confusion, and when you're writing, that should be your primary concern.

If you use *Merriam-Webster's,* what do you do? They recommend two words.

In cases like that—even when I feel strongly about the way a word should be used—I still go with my dictionary of choice. It may be begrudgingly, but I do it. It's not often that this happens but sometimes it *does* happen.

If you don't agree, you have plenty of reputable backup: the *OED* lists it as one word, as do *Collins Dictionary,* Dictionary.com, and others.

Hyphenation Questions and Dictionary Recommendations

Dictionaries have a huge effect on how a word is spelled and used, so it's always been a wonder to me why there doesn't seem to be more collaboration. If you look at the Google Ngram results for barcode when using British English, the difference is noticeable. The one-word version is used as often as the two-word variation.

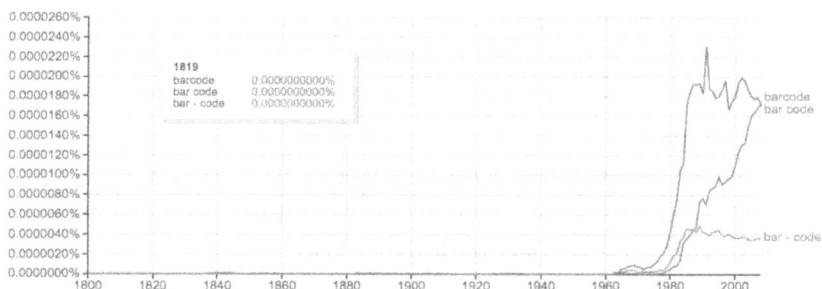

Barcode is one of the easy words, though. You decide on which variation you want to use (one word or two) and stick with it. With some words it's not so easy.

Using Hyphens with Prefixes and Suffixes

Post is always hyphenated when the second part of the word is capitalized, but it appears as one word when that is not the case.

Examples follow:

- post-Victorian
- post-Freudian

But you would say . . .

- postmodern
- postwar
- postdoctorate
- postseason

Words with *wide* at the end (suffixes) are hyphenated when used with proper nouns; otherwise they're not:

- European-wide mandate

But

- statewide

- countrywide
- nationwide

Co Words

Many style guides differ on this rule. I follow AP's suggestion, and that is to retain the hyphen when forming nouns, adjectives, and verbs that indicate occupation or status:

- co-author
- co-chairman
- co-defendant
- co-host
- co-owner
- co-partner
- co-pilot
- co-respondent (in a divorce suit)
- co-signer
- co-sponsor
- co-star
- co-worker

However, AP goes on to say that "several are exceptions to Webster's New World College Dictionary (their dictionary of choice), but in the interests of consistency we used hyphens."

Use no hyphen in other combinations:

- coed
- cooperate
- coeducation
- cooperative
- coequal
- coordinate
- coexist
- coordination
- coexistence

- copay

Cooperate, coordinate and related words are exceptions to the rule that a hyphen is used if a prefix ends in a vowel and the word that follows begins with the same vowel.

Semi Words

No hyphen is used after *semi* unless it is connected to a word beginning with the letter *i*:

- ☑ semiconductor
- ☑ semicircle

But

- ☑ semi-intelligent
- ☑ semi-inspirational

Non Prefixes

When faced with words beginning with the prefix *non*, the answer is usually use one word. This wasn't always the case, but there is a trend toward doing away with hyphens, and *non* prefixes are on the list.

While AP recommends almost all words beginning with *non* be one word, they stick with the rule regarding hyphens and proper nouns, so it would be *nonexistent, nonentity*, but he has *non-American* views.

I ran into an issue when writing a book about people who have been successful despite lacking a formal education—*Uneducated*. It dealt with the use of the word *non-degreed*, which I used frequently throughout the book. None of the dictionaries I checked with had it listed either as hyphenated or one word, and the spellcheckers insisted that the one-word version was wrong.

I finally found it listed as *non degree* in a couple of dictionaries and as one word, *nondegree* in *Merriam-Webster's*.

I couldn't find an answer in CMOS, but in the "Ask the Editor" section of the *AP Stylebook*, it used examples of "non-degreed" and said that if there is the possibility of confusion, use the hyphen.

Up or Down

Compound nouns that end with *up* can be either one word or hyphenated.

Examples follow:

- checkup
- roundup
- pileup
- close-up
- sign-up
- follow-up

This rule applies to nouns, not verbs. So, "I will *follow up* with you next week," but "I'll give you a *follow-up* call."

Most compound nouns that end with *down* are one word.

Examples follow:

- breakdown
- countdown
- meltdown
- showdown
- sundown

In and Out.

Compound nouns ending in *in* usually take a hyphen, but compound nouns ending in *out* are usually one word:

- break-in
- buyout
- drive-in
- dropout
- sellout
- sit-in
- standout
- trade-in

Compounds Preceding a Noun

Compounds with *well-*, *ill-*, *better-*, *best-*, *high-*, *little-*, *lesser-*, *low-*, etc., are hyphenated when they precede the noun (unless the expression carries a modifier, such as very).

Examples follow:

☑ Bob is a well-known engineer.

☑ He is well-known in his community.

☑ Susan does high-quality work.

✗ Susan does very high-quality work.

☑ Susan does very high quality work.

Because we used *very* to modify *high-quality*, we remove the hyphen.

In the English language, words are combined in many ways. Even then, the changing isn't done. Often, words continue to change as common usage demands.

A few modern examples of this are: *brunch* (a combination of breakfast and lunch) and *carjack* (a combination of car and hijack, which I hope you have no personal experience with on either side), and *firefly* (a combination of fire and fly).

Often, these words are joined by a hyphen for a while, but invariably they turn into one word. There is only one way to know for certain whether the word is one word, hyphenated, or two words—and that is to look it up in a reliable source. Yet even that isn't as effective as it once was because some dictionaries take longer to recognize a change than others, which is why you will find that one source will cite usage one way while another source will list it as another.

I strongly advise selecting a reputable source and sticking with it. If you're going to use *Merriam-Webster's* as your source, use it every time. If your choice is Dictionary.com, use that every time. No matter what you decide, be consistent.

Do the same with a style book. If you decide to use the *AP Stylebook* as your source, fine. If you decide on the *Chicago Manual of Style* (CMOS), that's okay too.

If you write a lot, you will invariably run into exceptions to the rules. Because of that, I suggest you get a good dictionary and keep it at hand!

Hyphens and Percent

When writing, the word *percent* is always spelled out. You don't write "He showed a 40% increase in sales"; you'd write "He showed a 40 percent increase in sales." There are certain style guides that would advise "forty percent" instead of "40 percent," but the guides agree on spelling out *percent* and not using the symbol.

And there's another thing they agree on—how to hyphenate *percent*. You don't. The word *percent* is always spelled out and never hyphenated. So it's a "20 percent hike" (or "twenty percent"), and not "20-percent" or "twenty-percent."

Hyphenate Words That Use *All*

And do this whether they precede or follow the noun.

Examples follow:

Most religious people will tell you that God is *all-knowing* and *all-seeing*.

She was an all-caring individual. You have to be careful with this because there are some words you might think fall under this rule—like all ready—but they don't, as *all ready* is the preferred choice.

Hyphenate Compound Words Containing Half Whether They Precede or Follow the Noun

Examples follow:

- I looked at Sally during the marketing meeting, and she was only *half-awake*.
- The police made a *half-hearted* attempt to find the burglar.

I cite this rule, but then I'll tell you there are exceptions. If there's anything consistent in grammar, it may be that there are always exceptions. So when you look up words like *half brother* or *half sister*, you'll see they are not hyphenated but listed as two words. So the rule will prevent you from making the combination one word, but it doesn't tell you not to make it two.

Do Not Hyphenate Like Words.

Like words can be listed as one word:

- She maintained her *childlike* sense of enthusiasm, and it made her all the more attractive.

Self Words Should Be Hyphenated:

- self-absorbed
- self-taught
- self-educated
- self-published

There are many more *self-words*, but they are easy to identify, so you should be able to handle it.

Like all grammar rules, there are exceptions, and this one is no different. If *self* is followed by a suffix (selfish, or selfless), or if it's combined with a pronoun (yourself, itself, myself), then those words are not hyphenated.

Words Ending in "ly"

We're going to start with a rule that works *most* of the time, but not always.

Do not hyphenate compound words that come before or after a noun if the word ends in *ly* (and it's an adverb). If it's not an adverb, proceed as normal.

Do not hyphenate compound words containing the word *very* either. So it was a very friendly dog, not a very-friendly dog.

Examples follow:

❌ That's a supposedly-easy exam.

✅ That's a supposedly easy exam.

❌ Her house is an utterly-disgusting mess.

✅ Her house is an utterly disgusting mess.

❌ They went to a family day picnic.

✅ They went to a family-day picnic.

You may wonder why we hyphenated "family-day" when it ends

in *ly*. Because it's not an adverb. The rule states, "Do not hyphenate *ly* words if they're adverbs," but to proceed as normal if they're not. *Family* is not.

Below is a short list of *adjectives* that end in *ly*. They are words that would be hyphenated. I got this list from the GMAT Club site, which helps prepare people for the GMAT (Graduate Management Admission Test).

- bodily
- chilly
- costly
- cowardly
- curly
- deadly
- disorderly
- easterly
- elderly
- family (noun)
- friendly
- ghastly
- ghostly
- grisly
- heavenly
- hilly
- holy
- homely
- jolly
- kindly
- leisurely
- likely
- lively
- lonely
- lovely
- manly
- measly

- melancholy
- miserly
- northerly
- oily
- orderly
- quarterly
- scholarly
- silly
- sly
- smelly
- southerly
- stately
- surly
- timely
- ugly
- unfriendly
- unlikely
- unruly
- unsightly
- untimely
- westerly
- wobbly
- woolly

With any of the words on this list, you *would* use a hyphen, assuming it was a compound modifier.

The same goes for nouns ending in *ly*, and while there aren't as many, I'm sure you will run across them at some time. Here are a few to consider.

- ally
- anomaly
- assembly
- barfly
- belly

- blowfly
- botfly
- bully
- butterfly
- doily
- dolly
- dragonfly
- family
- firefly
- fly
- gadfly
- gully
- hillbilly
- holly
- homily
- horsefly
- jelly
- lily
- mayfly
- medfly
- monopoly
- panoply
- potbelly
- rally
- reply
- supply
- tally
- underbelly

More on Hyphens and When to Use Them

Hyphens seem as if they should be easy to master, but there is a bit of learning to do.

The basics are easy. Hyphens are used to link words together. Classic hyphen usage was to separate things, such as when words at the end of a line reached the margin.

We no longer need to worry about that function. We have computer programs that do it automatically. But there are still hyphenation issues that must be dealt with manually, especially when it comes to compound modifiers.

A compound modifier is made up of two or more words—usually adjectives but sometimes nouns—and those words form a descriptive phrase otherwise known as a compound adjective or compound modifier.

When to Use a Hyphen

There are three main reasons to use hyphens.

• In compound words
• To join prefixes or suffixes to other words
• To show a word break

One more thing—a hyphen is almost always used to join individual letters to words.

- The plumber said we needed a T-joint.
- We drove for miles before coming to the T-junction.
- It was an L-shaped object.
- Once we saw it, we made a U-turn.
- He wore a T-shirt to the wedding!

One rigid rule is that hyphens should not be used as a substitute for en or em dashes. Those dashes have their own purposes and rules, and they should be used accordingly. I've included a look at each one below.

• hyphen -
• en dash –
• em dash —

Another rule is a typographical one: hyphens should not have spaces on either side of them, so it's not "re - create," it's "re-create." The same spacing rule holds true with both types of dashes. (CMOS recommends no spaces, *but AP Stylebook* recommends spaces on each side of an em dash.) Once again, I include a sample sentence using each:

- He claimed to be a hands-on manager (hyphen).
- He worked at Apple from 1999–2006 (en dash).
- She's a sympathetic—or empathetic—sort of person (em dash).

Clarification

The other function of the hyphen, and perhaps the most important, is to provide clarification or remove confusion. At it's simplest form, it's to clarify a word that may otherwise be confused with a similar-sounding word. A few classic examples are:

- recover and re-cover
- reform and re-form
- repress and re-press

Without the hyphen, *recover* means "to find or get back," as in "He recovered the stolen jewelry" or "to recover from an illness," as in "He had a heart attack, but he recovered."

With the hyphen, *re-cover* means to place new fabric on a chair or sofa or something similar, as in:

- She re-covered the antique chair with new material.
- Many things can be re-covered even books.

There is a lot of confusion when it comes to compound words. Here is an article I did on compound words, and here is the list available as a download. The main thing to understand is that a hyphen is used to clarify your meaning.

🐾 A tip: you typically hyphenate two or more words that come before a noun and present a single idea; however, you do not need to hyphenate them if they come after a noun. The sentences below may help to explain this:

- She was a runner and loved to run a *long distance*.

- She was a runner and loved *long-distance* races (long-distance is describing the kind of race).
- He often called his wife from France, which was a *long distance* away.
- He often made *long-distance* calls to his wife.
- He was a *self-made* man, having been born into the working class.
- He was a *working-class* man.
- You should *back up* your data so that if your computer crashes, you'll have a *backup*.

In the first few sentences, I hope the examples are self-explanatory—the hyphenated version is a compound adjective—it describes what kind of races and what kind of phone calls. In the third sentence, the hyphenated word describes the kind of man, a working-class man.

The fourth sentence is different. It shows the difference between using a one-word version versus a two-word version.

And so you know, *back up*, when used as a verb is always two words, but you'd say:

- "The army unit called for *backup*."
- "He made a *backup* of his hard drive."

As much as some people insist on using a hyphen with *backup* it doesn't make it right. Here is an example :

✗ "Make sure you copy everything to your *back-up* drive."

The hyphen is not needed, and, as you can see by usage results from a Google Ngram search, the use of *backup* as one word far exceeds *back-up*. Some people still use a hyphenated version, and if it's used as a replacement for the one-word version, it's not a huge error, but you should never use it as a replacement for the verb, the two-word version.

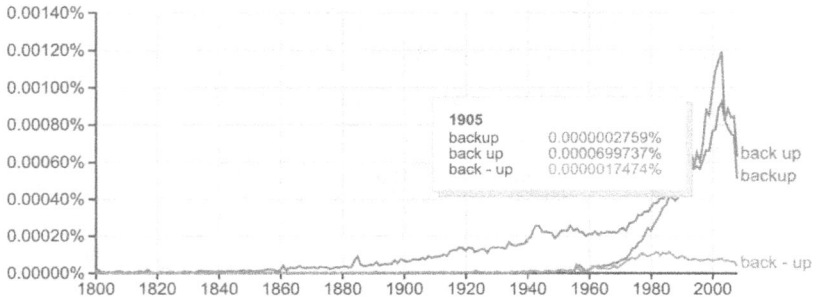

Here are a few of sentences to wrap up our discussion on when to use *back up* versus *backup*:

- He was the *backup* quarterback, and as such, he sat on the sidelines a lot.
- The police officer was under fire, so he called for *backup*.
- You should heed his advice and *back up* your hard drive.

As you can see, when used as an adjective to describe something else, such as "backup quarterback," it's one word. When used as a noun—a person, place, or thing, such as "He called for back-up,"—it's one word. But if used as a verb, denoting action, it's two words, as in "Back up your hard drive."

More Clarification

The main goal of writing should be to clarify things; in other words, convey your thoughts in the easiest, clearest manner possible. With that in mind, the proper use of hyphens goes a long way. Consider the following:

- She is an *infectious disease* doctor.
- She is an *infectious-disease* doctor.

In the first sentence, we're claiming she is a disease doctor who is infectious, and in the second sentence, we're claiming she is a doctor who deals with infectious diseases. That's a big difference. I think I'd prefer being treated by the second one.

Other Uses

Remember that hyphens can be used with more than one word. Their purpose is to provide clarity, and whether two, or three, or more words are needed for clarification makes no difference. Below are a few sentences that demonstrate this.

- Coffee is often considered a *pick-me-up* because of the effect caffeine has on some people.
- My *brother-in-law* recently bought a new car.

In both cases, we were speaking of one thing so a hyphen was needed to join the words to make it one thing.

Hyphens to join prefixes and suffixes to words

Whether we're talking about hyphens used to join compound words or about hyphens used for prefixes and suffixes, they're still being used to join words. And one of a hyphen's jobs is to do just that.

We've already talked about hyphens when used with a few *re* words. Now let's look at a few other rules of hyphen use regarding prefixes and suffixes.

Hyphens are also often used in words using *re* or *pre* that result in two of the same kind of vowels next to each other such as *re-engage* or *re-evaluate*. If we didn't hyphenate them, we'd have *reengage* and *reevaluate*, both of which are wrong. I found one dictionary that listed *reevaluate* as an alternative way to spell *re-evaluate*, but none of the dictionaries had *reengage* listed. It was consistently listed as *re-engage*.

Below are a few more words with a *re* prefix that require hyphens:

- re-extend
- re-establish
- re-encounter

- re-enable
- re-emphasise
- re-elevate

The above list consists of words that definitely need a hyphen.

Subjective Hyphen Use

Hyphens are often used subjectively; in other words, it's left up to the writer whether to use a hyphen or not. In more cases than not, the determining factor is clarity: If you think a hyphen will help make you message clearer, use it; if not, don't. Let's look a little deeper at that aspect of hyphenation.

There are a few rigid rules regarding hyphens, but often it's up to you. Many prefixed words can be written with a hyphen or without one. The school of thought is to avoid a hyphen with a prefix; however, if you feel the word looks awkward without a hyphen, or if your spellchecker flags it as wrong, use a hyphen.

A good example is the word *antiaircraft*. All the dictionaries I checked with listed it as one word—no hyphens—and yet many times writers hyphenate it.

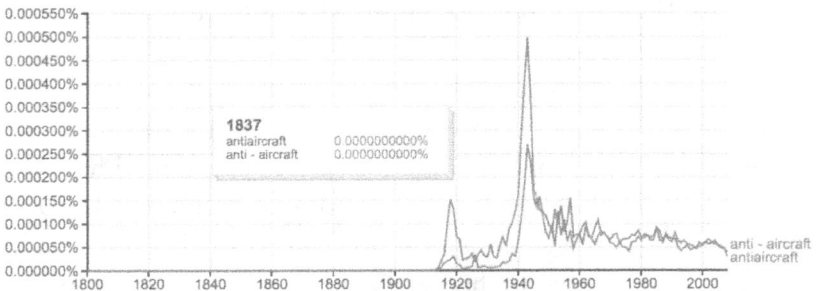

The above screenshot is the result of a Google Ngram search. As you can see, usage in general has dropped off dramatically, but when it was used, the hyphenated version (anti-aircraft) far outweighed the one-word version.

The bottom line is that using *antiaircraft* is not wrong, and you will find authoritative backup if you go that way, but if you're like many people, you may think it looks awkward and choose to hyphenate it. That's what the subjective use of hyphens is all about.

In the next chapter, I've listed a lot of compound words, many that are hyphenated and many that aren't. Below is a list of words beginning with *anti* that AP recommends using without hyphens as they have specific meanings.

antibiotic	antibody	anticlimax
anticoagulant	antidepressant	antidote
antifreeze	antigen	antihistamine
antiknock	Antimatter	antimony
antioxidant	antiparticle	antipasto
antiperspirant	antiphon	antiphony
antipollution	antipsychotic	antiserum
antiseptic	antithesis	antitoxin
antitrust	antitussive	

More Rules

A couple of these rules will be a repeat of what you've already learned.

1. If your prefix sits before a proper noun, use a hyphen: post-Nixon era, pre-Kennedy politics.

2. Do not allow the same vowel to double up: re-enter, re-evaluate. This is a rule with exceptions as evidenced by *preempt*. There are other exceptions, particularly when the vowel is an *o*. If you don't mind how the word looks without a hyphen then omit it. But if you do mind, leave the hyphen in.

The image below displays the Ngram search results for *cooperate/co-operate* and *coordinate/co-ordinate*. You can see that the majority of people use those words without the hyphen, though many do use the hyphen.

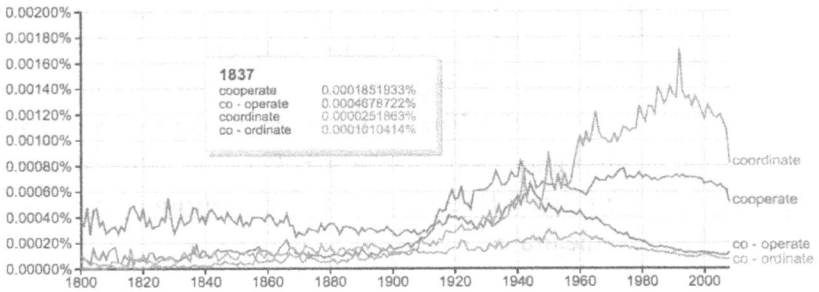

Sometimes your spellchecker may flag a word. Usually, it's best to accept the suggestion, but if you have doubts, check whatever dictionary you use. The final decision is yours. If you feel you need a hyphen to clarify words or to make them look better, use one.

1. Use a hyphen with *ex*

The prefix *ex* is usually followed by a hyphen:

- ex-husband
- ex-lover

Hyphens with *Fold*

If you're using *fold* and spelling out the number before it, use it without a hyphen, such as "a threefold increase"; however, if you're using numerals with *fold*, use a hyphen, as in "a 120-fold increase in the rodent population."

1. Also use hyphens anytime that the base word is:

- Capitalized
- A number
- An abbreviation
- When using two or more words to describe the same thing.

Below are a few sample sentences showing the above rules.

- He was voting in the pre-Nixon era.

- Heroin has been a problem since post-1990s
- He hasn't been around since pre-CIA.
- I want to compete in all the races: the two-, five-, and ten-meter runs.

That about covers it. If you question whether a word should or should not include a hyphen, look it up in your favorite dictionary, although they don't always agree.

Because of that, I'll give the same advice I do for other matters, like style guides. Pick a dictionary you like and stick with it.

Trends

There continues to be a tendency to shy away from hyphenated words, despite the demand for clarification. *Oxford English Dictionaries* reports that approximately sixteen thousand hyphenated words were removed in their latest edition, being replaced in most instances by the one-word variation, but sometimes two words. Oxford rigorously maintains that clarity is paramount. Here's an example.

- When we traveled to San Francisco, we saw *five-hundred-year-old* trees.
- When we traveled to San Francisco, we saw *five hundred year-old* trees.

In the first sentence, you're saying that you saw trees that were five-hundred years old. In the second sentence, you could be saying you saw five hundred trees that were a year old. You could further confuse this by saying:

- When we traveled to San Francisco, we saw five *hundred-year-old* trees.

In this case, you'd be saying you say five trees that were a hundred years old. So you see, the diminutive hyphen, much like the comma, *does* matter.

Hyphens Used with Years

Because we just discussed this, it may be a good time to cover how hyphens are used with years.

If the age is used as an adjective or as a substitute for a noun, then it should be hyphenated.

Example:

- He's a *24-year-old* intern.
- The dog is *three years old*.
- The game is for *six-year-olds*.

The Bottom Line

There are plenty of other rules and reasons why you do or don't use a hyphen. If you follow this guide, you'll be right most of the time, but you're still better off consulting a dictionary. You're always going to run into situations like *good night*, which can be found in three forms:

- *Goodnight*, dear. I'm going to bed.
- He gave her a *good-night* kiss.
- Their team won, so it turned out to be a *good night*.

Or how about these:

- I'm looking for the best *work-out* equipment.
- I just had a great *workout*.
- I'm going to the gym to *work out*.

Each one of the above six sentences is correct. It all depends how the word is used.

Exceptions

We've talked about a few exceptions, and there are more, but I felt it wise to mention at least one more as it is frequently used.

We cited an earlier rule that stated, "Don't use hyphens with adverbs as a part of compound modifiers." One exception is the word "well." The following sentences are all correct.

- He prefers the *well-known* brands of coffee.
- She wasn't a *well-known* person until after the election.

But you don't hyphenate them if they come after the noun, similar to other compound modifiers.

- Her books are *well known* in England.
- The Marlborough brand of cigarettes is *well known* throughout the world.

The difference is when you use *well-known before the noun, it is being used as an adjective.*

One Last Rule

I know I said *one* last rule, but this is a three-part rule, so bear with me.

1. When it comes to compound verbs, that is, when two or more nouns are combined to form a verb, the resulting word is hyphenated. Keep in mind, this applies to nouns that are combined to form verbs; it doesn't apply to all words. So the following is correct:

- Be careful, the place is one big *booby trap* (noun).
- Be sure to *booby-trap* (nouns combined to form verb) the cabin before we leave.

Don't use hyphens when the word is made of a verb and an adverb or a preposition (like *up, in, on,* etc.). A few examples follow.

- If you save ten dollars a day, you will quickly *build up* your savings.

- Your wife called. She said, "Don't forget to *drop off* the prescriptions."

3. If the above-mentioned words are used as a noun and not verbs, use a hyphen.

- The pipe was clogged due to a *build-up* of grease.
- The kidnappers were specific regarding where to make the *drop-off*.

I hope that helps. But please remember that if you're in doubt about anything, consult a dictionary or style guide.

A LITTLE HELP

How many times have you typed a word or were about to type a word, when you asked yourself—*Is that two words or one? Or does it need a hyphen?*

I don't know about you, but it happens to me all of the time. And, as we've mentioned, the spellcheckers don't always agree.

The question of whether to use two words or one comes up more times than you may think. And when you add hyphens to the mix, it becomes damn frequent—frequent enough to cost you a lot of time to ensure you get it right.

That's why, in this chapter, I'm going to include a long list of oft-questioned words. Feel free to use this list as a reference. It will be a lot faster than consulting a dictionary.

In fact, to make things even faster, I use a key combination (shortcut) linked to my list, so if I'm typing and have a question, all I have to do is type *hyphenwords*, (with no spaces), and it immediately takes me to the list. You can learn all about how to save precious time by using text shortcuts in the book I wrote about that—*No Mistakes Writing, Volume I—Writing Shortcuts*.

The Oxford-English Dictionary website addresses the issue of compound words and sheds some light on their usage. It shows that many of today's single-word forms, such as those listed below, were originally written as separate words.

- forever
- tomorrow
- instead
- nonetheless
- somewhat
- whatsoever

The merging of words appears to be a strong trend in American English, where it's standard practice to write *underway*, *anymore*, or *someday* as one word, whereas the two-word forms are still the norm in British English.

Compound words are primed for confusion, yet in most cases—at least in conversation—they do *not* cause confusion. Even in writing, they seldom make anyone stop and think, though they may make a person wonder about your grasp of the language.

What do I mean?

If you write, "I had *alot* to eat for dinner," people may know you used the word erroneously, but they will still know that *alot* means for *a lot*.

It's when we delve into other words where the meaning is different between the one-word and two-word version that we run into problems.

One of these is the first word on our list: along. *Along* and *a long* have different meanings. Let's take a look.

Along or a Long?

Let's look at these examples to understand the difference:

✅ The art critic should have seen that mistake *a long* time ago (correct).

As you can see, you cannot substitute *along* for that, or you'll have:

❌ The art critic should have seen that mistake *along* time ago (incorrect).

Similarly, look at these opposite examples.

✅ I held the umbrella for her as she walked *along* with me (correct).

✗ I held the umbrella for her as she walked *a long* with me (incorrect).

The two-word version is meant more as a measurement of time or distance, as in "He lives *a long* way off" or "Christmas is *a long* time away."

Along can mean several things, one of them is "beside or next to," as in "The sidewalk along the meandering creek."

Alot or A lot?

This one is easy, and yet I still see it misused *a lot*. It's easy to get right because *alot* is not a word. The way to write it is always as two words.

Any more or Anymore

Any more (two words) is reserved for "even the smallest amount," as in "I don't want any more to drink."

Anymore (one word) is reserved for "any longer." In other words, when used as an adverb, the one-word spelling *anymore* is used, as in "I don't go there anymore."

Whether there are an equal number of people using *any more* as there are *anymore* in the proper sense, I don't know. But proper or not, their usage is almost equal. It's also obvious that the one-word version has gained massive popularity during the past forty years.

Any Place or Anyplace

As you can see from the chart below, the proper usage of *any place* as two words has been slipping when compared to *anyplace* as one word. *Anyplace* as one word has been accepted for informal speech for a while, but it has been frowned upon in formal writing.

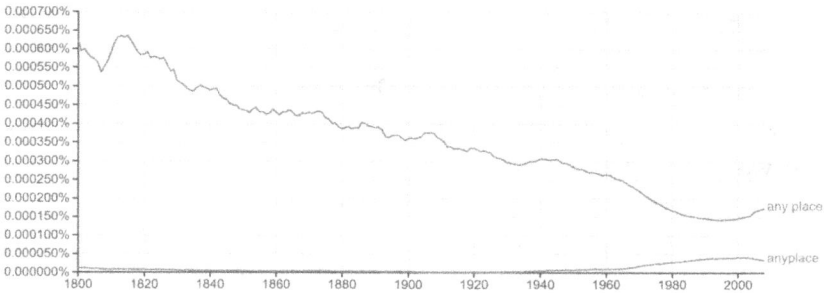

Any Time or Anytime

During the past twenty years, *anytime* has made headway but it is still far behind its two-word counterpart when it comes to usage.

Apart or a Part?

Apart means separated by a distance of time or space, as in "Dallas and Fort Worth are thirty miles *apart*" and "The innocent man stood *apart* from the others."

A *part* is a piece of something, a component, as in "I went to Auto Zone to get *a part* for my car."

🖢 The way to remember this (and some others) is by testing it with the plural use. *Apart* cannot be used in the plural sense. Try it. Dallas and Fort Worth are thirty miles *aparts*. That doesn't make sense.

However, "I went to Auto Zone to get three *parts* for my car" makes perfect sense.

If you can use a plural and still have it make sense, it's the two-word version. This works for other words also (mostly ones that use *a* as an indefinite article. Try it with the next example—*apiece* and *a piece*.

Apiece or A piece?

Apiece is used for an expression meaning "each." It's an adverb and means "for each one," as in "Give them one apple apiece (each)."

A piece refers to a piece of something, as in "I'd love a piece of that pie."

🖐 Remember that *a piece* is two words and refers to something that has, or had, more than one piece or part. *Apiece* is one word and refers to just one.

Best Seller or Bestseller or Best-seller

Merriam-Webster's lists it as two words. Dictionary.com lists it as one word, but offers the two-word option as an alternative. And Cambridge lists only the one-word option.

My editor uses the two-word option for a noun, although when it is used as an adjective, she hyphenates it. So it would be *best-selling*, as in "She is a best-selling author" or "That is a best-selling book." But when used as a noun, it would be the two-word option, as in "He is a best seller."

Broken-down or Broken Down

Every source I checked had it hyphenated: *broken-down*.

Copyeditor or Copy Editor?

Dictionary.com lists it either way, but *Merriam-Webster's* lists only the two-word version. The Free Dictionary lists both ways, while the *AP Stylebook* claims it is two words.

If the dictionaries and style books can't agree, how are we to know which is right?

Extensive research will only exhaust you. It seems like most resources recommend *copy editor* as two words, but few disapprove of the one-word variation. I would say—like so many compound words—that either form will work, but I would still go with the two-word option; that's what the American Copy Editor Society suggests.

🖐 The way I remember it is to remind myself that a copy editor is an editor that edits copy.

Copyright or Copy Right or Copywrite?

According to the *AP Stylebook*, a *copyright* (one word) is:

... the exclusive right to make copies, license, and otherwise exploit a literary, musical, or artistic work, whether printed, audio, video, etc.: works granted such right by law on or after January 1, 1978, are protected for the lifetime of the author or creator and for a period of 70 years after his or her death.

🖐 The way I remember it is simple. A copyright is one thing, so it's one word.

Copywrite

Copywrite is a rarely used derivative of copywriter—which refers to a writer of copy (used mostly in advertising). Most people would consider this an error, so you're safer saying that someone writes copy rather than that they copywrite.

🖐 The way I remember it is simple. A *copyright* is one thing, so it's one word.

Double Check or Double-Check

Cambridge dictionary lists it as a verb and hyphenated. *Merriam-Webster's* lists it both ways, the noun form (a *double check*) and the verb form (*double-check that*). Dictionary.com lists the verb and noun as hyphenated, but also lists the noun without hyphens.

I think you're safe if you use hyphenated, but to be *doubly safe*, I'd use hyphenated for the verb and two words for the noun form.

So . . .

- Please *double-check* that work.

But . . .

- Before you leave for the day, do a *double check* on the data.

E-book, ebook, eBook

As a term for books presented in electronic form, *eBook* is going out of style, at least in edited publications. As of early 2012, most American, Canadian, and Australian news publications that publish online are using the hyphenated, uncapitalized form: *e-book*. Meanwhile, most web-friendly British publications are using the one-word: *ebook*.

Login or Log in?

Login and *log in* have different meanings depending on whether they are used as a noun, adjective, or verbal phrase:

- —the place where you enter your username and password is the login page (adjective).
- —the information you use may be known as your login (noun).
- —but the action of signing on is called logging in (verb), as in "Log in to your account to access it."

One way to tell the verb form is if you can place a word between *log* and *in*, as in "The system will *log you in* automatically."

Nevermind or Never Mind?

Now let's tackle the ever-popular *never mind*. Or is it *nevermind*?

It is used so much as one word it's in danger of becoming accepted, but most spellcheckers still flag it when used as one word, and right they are. *Never mind* is meant to be used as two words, meaning "forget about it" or "pay it no mind."

In some instances, it's obviously meant to be used as two words:

- "It's going to be a scorcher today," her husband said. "That's okay. I never mind the heat."

When *never mind* is used like the above, it seems apparent that it is used appropriately. But there are cases where usage comes into question.

Nevermind as one-word has been creeping into the vocabulary, especially when used in the following context:

- "You want me to lock the door when I leave?" he asked.
- "Nevermind," she said. "I'll get it myself."

To set the record straight, *never mind* should be used as two words, but I wouldn't worry about it if you let it slip by as one.

Recent research has shown that *nevermind* as a one-word alternative is used fifty percent as much as the proper way, using two words. When the popular usage gets that high, it typically isn't long before it becomes recognized as an accepted way to express yourself.

The way I remember it is to think of the alternatives: "pay no attention," "pay no mind," "forget about it," etc., are all more than one word. And *never mind* is more than one word.

On-line or Online

There was a time when *on-line* was okay. Now usage favors *online*, used as one word.

Overtime or Over Time

Over time is used as follows: "I'll get to fixing that fence over time" (meaning "someday" or "over the course of time").

Overtime, as one word, means putting in extra hours. "He had ten hours of overtime last week."

Someday or Some Day?

This one is not a huge mix-up, but some people *do* get it confused, so let's take a look at it.

Someday is used for an indefinite time in the future, as in "*Someday* my ship will come in." Or "*Someday* I'll meet Mr. Right."

This is unspecific, only naming the future as a time when it will happen.

"Some day" is for a *specific* day that hasn't been named. as in "We'll go to the zoo *some day* next week." That statement tells you that it will be next week, but it doesn't name the day. Or, "*Some day* next month we'll visit the college dorms."

Start-up or Startup

This one is hotly debated, and there are many proponents on both sides. If you poll the major newspapers, *startup* seems to win, however, *start-up* isn't far behind. In fact, if you use Google's Ngram to compare, it's almost even, with *start-up* gaining ground in the past few years.

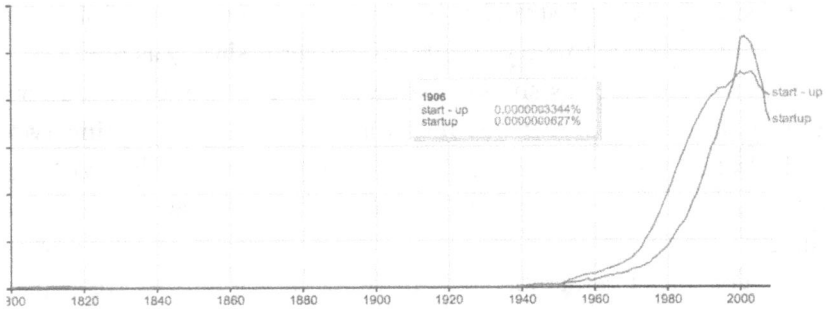

The people I spoke with about this seemed to favor *start-up* when it was used to describe a company, as in "Apple was a successful *start-up* company." But the favor shifted to *startup* for other usage. "Apple was once a garage-based *startup*."

Telltale or Tell-Tale or Tell Tale

This one was less controversial than I thought. Everywhere I checked, all agreed that it should be one word: *telltale*.

That surprised me because I see it so often as a hyphenated word, such as a *tell-tale sign,* but apparently, it should be a *telltale sign*.

All resources I checked with showed *telltale* as one word, yet the most famous example I know of using *telltale* is Edgar Allen Poe's short story "The Tell-Tale Heart," which uses a hyphenated version.

Rule of Thumb for All Words

A good rule to remember is that the verb form of a compound word is usually two words, or sometimes hyphenated. The noun form is usually one word, and the adjective form is usually hyphenated (or one word).

Examples are as follows:

- Noun (and adjective)—"Do the cleanup, and then you can go home."
- Verb—"Clean up that mess before you leave."

The bottom line is that common usage is forcing more words

than ever to evolve from two words or hyphenated words into one, but there are instances when things go the other way.

Examples of hyphenated words that have become two words are below. The first is one we're all familiar with. It's presented in the form of a screenshot from *Merriam-Webster's*.

income tax

noun

screenshot of income tax

Merriam-Webster's listing of "income tax" without hyphens.

I highlighted *income tax*, but there are more than a few words that have gone this route: *ice cream, high school*, and more.

Even when used as an adjectival phrase, the words remain separate. "He was a high school senior," not "He was a high-school senior." And "She was enjoying her ice cream cone," not "She was enjoying her ice-cream cone."

There remain a few holdouts, people who insist on the hyphen, but almost all credible sources agree that the hyphen is no longer needed.

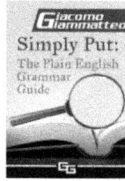

*H*ere is a list of words that can be either one or two words or possibly hyphenated.

- able-bodied
- about-face
- aboveboard
- absent-minded
- ad-lib (n.,v.,adj.)
- after-hours
- aftereffect
- afterglow
- after-hours
- afterimage
- afterlife
- afternoon
- afterthought
- aide-de-camp
- air base
- air show
- air time

- air-conditioned
- aircraft
- airfield
- airlift
- airline
- airmail
- airmen
- airplane
- airport
- airtight
- airtime
- airways
- a la carte
- a la king
- a la mode
- all ready
- already
- all-knowing
- all-seeing
- all-encompassing
- all-compassionate
- all-forgiving
- all ready
- all right
- all-time (n)
- all-time (adj)
- allover
- allspice
- alma mater
- alongside
- a lot
- already
- also
- also-ran (n)
- another

- anti-aircraft
- anti-bias
- antibiotic
- antibody
- anticlimax
- antidote
- antifreeze
- antigen
- antihistamine
- anti-inflation
- anti-intellectual
- anti-labor
- anti-slavery
- anti-social
- anti-war
- antibiotic
- antibody
- anticlimax
- antidote
- antifreeze
- antigen
- antihistamine
- antiknock
- antimatter
- antimony
- antiparticle
- antipasto
- antiperspirant
- antiproton
- antiseptic
- antiserum
- antithesis
- antitoxin
- antitrust
- antitussive

- anybody
- anyhow
- anymore
- anyone
- anyplace
- anytime
- anyway
- anywhere
- archbishop
- archdiocese
- archenemy
- archrival
- around
- art form
- art work
- artifact
- ashcan
- ashtray
- attorney general
- auto racing
- automaker
- autoworker
- awe-struck
- awhile (adv)
- baby sitter
- baby-sit
- baby-sitting
- babysitter
- back porch (n)
- back seat (n)
- back street (n)
- back up (v)
- backup (n)
- back yard (n)
- backache

- backbite
- backbone
- backbreaker
- backcountry
- backdrop
- backfire
- background
- backhand
- backhanded
- backlash
- backlog
- backpack
- back porch (n)
- back-porch (adj)
- backseat (adj)
- back seat (n)
- backside
- backslap
- backslide
- backspace
- backspin
- backstabbing
- backstage
- backstop
- back street (n)
- back-street
- backstroke
- backtrack
- backward
- backwoods
- backyard (adj and noun)
- bail out (v)
- bailout (n)
- ball carrier
- ball point pen

- ballclub
- ballpark
- ballplayer
- ballroom
- Band-Aid (trademark)
- bandleader
- bank robber
- bankbook
- bankroll
- bar mitzvah
- barhop
- barkeeper
- barmaid
- barrelhouse
- barroom
- barstool
- baseball
- basket case
- basketball
- beachcomb
- became
- because
- become
- bedclothes
- bedrock
- bedroll
- bedroom
- bellbottom
- bellboy
- bellhop
- bellybutton
- below
- best seller
- best-selling
- big time (n)

- Big-time (adj or adv)
- big-bang theory
- big-time (adj)
- bird watching
- bird's-eye
- blackball
- blackberries
- blackbird
- blackboard
- blackjack
- blacklist
- blackmail
- blackout
- blackout
- blacksmith
- blacktop
- blast off (v)
- blastoff (n adj)
- blood bath
- bloodhound
- blow up (v)
- blow-dryer
- blowgun
- blowup (n)
- blue blood (n)
- blue chip stock
- blue-blooded (adj)
- bluebell
- blueberry
- bluebird
- bluefish
- bluegrass
- blueprint
- boarding school
- boardinghouse

- boardroom
- boardwalk
- bodybuilder
- bodyguard
- bodywork
- boldface
- bona fide
- bonbon
- boo-boo
- bookcase
- bookdealer
- bookend
- bookkeeper
- bookmark
- bookmobile
- bookseller
- bookshelf
- bookstore
- bookworm
- boomtown
- bootstrap
- bowlegged
- bowlegs
- bowtie
- box office (n)
- box-office (adj)
- boyfriend
- brainchild
- brainwash
- brand-new
- break dancing (n)
- break in (v)
- break-out
- break up (v)
- break-dancing

- break-in (n adj)
- breakdown
- breakup (n adj)
- breast-feed
- bricklayer
- bridegroom
- bridesmaid
- broken-down
- brother-in-law
- brothers-in-law
- brownout
- brussels sprouts
- bugspray
- build up (v)
- buildup (n adj)
- bull's-eye
- bullet hole
- bulletproof
- bullfight
- bullpen
- Bundt cake
- bus line
- businesslike
- businessman
- businesswoman
- busload
- butterball
- buttercup
- butterfingers
- butterflies
- buttermilk
- butternut
- butterscotch
- buy out (v n)
- by-election

- bylaw
- byline
- bypass
- byproduct
- bystreet
- cabdriver
- cabinetmaker
- cakewalk
- call up (v)
- cameraman
- cancan
- candleholder
- candlelight
- candlemaker
- candlestick
- cannot
- car pool
- car seat
- card maker
- cardboard
- cardsharp
- cardstock
- carefree
- carefree
- caretaker
- careworn
- carfare
- cargo
- carhop
- carload
- carmaker
- carpetbagger
- carpool
- carport
- carrack

- carry over (v)
- carry-over (n)
- carryall
- carsick
- carsick
- cartwheel
- carwash
- caseload
- cash flow
- cashbox
- cast member
- catch all (v)
- catchall (n adj)
- cattail
- catwalk
- caveman
- cease fire (v)
- cease-fire (n)
- centerfold
- cha-cha
- chain saw
- chairman
- chairwoman
- change over (v)
- change up (v)
- change-up
- changeover (n)
- check up (v)
- checkup
- check in (v)
- check-in (n)
- check out (v)
- checkout (n)
- cheese maker
- cheeseburger

- cheesecake
- chief
- chock-full
- chowhound
- Christmastime
- church member
- churchgoer
- citizens band
- city hall
- citywide
- claptrap
- clean up (v)
- clean-cut
- cleanup (noun)
- clear-cut
- clearinghouse
- cloak-and-dagger
- clockwise
- close-up (n adj)
- closed shop
- co-author
- co-chairman
- co-host
- co-owner
- co-partner
- co-pilot
- co-respondent
- co-signer
- co-star
- co-worker
- coal mine
- coastline
- coatdress
- coattails
- Coca-Cola

- coed
- coeducation
- coexist
- coexistence
- coffee grinder
- coffee maker
- coffee table (n)
- coffeemaker
- coffeepot
- coleslaw
- colorblind
- comeback
- comedown
- commander in
- commonplace
- commonwealth
- con man
- concertgoer
- Confinement
- congressman
- congresswoman
- cooperate
- coordinate
- coordination
- cop-out
- copy desk
- copy editor
- cornmeal
- cornstarch
- cost-effective
- countdown
- counter top (n)
- counter-top
- counteract
- countercharge

- counterfoil
- counterproposal
- counterspy
- country-martial
- country-western
- countryside
- courthouse
- courtroom
- courtyard
- cover up (v)
- crack up
- crackup (n adj)
- crawfish
- crawl space
- crew member
- crewcut
- crisscross
- crock pot
- cropland
- cross country (n)
- cross fire
- cross over (v)
- cross section (n)
- cross-country
- cross-examination
- cross-examine
- cross-eye
- cross-section (v)
- crossbow
- crossbreed
- crosscut
- crossover
- crosswalk
- curtain raiser
- custom-made

- cut back (v)
- cut off (v)
- cutoff
- cut out (v)
- cutback (n adj)
- cutoffs
- cutout (n)
- D-day
- dairymaid
- daisywheel
- daisywheel
- dark horse
- date line
- day to day (adv)
- day-to-day (adj)
- daybed
- daybook
- daybreak
- daycare and day-care
- daydream
- daylight
- daylong
- daytime
- dead center
- dead end (n)
- dead-end (adj)
- deadline
- deathbed
- decade-long
- decision maker
- decision-making
- deep water (n)
- deep-sea (adj)
- deep-water
- Deepfreeze (trademark)

- degree-day
- derring-do
- desk top (n)
- desk-top (adj)
- die-hard (n adj)
- dinner table
- disease
- dishcloth
- dishpan
- dishwasher
- dishwater
- disk drive
- ditchdigger
- docudrama
- doghouse
- dogwood
- dollhouse
- door to door (n)
- doorstop
- double bind
- double-check
- double-faced
- double-parked
- down-home
- downbeat
- downdraft
- downside
- down under
- drawbridge
- drive in (v)
- drive-in (n adj)
- driveway
- drop out (v)
- duckbill
- duckpin

- duckweed
- dump truck
- Dutch oven
- Dutch treat
- dyed-in-the-wool
- earache
- eardrop
- eardrum
- earmark (v)
- earring
- earthbound
- earthquake
- earthward
- earthworm
- easygoing
- ebook
- e-book
- e-Book
- editor in chief
- egghead
- eggshell
- elsewhere
- email
- e-mail (I prefer this version but you can use any)
- empty-handed
- en route
- every day (adv)
- every one (each)
- everyday (adj)
- everything
- extra-base hit
- extra-dry
- extra-large
- extra-mild
- extralegal

- extramarital
- extraterrestrial
- eye to eye (adv)
- eyeballs
- eyeglasses
- eyelash
- eyelid
- eyesight
- eyesore
- eyewitness
- face lift
- face to face (adv)
- face-to-face
- fact-finding
- fade out (v)
- fade-out (n)
- fall out (v)
- fallout (n)
- far-fetched
- far-flung
- far-off
- far-ranging
- fare up (v)
- farm worker
- farmhouse
- farmland
- farsighted
- father-in-law
- fatherland
- feather bedding
- feather-bedding
- fee-table (adj)
- Ferris wheel
- ferryboat
- fiberglass

- field house
- field trip
- fieldwork
- film ratings
- film-making
- filmgoer
- filmmaker
- filmmaking (n)
- fingertip
- fire breather
- fire chief
- fire wagon
- firearm
- fireball
- fireboat
- firebomb
- firebreak
- firecracker
- firefighter
- fireflies
- firehouse
- fireproof
- firetruck
- firewater
- fireworks
- firsthand
- fishbowl
- fisherman
- fisheye
- fishhook
- fishlike
- fishmonger
- fishnet
- fishpond
- fishtail

- fistfight
- flagpole
- flagship
- flameout
- flare-up (v)
- flea market
- flimflam
- flip-flop
- floor-length
- flower girl
- flyswatter
- folk singer
- folk song
- follow up (v)
- follow-through
- follow-up (n)
- foolproof
- foot-and-mouth
- football
- foothill
- footlights
- footlocker
- footnote
- footprints
- footrest
- forbearer
- forbid
- fore-topgallant
- fore-topmast
- fore-topsail
- forearm
- forebear
- forebrain
- forecast
- foreclose

- foreclosure
- foredoom
- forefather
- forefeet
- forefinger
- forefoot
- forego
- foregoing
- foregone
- foreground
- forehand
- forehead
- foreknowledge
- foreleg
- foreman
- foremost
- forepaws
- foresee
- foreshadow
- foresight
- forestall
- forethought
- foretold
- forever
- forewarn
- foreword
- forget
- forgive
- forklift
- format
- fortnight
- fortuneteller
- fortunetelling
- forty-nine or '49er
- foul up (v)

- foul-up (n)
- four-flush
- frame up (v)
- frame-up (n)
- free on board
- free-for-all
- free-lance (v adj)
- free-lancer (n)
- freestanding
- freewheeling
- freewill offering
- freeze-dried
- freeze-dry
- freeze-drying
- friendship
- front line (n)
- front page (n)
- front-line (adj)
- front-page (adj)
- front-runner
- fruit grower
- fruit cup
- full house
- full page (n)
- full time (n)
- full-time (adv)
- full-dress
- full-fledged
- full-length
- full-page (adj)
- full-scale
- full-size (adj)
- full-time (adj)
- fund raising (n)
- fund-raiser (n)

- fund-raising (adj)
- G-string
- game plan
- gearshift
- get together (v)
- get-together (n)
- gift wrap (n)
- gift-wrap (v)
- giveaway
- glass (generic)
- glassmaking
- go ahead (v)
- go-ahead (n)
- go-go
- godchild
- goddaughter
- goodbye
- goodnight
- goose bumps
- grandaunt
- grandchild
- grandchildren
- granddad
- granddaughter
- grandfather
- grandmaster
- grandmother
- grandnephew
- grandnieces
- grandparent
- grandson
- grandstand
- granduncle
- grasshopper
- grassland

- graveyard
- ground rules
- ground water
- groundbreaking
- groundskeeper
- groundswell
- grown-up (n adj)
- guesthouse
- gumball
- gun battle
- gunboat
- gunfight
- gunfire
- gunpoint
- gunpowder
- H-bomb
- hair dryer
- haircut
- hairsbreadth
- hairstyle
- hairstyling
- hairstylist
- half dollar
- half note
- half sister
- half size (n)
- half sole (n)
- half tide
- half-baked
- half-blood
- half-brother
- half-cocked
- half-hour (n adj)
- half-life
- half-mast

- half-moon
- half-size (adj)
- half-sole (v)
- half-staff
- half-truth
- halfback
- halfhearted
- halftime
- halftone
- halftrack
- hamburger
- hammerhead
- hand to hand (n)
- hand to mouth (n)
- hand warmers
- hand-carved
- hand-held
- hand-painted
- hand-picked
- hand-set (v)
- hand-sewn
- hand-stitched
- hand-to-hand (adj)
- hand-to-mouth
- handbook
- handcrafted
- handcuff
- handgun
- handhold
- handmade
- handout
- hands off (n)
- hands-off (adj)
- handset (n)
- handwrought

- hang up (v)
- hang-up (n)
- hangover
- hanky-panky
- hard-bound
- hard-cover
- hard-line
- hardback
- hardworking
- harebrained
- harelip
- has been (v)
- has-been (n)
- head-on
- headache
- headdress
- headlight
- headline
- headlong
- headquarters
- heart-rending
- heartbeat
- heartfelt
- heartwarming
- helter-skelter
- hereafter
- hereby
- herein
- hereupon
- herself
- heydey
- hi-fi
- hide out (v)
- hide-out (n)
- hideaway

- high jinks
- high point
- high-rise (n adj)
- high-step (v)
- high-stepper (n)
- highball
- highchair
- higher-up
- highland
- highway
- himself
- hit and run (v)
- hit man
- hit-and-run (n)
- hitchhike
- hitchhiker
- ho-hum
- hoar-long
- hocus-pocus
- hodgepodge
- hold over (v)
- hold up (v)
- holdup (n)
- holdover (n)
- holdup (n adj)
- home builder
- home buyer
- home-baked
- home-grown
- homemade
- homemaker
- homeowner
- hometown
- honeybee
- honeycomb

- honeydew
- honeymoon
- honeysuckle
- hook up (v)
- hookup (n)
- hookworm
- horse race
- horse rider
- horse-trader
- horseback
- horsefly
- horsehair
- horseman
- horseplay
- horsepower
- horseradish
- hot line
- hot seat
- hot spot
- hot tub
- hotbed
- hotheaded
- house call
- houseboat
- housecleaning
- household
- househusband
- housekeeper
- houseplant
- housetop
- housework
- however
- hurly-burly
- hush-hush
- hydroelectric

- hyperactive
- hypercritical
- ice storm
- in-depth
- in-group
- in-house
- in-law
- inasmuch
- inbound
- individual
- Indochina
- indoor (adj)
- indoors (adv)
- infield
- infighting
- infrared
- infrastructure
- inpatient (n adj)
- inside
- insofar
- intake
- inter-American
- international
- interracial
- interstate
- intramural
- intrastate
- ironwork
- itself
- jackpot
- jai alai
- jailbait
- jellybean
- jellyfish
- jerry-built

- jet plane
- jetliner
- jetport
- job hunting (n)
- job-hunting
- jukebox
- jumbo jet
- jump shot
- jury-rigged
- Kmart
- keyboard
- keyhole
- keynote
- keypad
- keypunch
- keystone
- keystroke
- keyway
- keyword
- kick off (v)
- kickoff (n)
- kilowatt-hour
- kindhearted
- knock off (v)
- knock-off (n)
- know-how
- kowtow
- lad
- lame duck (n)
- lame-duck (adj)
- lamebrain
- last-ditch effort
- latecomer
- lawsuit
- left wing (n)

- left-handed
- left-hander
- left-wing (adj)
- let up (v)
- letup (n adj)
- life jacket
- Life Savers (trademark)
- life vest
- life-size
- lifeblood
- lifeboat
- lifeguard
- lifelike
- lifeline
- lifelong
- lifesaver
- lifestyle
- lifetime
- lifework
- lift off (v)
- liftoff (n)
- light bulb
- light-year
- lighthearted
- like-minded
- like-natured
- likewise
- limelight
- limestone
- long distance (n)
- long shot (n)
- long term (n)
- long time (n)
- long-distance
- long-lasting

- long-lived
- long-range
- long-run
- long-shot (adj)
- long-term (adj)
- longhand
- longhouse
- longstanding
- longtime (adj)
- look-alike
- lovemaking
- lukewarm
- lumberyard
- lunch box
- lunchtime
- machine gun (n)
- machine-gun
- machine-gunner
- machine-made
- mah-jongg
- mainland
- mainline
- make up (v)
- makeshift
- makeup (n ad)
- man-made
- map maker
- meantime
- meanwhile
- meat loaf
- meatball
- meat cutter
- *ménage a trois*
- menswear
- mental

- merry-go-round
- metalwork
- mid-America
- mid-Atlantic
- midterm
- mind-set
- mine shaft
- miners
- minibus
- miniseries
- miniskirt
- mix up (v)
- mix-up (n)
- mock-up (n)
- money-saving
- moneymaker
- monthlong
- moonbeam
- moonlight (n v)
- moonlit
- moonscape
- moonshine
- moonstruck
- moonwalk
- mop up (v)
- mop-up (n adj)
- moreover
- mothball
- mother-in-law
- motherhood
- motor home
- motorcycle
- mountain man
- mousehole
- movie house

- moviegoer
- moviemaker
- moviemaking
- mud slide
- multicolored
- multilateral
- multimillion
- multimillionaire
- muscle ache
- music
- nail clippers
- name tag
- narrow gauge (n)
- narrow-gauge
- narrow-minded
- nationwide
- nearby
- nerve-racking
- nevermore
- new wave (n)
- new-wave (adj)
- newborn
- newfangled
- newfound
- news writer
- news writing
- newsboy
- newsbreak
- newscaster
- news dealer
- newsletter
- newsmagazine
- newsman
- newspaper
- newsperson

- newsprint
- newsreel
- newsroom
- newsstand
- newsworthy
- nickname
- night shift
- nightclub
- nightfall
- nightspot
- nighttime
- nitpicking
- nitty-gritty
- no one
- nobody
- noisemaker
- nonaligned
- nonrestrictive
- nonchalance
- nonchalant
- nondescript
- nonentity
- nonsense
- nonsensical
- northeast
- notebook
- noteworthy
- nowhere
- nursemaid
- nutcracker
- oceangoing
- oddsmaker
- off-Broadway
- off-color
- off-duty

- off-off-Broadway
- off-peak
- off-road
- off-season
- off-white
- offhand
- offset
- offshore
- offside
- offstage
- oilman
- old times
- Old West
- Old World
- old-time
- old-timer
- on-line
- one time (n)
- one-sided
- one-time
- oneself
- onetime
- ongoing
- only
- open-minded
- out of bounds (n)
- out of court (adv)
- out-of-bounds
- out-of-court
- outact
- outargue
- outbluff
- outbox
- outbrag
- outclimb

- outdated
- outdistance
- outdrink
- outfield
- outfight
- outfox
- outhit
- outleap
- outmatch
- outpatient (n adj)
- outperform
- outpitch
- outpost
- outproduce
- output
- outrace
- outscore
- outshout
- outstrip
- outswim
- outtalk
- outwalk
- ovenproof
- overabundance
- overall
- overboard
- overbuy
- overcoat
- overexert
- overflow
- overland
- overrate
- override
- overshoes
- oversize

- overtime
- overview
- pacemaker
- pacesetter
- paddy wagon
- painkiller
- pancake
- panchromatic
- pantheism
- pantsuit
- pantyhose
- Pap test (or smear)
- paper bag
- paper clip
- paper towel
- paperwork
- pari-mutuel
- parkland
- part time (adv)
- part-time
- partygoer
- passbook
- passerby
- passkey
- Passover
- passport
- patrolman
- patrolwoman
- paycheck
- payday
- payload
- peace offering
- peacekeeper
- peacekeeping
- peacemaker

- peacemaking
- peacetime
- pell-mell
- pen pal
- penny-wise
- peppermint
- percent
- pet store
- petty officer
- pickup
- pile up (v)
- pileup (n adj)
- pillowcase
- pin up (v)
- pinch hit
- ping
- Ping-Pong (trademark)
- ping-pong (v) as a verb, no caps
- pinhole
- pinstripe
- pinup
- pinup (n)
- pinwheel
- pipeline
- place mat
- playback
- playboy
- playhouse
- playoff
- playthings
- pocket watch
- pocketbook
- point-blank
- police officer
- policy-maker

- policy-making
- policyholder
- pom-pom
- pompon
- ponytail
- pooh-pooh
- popcorn
- post office
- postcard
- postdate
- postdoctoral
- postgraduate
- postnuptial
- postoperative
- postscript
- postwar
- pothole
- potluck
- potshot
- powder keg
- power line
- pre-convention
- pre-cut
- pre-dawn
- pre-election
- pre-eminent
- pre-empt
- pre-establish
- pre-exist
- pre-menstrual
- pre-register
- pre-wash
- prearrange
- precondition
- precook

- predate
- predispose
- prefix
- preflight
- preheat
- prehistoric
- preignition
- prejudge
- premarital
- prenatal
- preschool
- preset
- pretest
- pretrial
- prewar
- price tag
- prima-facie (adj)
- prizewinner
- prizewinning
- pro-business
- pro-labor
- pro-life
- pro-war
- profit-sharing
- pull back (v)
- pull out(v) pullout
- pullback (n)
- purebred
- push up (v)
- push-button (n)
- push-up (n adj)
- put out (v)
- putout (n)
- quick-witted
- racquetball

- railroad
- railway
- rainbow
- raincheck
- raincoat
- raindrop
- rainstorm
- rainwater
- ranch house
- ranchland
- rangeland
- rank and file (n)
- rattlesnake
- rattletrap
- rawhide
- razor strop
- razzle-dazzle
- razzmatazz
- re-cover
- re-elect
- re-election
- re-emerge
- re-employ
- re-enact
- re-engage
- re-enlist
- re-enter
- re-entry
- re-equip
- re-establish
- re-examine
- re-form
- re-sign
- ready-made
- rearview mirror

- recording
- recover (regain)
- red-haired
- red-handed (adj)
- red-hot
- reform (improve)
- rendezvous
- repairman
- resign (quit)
- riffraff
- right hand (n)
- right wing (n)
- right-handed (adj)
- right-hander (n)
- right-to-work
- right-wing (adj)
- ring bearer
- rip off (v)
- rip-off (n adj)
- riverbanks
- riverboat
- roadside
- rock 'n' roll
- roll call (n)
- roll-call (adj)
- roller coaster
- roller skate (n)
- roller-skate (v)
- roly-poly
- round table (n)
- round trip (n)
- round up (v)
- round-table
- round-trip (adj)
- round-up (n)

- rubber band
- rundown
- runner-up
- running mate
- rush hour (n)
- rush-hour (adj)
- safe-deposit box
- sailboat
- sales pitch
- salesclerk
- sandbag
- sandlot
- sandstone
- sandstorm
- saucepan
- scapegoat
- scarecrow
- school bus
- schoolbook
- schoolboy
- school bus
- schoolhouse
- schoolteacher
- schoolwork
- scot-free
- seashore
- seat belt (n)
- seat-belt (adj)
- seawater
- second guess (n)
- second hand (n)
- second-guess
- second-guesser
- second-rate
- secondhand

- secretary-treasurer
- seesaw
- self-assured
- self-defense
- self-esteem
- semiannual
- semicolon
- send off (v)
- send-off (n)
- Seven-Up or 7UP
- sewer line
- shady side
- shake up (v)
- shake-up (n)
- shape up (v)
- sharpshooter
- sheepskin
- Sheetrock
- ship bottom
- shirt sleeve (n)
- shirt-sleeve
- shoelace
- shoemaker
- shoeshine
- shoestring
- shoot-out (n)
- shootout (v)
- shopworn
- short-handed
- short-lived
- shortbread
- shortchange
- shotgun
- show off (v)
- showcase

- showoff
- showplace
- showroom
- showstopper
- shut down (v)
- shut in (v)
- shut off (v)
- shut-in (n)
- shut-off (n)
- shutdown (n)
- side by side (adv)
- side-by-side (adj)
- side dish
- side effect
- side street (n)
- side trip
- side-by-side
- sideburns
- sidekick
- sideshow
- sidestep
- sidetrack
- sidewalk
- sightseeing
- sightseer
- sign up (v or n)
- silversmith
- single-handed
- single-handedly
- sister-in-law
- sisterhood
- sit down (v)
- sit in (v)
- sit-down (n)
- sit-in (adj n)

- sixfold
- skateboard
- skintight
- skylark
- skylight
- skyrocketing
- skyscraper
- slantwise
- slapstick
- sledgehammer
- sleight of hand (n)
- sleight-of-hand
- slide show
- slowdown
- slumlord
- slush fund
- small-arms fire
- smash up (v)
- smashup (n)
- smoke bomb
- smoke screen
- snakeskin
- snowball
- snowbank
- snowbird
- snowdrift
- snowfall
- snowflake
- snowman
- snowplow
- snowshoe
- snowstorm
- snowsuit
- so called (adv)
- soft-cover

- soft-pedal
- soft-spoken
- softball
- software
- somebody
- someday
- somehow
- someone
- someplace
- something
- sometimes
- somewhat
- somewhere
- son-in-law
- songwriter
- sound stage
- soundtrack (n)
- soundproof
- southeast
- southwest
- soybean
- space shuttle
- spacecraft
- spaceship
- spacewalk
- spearmint
- speech writer
- speech writing
- speechmaker
- speechmaking
- speed up (v)
- speedup (n adj)
- spillway
- spokesperson
- sportswear

- spot-check
- spotlight
- stagehand
- stained glass (n)
- stained-glass
- stand in (v)
- stand off (v)
- stand out (v)
- stand up (v)
- stand-in (n adj)
- stand-up (n)
- standard-bearer
- standby
- standing room
- standoff
- standoff (n adj)
- Standout
- standpipe
- standpoint
- starfish
- start up (v)
- start-up (n adj)
- state police
- statehouse
- states' rights
- statewide
- station wagon
- steamboat
- steamship
- step family
- stepbrother
- stepchild
- stepdaughter
- stepfather
- stepmother

- stepparent
- steppingstone
- stepsister
- stepson
- stockbroker
- stockroom
- stone carver
- stonewall
- stool pigeon
- stop off (v)
- stop-off (n)
- stopgap
- stoplight
- stopover
- stopwatch
- storerooms
- story line
- storyteller
- stove top (n)
- stove-top (adj)
- straight-laced
- strait-laced
- straitjacket
- street dance
- street gang
- street people
- street sweeper
- streetwise
- street-smart
- streetlamp
- streetlight
- streetwalker
- strikebreaker
- strong-willed
- stronghold

- subbasement
- subcommittee
- subculture
- subdivision
- submachine gun
- subtotal
- subway
- subzero
- summertime
- sun porch
- sunbaked
- sunbathe
- Sunday
- sundial
- sundown
- sundress
- sunfish
- sunflower
- sunglasses
- sunlit
- sunroof
- sunup
- supercarrier
- supercharge
- supercool
- superego
- superfine
- supergiant
- superhero
- superhighway
- superhuman
- superimpose
- superman
- supermarket
- supermen

- supernatural
- superpower
- superscript
- supersensitive
- supersonic
- superstar
- superstructure
- supertanker
- superwoman
- sweat pants
- sweatshirt
- sweetheart
- sweetmeat
- T-shirt
- table tennis
- tablecloth
- tablespoon
- tabletop
- tableware
- tadpole
- tagalong
- tail wind
- tailbone
- tailcoat
- tailgate
- taillight
- taillike
- taillike
- tailpiece
- tailspin
- take off (v)
- takeoff
- take out (v)
- take over (v)
- take up (v)

- take-home pay
- takeout (n adj)
- takeover
- talebearer
- taleteller
- tape
- tape-record (v)
- tapeworm
- taproom
- taproot
- target
- task force
- taskmaster
- tattletale
- taxicab
- taxpayer
- teacup
- teakettle
- teammate
- teamwork
- teapot
- tear gas
- teaspoon
- teen-age (adj)
- teen-ager
- teenager
- telex (generic)
- telltale
- tenderfoot
- tenderhearted
- tenfold
- terry cloth
- textbook
- theatergoer
- themselves

- therefore
- Third World
- three R's
- throw away (v)
- throwaway
- throwback
- thumbtack
- thunderbolt
- thunderstorm
- tidbit
- tie up (v)
- tie-in (n adj)
- tie-in (v)
- tie-up (n adj)
- tiebreaker
- time sharing (n)
- time-sharing
- timekeeper
- timepieces
- timesaver
- timesaving
- timeshare
- timetable
- tiptop
- titleholder
- today
- together
- tollhouse
- Tommy gun
- toolbox
- toothpaste
- toothpick
- top-notch
- touch up (v)
- touch-up

- touchdown
- township
- toy makers
- trade in (v)
- trade off (v)
- trade-in (n adj)
- trade-off
- trademark
- trans-Atlantic
- trans-Pacific
- transcontinental
- transmigrate
- transoceanic
- transsexual
- transship
- trash can
- trendsetter
- trigger-happy
- truck driver
- truck stop
- try out
- tryout (n)
- tune up (v)
- tuneup (n adj)
- turboprop
- turn off (v)
- turnabout
- turnaround
- turnbuckle
- turncoat
- turndown
- turnkey
- turnoff
- turnpike
- turntable

- twofold
- typewriter
- U-boat
- U-turn
- ultramodern
- ultrasonic
- ultraviolet
- un-American
- unarmed
- underway
- underachieve
- underact
- underage
- underarm
- underbelly
- underbid
- undercharge
- underclothes
- undercover
- undercurrent
- undercut
- underdog
- underestimate
- underexpose
- underfoot
- underground
- undersheriff
- undersold
- up-tempo
- upbeat
- upbringing
- upcoming
- update
- upend
- upgrade

- upheaval
- upheld
- uphill
- uphold
- upkeep
- upland
- uplift
- uplink
- upload
- upmarket
- upon
- upper hand
- uppercase
- upperclassman
- uppercut
- uppermost
- upright
- uprising
- uproar
- uproot
- upscale
- upset
- upshot
- upside
- upside down (adv)
- upside-down
- upstage
- upstairs
- upstanding
- upstart
- upstate
- upstate
- upstream
- upstroke
- uptake

- upthrust
- uptight
- uptime
- uptown
- upturn
- upward
- upwind
- V-8
- V-J Day
- V-neck
- vice chancellor
- vice consul
- vice president
- vice principal
- vice regent
- vice secretary
- vice versa
- video game
- videocassette (n adj)
- videodisc
- videotape (n v)
- voodoo
- vote-getter
- wagon master
- wagonmaker
- waistline
- walk on (v)
- walk up (v)
- walk-on (n)
- walk-up (n adj)
- walkways
- wall covering
- wall hanging
- walleyed
- wallpaper

- war horse (horse)
- wardroom
- warehouse
- warfare
- warhead
- warhorse (veteran)
- warlike
- warlord
- warm-up
- warm-blooded
- warmhearted
- warning
- warpath
- wartime
- wash out (v)
- washboard
- washbowl
- washcloth
- washed up (v)
- washed-up (adj)
- washhouse
- washout
- washout (n)
- washrag
- washroom
- washstand
- washtub
- waste water
- wastebasket
- wasteland
- wastepaper
- wastewater
- watch
- watchband
- watchdog

- watchmaker
- watchman
- watchtower
- watchword
- water bed
- water ski (n)
- water tank
- water-ski (v)
- water-skiing
- watercolor
- watercooler
- watercraft
- waterfall
- waterfowl
- waterfront
- waterline
- waterlog
- watermark
- watermelon
- waterpower
- waterproof
- waterscape
- watershed
- waterside
- waterspout
- watertight
- waterway
- waterwheel
- waterworks
- wavelength
- wavelike
- waxwork
- waybill
- wayfarer
- waylaid

- wayside
- wayward
- weak-kneed
- weather vane
- weather-beaten
- weathercock
- weatherman
- weatherproof
- week-nights
- weekday
- weekend
- weeklong
- weeknight
- weightlifting
- well-being
- well-to-do
- well-wishers
- wet bar
- whatever
- whatsoever
- wheelbarrow
- wheelbase
- wheelchair
- wheeler-dealer
- wheelhouse
- whereabouts
- wherever
- whirlwind
- white collar (n) white-collar (adj)
- white paper
- white water (n)
- white-water (adj)
- whitecap
- whitefish
- whitewall

- whitewash
- whole-wheat
- wholehearted
- wholesale price index
- wide-angle
- wide-awake
- wide-eyed
- wide-open
- wide-brimmed
- widespread
- wifebeater
- willpower
- windchill index
- wind power
- wind up (v)
- wind-swept
- window-dress (v)
- window-shop (v)
- wine taster
- winemaking
- wingspan
- winter storm
- wintertime
- wipeout
- wiretap
- without
- wood heat
- wood-burning
- woodcarver
- woodcarving
- woodshop
- woodsmoke
- woodstove
- woodwork
- word-of-mouth

- work force
- workday
- working class (n)
- working-class
- workout
- workplace
- workweek
- worldwide
- worn-out
- write in (v)
- write-in (n adj)
- wrongdoing
- X-ray
- yard sale
- year-end (adj)
- year-round
- yearlong
- yesteryear
- yo-yo
- yuletide
- zigzag

This is not a comprehensive list. In order to get all the words, I'll need your help, so send in suggestions of any that are missing.

But no matter how you look at it, it's a hell of a good start. If you make a few text shortcuts using a text expansion app like I described in *No Mistakes Writing Volume I—Writing Shortcuts,* you'll have access to this list within seconds. That way, if you have doubts about which form to use, hit the keystroke that pulls up the list, then simply do a quick search for the word you're looking for.

Also, as always, if in doubt, consult a dictionary. Example—one of the words on this list—*archrival*—my spellchecker insists is wrong, but when you check it with *Merriam-Webster's*, it shows it as spelled correctly. *Oxford English Dictionary*, however, lists it as *arch-rival*, with a hyphen.

. . .

ONE MORE EXAMPLE OF WHY YOU NEED TO CONSULT A dictionary.

Note:

One thought is that if your favorite writing app has a spellchecker you like, use it to *learn* the words you have issues with. For example, if it flags a word like *archrival* as being inaccurate, and you know it's right, add it to the spellchecker's corpus so it won't flag it again.

I've had to do this with numerous words, but it's a good way to conform to the dictionary you want to use.

Chapter Twenty-Eight

QUIZ 6

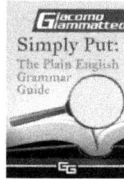

Quiz 6 (only two of the following are correct)

The onset of the clinical trial showed patients' tolerance for the new drug as "unacceptable;" the conclusion was quite different.

The onset of the clinical trial showed patients' tolerance for the new drug as "unacceptable"; the conclusion was quite different.

The onset of the clinical trial showed patient's tolerance for the new drug as "unacceptable;" the conclusion was quite different.

THE THIRD CHART FROM THE LEFT, (SEE FIGURE TWO), IS THE correct one.

The third chart from the left (see figure two,) is the correct one.

The third chart from the left (see figure two) is the correct one.

The third chart from the left (See figure two), is the correct one.

The third chart from the left (see figure two), is the correct one.

Chapter Twenty-Nine

EN AND EM DASHES

En Dashes and Em Dashes and How to Use Them

We recently discussed hyphens, so it may be a good time to go over en dashes and em dashes. After all, they're kind of the same, right?

Not really.

They may look similar, but they have different functions and different rules regarding when and how to use them, not to mention how to type them on a keyboard.

Hyphens, En Dashes, Em Dashes

To understand dashes and how they're used to punctuate sentences, it's important to grasp what they're used for and, just as importantly, what they're *not* used for. I'm going to let CMOS (*Chicago Manual of Style*) do that, though I may remove some of their grammatical terms and two-dollar words. All three of the following definitions came from *Chicago*.

Hyphen

The hyphen connects two things that are closely related, usually words that work together as a single concept or work together as a joint modifier (e.g., tie-in, toll-free call, two-thirds).

En dash

: The en dash connects things that are related to each other by distance, as in the May–September issue of a magazine; or the dates of employment on a résumé, such as 2002–2015; or even a range of pages in a book, 155–193.

Em dash

The em dash allows, in a manner similar to parentheses, an additional thought to be added within a sentence by sort of breaking away from that sentence.
: 1B. Em dashes also substitute for something missing.
: 1C. Also, the em dash may serve as a sort of bullet point.

Note: In all instances, you don't use spaces on either side of any dashes (hyphens included), although that is *Chicago's* recommendation. Some style books may disagree. Below is a screenshot comparing the relative sizes of hyphens, en dashes, and em dashes. Below the dashes are the letters *I, n,* and *m* to show the approximate size.

Hyphen, en dash, em dash

- — ——

I n m

En Dashes and Labeling Times

In almost any form of business writing or, for that matter, any form of writing, you will find it necessary to list a time, or times, in the communication. Here is the proper way to do it:

- The interviews will be conducted between 8:00 and 4:00.

You would not say "The interviews will be conducted between 8:00–4:00."

If you use the words *between* or *from*, you do not use an en dash; however, if you do not use either of those words, an en dash is not only fine but required.

- The interviews will be conducted 8:00–4:00.

This rule isn't followed often, but it is a rule. If you want to look as if you know your grammar, stick to it.

An en dash is longer than a hyphen and shorter than an em dash. The en dash's name derives from the fact that it is approximately the same width as the letter *N*.

Another point about en dashes is whenever you would say the words *to* or *through* where the dash is, it is likely an en dash that's needed, not a hyphen or em dash. Examples follow:

✖ He was a hands-on manager. (hyphen)

✖ It wasn't him—it was her! (em dash)

☑ I took the Houston–Philly–Boston flight. (en dash)

☑ Director of Sales, 1994–2017. (en dash)

☑ We travel to Europe every year, usually May–August (en dash).

Notice that in each situation where we used the en dash (green checked sentences) you could have substituted the word *to* or *through* and it would have sounded right.

- I took the Houston *to* Philly *to* Boston flight.
- Director of Sales, 1994 *to/through* 2017.
- We travel to Europe every year, usually May *to/through* August.

There is something to be aware of, though (as discussed above). If you use the words *from* or *between* to introduce a phrase that would ordinarily contain an en dash, you need to use the words *to* or *and* (respectively) instead of the en dash. Let's use the above sentences as examples. (Some rewording may be necessary to be grammatically correct.)

☑ I took the flight *from* Houston *to* Philly *to* Boston.

☑ Director of Sales *from* 1994 *to/through* 2017.

☑ We travel to Europe every year, usually *from* May *to/through* August.

✖ I took the flight *from* Houston–Philly–Boston.

✖ Director of Sales, *from* 1994–2017

✗ We travel to Europe every year, usually *from* May–August.

✓ He smokes *between* two *and* three packs of cigarettes per day.

✓ She takes the connecting train *between* Rome *and* Naples every night.

✗ He smokes *between* two–three packs of cigarettes per day.

✗ She takes the connecting train *between* Rome–Naples every night.

✓ The Yankees beat the Red Sox 6–2 (six *to* two) last night.

✓ The Philly–NY (Philly *to* NY) train ride only takes ninety minutes.

We mentioned earlier that you don't use spaces on either side of a dash, but some style guides suggest you do. CMOS recommends no spaces before or after a dash, so it would look like this:

- . . . it's him—not her.

AP recommends spaces around dashes, but their recommended dictionary (Webster's New World College Dictionary), does not. Their recommended style looks like this:

- . . . it's him — not her.

Some style guides, including a lot of British ones, recommend using the en dash *with* spaces instead of the em dash, so the same sentence we listed first, would look like this:

- . . . it's him – not her.

You may also use en dashes to refer to an "open-ended date"; that is, an unfinished date range (where the closing date has not been established), as would be the case when citing the range of years someone has been alive when they haven't died yet. Or the publication date for a magazine still in circulation. Examples follow:

- Robert De Niro (1943–)

- Steven Spielberg (1946–)
- Sports Illustrated (1954–)

Sometimes an en dash is used to denote different places for universities (or companies, etc.) that have more than one location. The examples below show how it's written using en dashes.

- The University of California–San Diego
- The University of Texas–Austin
- Texas A&M University–College Station

That's not the only way such locations may be listed, though, so check to make sure beforehand. Commas could be used just as efficiently.

- The University of California, San Diego
- The University of Texas, Austin
- Texas A&M University, College Station

The institutions may also choose to simply use words:

- The University of California at San Diego
- The University of Texas at Austin
- Texas A&M University at College Station

That sums up en dashes. Now on to the en dash's big brother—the em dash.

The Most Common Use of Em Dashes

For clarification, here are a few real-life examples of the three *primary* functions of an em dash.

1. To take the place of a colon, but with more punch.

Carla hated three things—deception, falsehoods, and lies.

Notice how that one piece of punctuation adds emphasis to the sentence. Yes, the words helped, but a colon wouldn't have been the same.

Carla hated three things: deception, falsehoods, and lies.

I don't know about you, but I can almost *feel* the disgust in the first example, and the second is pretty bland, as if she's citing a list of things she needs at the grocery store.

2. To offset a parenthetical phrase or thought.

No matter what happened—good, bad, or indifferent—in Uncle Dominic's house it was cause to put espresso on the stove.

3. To indicate an interruption in dialogue.

"I'm through talking," he said. "The next time—"

"There won't be a 'next time,'" she said, and slammed the door.

Note

I know there should be no comma following *said* in the sentence above (repeated below):

- "There won't be a 'next time,'" she said, and slammed the door.

I didn't use the comma because it's the way I punctuate dialogue, and I like it. I explain it in one of my books: *Editing Made Easy*.

DON'T THINK THE EXAMPLES ABOVE ARE THE ONLY USES OF THE em dash; there are many more. Along with the above reasons, there are other situations where you may see em dashes used frequently:

- To introduce a phrase or clause that summarizes what has just been said.

Exercising, drinking a lot of water, and throwing away your cigarettes—these are three simple things to keep you healthy.

To introduce several expressions, such as "that is," "namely," and "for example." As usual, examples follow:

☀ "My husband loves most working dogs—namely, Australian shepherds, Australian cattle dogs, and Anatolian shepherds."

☀ "I used to breed fish, and I loved the aggressive ones—for example, African and South American cichlids."

☀ During World War I, the Ottoman Empire and Hungary fought against the Allies—that is, they fought with the Germans.

One thing to note in the sentences above is that commas would normally precede *namely*, *that is*, and *for example*; however, you *do not* precede an em dash with a comma. The em dash serves in place of the comma. Under certain circumstances, it's acceptable to use an exclamation point or a question mark, and you may use a period if it concludes with an abbreviation. You also don't use semicolons or colons immediately preceding an em dash.

- For no reason he left—was he warned?—and he took his gun with him.
- The only reason for you to drive—God forbid!—is if everyone else is drunk.
- He insists on being addressed by his full title—Dr. Milton Abrams, M.D.—and we must abide if we want him to stay.

In the cases above, note the use of the punctuation preceding the em dash. It's rare you'd see this construction, but if you run across examples like the above, this is how to punctuate them.

One more thing about em dashes is that in special circumstances they may be used in place of a word. It may be a curse word you don't want to list, or it may be the name of someone you want to keep confidential.

In circumstances such as this (when an em dash is used in place of one or more words), use two or three em dashes to let the readers know (just be consistent).

- The foreman of the jury——read the guilty verdict today

at 11:00 a.m. (The em dashes represent the foreman's name).

- The young woman——was attacked and raped just before midnight while on her way home (same thing).
- When the foreman read the verdict, the defendant, noted mobster Carlo Giannini became vocal. "I'll kill you for this, you——rat. You're dead meat." (The em dashes are in place of the foul language he used.)

Bottom Line

To neatly wrap up dashes:

- A hyphen is used to connect compound modifiers (among other things), such as "hands-on manager," and "high-volume manufacturing."
- An en dash is used to show a range of dates (among other things), such as "2003–Present."
- An em dash might be used in a cover letter for a job application, such as this: "As general manager—and temporary vice president of sales—drove profits to record levels."

One more note about em dashes—they are often used in regular prose to add a little punch. I'll give you an example.

Imagine you're writing a scene where a family is having dinner at a restaurant someone's recommended. Let's imagine the maître d' approaches the table and asks how things are going. You might write the following:

- We ordered dinner an hour ago, and it hasn't arrived yet.

But if you wanted it to carry more punch, you might write:

- We ordered dinner—about an hour ago—and it hasn't arrived yet.

I don't know about you, but I think the second example carries more emphasis.

Technical Details

- To make hyphen (-), press the hyphen key on the keyboard.
- To make an en dash (–), press *option-* on a Mac or *control* and *minus sign* on the numeric keypad.
- To make an em dash (—), press *option/shift/hyphen* on a Mac or *control/alt* and *minus* key on the numeric keypad of a PC.

Chapter Thirty

QUIZ 7

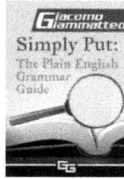

Quiz 7

This quiz is for *you* to punctuate. Each sentence deals with subject-verb agreement.

- Bob and his dog (do/does) everything together.
- My mom, as well as my dad, (are/is) going to the party.
- (There's/there are) a lot to do before we're done.
- He, my sister, and my dad (jog/jogs) every morning.

Chapter Thirty-One
QUIZ 8

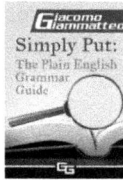

Q uiz 8 (Select the sentences that are correct.)

HE SAID HE'D GO TO THE THEATER. (WILL HE?)
> He said he'd go to the theater. (will he?)
> He said he'd go to the theater (Will he?).
> He said he'd go to the theater (will he?).
> He said he'd go to the theater. (Will he?).

"SHE SAID (AT LEAST, I THINK SHE SAID), 'LET'S GO TO THE beach.' "
> "She said (at least I think she said), 'Let's go to the beach.' "
> "She said (at least, I think she said), "Let's go to the beach."
> "She said, (at least, I think she said), 'Let's go to the beach.' "

. . .

WE SAW A KOALA BEAR (HAVE YOU EVER SEEN ONE?) WHEN WE went to the zoo.

We saw a koala bear, (have you ever seen one?) when we went to the zoo.

We saw a koala bear, (Have you ever seen one?) when we went to the zoo.

We saw a koala bear (Have you ever seen one?), when we went to the zoo.

We saw a koala bear (have you ever seen one?) when we went to the zoo.

Chapter Thirty-Two

SLASHES

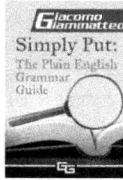

The forward slash (/) is not recommended for formal writing; however, it is used frequently with informal writing. Here are a few examples of how it's used.

Perhaps the most frequently seen usage is for fractions or dates, as the first few examples show.

- ½
- 11/17/16

It is also used in place of *or* in some cases.

- He/she was the one who robbed me.

A slash may also be used with abbreviations:

- w/o [for without]
- c/o [*for* care of]
- w/w [*for* wall-to-wall]

And from the *Merriam-Webster's Manual for Writers and Editors*:

If the letter is being used to refer to its sound and not its
printed form, slashes or brackets are used instead of italics in
technical contexts.

>The pure /p/ sound is rarely heard in the mountain
dialect.

— MERRIAM-WEBSTER'S

You may think this is an extremely rare case, but it's not. For
people who deal with teaching phonics by the sounds letters make
(phonemes), it is an everyday practice.

If you ever browsed a dictionary or looked up a word you didn't
know how to pronounce, invariably, phonemes were used to sound
it out. I've shown *through, cow,* and others below as they are listed
by *Merriam-Webster's*. (I removed the parts of speech designation so
it didn't confuse anyone.)

- through: \\'thrü\\
- cow: \\'kaủ\\
- fan·tas·tic: \\fan-'ta-stik, fən-\\
- cat: \\'kat\\
- pho·neme: \\'fō-ˌnēm\\

By the way, the above examples are the only times I know of
other than computer programming, where a backslash (\\ ) is used
on a regular basis.

THE "VERTICAL SLASH" OR "UPRIGHT SLASH" (|) IS USED IN
mathematical expressions and computer programming.

Part Three

GRAMMAR MYTHS

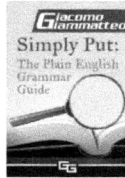

There are a lot of people who love to correct other's grammar. It's not something I'd recommend as it tends to piss people off; however, if you *are* going to correct someone else's grammar, make sure you're right. With that in mind, this section contains a few of the worst grammar myths—words or sayings that people love to *correct* even though they're not wrong.

Like a lot of issues dealing with grammar, the rules are more like guidelines, though sometimes they're viewed as strict.

I've tried to point out the accepted way to deal with grammar issues, but I also mention when those rules are seldom followed.

A couple of items that were intended for inclusion here were moved to the "Usage" section.

Chapter Thirty-Three

BETWEEN AND AMONG

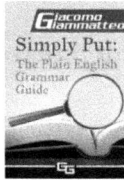

*B*etween—there can be only two.

This age-old myth reminds me of the movie *Highlander* where the theme was "There can be only one."

Between and Among

This is another long-standing, entrenched grammar myth. The legend states you can only use *between* for choices regarding two items or people. You are to use *among* for choices of more than two.

This is simply not the case. There are instances where you should use *between* and instances where you should use *among* outside these rules, and it's time to debunk the myth.

First, let's look at what the *Oxford English Dictionary* has to say about it:

> 'In all senses, between has been, from its earliest appearance, extended to more than two': there's an example of this from the year 971 (yes, not 1971!). Contemporary authorities (such as Pocket Fowler's Modern English Usage) advise that it's perfectly acceptable to use between or among

in certain contexts when referring to more than two participants:

Now let's look at a few examples.

☑ A noncompete agreement was drawn up *between* Apple, Google, Facebook, and Twitter.

✘ A noncompete agreement was drawn up *among* Apple, Google, Facebook, and Twitter.

✘ There was an agreement *between* members of the board that prices should remain stable.

☑ There was an agreement *among* members of the board that prices should remain stable.

☑ The shark is unique *among* all the predators of the sea.

✘ The shark is unique *between* all the predators of the sea.

☑ Sheila went to dinner, and she sat *among* her family members.

☑ Sheila went to dinner, and she sat *between* her family members.

Let's look at the last two examples.

In the first of those two, we're implying Sheila was sitting at a table with family members—she was sitting among them. So there was a table with, say, eight people, and she was one of them.

In the second example, we're implying she was sitting at a table with others, but they may not all have been family, however, she did sit *between* family; in other words, the people on either side of her were family members.

Looking now at the very first example, notice we used *between* with four choices: Apple, Google, Facebook, and Twitter. There's nothing wrong with that usage. According to CMOS (*Chicago Manual of Style*), you can use *between* with any number of items. Here's what they have to say about it:

Between indicates one-to-one relationships {between you and me}. *Among* indicates undefined or collective relationships {honor among thieves}. *Between* has long been recognized as being perfectly appropriate for more than two objects if multiple one-to-one relationships are understood from the context {trade between members of the European Union}. *Amid* is used with mass nouns {amid talk of war}, *among* with plurals of count nouns {among the children}. Avoid *amidst* and *amongst*.

— CMOS

When this myth started and how it started are a mystery, but I wonder if it doesn't have something to do with so many idiomatic expressions using *between* with only two items.

- Between a rock and a hard place.
- Between you and me.
- Between the devil and . . .
- There's bad blood between . . . (two people or families).
- He doesn't have much between the ears (two ears).
- I need to choose between jobs.
- Alternate between . . . (alternate means to go from one to the other).
- There's a fence between his property and mine.

One more example to show how using between with more than two choices is fine:

- If my grandson had to choose *between* a red, gold, blue, or green Power Ranger, he'd choose red every time.

The rules for use are not clear to most people, but if you want to be safe, I'd use *between* when choosing between specific, named items (regardless of number) and *among* when choosing between unnamed options.

Chapter Thirty-Four
DANGLING MODIFIERS

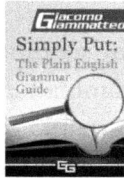

Dangling modifiers do not fall into the "grammar myths" category like the other topics. And while we're at it, a dangling modifier is not the same as a misplaced modifier, which is usually an easy fix. A few examples of misplaced modifiers follow.

- Mom was at the beach today, and she found a *gold* man's wedding ring.

First of all, I doubt it was a ring that belonged to a *gold* man, and if it was, how did she know that? The way to fix it is simply move the modifier.

- Mom was at the beach today, and she found a man's *gold* wedding ring.

It's as simple as that. Move one word and the sentence is correct. Along those same lines, consider the following:

✗ It was a *platinum* man's watch, and it was worth a lot of money.

☑ It was a man's *platinum* watch, and it was worth a lot of money.

I think you see the problem with sentences that contain misplaced modifiers, and I hope you also see how easy it is to fix.

But most of the fuss you hear from editors and grammarians is not about misplaced modifiers but *dangling modifiers.*

Many people come down on dangling modifiers, but they're not all bad.

According to a recent article in The Guardian, by well-known linguist Steven Pinker, dangling modifiers (as well as other so-called rules) are not necessarily ungrammatical.

When I said Pinker was "well-known," I didn't mean to imply by common folk. His name is in no danger of being tossed around during a Saturday-morning pick-up game on a Bronx basketball court, but it may be heard being bandied about at a Beacon Hill social club by a few Ivy League types while discussing the merits of using *shall* as opposed to *will*. Now back to what Pinker had to say.

The decision of whether to recast a sentence to align its subject with the subject of a modifier is a matter of judgment, not grammar.

— STEVEN PINKER

The following isn't about modifiers, but it serves the point that Pinker was trying to make—that, sometimes, strict grammarians complain about something simply to have something to complain about.

Pinker brings up excellent points in the article. One point involves a well-known advertising campaign back in the days when cigarette advertising nearly dominated the airwaves. When the campaign came out, grammarians threw a fit. Here's what all the fuss was about:

- "Winston tastes good *like* a cigarette should."

What caused such a furor was that the grammarians said the ad should have been worded "Winston tastes good *as* a cigarette should." (They should have paid more attention to what they were selling, not how they worded it.)

While we're speaking of ad campaigns, remember the stink raised by the grammarians when Apple's "think different" campaign came out? The purists were furious. They insisted it should have been "differently" that was used.

Pinker also made another good point regarding dangling modifiers, and he made the point much better than I could have, so I'll use his example.

Do you see a problem with the sentences that follow?

- "Checking into the hotel, it was nice to see a few of my old classmates in the lobby."
- "Turning the corner, the view was quite different."
- "In order to contain the epidemic, the area was sealed off."

According to an old rule about "dangling modifiers," these sentences are ungrammatical. The rule decrees that the implied subject of the modifier (the one doing the checking, turning, and so on) must be identical to the overt subject of the main clause (it, the view, and so on). Most copy editors would recast the main clause, supplying it with a subject to which the modifier can be properly fastened:

- "Checking into the hotel, *I* was pleased to see a few of my old classmates in the lobby."
- "Turning the corner, *I* saw that the view was quite different."

The kind of dangling modifier I often see is innocent enough. This kind of mistake listed below can elicit a chuckle, but I'm sure readers understand what is intended.

- After lighting the fire, the coyotes stopped howling.

I'm certain everyone understands what the writer intended, and they didn't mean the coyotes lit the fire.

My advice is simple. If you spot a dangling modifier, and it seems as if it could cause confusion for the reader, by all means, change it. Clarity is what we're after.

But if you see a dangling modifier (like in the first examples above), and they read with clarity, leave them alone and move on.

Chapter Thirty-Five

DON'T BEGIN A SENTENCE WITH THE WORD HOWEVER

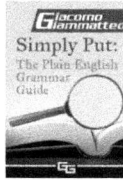

$\mathcal{G}$rammarians of all types have long asserted that you shouldn't begin a sentence with *however*; however, they weren't necessarily correct.

There is nothing wrong with starting a sentence with *however* as long as you know how to do it. Look at the examples below.

☑ However you want to do it is fine by me.

☑ His mother told him he couldn't go to the party without his brother. However, he went anyway, and he went alone.

☑ However you got that computer, I'm certain it wasn't legal, so I don't want to hear about it.

The second sentence could have been reworded so that a semi-colon came before *however*.

☑ His mother told him he couldn't go to the party without his brother; however, he went anyway, and he went alone.

Merriam-Webster's has a usage note on *however*." Look at what they have to say regarding Strunk and White's advice against it:

This is a stylistic choice, more than anything else, as we have a considerable body of evidence of writers using *however* to

begin   sentences,   frequently   with   the   meaning   of
"nevertheless."

_____

_____

"However, I am sure James does not drink so much."
> — —JANE AUSTEN, *NORTHANGER ABBEY*,
> 1818

_____

_____

Oh,   there   is   no   accounting   for   the   caprice   of
women. However, I was talking about Miss Moore.
> — —CHARLOTTE BRONTË, *THE DUKE OF*
> *ZAMORNA*, 1838

_____

Merriam-Webster's goes on to say that it is perfectly acceptable to
use at the beginning or middle.

_____

However may be used to begin a sentence, it can be used in
conjunction with *but*, and you can place it pretty much
anywhere you want in a sentence, so long as you do so with
care.

> — MERRIAM-WEBSTER'S

_____

Chapter Thirty-Six

DON'T END A SENTENCE WITH A PREPOSITION

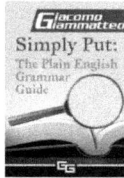

*I*f you were born before 1990, you were probably instructed—or even admonished—against ending sentences with prepositions. Most likely there wasn't a reason why you shouldn't, simply a stern warning not to do it. And you know what? It worked.

You have probably spent the years since then cringing when you hear someone say "Where are you at?" or "Where are you going to?"

I doubt many people go so far as to carry a list of prepositions in their pocket, but, with the proliferation of smart phones, I doubt if anyone needs to (there's that pesky preposition again).

The truth about structuring sentences to be grammatically correct is that you usually shouldn't worry about it.

While sentences like the ones I used as examples are somewhat grating, they can be easily fixed by simply dropping the preposition.

✕ Where are you at?
✓ Where are you?
✕ Where are you going to?
✓ Where are you going?

There are other examples that aren't as offensive, even to the nerdiest grammarian; however, they would be more difficult to fix. But then again, who says they need to be fixed? Let's take a look.

- She loves to fuss *over* her cat (no problem).
- Her cat loves to be fussed *over* (uh-oh).

When you ask someone a question that begins with *who*, *what*, or *where*, it often results in the sentence ending with a preposition. But who's to say that's wrong?

- Who did you invest *with*?
- What play are you going *to*?
- Which side is *up*?
- When are they going to let us *in*?

You could easily rearrange these sentences so they didn't end in prepositions, but why bother? They're fine as they are, and it's the natural way of speaking.

If you have to have a rule for this, consider the following, but only as a guide.

👈 If the sentence that ends in a preposition keeps the same meaning when you remove the preposition, then remove it.

For example, take a look at the first two sentences I used as examples. I'll repeat them here.

✖ WHERE ARE YOU AT?
   ✅ Where are you?
   ✖ Where are you going to?
   ✅ Where are you going?

These sentences are wrong for a different reason. They're wrong because you don't need those prepositions; they're redundant. However, there are prepositions that are an integral part of the sentence, and to remove them would change the meaning, and to re-arrange the sentence may be ridiculous.

- Who are you waiting *for*?
- They were best friends until the fight, but then they made *up*.
- Do you want to tell me what that was *about*?
- Where are you *from*?

My advice is simple. If a sentence grates on you or doesn't sound right, change it or find something more important to worry *over* or worry *about* or drown your sorrows *in*.

List of Prepositions

This list is from The Free Dictionary. It doesn't include prepositional phrases, but it shows the more common prepositions and even the less common ones.

- aboard
- about
- above
- across
- after
- against
- along
- amid
- among
- around
- as
- at
- before
- behind
- below
- beneath
- beside
- between
- beyond
- but
- by
- concerning

- considering
- despite
- down
- during
- except
- following
- for
- from
- in
- inside
- into
- like
- minus
- near
- next
- of
- off
- on
- onto
- opposite
- out
- outside
- over
- past
- per
- plus
- regarding
- round
- save
- since
- than
- through
- to
- toward
- under

- underneath
- unlike
- until
- up
- upon
- versus
- via
- with
- within
- without

Chapter Thirty-Seven

DOUBLE NEGATIVES ARE ALWAYS WRONG

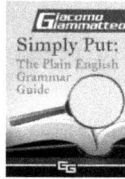

Giacomo Giammatteo
Simply Put:
The Plain English Grammar Guide

*C*hildren learn this so-called rule right after their "ABCs" or it seems that way. When I was a kid, if a teacher heard you say "I don't got no . . ." or anything resembling that phrase, you were bent over the desk and rewarded with a beating (usually with a fiberglass yardstick).

I realize teachers aren't allowed to administer corporal punishment nowadays, but some of them have a glare that's almost as bad.

We were taught that using double negatives makes a statement positive; therefore, don't use them.

As an example, our teacher would explain that "I don't have no apples" technically means "I do have apples."

I agree that *most* double negatives are wrong and should be avoided in formal writing; however, they may have a place in informal writing, dialogue, and everyday speech. There is no denying their presence.

There is also one instance I can think of where a double negative even has a place in formal writing. Consider the following sentences:

- I *didn't* want to go to the play, but after she bought the tickets, I *couldn't not* go.
- My drug-addict brother asked for help again, so I gave him the money. I had to. I *couldn't not* help him.
- I *can't* imagine it's *not* real.

These sentences could have been reworded, but they wouldn't have carried the same weight. Take a look:

- I didn't want to go to the play, but after she bought the tickets, I had to go.
- My drug-addict brother asked for help again, so I gave him the money. I had to. I had to help him.
- I find it difficult to believe it's not real.

Whether you agree that the sentences sounded stronger with the double negatives or without them makes no difference. If someone wanted to word them that way, others shouldn't complain.

Writers who understand their craft may wish to use double negatives to their advantage, especially for character development, for emphasis, or to make a stronger point. Consider the following:

- Hector was a *happy* fellow (normal usage).
- Hector was *not an unpleasant* fellow (double negative).

While grammarians will tell you that a double negative cancels out and turns the sentence into an affirmative, saying Hector was *happy* paints him as a nicer person than saying he was *not unpleasant*.

The second sentence gives the impression of a person who may not be unfriendly or dour, but the word choice doesn't necessarily paint that person as someone you'd want to be around.

Many other examples could be made. Suppose someone asks your opinion about a friend.

- Braden asked me out, but I haven't decided if I'm going. Is he a *kind* person?

This is a question posed to you by Sally, your friend. She is asking about Braden, another friend.

- I've known Braden a long time. He's not *un*kind.

Saying someone is *not unkind* falls far short of saying they are a nice person. To me, that statement implies that while Braden may not go out of his way to be mean to others, he isn't necessarily nice to them.

And to cite an example of a double negative in recent use:

In 2012, when President Obama was speaking at the United Nations regarding the Iran nuclear issue, he said the following:

"America wants to resolve this issue through diplomacy, and we believe that there is still time and space to do so. But that time is not unlimited.*"*

— PRESIDENT BARACK OBAMA

This tactic is often used by politicians, salesmen, negotiators, et al. It's similar to giving someone an ultimatum, then saying "I'm *not* saying you have to decide in five minutes, but you *don't* have all day."

Chapter Thirty-Eight

FLAT ADVERBS

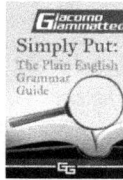

What is a flat adverb? Don't be embarrassed if you don't know. I didn't know until about a year ago, when I was doing research for one of my grammar books. The editor I used corrected me for using them.

At the time, I didn't know better, so I changed the words. Now I wouldn't do that. And while most editors will know better, a lot of readers won't, so learn the basics and don't let people tell you different (or differently).

Flat Adverbs

A flat adverb is an adverb that assumes the form of a related adjective, most often when words ending in *-ly* are used without the *-ly*.

Though once quite common, flat adverbs have been largely phased out by their *-ly* counterparts. This shift is owed to eighteenth-century grammarians who insisted that adverbs end in *-ly*. Nonetheless, flat adverbs are preferred in some cases, such as "Take it easy" and "Sleep tight." We don't say "Take it easily" or "Sleep tightly."

I found out what a flat adverb was by accident. I had given a first draft of my new novel to a group of beta readers, and a couple of them chided me for using *slow, fast, quick,* and *hard* instead of their normal adverbial forms (*slowly, quickly,* and *hardly*). In this case, *hardly* would not have worked; there is no normal counterpart for *fast*; and *slow* and *quick* sounded a lot better to me than *slowly* and *quickly.*

But was I wrong?

I wondered, so I did some research. Here's what I found: The first thing was that flat adverbs have been persecuted for a long time. The most famous of these, and one that drew considerable attention, was from an ad campaign Apple ran in the 1990s. It suggested that people *think different.*

Grammarians the world over raised a stink. "It should be *think differently,*" they said.

They were met by an even more vocal rebellion from the common people, who insisted that nothing was wrong with *different.* It turns out that the common people were correct.

Different turned out to have been used as an adverb for hundreds of years, and the ad went on to become a tremendous success. Also, as a result of the initial uproar, many other flat adverbs were brought to light, including *bright, high, clean, slow, fast, quick, hard, sharp, soon,* and *tough,* among others.

Much of the criticism I caught referred to my use of the flat adverbs in dialogue (imperatives), and, oddly enough, that's where I found flat adverbs used the most. Examples follow.

- Drive slow.
- Be quick.
- Breathe deep.
- Hit him hard.
- Be kind.
- Run, Maria. Run fast!
- Aim high.
- Look sharp.

Let's look at how these would appear if we used their normal adverbial forms (where they have them).

- Drive slowly. (Not so bad—about the same)
- Be quickly? (Doesn't work)
- Breathe deeply. (Sounds the same)
- Hit him hardly? (Doesn't work at all)

You could say "I hit him hard" or "I hardly hit him," but the meanings are almost opposite.

- Run, Maria. Run (fast)? (No counterpart)
- Aim highly? (Doesn't work at all)
- Look sharply. ("Look sharp" and "look sharply" have different meanings)

Let's look at a few sentences where we can and can't use them interchangeably.

Bright

☑ The lights of the city shine bright at night.

☑ The lights of the city shine brightly at night.

Clean

☑ "You need to come clean," he said.

✗ "You need to come cleanly," he said

☑ "Make sure and go to the reception cleanly groomed."

✗ Make sure and go to the reception clean groomed.

Deep

☑ "Breathe deep," the diving instructor told her.

☑ "Breathe deeply," the diving instructor told her.

Hard

☑ He hit him hard.

✗ He hit him hardly.

☑ He hardly hit him.

✗ He hard hit him.

Fast

✗ Run fast, Maria.

Run (no counterpart)

High

☑ Jump high, Tom.

✗ Jump highly, Tom.

Sharp

☑ He dresses sharp.

✗ He dresses sharply.

☑ He was sharply dressed.

✗ He was sharp dressed.

As you can see, all of the flat adverbs worked but not all of the *normal* adverb forms (*ly*) worked except where we rearranged the sentence and placed the adverb in front of the verb. In those cases, the sentence took on a new meaning.

☑ He was sharply dressed.

☑ He was sharply dressed.

☑ "Make sure and go to the reception cleanly groomed."

You know the saying: "A little knowledge is a dangerous thing." Well, that applies here. Most people don't know if something is wrong with your grammar, but if they think it's wrong, you're likely to hear about it.

And yet the flat adverb has been with us for a long time. Consider these expressions: "He holds his cards close," or "Sit tight," or "Hang tough." Each of these words—*close, tight,* and *tough*—are functioning as flat adverbs, yet these sayings are used all the time and accepted.

So the next time someone tells you you're using the wrong word and they're referring to a flat adverb, tell them to go to . . . here

Chapter Thirty-Nine

"IT IS HE" OR "IT'S ME"

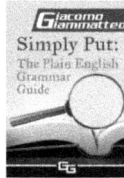

One of the rules teachers also drummed into our heads when we were young (so long ago) was the proper way to answer the phone, door, etc., when asked who it was.

If someone called you on the phone, and when you answered, they asked: "Is this Jim?" you were taught to answer, "This is he."

Or if you knocked on someone's door, they may have called out, "Is that you, Jim?" And you may have responded, "It is I."

The problem is that it doesn't work that way in the real world. It may be used less than the proper way to use *whom*. You don't come home from work and call to your spouse, "Hey, babe, it's I."

Of course not. You'd say "Hey, babe, it's me."

Or if someone asks you, "Is this Jim?," you'd likely answer, "It's me," not "It is I" or "It is he."

This is another example of a rule that should never have been a rule. My advice is if you want to sound like a stiff-collared, ancient butler, stick to the "It is I" response, but if you want to sound as if you're part of the everyday world, just say "It's me."

Chapter Forty

MYTHS THAT AREN'T MYTHS, THAT AREN'T NOT MYTHS

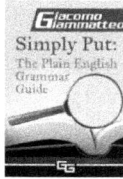

*N*ow that I've confused the hell out of you with that chapter title, let me explain—or at least try to explain.

Many people use qualifiers with words that are absolutes, which drives others, especially sticklers for the language, up the wall. One of the worst offenders is "very unique" or any qualifier or intensifier with the word *unique*.

I can be a stickler myself, so I'm not saying the grammarians are wrong; however, their anger and frustration may be misplaced. While I'm opposed to a lot of changes, I realize that the adaption of language (any language) is inevitable. I also prefer that words change as opposed to sensible rules regarding structure.

Most who use phrases like "very unique" are the same people who misuse the primary word *unique*; in other words, they view their use of *unique* to mean "rare" or "uncommon" but not necessarily "one of a kind."

Because they view it only as rare, it can be qualified. A rare item can be rarer than another, and somewhere out there can be found the rarest of something. Based on this theory (even though the use of *very* is questionable), the use of the phrase "very unique" is not incorrect.

It's not incorrect because the person doesn't view *unique* as being one of a kind, so in their mind, it can be qualified. That doesn't make it right to the rest of the world, but it makes it right to them.

The same logic applies to all absolutes. Take the phrase "absolutely perfect." If we assume the user considers "perfect" a state of bliss, a goal they aspire to, and that's what they consider perfect, then it could take a qualifier.

Imagine a young couple from humble beginnings. Now imagine their idea of a perfect house. *Perfect* to them may be a two-story colonial on a cul-de-sac with 2,400 square feet. To them, that's absolutely perfect.

Now imagine a couple who grew up in mansions, with servants and multiple vehicles stored in an eight-car garage. To them, that same 2,400-square-feet house may be smaller than the garage they grew up with.

As we've stated, language changes. Words we currently use every day and consider acceptable may have made a linguist from Shakespeare's time shudder and curse.

Let's look at a few and how their usage has changed. Some of the following has been paraphrased from an outstanding article I saw in *The Telegraph*.

- *Bedroom* is now a place where a person sleeps or keeps their bed (a separate room).
- *Bed-room* used to refer to anyplace a person slept; in other words, where there was room to bed, as in "Do you have any bed room?"
- *Housekeeper* is now someone who keeps house or perhaps a member of a household who manages the household.
- *Housekeeper* in Shakespeare's day was more of a guard or a watchdog.
- *Customer* now means a person who purchases a product or service or a person you may sell something to. It can

also refer to a character trait, as in "He's a tough customer."

- *Customer* in Shakespeare's day meant anyone involved in a negotiation, deal, or transaction regardless of whether they were buying or selling.

If you ever want to see just how much the language has changed, take a few minutes to read some of Shakespeare's work. It's not as difficult as reading an unknown language, but it is usually a struggle. Below is a sample (an easy one) from *Antony and Cleopatra*:

"If he filled his vacancy with his voluptuousness, full surfeits and the dryness of bones call on him for't."

The Bottom Line

To finish up this chapter, let's look at a few other sayings similar to "very unique."

- absolutely perfect
- completely perfect
- totally perfect

Regardless of how we feel about phrases like these, I'm convinced they're here to stay. The way I figure it, in four hundred years, people won't be able to read our works any better than we can read the works of Shakespeare.

Chapter Forty-One

"NONE" ALWAYS REQUIRES A SINGULAR VERB

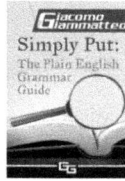

Giacomo
Giammatteo
Simply Put:
The Plain English
Grammar
Guide

*N*one **always requires a singular verb**
A long-standing belief is that *none* always takes a singular verb because *none* is short for "no one" or "not one," but it can also mean "not any" in which case it would take a plural verb.

I've provided a few examples below. In the first sentence, *none* is used with a mass noun, a noun that cannot be made plural or counted; therefore, it takes a singular verb. You can't say "None of the *butters were* eaten."

- ☑ None (not any) of the butter *was* eaten.
- ☑ None (not one) of the apples *were* eaten.

As you can see, *none* works well with either a singular or plural verb, depending on the circumstance. The following is from the Oxford English .Dictionary
  Usage

It is sometimes held that none can only take a singular verb, never a plural verb: none of them is coming tonight rather than none of them are coming tonight. There is little justification, historical or grammatical, for this view. None is descended from Old English nān meaning 'not one' and has been used for around a thousand years with both a singular and a plural verb, depending on the context and the emphasis needed.

Chapter Forty-Two

SPLITTING A VERB WITH AN ADVERB

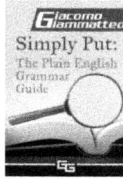

Simply Put:
The Plain English Grammar Guide

*L*ater on we talk about the effects of placing *only* in different positions in a sentence, so it's only right that our first example is using *only*. This example points out what happens to the meaning of the sentence when you use *only* to split the verb.

- I like swimming at the beach *only*.

Here you're saying you like swimming but at the beach only; in other words, not at the lake, or the creek, or in a backyard pool. When you change the position of *only*, though, you drastically change the meaning of the sentence.

- I like *only* swimming at the beach.

Now you're saying that you like swimming (again), but you like nothing else at the beach. You don't like surfing, or building sand castles, or even sunbathing—*only* swimming.

Not all words affect the meaning of a sentence the way *only* does, but the placement of adverbs usually has some effect, even if it's only how it sounds to others.

On to splitting compound verbs

There have been, and still are, grammarians who advise against splitting compound verbs, not with the level of vehemence that they rail against split infinitives, such as "to boldly go," but their protests are only slightly less aggressive.

There is more than enough evidence to support the splitting of verbs with adverbs, and it's not just in everyday speech. Consider the first line from the oath sworn by the president during an inauguration.

I do solemnly swear that I will faithfully execute the Office of President of the United States

---

- I *do* **solemnly** *swear* that I *will* **faithfully** *execute* the office . . .

In this example of the president swearing his oath, we have not one, but two examples of verbs being split by another word:

- I *do* **solemnly** *swear* that I *will* **faithfully** *execute* . . .

In the example above, the words in italics are the verbs, and the words in bold formatting are the adverbs splitting them.

The oath could have been reworded to something like: "I solemnly do swear" or "I will execute the office of the president faithfully," but it would mean the same thing, and it wouldn't sound as good.

Some authorities have long fought against this *rule* regarding splitting compound verbs, and they've been as vocal as they have been regarding the *rule* about not splitting infinitives.

As far back as the 1920s, H.W.Fowler (*A Dictionary of Modern American Usage,* 1926), spoke out against it, and more recently B. A. Garner (*A Dictionary of Modern American Usage,* 1998), did the same.

— BALTIMORE SUN

Some people agree

While researching this, I came across several university sites that not only objected to the "rule" of not splitting compound (multiple) verbs, they had rules that suggested the reverse.

- "When the verb consists of an auxiliary, the adverb goes after it."

- He *has **always** wanted* to be a politician.

I agreed wholeheartedly with them. You'd be hard pressed to rephrase that sentence where it means the same and sounds as good. Look at the alternatives:

- He always has wanted to be a politician.
- He has wanted always to be a politician.
- He has wanted to be a politician always.
- Always, he has wanted to be a politician.

None of them sounds as good as the original: "He has always wanted to be a politician."

One guideline that's fairly strict is that you shouldn't place an adverb between the verb and its object:

✗ I understand completely the test results.

✓ I completely understand the test results.

✓ I understand the test results *completely*.

I'm sure you know by now that there are usually exceptions to any rule, and this rule is no different. Below is the exception.

- If there is a preposition before the verb's object, you can place the adverb before the preposition *or* after the object.

☑ The lost child ran *happily* **toward** his mother.
☑ The wayward son looked *hungrily* **around** the table.

Not to beat a dead horse, but I'm going to provide one more example. This may sail past the younger audience, but maybe not.

In *Casablanca*, one of the better films ever made, Bogart says something to Ingrid Bergman near the end that has become a somewhat-famous phrase "We'll always have Paris."

This has grown to be one of the more quoted lines from movies, and it fits right in with the topic of discussion. It may not appear so at first, but look closer.

- "We'll *always* have Paris."

Upon inspection, we see that *we'll*, a contraction meaning "we will" is separated from the other part of the verb (have) by the adverb *always*. This placement is crucial; it's the only one that sounds right. Look at it if it's moved.

- *Always*, we'll have Paris.
- We'll have Paris, *always*.
- We *always* will have Paris.

They all sound stilted, as if a stodgy old grammarian was saying them, not a romantic younger couple who love each other. I doubt dialogue like that would have stirred emotions with theater goers. And if they had used one of those lines, I can almost guarantee it would not be an often-quoted movie line.

The bottom line is that regardless of what anyone tells you about not splitting a compound (multiword) verb with an adverb, if it sounds better, do it.

Chapter Forty-Three

THAT IS FOR THINGS AND WHO IS FOR PEOPLE

*W*hether used verbally or in written form, it can be tricky to know when *that*, *which*, or *who* should be used. But if you understand the differences and the rules that govern them, it's not that difficult.

By the way, when you do a Google search for *that* and *who*, you'll get results in the billions. I got more than five billion. No matter how you look at it, it means a lot of people are confused about how to properly use these words.

The first rule is simple:

• *Who* refers only to people:

Examples follow:

• Margaret yelled at Sam, *who* had eaten the dessert without permission.

• He is the one *who* dropped his wallet.

That refers primarily to things, although it can also refer to a *class* or *type* of person or to a *team*:

• The Patriots seem to be the team *that* always wins (team).

• He is the kind of coach *that* is hands-on (type of person).

• He has the kind of gun *that* I want (thing).

Note:

Regarding sentence number two, some think it's better to say "He is the kind of coach *who* is hands-on"; however, using *that* is acceptable because you're talking about the "kind" of person, not the person.

Something else to note is that while *who* is used for people, it is not used for companies or organizations.

So you wouldn't say "The company *who* pays *their* employees well is bound to succeed."

It would be "The company *that* pays *its* employees well is bound to succeed."

And while the rule states that *who* is only used for people, exceptions are made for animals *who* would otherwise be referred to by name or gender, although there are rules governing that as well:

☑ The brown one is the dog *that* bit me.

The simple rule is that in most adult-oriented writing, you refer to an animal as *it* unless you have already given it a name or referred to it by gender.

The "not so simple" rule usually occurs with children's books (though it could with adult books as well).

When the book has talking animals as characters, you refer to them using *he* or *she* and *who* because you are giving them personalities by granting them the ability to speak. Once you go that far, it's only fair to assign them names and genders.

The following are two examples:

☑ The dog defied *its* nature and fought the other animal (generic).

☑ *He* defied *his* nature and fought the other animal (presuming the dog has been given a name or that at least gender was established).

Let's look at a few more examples.

If you're sitting around the house talking about one of your pets or an animal you are familiar with, it's all right to say the following:

☑ *Bear* was out late last night; *he* must have been roaming the woods.

But if you're speaking of a stray or a dog you don't know, you'd say it this way:

☑ Yesterday, *some* dog came onto the property, and *it* caused a ruckus with our dogs. It's a good thing we had *Bear* locked up, or *he* would have attacked *it*.

As you can see, when we had a gender and a name (Bear), we used *he*, or the name, but when we were speaking of the stray, we referred to it as "it."

This makes it easy for me. My wife and I have an animal sanctuary, and if an animal is living there, he or she gets a name.

One More Time

Not to beat a dead horse, but let's review this one more time. If a stray dog bit you, you'd tell the doctor, "I was walking down the street, and the dog bit me. *It* just came up and bit me."

On the other hand, if you knew the dog, you might say "I was walking down the street, and *Mollie* ran up and bit me. For no reason, *she* bit me."

You might also say "*She* is the one *who* bit me."

So a saying you probably hear frequently—"Who is that?" —is questionable. According to some, it should be "Who is he?" or "Who is she?" By saying "Who is that?" you're referring to the person as *that* instead of *he* or *she*.

But regardless of what people think, I don't believe sayings like that are going away. Think about what most people say when someone knocks on their door: "Who is it?" Or if someone tells you "Someone's at the door" or "Someone's on the phone" and you ask "Who is it?"

We've already talked about the astounding number of Google searches regarding these words, which means a large number of people have questions regarding their proper use.

The Bottom Line

With all of these explanations, the bottom line is simpler. Try to use *who* when referring to people, but if you mess up and use *that*, I wouldn't worry about it. People have used *that* to refer to other people for centuries; in fact, if you listen closely to people speak, I'll gamble that you will notice many of them use *that* when referring to people.

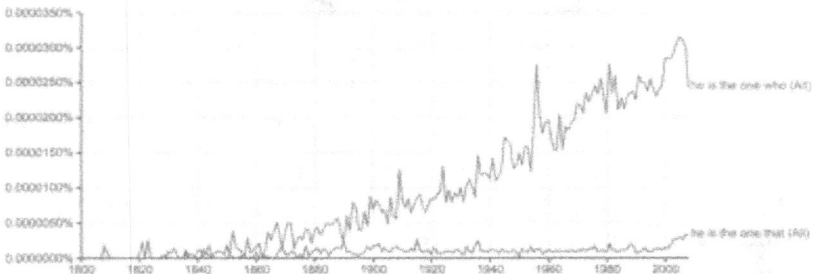

Looking at the Google Ngram above, you'll see that using *that* is making a minor comeback while using *who* is on a slightly downward path. I predict the gap between the two will grow shorter in the years to come.

There are plenty of other grammar myths out there, but there are also plenty of grammar misuses. If you have any interest in the language, learn what's right and what's not. And if you're interested in learning about grammar the easy way, look up one of my grammar bites books.

Chapter Forty-Four

THEN CAN'T BE USED AS A CONJUNCTION

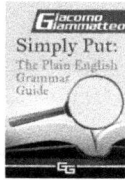

*M*any people advise against using *then* as a conjunction, and some of those people are adamant about it. Consider the following statement from Jonathan Franzen, listed in his "rules of writing."

Never use the word "then" as a conjunction – we have "and" for this purpose. Substituting "then" is the lazy or tone-deaf writer's non-solution to the problem of too many "ands" on the page.

— JONATHAN FRANZEN

Consider this sentence:

- Rose cleared the table, then did the dishes.

I see nothing wrong with that sentence as it is, and yet, according to Jonathan Franzen, it's wrong.

But according to Cambridge English Dictionary, using *then* in a sentence such as that, is merely using it to mean "next."

From Cambridge English Dictionary:

We can use then to mean 'next':

He opened the door, then the lights came on and everybody shouted, 'Happy Birthday'.

Heat some olive oil in a pan, then add some chopped garlic and some salt.

Cambridge English Dictionary

I agree with Cambridge. I see nothing wrong with the sentences they used as examples; in fact, I use *then* with all my writing in such a manner, and I think it makes the writing flow smoother in most cases. It sounds more natural to me.

Here's what *The Chicago Manual of Style* has to say:

The adverb then is often seen between independent clauses as shorthand for and then, preceded by a comma. This usage is perfectly acceptable, and it is more or less obligatory in the imperative (as in the first example below); some writers, however, may prefer to use a semicolon, which is strictly correct.

Touch and hold the icon, then drag it to the trash.

First we went out for shiitake burgers, then we enjoyed vegan sundaes.

or

First we went out for shiitake burgers; then we enjoyed vegan sundaes.

but

First we went out for shiitake burgers, and then we enjoyed vegan sundaes

— CHICAGO MANUAL OF STYLE (CMOS)

And this is what the American Heritage Dictionary has to say:

Sticklers for grammar sometimes assert that *then* is not a coordinating conjunction, and that the sentence *She took a slice of pie, then left* is thus incorrect; it must be rewritten as *She took a slice of pie and then left,* in which the *then* acts as an adverb and the halves of the compound predicate are linked by the coordinating conjunction *and.* But this use of *then* as a coordinating conjunction is actually both widespread and widely accepted; in our 2012 survey, more than three quarters of the Usage Panel found the sentence *She took a slice of pie, then left* completely acceptable.

— AMERICAN HERITAGE DICTIONARY

The next time you have an urge to use *then* in such a manner, go ahead and do it. You have plenty of reputable resources to back you up.

And while we're at it, I might mention that Franzen's use of *non-solution* as a hyphenated word amounted to a style choice. There's nothing wrong with that. I often make such choices myself. But none of the dictionaries I looked in had *non-solution* listed with a hyphen; all of them had it as one word: *nonsolution.*

It's no different than an author deciding to use *then* in the manner discussed above.

Chapter Forty-Five

WHICH AND THAT

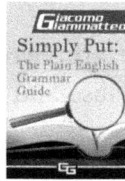

*T*he title of this section is "Grammar Myths," and while some of the chapters are myths, this one is only partly a myth.

It's not that difficult to know when to use *which* versus when to use *that*; they follow a fairly strict set of rules.

You would say "My van, which has a wheelchair ramp, is black." Or you would say "My van that has a wheelchair ramp is black."

Examples: "My van, which has a wheelchair ramp, is black." As you can see, you didn't need to state it had a wheelchair ramp. "My van is black" would have worked on its own.

But suppose you had two vans and only one had a ramp. In that case, you might say "My van that has a wheelchair ramp is black." In this case, your explanation of the ramp is necessary in designating the proper van, especially if both are black.

The first uses *which* and takes a comma before and after the "wheelchair ramp" clause. The second uses *that* and does not use commas.

Whenever you use *that* to start a clause, the clause is usually necessary and, therefore, needs no commas.

Now on to a more prickly subject. It has long been a *rule* that you use *that* to introduce essential clauses (necessary ones), and you use "which" to introduce nonessential clauses (unnecessary ones). When the clause in question requires *which*, you offset the clause or phrase with commas as well. I'll use the same examples we used earlier to show this.

- "My van, which has a wheelchair ramp, is black."
- "My van that has a wheelchair ramp is black."

All good so far. But there are plenty of cases where you could use *which* with an essential clause and have it sound fine. Consider the following.

- The ice cream which I like best is vanilla.

By all accounts, the sentence above should have used *that* and not *which*. It should have read, "The ice cream that I like best is vanilla." But there's nothing wrong with the sentence as it stands.

And when considering that sentence, it's worth mentioning that neither *which* or *that* were needed. You could have simply written:

- The ice cream I like best is vanilla

Getting back to *which* and *that*, I think this practice may have started as a guide for people to recognize essential and nonessential clauses in a sentence, but using the comma or not using the comma should suffice. If a clause or phrase is offset with commas, the phrase is nonessential (if done right), and if there are no commas, the phrase is essential.

This is what CMOS has to say about it.

Although *which* can be substituted for *that* in a restrictive clause (a common practice in British English), many writers preserve the distinction between restrictive *that* (with no commas) and nonrestrictive *which* (with commas).

— CMOS

I would still steer clear of using *that* with nonessential clauses, but I see no reason to avoid using *which* in place of *that* if it seems appropriate; in fact, we have many famous examples: "That which doesn't kill you makes you stronger." If you wanted to write that according to the recommended rules, it would be "That that doesn't kill you makes you stronger." Sounds pretty bad, doesn't it?

The Guardian made note of several other cases that have been accepted for years:

- Render unto Caesar the things *which* are Caesar's, and unto God the things *that* are God's

Shakespeare wrote this in a play hundreds of years ago, and not only has it been accepted, it has been taught to millions of students studying his plays. If you search for the quote now, you're likely to find *that* has been substituted for *which*, and it's probably been to keep up appearances of what is considered correct.

But The Guardian pointed out another example that is a little more difficult to brush over. It occurred during President Franklin Roosevelt's famous fireside chats in World War II. Here is the saying:

- . . . a day which will live in infamy.

There's nothing wrong with that statement, just like there was nothing wrong with the earlier example regarding which ice cream I like best.

- "The ice cream which I like best is vanilla."

The absence of commas offsetting the clause indicates there is more than one flavor. With commas, it would indicate otherwise.

OR HOW ABOUT THIS ONE?

You're at the ice cream shop with your kids, and you see your son staring at the menu. He looks up at you and says the following.

- I don't know *which* one I want.

Technically, that is an essential phrase. If he had simply said, "I don't know," it wouldn't have told us enough. "You don't know what?"

According to existing grammar rules, *which* should not have been used, but using *that* would have been an obvious mistake.

Like a lot of things, the decision whether to use *that* or *which* with essential clauses is mostly a choice of style. If it sounds right, do it. Just make sure to use your commas (or other punctuation).

Rules Regarding Which and That

The first rule is simple. We've already mentioned it and seen it used.

- *That* always introduces an essential clause (which means no commas).

The second part of the rule is not only debatable, it's downright wrong.

- *Which* is used to introduce nonessential clauses.

While it's true that *which* is used for nonessential clauses, it can also be used with essential clauses. We've already seen *which* used this way in a few sentences in the Shakespeare and Roosevelt examples, but let's look at a few more. You'll see that those two were not simply examples that escaped notice.

By the way, in British English, it is acceptable to use *which* to introduce essential clauses.

THERE IS AN EXCEPTION THAT NULLIFIES THE *RULE* REGARDING using *which* in this manner, and that rule is as follows.

If *which* is combined with a preposition, a noun, or a pronoun, it can't be replaced by *that* even when it introduces an essential clause. Let's look at a few examples to see how this works.

- The company *in which* he placed his faith has failed him (preposition).
- My wife didn't tell me *which* car she drove to work (car).
- I don't know *which* one I want (pronoun).

If you try to substitute *that* for *which* in any of the examples above, you'll see it doesn't work.

Chapter Forty-Six

YOU CAN'T SPLIT INFINITIVES

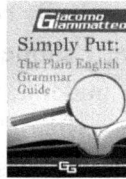

*I*n my early years of school, teachers began drumming this rule into students' heads—usually right after ensuring we wouldn't end sentences with prepositions. Let's first look at the issue, and then we'll show why it isn't an issue.

I realize I said I wouldn't resort to grammatical terms, but some things demand it.

You know what an infinitive is; you simply may not know what it's called. An infinitive is a verb in its simplest form coupled with the word *to*. Examples are "to talk," "to eat," "to be," "to see," etc. When people say you shouldn't split an infinitive, they mean you shouldn't put words between *to* and the verb.

Perhaps the most discussed example of this is the lead-in to the 1960s *Star Trek* show: "*To boldly go* where no man has gone before."

Grammar purists insist it should be "To go boldly . . ." stating that *boldly* is splitting the infinitive. The problem is that there isn't a hard-and-fast rule against splitting an infinitive. In fact, many people believe it sounds more natural not to split them (in some circumstances).

It may not sound better in all cases, but my opinion is if you like a sentence better with the infinitive split, then split away. If not, change it.

You can see more about a related subject—splitting a compound verb—in the chapter dealing with that.

In order to better understand why splitting infinitives isn't such a grave sin, just listen to everyday speech. You'll hear them used a lot, and often, they not only don't sound bad, they sound *normal*.

Think of the phrase "to magically appear." It sounds fine. It sounds better than the grammatically correct "to appear magically." But so does the split infinitive I slipped in at the beginning of the previous paragraph: "to better understand."

Or consider the following, which I read on the Science Daily site in a blog discussing the opioid crisis.

. . . population of residents ages 65 and older is expected *to more than double* by 2030 . . .

You would be hard pressed to rearrange that sentence by placing "more than" somewhere else and have it still make sense and keep the same meaning.

I saw a similar example in a financial report for a new tech company where the analyst said, ". . . profits increased to greater than anticipated results . . ."

There's nothing wrong with split infinitives. In many cases, they sound better. And in some cases, like the two above show, they're necessary.

Chapter Forty-Seven

YOU CAN'T START A SENTENCE WITH A CONJUNCTION

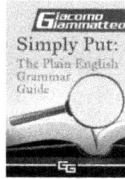

There's that *conjunction* word again. We've talked about it before. Remember? It's the one I referred to as a *connecting* word. I may refer to the words as *conjunctions* but remember they're only connecting words.

I'll also provide a list of conjunctions at the end of this chapter.

Connecting words

This is a long-standing taboo (beginning sentences with them), but it has never been an absolute no. Most teachers would advise against starting a sentence with a conjunction—some of them would strongly advise against it—but it wasn't forbidden.

I don't know where this objection to using a conjunction to start a sentence came from, but it doesn't hold water. It's fine to do so, but like anything, do it in moderation.

And, *but*, *so*, and other conjunctions are more commonly seen in their usual role of connecting clauses, but they can function just as well in leading the way.

- Jamie said no when I asked her to the prom. But as I walked away, I wondered why.

That sentence could have been constructed using *but* as a coordinate conjunction (connecting word), but I feel it would have lost some of the punch. There's more of a pause in the first example:

- Jamie said no when I asked her to the prom, *but* as I walked away, I wondered why.

Let's look at another example.

- My buddy Frank and about a million others think The Beatles were the best band ever. And who am I to argue?

Now, look at starting a sentence with a different type of connecting word—a subordinate conjunction.

- *Because* it was snowing, we stayed home from school.
- *Until* I see her again, I'll be worried.

As you can see, there is nothing wrong with any of those examples. The words work fine at the beginning of a sentence; they sound fine, and they are grammatically correct.

Like everything, do this in moderation, but if you think using a connecting word to start a sentence sounds good, by all means, do it.

A list of conjunctive adverbs is shown below or on the next page. You already have a list of the seven coordinating conjunctions: FANBOYS (for, and, nor, but, or, yet, so).

accordingly	additionally	also	anyway	besides
certainly	comparatively	consequently	conversely	elsewhere
equally	finally	further	furthermore	hence
henceforth	however	in addition	in comparison	in contrast
incidentally	indeed	instead	likewise	meanwhile
moreover	namely	nevertheless	next	nonetheless
now	otherwise	rather	similarly	still
subsequently	then	thereafter	therefore	thus
undoubtedly	yet			

Part Four

MISCELLANEOUS

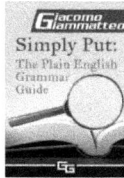

This section covers a lot of territory:

Chapter Forty-Eight
ABSTRACT NOUNS

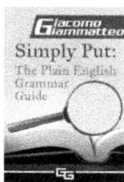

*A*bstract nouns are a special category of nouns, and they have special rules to govern them.

Other types of nouns are concrete nouns, collective nouns, proper nouns, etc.

Concrete nouns consist of people, places, or things we experience with one or more of our five senses. Abstract nouns are the opposite. If a noun is abstract, it describes something you can't see, hear, taste, touch, or smell. One more thing to note, and the reason for all of this verbiage: abstract nouns always use a singular verb—*is*, *was*, etc.

Below are a few examples of abstract nouns. Try out the verb with some and you'll see a plural form doesn't work.

Please remember that in the present tense, nouns and verbs form plurals differently: nouns add an *s* and verbs remove the *s*. It would be "The king *rules* the country" and "They *rule* the country."

- anger ("His anger *was* annoying" not "His anger *were* annoying.")
- chaos ("Chaos *rules* the universe" not "Chaos *rule* the universe.")

- conduct ("The children's conduct *was* atrocious.")
- courage
- culture
- death
- democracy
- education
- evil
- experience
- friendship
- grief
- hospitality
- information
- justice
- knowledge
- leisure
- liberty
- melancholy
- peace
- piety
- progress
- safety
- shopping
- softness
- speed
- taste
- time
- trouble
- violence
- virtue
- warmth
- work

As you can see, you can't touch or smell any of these things, and as previously mentioned, they all take a singular verb.

- "Love *cures* all."
- "Taste *is* one of the five senses."
- "Violence *has* never solved anything."
- "Work *is* rewarding."

Chapter Forty-Nine

ACRONYMS AND INITIALISMS

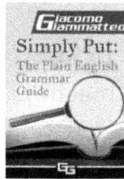

Giacomo Giammatteo
Simply Put:
The Plain English
Grammar
Guide

*T*he English language is full of redundancies, both written and verbal, so it's no wonder I've addressed this issue more than once. But this time it's different (at least I hope so). This time I'll be discussing a special kind of redundancy, one that has become prevalent in verbal communication.

Both acronyms and initialisms are abbreviations, but there is a key difference. An acronym is an abbreviation formed by using (usually) the first letters of the words—and they form a word, as in RAM (random access memory) or *laser* (light amplification by stimulated emission of radiation), but an initialism, while formed the same way, does not have to form a word.

Examples of initialisms are:

- FBI (Federal Bureau of Investigation)
- CIA (Central Intelligence Agency)

Note how in these examples you say the word by using the initials F_B_I and C_I_A.

Style guides differ on whether to use periods after each letter, so I'll leave that up to you and your style guide.

One thing style guides are in agreement on is capitalization. Both acronyms and initialisms are to be capitalized—with a few exceptions (of course).

Initialisms and acronyms are great and save a ton of time. After all, it's easier to say "laser" than "light amplification by stimulated emission of radiation" and to say "FBI" than "Federal Bureau of Investigation."

While all that is great, it brings another set of problems—our old friend redundancy. Many of the abbreviations are prone to be redundant:

• **ATM** We addressed this before, but let's do it again.

Many people say, "ATM machine" when the word *machine* is included in the initialism. That's like saying "automated teller machine machine."

• **PIN** Same thing. We've addressed it before, but it's prevalent, so let's do it again.

How often do you hear people say "I forgot my PIN number" or "I don't remember the PIN number"?

Since *number* is implied in the abbreviation—PIN—there is no need to repeat it. It's like saying "I forgot my personal identification number number." Sounds pretty ridiculous, doesn't it?

Despite this, hundreds of thousands of times per day, people refer to PIN numbers. In fact, if you do an internet search on "PIN number," you'll be presented with more articles than you'd care to count listing it as such, many of them even from banks.

• **ATCS**—air-traffic-control system

• **SAT**—Originally called the "scholastic aptitude test," now it supposedly refers to nothing. Still, there is no reason to say "test.") So it's not the SAT test, it's the SAT.

• **UPC** —No need to say UPC code. The C stands for code, as in "universal product code."

• **ISBN**—ISBN number. *Number* is redundant.

• **HIV**—HIV virus. HIV suffices. No need for *virus*.

• **VIN**—VIN number. Same as ISBN. Number is not needed. Don't tell me you haven't heard people use "VIN number." I hear it all the time, even on TV when someone asks, "Did you get the VIN number?" or "Get the VIN number. We'll run it through the system." The problem is the same as in the previous example. Since *number* is already implied by the *N* in VIN, there is no sense repeating it. It's like saying "Don't forget to check the vehicle identification number number."

I said earlier there would be exceptions to the capitalization rule. Let's look at a few.

An initialism is a type of acronym that cannot be pronounced as a word but must be read letter by letter, like FBI or UCLA.

The below is from Yourdictionary.com.

An acronym, technically, must spell out another word. This is a good point of reference to help you distinguish between abbreviations and acronyms.

— YOURDICTIONARY.COM

I checked with two more sources: *OED* and *Cambridge Dictionary*. Their entries are listed below.

An abbreviation formed from the initial letters of other words and pronounced as a word (e.g., ASCII, NASA).

— OED

---

a word made from the first letters of other words:
AIDS is the acronym for "acquired immune deficiency syndrome."

> an abbreviation consisting of the first letters of each word
> in the name of something, pronounced as a word.
>
> — *CAMBRIDGE DICTIONARY*

Sources indicate that an acronym is formed by using the first letters from other words, but *OED* goes on to say "And pronounced as a word," as does the advanced version of *Cambridge*.

I have a problem with both. First, dictionaries don't agree, but that's neither here nor there. Specifically addressing these two definitions, their interpretation of the word goes against fact. Consider the following words, formed not from initial letters but from initial syllables.

• radar
• Nabisco (National Biscuit Company)
• sonar

If you look up the words *sonar* and *radar* using *OED*, you'll see the information below, which is included in the word's origin:

• from so(und) na(vigation and) r(anging), on the pattern of radar.
• from ra(dio) d(etection) a(nd) r(anging).

As far as I can see, these explanations constitute more than initial letters.

And before anyone argues that initial letters can mean more than the first letter, take a look at *OED*'s definition of *initial*:

> The first letter of a name or word, typically a person's name
> or a word forming part of a phrase.
>
> — OED

And here is *Cambridge*'s take on *initial*:

first, or happening at the beginning:

— *CAMBRIDGE DICTIONARY*

Since the dictionaries can't seem to agree on what an acronym is, let's do it ourselves.

I think it's important to understand that all initialisms, acronyms, and abbreviations are related. All involve the shortening of a word, or words, for brevity's sake. If it were me defining them, I'd say all initialisms are acronyms, which are all abbreviations. Acronyms are a type of abbreviation, and initialisms are a type of acronym. Let's look at a few of the more common ones, though there are thousands to consider

Abbreviations

- Dr. = doctor
- Mr. = mister
- exam = examination
- memo = memorandum
- decaf = decaffeinated
- lo-cal = low calorie

As you can see, abbreviations can be formed using the first and last letters of a word, such as *doctor*, *mister*, *road*, etc.

Abbreviations can also include random letters, such as "blvd" for "boulevard."

You should capitalize the abbreviation if the word would be capitalized in that use. Examples show this better.

- She lives on a beautiful tree-lined boulevard.
- She lives on Baynard Boulevard
- She lives on Baynard Blvd.
- He always wanted to be a doctor.

- My cardiologist is Dr. Magnus.
- My cardiologist is Doctor Magnus.
- I forgot to tell you that Mr. Sharkey is my neighbor.
- I forgot to tell you that Mister Sharkey is my neighbor.

Acronyms

- NATO = North Atlantic Treaty Organization
- NASA = National Aeronautics and Space Administration
- scuba = self-contained underwater breathing apparatus
- radar = radio detection and ranging
- sonar = sound navigation and ranging
- GEICO = government employee insurance company

Acronyms are usually capitalized, but despite what some resources may tell you, they are not *always* capitalized. Once an acronym becomes accepted and used by the public, it doesn't take long to become part of the language. Consider the following, which many people have forgotten were originally acronyms.

- scuba
- radar
- sonar
- laser
- amphetamine

Amphetamine is short for its chemical name, "a (lpha-) m (ethyl) phe (ne) t (hyl) amine." None of the above words are capitalized, yet they are all undoubtedly acronyms.

Some acronyms are capitalized in the United States but may not be elsewhere. *NATO* and *NASA* are often seen in British English as *Nato* and *Nasa*.

Initialisms

- FBI

- CIA
- NBC
- CBS
- HBO

Abbreviations can sometimes form a word also, but the difference is an abbreviation is formed from only one word, as is shown in the examples of *exam*, *decaf*, and *memo* above, whereas an acronym would use letters from more than one word.

An initialism is formed from the letters of various words also, but they are pronounced as individual letters, such as

- FBI = "ef-bee-eye"
- NBC = "en-bee-cee"
- CEO = "cee-ee-oh"

Initialisms usually require the definite article *the* to precede them. You would say "the FBI" and "the NBA."

- *The* NBA has the best athletes.
- He's on *the* FBIs most-wanted list.
- *The* CIA operates internationally.
- *The* CEO wants to see you now!

But, like most rules, there are exceptions. Consider HBO (Home Box Office). It is often heard without any article preceding it.

- Game of Thrones is shown on *HBO*.
- *HBO* has the best movies.
- I watched it on *HBO*.

The same applies when using initialisms such as NBC or CBS or CVS (the drugstore chain). You'd tell your husband to "Stop at CVS and pick up our prescriptions on your way home." You wouldn't say "Stop at *the* CVS . . ."

Writing these examples brought up another thought—the pluralization of acronyms and initialisms. While you'll find style guides that offer various suggestions, I think the following works best:

Use a lowercase *s* and *do not* use an apostrophe when making a plural.

- Ten CEOs got together to discuss the situation.
- All the CFOs had to file their reports by mid-April.

However, if possession is implied, use an apostrophe.

- The mass murderer is on the FBI's most-wanted list.
- The NBA's salary cap was recently raised.

People use abbreviations, acronyms, and initialisms every day, and often without knowing what they stand for. We've already mentioned some like *scuba* and *radar,* but how about the following?

- A.M. (from Latin, *ante meridian*, meaning *before noon*)
- P.M. (*post meridian*, meaning *after noon*)
- AD (*Anno Domini,* meaning *in the year of our Lord*)
- BC (before *Christ*)
- PDF (portable document format)

I usually use *p.m.* and *a.m.* as opposed to *P.M.* or *A.M.*, however, since we started the sentences with the words, I felt it would look awkward to have *A.m.* and *P.m.*, so I opted to capitalize both letters.

Corporations are big on acronyms whether it's for brand names or the name of the company.

- Nabisco (National Biscuit Company)
- 3M = (Minnesota Mining and Manufacturing)

- Esso (Standard Oil)
- Sunoco (Sun Oil Company)
- OEM (original equipment manufacturer)

Going back to initialisms we can see not all of them are capitalized. Consider the following.

- mph = miles per hour
- rpm = revolutions per minute
- mhz = megahertz

Technical terms are often capitalized differently, even as initialisms, so it's better to check your preferred dictionary or style guide.

Just when you think you've covered all the bases, another exception turns up. Consider JPEG, which may be considered part initialism and part acronym.

It is pronounced using the first letter, *j,* but the rest uses the remainder as a word. So it's pronounced "j-peg."

Technology has added hundreds of acronyms, including the ubiquitous "LOL," "BRB," "PM," and more.

One you may not have thought of though is CAPTCHA, the code you need to type in for security purposes. It stands for completely automated public Turing test and is used to tell computers and humans apart.

Or how about Gestapo? (it is an acronym for *Geheime Staatspolizei*—secret state police)

And of course, one of the major initialisms: USA.

Chapter Fifty

ALTHOUGH, THOUGH, EVEN THOUGH

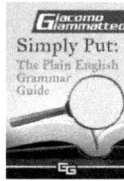

*C*OMMAS WITH ALTHOUGH, THOUGH, EVEN THOUGH, WHEREAS, AND WHILE

There is a rule that states you shouldn't use a comma to precede a dependent clause when it follows an independent clause. Phew! That's a lot of unnecessary grammar terminology. But now that we've gotten it out, I need to tell you that like most rules, there are exceptions.

We'll be looking at a few words and how they're used, then we'll look at what part they play in the exception to the rule we just stated.

Though, although, even though, while, and whereas

Though is a conjunction (connecting word) defined by <u>Yourdictionary</u> as:

---

even if, or in spite of, the fact.

Though is used more often than *although,* though they're frequently used interchangeably. If anything, *although* is seen in formal writing more than it's heard in everyday speech, but that doesn't mean *though* is forgotten when it comes to writing.

The screenshot of a Google Ngram search for *although*, *though*, and *even though* is shown below. It shows that while *though* has declined in usage when it comes to published works, it is still far ahead of *although*, and it's making a comeback.

Although is defined by <u>Yourdictionary</u> as:

Regardless of the fact that; even though: Although the room is big, it won't hold all that furniture. But; however: He says he has a dog, although I've never seen it.

I included "even though" in the search because it is used the same way, *even though* it is often used to show more emphasis between the clauses it connects.

Note that while we use *even* with *though* to show emphasis, *even* is never used with *although*.

☑️ *Even though* he stole the money, I would not call him a thief.

❌ *Even although* he stole the money, I would not call him a thief.

As you can see, it doesn't work when you pair *even* with *although*.

All three words are often used to introduce a phrase or clause, and when that comes before an independent sentence, the phrase is followed by a comma:

- *Although* he was in love with her, he couldn't bring himself to pop the question.
- *Though* he was in love with her, he couldn't bring himself to pop the question.
- *Even though* he was in love with her, he couldn't bring himself to pop the question.

But accepted practice states that if it is the other way around, no comma is needed. Let's look at a few examples with various subordinate conjunctions.

☑ He was in love with her *because* she was beautiful.

☑ He did his homework early *since* he was forbidden to leave the house.

☑ He was in love with her, *although* he often despised her.

☑ He was in love with her, but admitting it was difficult.

☑ He was in love with her, however, admitting it was difficult.

Now let's get to the exceptions. *Although* has two meanings, and how you use it determines if a comma is needed.

When it is used to give additional information that negates, contradicts, or contrasts what has been said, you need a comma. In cases like this, you can substitute *but* for *although,* and the sentence should remain the same.

- Building a bridge over the raging river was difficult, *although* not as difficult as we had presumed.

If you look, you can see the sentence remains the same when *although* is replaced with *but.*

- Building a bridge over the raging river was difficult, *but* not as difficult as we had presumed.

While is another word with two meanings, and like *although*, usage will determine how it is punctuated within the sentence.

While sometimes means "at the same time as," as in "I drove home while it was snowing."

In that sentence, you're saying that you drove home during a snowstorm (or at least as it snowed). Here's another one showing a different meaning.

- My wife loves traveling to Italy, while I prefer Ireland.

In this sentence, *while* is being used to mean "whereas."

Whereas

Now on to *whereas*, and that elusive rule.

Whereas is used to *contrast* things, and the rule states that when you contrast things, you should use a comma. We'll use a similar example to the one we just used with *while*.

- I love traveling to Ireland, *whereas* my wife loves going to Italy.

Notice that the clause following *whereas* is not essential; in other words, we could remove it, and the sentence would still retain the primary meaning. We won't have the additional information, but we will have what's necessary.

"I love traveling to Ireland" still gives us the intended meaning. What we don't know is that his wife loves going to Italy.

Let's examine this exception to the rule, then look at a few more example sentences.

We put commas before these connecting words (*although, even though, though, whereas, while*) because they constitute a group of conjunctions known as "adverbs of concession," and they indicate contrast between what was stated before the conjunction and what comes after it. You should use commas with these words even when the independent clause comes first.

Now it's time to look at a few more examples.

- I didn't hear him, although his voice was loud. (See the contrast?)
- The skunk smell remained, though we bathed the dog twice.
- He decided to go to the prom, *though* he disliked dancing.
- Her husband loved traveling to Italy, *whereas* she liked going to Ireland.

In each of the above examples, we need a comma prior to the connecting word because they function as an *adverb of concession* or a *means of contrast*.

Look at each sentence. If the meaning of the connecting word is *but*, as in "The skunk smell remained, though we bathed the dog twice," then use a comma.

Use a comma before *although, even though, though, whereas,* and *while* when they are used with a contrasting statement and fall in the middle of the sentence. Do not use a comma before *while* when it is used to mean "at the same time" or "during." Also, do not use a comma after the word when it is being used to introduce a clause at the beginning of a sentence. (Do use a comma after the *clause* though.)

And remember, if the clause is nonessential, it needs a comma before it and after it (if it occurs mid-sentence).

More examples follow.

☑ James ate hot dogs for dinner, while his sister had steak (used as *whereas* or *although*, needs comma).

☑ James ate hot dogs for dinner while his sister ate steak (used to mean "at the same time," so no comma).

☑ She went to the beach by herself, although she planned on going with friends. (contrasting statement; comma needed).

☑ While his sister ate steak for dinner, James ate hot dogs.

☑ She went to the beach, even though her friends didn't go.

Chapter Fifty-One

DATES

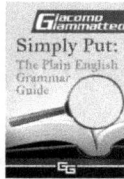

*D*ates
BC (before Christ) is used *after* the date.

AD (*Anno Domini*, "in the year of the Lord") appears *before* the date.

- You write "Julius Caesar died in 44 BC (or BC), and his nephew, Octavius Caesar, Emperor Augustus, died in AD (AD) 14.

There has been a lot of debate lately about the use of BC (before Christ) and AD (Anno Domini) [in the year of our Lord]. People want to substitute them for CE (Common Era) and BCE (Before Common Era) but in their proposal, they keep the dates the same.

So the year one, the year of our Lord, is still the divider, but instead of saying why—that Christ was born then—they refer to it as the "common era." A bit ridiculous, if you ask me. I'm for sticking with what we have.

Chapter Fifty-Two

EUPHEMISMS AND ANACHRONISMS

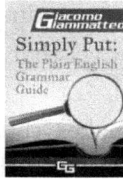

*E*veryone knows what these words are, even if you don't know what the true definition is. To get this over with, let's look at them.

Euphemism

---

the substitution of a milder, vaguer, or pleasanter word or expression for one considered to be offensive or unpleasant. definition 2: the word or expression so substituted. "Put to sleep" is a euphemism for "kill" when referring to animals.

Anachronism

- the representation of something as existing or happening at a time when that thing did not exist or happen, or a similar presentation done in error.

A clock in a play about ancient Rome is an anachronism.

definition 2: something that is or appears to be out of its appropriate time period. People in industrial countries tend to think of travel by horse as an anachronism.

Now that we know what the words mean, what do they have to do with anything?

I brought these up because they can present issues with a lot of writing: any kind of history (including historical fiction), fantasy that is set in past times, any novel that makes use of flashbacks, and all novels involving time travel.

One of the things that makes these so dangerous is the ease with which they can be misused and the furor it causes with dedicated readers of such novels.

Let's look at each one and how it may be misused.

Anachronism

The obvious anachronisms are things that are ludicrous, such as a person from a middle-aged time period wearing a wristwatch or looking at a clock on a wall.

A less-noticeable one may be someone from the year 2006 talking on an iPhone—they weren't released until June 2007. Not a horrendous mistake, you think. But to a serious reader, that is almost as bad as Caesar reading a printed book.

Time-travel novels are rife with potential pitfalls, and the people who write those novels need to continually be on the alert for mistakes. If the writers don't find the mistakes, the readers will.

The types of anachronisms many writers don't pay attention to are the innocuous ones, at least they seem that way. The writer may mention the aftermath of a natural disaster, such as an eruption, when it hasn't happened yet. Or they may refer to an island that hadn't been discovered at that time.

I remember reading a mystery that took place in Boston, and the writer mentioned a breed of dog that wasn't around at that time. The same novel had a song playing on the radio, and that song hadn't been recorded at that time.

Any novel that deals with historical fiction, flashbacks, and especially time travel is subject to mistakes like these—one more reason why it's good to have a small army of beta readers. They are likely to catch things like this.

Euphemisms

I mention euphemisms because they can be a form of an anachronism. Each euphemism (or "minced oath") began somewhere and sometime. What that means is you can't have one of your characters using a euphemism that hasn't been established yet.

Several euphemisms heard frequently are: *friggin, frickin, freaking*. All of them can be interpreted as fill-ins for *fucking*. But you don't want to have a character prior to the early 1900s using any of those words because they didn't exist. It would be no different than having them use a smart phone or a computer.

Chapter Fifty-Three

HALF SPACES OR THIN SPACES

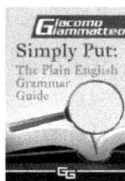

Half spaces

What they're used for and how to make them.

Before we start, I need to let you know this advice is for people who own a Mac. There's a workaround for PCs, and I'm sure there's a way to make a thin space naturally on a PC, but I don't use a PC, so I don't know the details.

If you own a PC and can't find a way to do it, you can get someone with a Mac to email the half space to you. If you don't know someone with a Mac, email me.

I suppose I should explain what a thin space is and when and why you need to use one.

One of the only times you use single quotation marks in American English is when you cite a quote within a quote:

- Jim said, "Mom's exact words were 'Tell him to come home now.' "

The entire sentence had to be put in quotation marks, and the "Tell him to come home now," had to be in single quotes because those are the words his mother spoke. That's using a quote within a quote. The problem comes at the end of the sentence.

Typographical rules say there should be a small space between the single and double quotation marks. A regular space is too wide, so you're supposed to use what's called a "thin space" or a "half space." The problem is that most people don't know how to make one.

I searched for days. I even called Apple, but no one could tell me how to make a "thin space." Then I ran across an article written by Steve Sande from AppleWorld Today. I wrote him, and he graciously responded with instructions on how to make a thin space. I'll share that with you. (By the way, that is a thin space separating the quotation marks above.)

GETTING READY

Remember, these instructions are only for a Mac, and know that you can't type this in from the keyboard. You'll need to open "Systems Preferences" > "Keyboard" > "Input Sources" and check the box that says "Show input menu in menu bar."

The menu bar will offer two choices: "Show emoji and symbols" and "Show Keyboard Viewer." Select "Show Emoji and Symbols," which brings up the Character Viewer. It should look something like this:

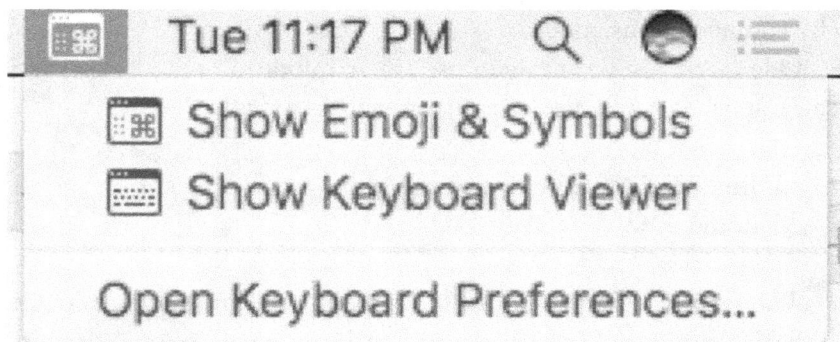

Now click on "Show Emoji and Symbols" and it will open up a window similar to the image below.

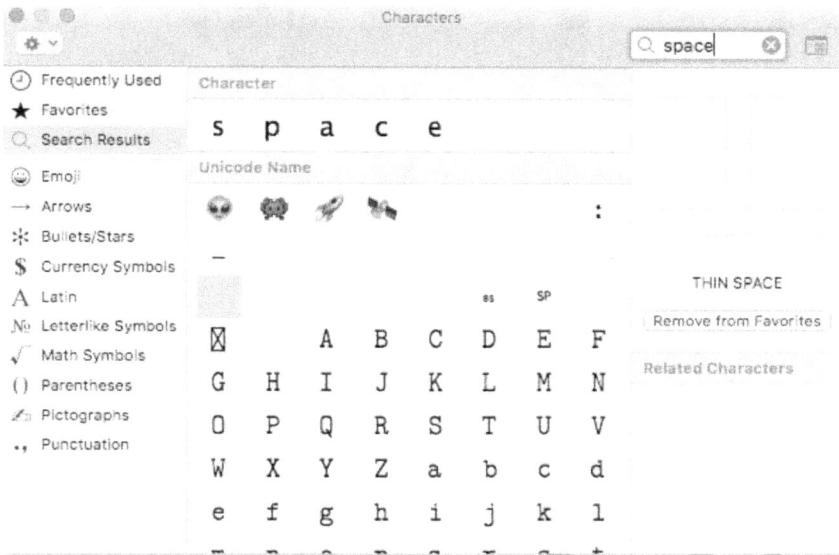

Type "space" in the top right search bar and you should be rewarded with an image that looks like the above. Notice the highlighted item on the far left, third row down. If you look to the right side of the image, you'll see it lists it as a "thin space."

This is the item you want. Click to add it to "Favorites." You'll notice my window says, "Remove from Favorites," but that's because I already added it.

Once you add the thin space to your favorites, click on "Favorites." It won't look like this because this is showing how mine looks, displaying the favorites I have chosen, but it will show the highlighted "thin space." To insert the space into your document, place the cursor where you want the space to go, then double-click.

You may think, "That's a lot of trouble to go through for a space," but there are ways around that.

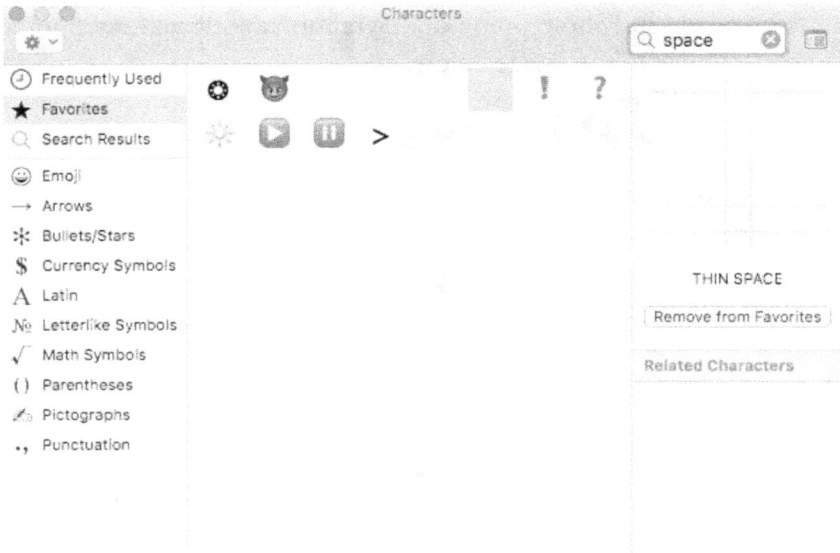

The first is a simple solution that will save you time. Much of the time, you'll encounter the need for a thin space when quoting someone else, which often happens in books or long documents.

Write the entire project without using thin spaces, then, when you're done, use the "Find and Replace" function to search for every situation where there is a single quote (') next to a double quote ("). It should look something like this: ('"). Now replace the single and double quotes with a single quote, thin space, and double quote.

This method is a lot easier than having to deal with the keyboard viewer for every occurrence, but it's still not ideal. Let's look at a few other ways to handle it.

The easiest way, in my opinion, is to use a text-expansion program. I use one called Text Expander™. You can check it out here:

This may also be a way for people with PCs to use a "thin space" as Text Expander™ makes a PC version.

If that's an acceptable option, find a way to copy the space from a Mac. (The easiest way I can think of is to have someone with a

Mac email it to you.) Once you have the thin space, copy it to your text-expansion program and you'll have it permanently.

Once it's in your text-expansion program, assign it a shortcut you'll remember. I gave mine a simple one: "thinspace," with no space between *thin* and *space*, and I set it to expand immediately. You could also assign it something like "halfspace" or anything you'll remember easily.

Text Expander makes it so easy to do almost anything faster that I even wrote a book about it: *Writing Shortcuts.*

Option number two makes things easy as well, and that is using an app called "Paste" that allows you to have unlimited copy and paste functions, and it's as simple as using ⌘, ⇧, and *v* simultaneously. Below is a screenshot.

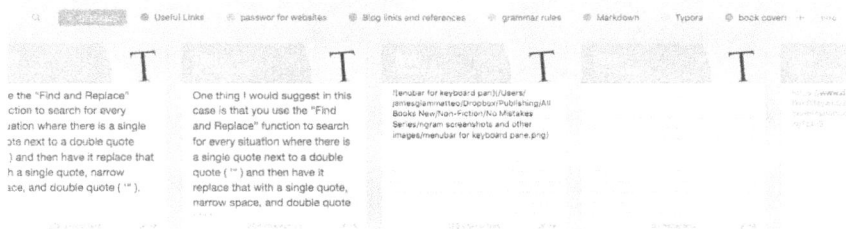

Each new item you copy will show up on the left. There are also places to store an item permanently as shown above in the areas marked with red and green dots. I have my "thin space" stored with other things I may find a need for like ! ? and many more.

So there you have it: a way to type a "thin space" as well as three alternatives, and even a way for those with a PC to do it (assuming they know someone with a Mac who is willing to share the *thin space* with them).

Now that I've put you through all this, I have found a way to make a thin space in Microsoft Word. And it's not difficult.

Type any sentence, then highlight a space between two words only. If you want to have a copy of the single quote/thin space/double quote, then type that using a full space. It should look like this: ' ".

Highlight the space portion only, not the quotes.

If you're using a PC, type "Control D" (^ D). On a Mac, type "Command D" (⌘ D). It will bring up a dialogue box similar to the one below. (This is from a Mac.)

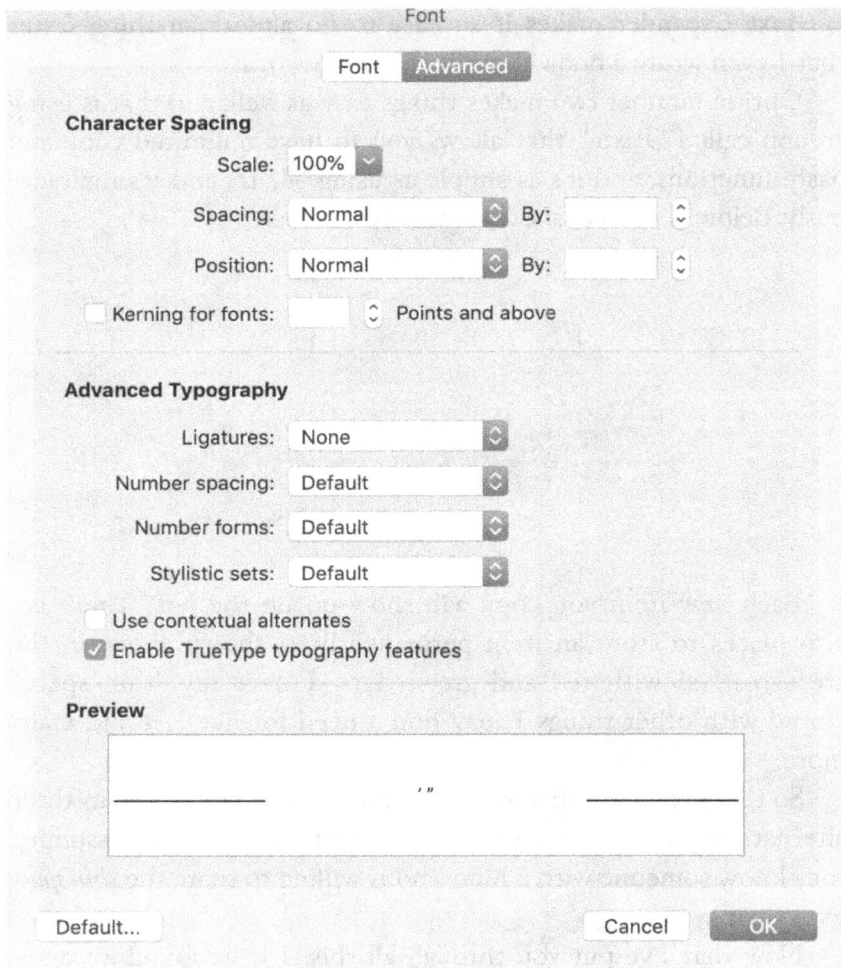

Font

Font   Advanced

Character Spacing

Scale: 100%

Spacing: Normal   By:

Position: Normal   By:

Kerning for fonts: Points and above

Advanced Typography

Ligatures: None

Number spacing: Default

Number forms: Default

Stylistic sets: Default

Use contextual alternates

✓ Enable TrueType typography features

Preview

————————   ' "   ————————

Default...   Cancel   OK

Go to the "Advanced" tab up top and then access the "Scale"

dropdown menu (It will initially show 100%). Set it to the scale you want. Fifty percent is recommended for this.

That's it; you're done. This would be a chore to do every time, so if you don't have a text expansion app or an app like *Paste*, create a new *Word* document and make your '" the only thing in the document, then put it somewhere that it's easy to access so you can copy and paste.

Part Six

NUMBERS

A lot of writers simply skip over the recommendations of how to use numbers when writing.

It's not something that should be ignored though. The practice of when to use digits and when to spell out the numbers is fairly specific and different style guides recommend different styles.

I've tried to list the major differences between AP and CMOS, but not all are covered. In addition, if you use a different style guide, it may call for something not mentioned here. It's yet again another reason to pick a guide and stick with it.

Chapter Twenty-Seven

HOW TO USE NUMBERS WHEN WRITING

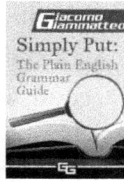

$\mathcal{B}$efore we get started, I'm going to briefly discuss numbers and numerals. By definition, a numeral is:

- A word, letter, symbol, or figure, etc., expressing a number.

There are rules regarding when to use the word numeral versus number. I'm going to ignore those rules and use *number* or *numbers* for most things, however, if I do use *numeral* it will refer to the symbol. *Figure* may also be used to represent a numeral.

Another note is that while I may say "Do it this way," whether you decide to spell out the numbers or use numerals is up to you. No matter what you do, be consistent. Pick a style guide and follow it.

How to Use Numbers When Writing

When writing, I like to spell out the numbers one through ten and use the actual numerals for those over ten. Most style guides agree on spelling out numbers one though nine, so you're safe doing that.

They begin to differ immediately after, though. CMOS recommends spelling out numbers up to one hundred and using numerals after that, except for round numbers, and *AP Stylebook* recommends spelling out the numbers zero through nine and using numerals thereafter—until one million is reached.

An example might be, "The farmer had six cows. But you might write, "The farmer had 34 chickens," or you could stick to the CMOS recommended "thirty-four" chickens.

One occasion when numbers are used extensively is when you are writing résumés. Résumés are filled with dates, dollar amounts, sales figures, and percentages lost or saved. Because of that, how to use numbers on a résumé is a good way to learn about the many options. When I worked in that business, I wrote a blog about using numbers on a résumé, so I thought I'd include it here.

Everything You Need to Know about Numbers on Résumés

Reading Résumés . . .

. . . is a boring job, the kind of job that can put you to sleep if you're not careful. That's why it's important that the person writing the résumé does everything in their power to keep the résumé screener awake and to make sure the screener doesn't get frustrated.

One of the worst offenders on résumés is inconsistency, and when we talk inconsistency—numbers (and everything dealing with them), take home the prize.

Dates

Résumés are full of dates: the year you graduated, the date range you worked at each company, the date range of the positions you held, dates of accomplishments, dates of awards, etc.

Quite often, these dates are expressed in as many different ways as there are dates.

Many ways are acceptable. The important thing is to be consistent.

Months Spelled out? Or Numbers?

The place where dates are used most are in the "Work History" section, and the biggest problems are that some people use numbers to represent months, and some spell the months out. Either way is right, as long as you are consistent.

Obviously this doesn't apply just to résumés; it is a guide for all usage.

August 1999–May 2003 is perfectly fine, but so is 08/1999–05/2003, or even 8/99–5/03. Problems come up when someone starts out with one style and switches to another—usually to save space or to make the date fit on one line.

I strongly suggest picking one style and sticking with it, regardless of formatting. My personal preference is using numbers for months combined with the full year, like this: 08/1999–05/2003.

On a side note, the punctuation separating the dates should be an *en dash*, not a hyphen or an em dash, and the en dash should be used with no spaces surrounding it.

✗ 08/1999-05/2003. (Do not use a hyphen.)

✗ 08/1999—05/2003. (Do not use an em dash.)

✗ 08/1999 – 05/2003. (Do not use spaces to surround punctuation.)

✅ 08/1999–05/2003. (Use an en dash, with no spaces.)

Note, I said no spaces, but *AP Stylebook* recommends a space preceding and following the dash.

Alignment

I suggest right-aligning the date range for each company. If you don't know how to do that, take a look at this video. And I suggest offsetting the dates for each position one or two tab stops left of the others.

Percentages

Before we start, this may be a good time to discuss the difference between *percent, percentage,* and *per cent.*

A *percent* is one one-hundredth of something. The online etymology dictionary shows this:

1560s, *per cent*, from Modern Latin *per centum* "by the

hundred" (see **per** and see **hundred**). Until early 20c. often treated as an abbreviation and punctuated accordingly

---

A *per cent* is the same as *percent* except that when used as two words, it's mostly British.

A *percentage* is the result obtained by multiplying a number by a percent. It is also used when referring to odds, as in "There's no percentage in betting on that."

The easiest way to determine which word to use is to use *percent* when a number accompanies it and *percentage* if there is no number:

- Thirty *percent* of the class was out sick.
- What *percentage* of the class was out sick?

Back to Numbers on Résumés

The most powerful parts of a résumé are often represented by percentages—showing how much money you saved, how many new accounts you brought in, or how much you improved yields, etc. It can be very persuasive. And using percentages can be even more powerful when combined with dollars:

- Increased sales by $6 million, a 24 percent increase from previous year.

I used *6* instead of *six* to stay consistent within the sentence. Regardless of any of the rules cited above, I recommend consistency within a sentence whenever possible.

✗ Cut costs by $1.5 million on a seven million dollar budget.

✓ Cut costs by $1.5 million on a $7 million budget.

Bottom line

A résumé is a simple document with a lot of complexity. One of the most important things you can do to improve your résumé is to eliminate mistakes. The other is to make it consistent. If you follow the advice presented here, and take a close look at all the numbers you use, you'll be ahead of the crowd.

Now back to rules on writing numbers.

Rules (or one version of the rules)

The rules governing writing numbers can be long and complicated. But even worse than that, the rules are often in conflict. The few that seem to be fairly consistent are the following:

- Spell out numbers from one to nine.
- Hyphenate compound numbers from twenty-one to ninety-nine. (AP and CMOS style guides differ.)
- Don't start a sentence with a numeral.
- Use commas for numbers with more than three digits (4,377, not 4377—although the United Kingdom is different).
- If you use fractions, hyphenate them (two-thirds, not two thirds).
- When writing about sums of less than a dollar, decimal points are not needed (85 cents or sixty-seven cents).
- Do not add the word *dollars* when the number contains the $ sign.
- When writing times of the day, it is recommended to use *noon* and *midnight* as opposed to 12:00 AM or 12:00 PM.
- When designating *AM* and *PM* there are a variety of ways to do it, but be sure to be consistent. You can use *am* and *pm*; *AM* or *PM,* you can put a period after the abbreviation or not, such as *a.m* or *p.m.*; and you can elect to follow the numbers with a space or not: 11:32am, 11:32 am, 11:32 A.M., or 11:32 AM.
- Most writers nowadays use numerals to designate the times of day. He has a meeting at 3:25 or she didn't get in until 8:44.
- When using fractions, whole numbers are often spelled out, while mixed numbers use digits; however, if both occur in the same paragraph, stick to one format. He

sold 10 percent more this year, but his increase was only
6 ½ percent.

- Always spell out *percent*. Don't use the symbol. It would
  be 19 percent or nineteen percent, not 19% or nineteen
  %. (Most style guides make allowances for writer's
  choice; in other words, if a writer wants to use the
  symbol, it's fine as long as they are consistent.)
- When using decimals, it is preferable to use figures. It
  would be 4.77 inches or 15.6 feet. Also, when writing a
  number less than zero, use the *0* numeral preceding the
  decimal point.
- Do not use commas with spelled-out numbers of four
  digits or more. It's six thousand five hundred twenty-six,
  not six thousand, five hundred twenty-six.
- When using complete dates, a comma precedes the year.
  August 6, 2012. It is never August sixth, 2012.
- When referring to decades there are several ways of
  dealing with it. Decide which one you like and stick with
  it. If you use all four numbers to represent a decade, do
  not use an apostrophe. You can represent decades in the
  following ways: 1960s, 1990s, '80s, 40s, 70's, 50's.
- Write the numbers of kings and queens in Roman
  characters, such as Elizabeth I or Henry VIII.
- Spell out ordinal numbers up to twelve, but with dates
  you can use them in this order: "March 5th is my son's
  birthday" or "He came in first." But you'd say, "He was
  born on the fifth" or "She's getting married on the
  tenth," but "The funeral will be on the 14th."

How to Write Numbers with Measurements

Follow the same guideline when writing numbers used with
measurements. There is one thing to note though. Many people use
the standard 4' 6" or 17' 3". The problem is that many people have
the preferences set on their writing app so that it automatically
converts straight quotes to curly quotes or quotation marks.

It's easy to fix.

The simplest way to fix this is to type a single or double quotation mark, then immediately *undo* it. (On a Mac, you type ⌘ Z.) It then converts the curly quotes to straight ones. Another way to do it is shown below.

If you work on a Mac, type " ^+⌘" (control and command) with the spacebar simultaneously. You'll be rewarded with a character palette similar to below. From there, you can insert any punctuation, emoji, symbol, etc.

If you plan to access this often, take the symbols you use frequently and put them in the *favorites* section for quick access.

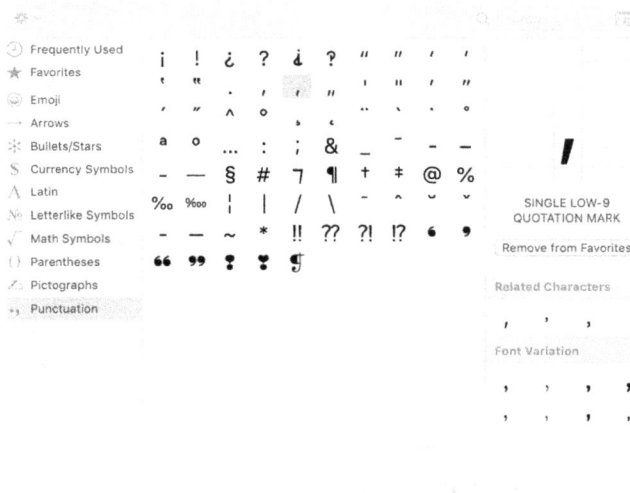

I don't use a PC, but if you do, I believe you hold down the *Ctrl* and *Shift* keys as you press the spacebar.

By the way, when using measurements, periods and commas are placed *outside* the punctuation. (I know we said earlier that periods and commas go *inside* quotation marks, but this is a single mark of punctuation, hence the exception.)

- We took another measurement and 7' 5", not 7' 3", is the correct distance.

Also, make sure you use a non-breaking space if the number may be split and moved to the next line.

- We took another measurement of the lumber set to the side for studs and 7' 5", not 7' 3" is the correct distance.
- We took another measurement of the lumber set to the side for studs and 7' 5", not 7' 3" is the correct distance.

Depending on which device you read on, the following may or may not apply.

See how in the first example, the 7' 5" is split and shown on two lines, but in the second example, the non-breaking space doesn't allow that to happen.

You make a non-breaking space on a Mac by typing ⌥ (option) and spacebar simultaneously. On a PC, I believe you hold down the Ctrl and Shift keys as you press the Spacebar.

Consistency

Be consistent no matter what. If you have a sentence, or even a paragraph, where you have need of one numeral and one spelled-out number, use two numerals instead. An example follows.

✕ He sold six machines last week, but he only sold 13 all month.

✓ He sold 6 machines last week, but he only sold 13 all month.

You've already seen there is a great degree of flexibility in how a writer may express themself, but I'll say again that no matter what style choices you make, be consistent.

Numbers Next to Numerals

If you deal with numbers a lot, a tricky situation *will* present itself sooner or later.

✕ There were twenty-seven twenty-one-year-old patients.

✕ There were 6 5-year-old trees.

Neither of those scenarios is good. It is immediately confusing to see numbers next to each other with no punctuation in between. The solution is to use a numeral for one and a spelled-out number for the other.

✅ There were 27 twenty-one-year-old patients.

✅ There were six 5-year-old trees.

Please note the hyphenation in both sentences. As we mentioned before, it's not *"twenty-one-year old,"* but *"twenty-one-year-old."*

An Often-ignored Rule:

- If you're writing dialogue or quoting someone, numbers should be spelled out as opposed to using numerals.

So in a scene where the mother is arguing with her daughter, she may say:

❌ "You're only 16, and you're *not* going to that party."

✅ "You're only sixteen, and you're *not* going to that party."

Other Rules

AP Stylebook as well as *CMOS* both have extensive *rules* or guidelines for using numbers. Below is a list of some of them from *AP Stylebook*.

There are rules about using numbers for any situation you can think of.

- Academic course numbers
- Addresses
- Ages
- Amendments to the constitution
- Cardinal numbers
- Centuries
- Court names
- Dates, years, and decades
- Decimals, percentages, and fractions with numbers larger than 1
- Dimensions, to indicate depth, height, length and width
- Distances
- Election returns
- Fleets

- Formulas
- Golf clubs
- Highway designations
- Latitude and longitude
- Mathematical usage
- Miles
- Monetary units
- Odds, proportions, and ratios.
- Parallels
- Proportions
- Ranks
- Recipes
- Roman numerals
- School grades
- Serial numbers
- Sports scores, standings and standards
- Telephone numbers
- Temperatures
- Times
- Weights

Yes, AP has rules for all of those situations. I won't attempt to cover them all, but if you have a question, look it up in whatever guide you use.

Written Numbers and Hyphens

Written numbers only use hyphens following words that end in —*ty* (twen*ty*, thir*ty*, for*ty*, fif*ty*, six*ty*, seven*ty*, eigh*ty*, and nine*ty*), however, no hyphen is needed for written words that do not end in —*ty* (six hundred fourteen, two hundred sixty-three, five thousand four hundred twenty-seven).

Note that the word *and* is not used following *hundred* or *thousand*. Also note that no comma is needed after *thousand* even though if that number had been written out using numerals (5, 427), a comma would have been required.

One Last Thing About Numbers

Another thing to note is when writing dates, it is advisable to use months in conjunction with numbers to ensure the dates are understood clearly by all. Europeans write dates differently than people from the U.S., so spelling the month will avoid confusion. Examples are below:

- Write April 4, 1997, not 4/1/1997.

In the first part of the example, using the month, there should be no confusion. However, if 4/1/1997 were used, it would read to someone from the U.S. as April 1, 1997, but to a European, it would read as January 4, 1997.

Chapter Twenty-Eight

USING NUMBERS WHEN WRITING

More on Using Numbers When Writing
There are rules, or at least recommendations, regarding how to use numbers. As we've already seen, there are quite a few rules. Following are a few more.

One thing to remember is that different style guides recommend different ways to use numbers. Even the two primary guides, AP and CMOS, differ greatly in some areas. Except where noted, the recommendations listed follow CMOS.

Using Numbers Adjacent to Each Other

When faced with a situation where two or more numbers are placed next to each other in a sentence, the recommendation is to use written text for one of the numbers (preferably the one with the fewest letters) and a numeral for the other.

☑ He ordered four 55-gallon drums of grease.

Not . . .

✗ He ordered 4 55-gallon drums of grease.

☑ The plumber bought thirteen ¾" pipes.

Not . . .

✗ The plumber bought 13 ¾" pipes.

As you can see from the examples above, when numbers are used next to each other, it may lead to confusion.

When numbers are used in pairs, they are typically formatted similarly, though not always. The first example below is the preferred one, but the two examples that follow are also acceptable.

☑ Three or four weeks' vacation is standard for people who have more than five years' experience.

☑ Three or four weeks' vacation is standard for people who have more than 5 years' experience.

You could even write it as follows:

☑ Three or 4 weeks' vacation is standard for people who have more than 5 years' experience.

However, as discussed elsewhere, you wouldn't start out with a numeral.

✗ 3 or 4 weeks vacation is standard for people who have more than five years' experience.

If you have a series of related numbers in the same sentence, the formatting for all the numbers should remain the same. If numerals are required for one, they should all be formatted as numerals.

- She had three babies: one weighed 7 pounds, one 9 ½ pounds, and the other 6 pounds.

Rounded Numbers

Rounded numbers or approximated numbers are often spelled out, though they can be represented by numerals as well.

- By his estimates, he has caught about four hundred fish during the past two years.
- The city wasn't heavily populated, but it did have about sixty thousand residents.
- With a population of less than 500 thousand, the island nation was smaller than many major cities.

Numbers in the millions or greater are usually expressed as

figures (numerals) followed by the appropriate words (million, billion, etc.). If the figure needs more than two numerals following the decimal point, use all figures instead.

- 4.66 million

But . . .

- 4,667,300

Roman Numerals

Roman numerals are seldom used these days, but there are a couple of situations when they are standard. Roman numerals are used to indicate order of succession for rulers (kings and queens), popes, and families who follow such procedures.

- Queen Elizabeth III
- Duke Marmont IV
- Pope John XXII
- James Wesley III

Outlines are another place where Roman numerals are used. Formatting for outlines is often designated with Arabic numerals, with capital letters, or with Roman numerals; sometimes all three are used.

- IV. Parts of Speech.
A. Verbs.
1. Action verbs.
2. Sense verbs.
B. Nouns.
C. Adverbs.
V. Punctuation.
A. Commas.
B. Dashes.
1. En dashes.

2. Em dashes

C. Periods

Roman numerals are also used with some scientific and medical terms as well as historical documents, including the Constitution.

- Blood factor VIII.
- Cancer stage III.
- Act II was where all the action took place.
- Amendment XIV is a crucial piece of lawmaking.

Lowercase Roman numerals are used even less frequently, but there's one place they are almost always used, and that is in representing page numbers in a book when those pages precede the ordinary Arabic numerals, as in the table of contents.

- See introduction, pp. ix–xii.

Keeping Numbers Together

When numerals are used instead of written numbers, keep them together if possible. If it's unavoidable to keep the number on the same line, split them at a naturally occurring point, such as a where a comma would come between three digits.

When numbers are used to indicate ranges of items (money, degrees, prescription dosages, etc.) the type of item does not have to be repeated under normal circumstances, and that applies whether you use written-out numbers or figures.

- Smart phones cost an average of three hundred to nine hundred *dollars*.
- My doctor increased the dosage of my prescription from 10 to 40 *mg*.
- Temperatures reached 95 to 100 *degrees* Fahrenheit for the third day in a row.

There is an exception to this rule, though. (Isn't there always?) If symbols are used to designate the item, those symbols are repeated. We'll use a couple of the sentence from above for examples.

- Smart phones cost an average of $300 to $900.
- Temperatures reached 95° to 100° Fahrenheit for the third day in a row.

Notice that both the symbol for dollars and for degrees was repeated. One other thing to note when writing about degrees: while it is often acceptable to either spell out the numbers or use figures, it affects whether you use a symbol to follow. If you spell out the number, you also need to spell out *degrees*.

- The temperature reached *113*° today.
- The temperature reached a low of *six degrees* yesterday.

Numbers with Dates

When writing dates, it is advisable to use months in conjunction with numbers to ensure the dates are understood clearly by all. Europeans write dates differently than do people from the United States, so spelling the month will avoid confusion. Examples are below:

- Write April 4, 1997, not 4/1/1997.

In the first part of the example, using the month, there should be no confusion. However, if 4/1/1997 were used, it would read to someone from the United States as April 1, 1997, but to a European, it would read as January 4, 1997.

BC and AD

When using dates inclusive of both BC and AD eras, use the designations each time a date is used.

- Julius Caesar died in 44 BC, and Augustus Caesar died in
  AD 14.

If it's obvious which era you're speaking of, you can skip the
designation, as in the example below.

- The Carthaginians ruled the Mediterranean Sea from
  650 to 200 BC.

Note also that if referring to an era by citing *centuries,* the terms
BC and AD follow; they don't precede.

- The Caesars started their rule in the first century BC,
  but they lasted long into the first century AD.

Numbers with Units of Measurement (Numbers used with
fractions are listed separately.)

Numbers are most frequently used to describe units of some
kind of measurement, whether miles, pounds, dollars, feet, inches,
yards, meters, etc. Now, let's look at how they're used.

- His best performance was a 10-second run for 100 meters,
  but his sights were set on beating the 9.58-second record.
- The new fence was 6' 2" high, replacing the 5'-high fence
  that was there.
- The trip to Dallas, a 195-mile journey, turned into a 6-
  hour drive due to accidents.
- It's amazing that such a small woman delivered a 9-
  pound baby.

Please note the use of hyphens when the measurement was used
as a modifier.

If a large amount of money (usually more than a million) is used
with the dollar sign, the number is often written with figures as well

as spelled-out text, and even when used as a modifier, no hyphen is needed.

- He purchased a $2 million home with his drug money, and he insured it for $4 million.
- Some authorities claim illegal sex trade generates more than $20 billion per year.
- The pharmaceutical company suffered its first loss due to bad publicity—a $100 million loss.

Note:

Remember that when the $ is used with a number as an adjective, describing something, you pronounce the word using the singular form: *dollar*, but when used otherwise, it's pronounced as plural.

- He purchased a $2 million house would be pronounced "He purchased a 2-million-*dollar* house."
- His house is insured for $4 million would be pronounced "His house is insured for 4 million *dollars*."

Numbers with Addresses

Addresses, especially in larger cities, are where you may encounter the problem of numbers needing to be next to other numbers. An example is below.

- He said he lives at 1447 9th Street.
- The preferred way to write that would be:
- He said he lives at 1447 Ninth Street.
- You could have also used a hyphen with spaces.
- He said he lives at 1447 - 9th Street.

Also, when numbers are used with suite, room, apartment, building, etc., make sure you're consistent with how you capitalize the designation preceding the number. CMOS recommends lower-case and AP uses capitalization.

- She said she's in Apartment 331.
- He works in Park Place, Building 6.
- "You'll be in Room 715," the clerk said.
- "I'd like a suite, please. Preferably Suite 1010."

Numbers with Fractions

You don't run across the need to use numbers as fractions too often, but just in case, here are a few tips.

Fractions used as nouns should be kept open (no hyphen needed), although many writers hyphenate them anyway, and as long as you're consistent, there isn't a problem.

☑ Three quarters of the pie was already gone.

Or . . .

☑ Three-quarters of the pie was already gone.

Fractions should always be hyphenated when they are functioning as modifiers.

☑ The bank robbers each got a one-fifth share of the take.

☑ The bank robbers each got a ⅕ share of the take.

It is customary to use spelled-out numbers for common, simple words.

- He was accustomed to running half-mile races; he didn't even get winded anymore.
- It was a cool evening, so she took a quarter-mile walk after dinner.
- It was ⅞ of a mile to the mall, so he drove instead of walking.
- I need a wrench, please. It looks like a ⅝.

If in doubt about whether to hyphenate a fraction, it's probably wiser to err on the side of caution and insert the hyphen. I doubt anyone would fault you, and that's *if* they notice.

One more note on fractions. Mixed numbers containing fractions use figures.

- She baked 2½ pies.
- He ran the race in 10¾ minutes

If you have a situation where a regular fraction is contained in the same sentence as a mixed fraction, use figures for both.

- She baked 2 ½ pies and ¾ pound of meatballs.
- He ran the race in 10¾ minutes, which was ⅔ of a minute better than his last performance.

Numbers Used with Decimal Fractions

Numbers used with decimal fractions as well as mixed decimal fractions use figures. Perhaps the most famous of the mixed-decimal fractions is the definition for π (pi): 3.1416 . . . but true decimal fractions abound in writing, especially mystery writing.

- Once the medical examiner performed the autopsy, he discovered the victim had been shot with a .45-caliber gun.
- A kilometer is equal to 1,000 meters or .621 miles (approximately).
- The new needles used for insulin are 30-gauge needles and are only about 0.01225 inches thick.

Note that the other numbers used in the same sentence as decimal fractions are written as figures also. It helps to be consistent in this manner. While you could have said, "A kilometer is equal to one thousand meters, or .621 miles (approximately)," it would be better to use all .

Numbers with Lists and Outlines

We discussed earlier about Roman numerals used with outlines, but let's look at how regular Arabic (Many dictionaries do not capitalize *Arabic*.) numbers are used with both lists (run-in and vertical lists) and outlines.

Run-in Lists Some lists in running text use numbers (enclosed in parentheses) to introduce each item.

- The interviewer said to bring three things: (1) a résumé; (2) a lot of stamina, a sense of humor, and a can-do attitude; (3) a list of references he could check.
- Mom said to get busy packing. She said to make sure we remembered everything: (1) a shovel and bucket for the sand, (2) towels, (3) sunglasses, (4) protection from sunburn.

Notice, too, the use of semicolons in the first example and not in the second. That's because the first example is more complex, containing commas within the listed items, while the second is a simple list.

Vertical Lists In vertical lists that use numerals (figures), the numbers are usually followed by periods, and the items that follow are capitalized if they form complete sentences. They are often capitalized even if not a complete sentence, though the key is to be consistent.

There are eight states that begin with the letter *m*:

1. Maine
2. Maryland
3. Massachusetts
4. Michigan
5. Minnesota
6. Mississippi
7. Missouri
8. Montana

If you wanted to end each item listed with a period, that would be okay, but you would not only need to do it in this listing, it should be done in all lists to remain consistent.

1. Maine.
2. Maryland.
3. Massachusetts.
4. Michigan.
5. Minnesota.
6. Mississippi.
7. Missouri.
8. Montana.

The above may have seemed easy because we used U.S. states and they are capitalized regardless of position or function in a sentence, but what we discussed about the capitalization option has nothing to do with proper nouns. Consider this:

1. Cattle & bison.
2. Cotton.
3. Timber.
4. Oil.

Times have changed, though. Now the Texas economy thrives on the following:

1. Information technology.
2. Oil and natural gas.
3. Aerospace.
4. Defense.
5. Biomedical research.
6. Fuel processing.
7. Electric power.
8. Agriculture.
9. Manufacturing.

Vertical lists may also be introduced by bullets (•), but that's another discussion.

Numbers and Outlines

We previously discussed Roman numerals with outlines, but let's look a little closer. It's considered standard to use a combination of numerals and letters to designate parts of an outline. The normal order is this:

1. Roman numerals.
2. Capital letters.
3. Arabic numerals.
4. Lowercase letters.

A typical outline may look like this:
II. Simply Put, the Plain English Grammar Guide
A. Parts of Speech.
1. Verbs.
2. Adjectives.
3. Prepositions.
B. Punctuation
1. Commas.
a. With lists.
b. With appositives.
2. Parentheses.
a. With other punctuation.
III. Misused Words.

Numbers with Money

If you're dealing with money that can be written out in a few words, then write it out. However, if it's more complicated, you may wish to use figures.

- While away at college, he called his father every week asking for fifty dollars.
- A new dryer will cost $400 or more. (You could also use four hundred dollars; just be consistent.)

- Her new refrigerator set her back $2,500.
- At the garage sale, she found things she needed for 50c, 75c, and 25c, and all of them turned out to be a bargain.

When you want to express a sum in mixed dollars and cents, use figures.

- The lunch bill came to $24.75.
- The vet bill was $215.99.

If you mention an even dollar amount, it is written without the decimal point, however, if another number is used with it, whether in comparison or included in a list, and it contains both dollars and cents, then both should be written out in full. Below are a few examples:

✅ He bought a Great Dane and paid $500 for it.

❌ I remember when $1 bought you a dozen eggs; now that same dozen costs $2.95.

✅ I remember when $1.00 bought you a dozen eggs; now that same dozen costs $2.95.

Numbers with Time of Day

The time of day is written out when followed by *o'clock* and often when the time is on the hour or half hour.

- It's one thirty; time to pick up the kids.
- What time is dinner? It should be ready by seven.

But when a more specific time is referred to, figures are used.

- The train leaves at 4:25.
- Fireworks start at 9:05 precisely.

Figures are also used with *a.m.* and *p.m.*

- The play starts at 7:00 p.m.

- The pool doesn't open till 1:00 p.m.

If you use what is known as *military time* (the 24-hour clock), no punctuation is included, and *a.m.* or *p.m.* are not necessary, though some people use *hours* following the figures.

- "Sergeant, have the men ready at 1800 hours."
- "Captain, I thought you said to be ready at 0800."

That wraps up *numbers*. By now you should have a good grasp on when to use figures (numerals) and when to write out the numbers. Don't worry if you make a mistake. I don't think anyone will challenge you to a duel over it.

Chapter Fifty-Four

ITALICS OR QUOTATION MARKS

*T*here continue to be questions regarding how, and when, to use quotation marks and italics in writing, whether it's informal or formal.

Let's try to clear up some of the misunderstandings as well as put an end to several myths.

Let's deal with the myths first. I have seen many people proclaim that "if you do this . . . you need to use quotations." And I've seen just as many people counter with "You should use italics for that."

Without getting into what they were talking about, I can tell you they were likely full of . . .

The arguments about whether to use italics or quotations usually stem from one of two issues. Most people know when and how to use quotation marks when it relates to dialogue, and they know when and how to use italics to emphasize a word within that dialogue (or to express someone's inner thoughts).

Where the problems typically occur are when dealing with using words as words or letters as letters. CMOS has a stand on this, of course, so let's see what they say.

CMOS

When a word or term is not used functionally but is referred to as the word or term itself, it is either italicized or enclosed in quotation marks. Proper nouns used as words, as in the third example, are usually set in roman (see also 7.64).

The term critical mass is more often used metaphorically than literally. What is meant by neurobiotics? You rarely see the term iPhone with a capital *i*.

Although italics are the traditional choice, quotation marks may be more appropriate in certain contexts. In the first example below, italics set off the Spanish term, and quotation marks are used for the English (see also 7.53). In the second example, quotation marks help to convey the idea of speech.

The Spanish verbs *ser* and *estar* are both rendered by "to be."

Many people say "I" even when "me" would be more correct.

As you can see, CMOS says it's an either-or situation—that you can use italics or quotation marks.

The trick, like everything, is to be consistent (and ideally logical).

When I started writing my No Mistakes Grammar Bites books, they required a lot of instances of using words as words, word definitions, or phrases relating to something previously referred to.

My amazing editor Michele helped me out by coming up with a sensible solution, and it was one that could be used consistently.

She suggested we use italics when we were dealing with one word and use quotation marks with two or more words. Because I'm a big proponent of examples, I'll list a few.

Dalmatian is often seen capitalized, but it is also listed in some dictionaries as *dalmatian*, even though the rules say ". . . if a name derives from a proper noun, capitalize it."

However, when you look up "Great Dane," it is almost always going to be listed with an uppercase *G* for *Great* and an uppercase *D* for *Dane.*

And now for the exceptions. (you knew there'd be some). While editing my *How to Capitalize Anything* book, we ran across a situation that didn't look right.

It followed the guidelines we had established, but it fell just outside the line regarding keeping things consistent. I was writing about capitalization of foods, and we ran across the following paragraph.

> I checked a few more dictionaries after making that chart and, to my surprise, found the American Heritage Dictionary had "Caesar salad" listed as lowercase. They also had *cheddar* and "french fry" listed as both lowercase and capitalized. The Lookup dictionary on my iPhone listed "caesar salad" as lowercase also.

By all rights, the words that are italicized and wrapped in quotes are done correctly, but it doesn't look right to have cheddar in italics and the others in quotes. To keep things consistent, and since we were speaking of the same types of items in the same paragraph, we put cheddar in quotes as well.

Also, here's an example from the current book, which has a lot of occasions to use both italics and quotations.

> Many of the online grammar sites, and even the style guides and dictionaries I checked refer to a lot of rules using the terms *always* or *never* when what they should say is *usually* or *seldom.*
>
> *Always* means "on every occasion" or "all the time." *Never* means "not at any time" or "at no time."

If a rule has exceptions (and most do), then you shouldn't use *always* or *never*.

We both thought that was clear enough to leave as it is.

MORE ON THE USE OF ITALICS AND QUOTATION MARKS

You didn't think we were done, did you?

There are plenty of other times to use italics. Here are a few.

- To mark a word so that its meaning is emphasized (like the dialogue below).
- "You're not telling her about *that*, are you?"
- I wanted to go to the prom, but I *had* to go to Jane's party.

To mark foreign words that are not well known.

- *Ti amo con tutto amore.*

But if foreign words are well known, there is no need to italicize them. Such is the case with the following.

- ciao
- amigo
- mucho
- risqué
- sfogliatella (or sfogliatelle)
- cannolo (or cannoli)

The list above is mixed. The first two I'm sure most people are familiar with: the Italian word used for goodbye (and hello), and the Mexican word used to mean friend.

Those two words will be recognized by the majority of English readers (at least in the States). However, the last two may or may not be recognized. It depends on the audience.

Sfogliatella is the singular form of an Italian pastry originally made in Naples, Italy. If you're addressing an Italian or an Italian-American audience, they will likely know what you're speaking of, and no italics will be needed. However, if the majority of your audience is non-Italian, you may want to italicize it.

Cannolo brings up a more interesting dilemma. Cannolo is the singular form of the well-known cannoli, made famous by the line in *The Godfather* when Clemenza said "Leave the gun. Take the cannoli."

Despite that line, and the fact that a person can buy cannoli in almost any shop that sells pastry, many people will not know that a cannolo is the singular form of cannoli.

Cannoli refers to more than one cannolo just as sfogliatelle refers to more than one sfogliatella.

One way to check if a foreign word should be italicized is to look it up in the dictionary. If it has an entry, it doesn't need to be italicized. But when you look up cannolo, none of the dictionaries have it; however, they all have cannoli.

The surprising thing is that many of the dictionaries listed cannoli as the plural form of cannolo, but they didn't have cannolo listed as an entry. And to top it off, *American Heritage Dictionary* had cannoli listed as the plural of cannolo, but they had cannolis listed as the plural of cannoli.

That kind of mistake is forgivable for the everyday person, but it shouldn't be made by a dictionary. It's like an Italian dictionary saying someone had a few *steakss* for dinner or a few *cupss* of coffee.

But enough about Italian desserts; that talk is making me hungry. Let's look more at italics.

If you italicize a word, and you intend to use it frequently, it only needs to be italicized the first time.

If you are using several foreign words and one is well-known while the other is not, you should italicize both of them. An example is below.

- He went to the pastry shop and ordered six *cannoli* and four *sfogliatelle*.

If he had just ordered cannoli, no italics would have been necessary, but if the writer felt the need to use italics with *sfogliatelle*, then both words should be italicized.

Short phrases of foreign words should also be italicized. As an example, I use the phrase *ti amo con tutto amore* in one of my mystery series, and I always italicize it, even the second and third time it's used.

Italics can also be used to refer to what may be an unknown word to your audience. If you're writing an article about a blackjack dealer and he's referring to an *anchorman*, you can elect to italicize it. Another option is to wrap it in single quote marks, like this: 'anchorman.' Note that this is one of the few times single quotes are used in American English.

Italics are often used to denote works of art as well. The following are typically italicized (by CMOS guidelines), although AP recommends almost all works of art be put in quotes.

"Aircraft and spacecraft, albums, ballets, operas, symphonies books cartoons, comic strips, exhibitions at a museum, films, journals, magazines, newspapers, paintings, pamphlets, plays, sculptures, and ships."

When writing about ships, the name of the ship is in italics, but not the preceding terms such as HMS or USS. So a ship's name would be written as the following.

- HMS *Windsor*
- USS *Arizona*

The items in the list below would be in quotes (according to CMOS).

- book chapters
- lectures and manuscripts (unpublished writing)

- radio shows
- short stories and short poems
- songs (album tracks)
- TV episodes
- video games

The thing to remember is what I've said all along: pick a style guide and stick with it. If AP says to use quotes, use them. If CMOS says to use italics, use them.

When it comes to what are known as scare quotes, most everyone agrees that the words should be wrapped in quotes, not italicized. This is the CMOS suggestion on what are known as scare quotes.

Quotation marks are often used to alert readers that a term is used in a nonstandard (or slang), ironic, or other special sense. Such scare quotes imply "This is not my term" or "This is not how the term is usually applied." Like any such device, scare quotes lose their force and irritate readers if overused.

A word or phrase preceded by *so-called* need not be enclosed in quotation marks. The expression itself indicates irony or doubt. If, however, it is necessary to call attention to only one part of a phrase, quotation marks may be helpful.

So-called child protection sometimes fails to protect.

Her so-called mentor induced her to embezzle from the company. but ...

These days, so-called "running" shoes are more likely to be seen on the feet of walkers.

— CMOS

I'VE NOTICED THAT SOME WRITERS DO THINGS DIFFERENTLY when it comes to writing individual letters. I believe you should stick to whichever method you use for "words as words." If you use italics for individual words when used as words, then use them for the letters also. Examples follow:

- All the *d's* at the beginning of words in that article should have been written using *D*.
- To pluralize most words, add an *s* though some words requires adding *es*.

Note in the first example, the way to pluralize an individual lowercase letter is to use an apostrophe. When the letter is uppercase, there is no need.

- All the capital *D*s should be made into lowercase *d*'s.

Here are the rules.

- All lowercase letters when written as themselves, require an apostrophe *s*.
- All uppercase letters when written as themselves, should be pluralized by adding *s* only (no apostrophe).

And now for the exceptions. There are four letters that, when written as capitals, require an apostrophe to make them plural.

- A
- I
- M
- U

The reason is simple and logical. If you simply add an *s* to those words, they form another word, thereby greatly increasing the risk of confusion.

- *As*
- *Is*
- *Ms*
- *Us*

When you use the apostrophe, however, it clarifies things.

- *A's*
- *I's*
- *M's*
- *U's.*

When you write out sounds, they are put in italics.

- She heard a *thump-thump* that sounded as if it were nearby. It frightened her.
- He woke to that unmistakable mosquito sound— *bzzz*— and it was close to his ear.

Remember, you can use italics and quotation marks several ways, but decide on a style guide and follow it. Don't deviate.

Chapter Fifty-Five

LATIN ABBREVIATIONS AND EXPRESSIONS

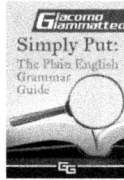

I went back and forth on whether to include this, and I was almost convinced not to when I stumbled across *etc.,* used the wrong way in a book. That convinced me I should include it. If you never use Latin abbreviations, you can safely ignore this chapter.

By the way, the first few examples have been covered previously. If you read them, and you feel as if you have a grasp on the ones discussed, skip over them.

E.G./I.E./Ergo/Et Al./Etc.

There are some, especially those in the legal and insurance professions (as well as writers), who love to use Latin abbreviations. There's nothing wrong with that, but far too often I have seen the abbreviations used improperly. The problem with using Latin terms is that many people won't know right from wrong, but with those who do, you'll look like an ass if you use them the wrong way. So for those of you who would like to use the terms, here is the proper way:

e.g.,

A Latin abbreviation for *exempli gratia*, *e.g.* means "for example." It is not necessary to place it in italics, but you should write it with periods and lowercase letters, and it is standard to follow it with a comma. Remember that *e.g.,* should not be used for clarifying what you mean to say. Leave that job to *i.e.,* Remember that *e.g.,* and *example* both start with the letter *e*.

- "Working dogs, *e.g.*, Great Danes English mastiffs, and boxers typically like to be active."

Use *e.g.,* when you want to give a few examples but not a complete list. As you can tell from the sample sentence, this is nowhere near a complete list. I could have added Bernese mountain dogs, Rottweilers, Doberman pinschers, and many more. If I had wanted to include the entire list, I would have used *i.e.*, not *e.g.*

i.e.

A Latin abbreviation for *id est*—*i.e.* means "that is" or "in other words" and is used to clarify the meaning of something. It is written similarly to *e.g.*, and is followed by a comma as well. It should precede a clarification, not an example. It should also be preceded by a comma.

Use *i.e.* when you want to provide further explanation for something.

"The fish expert recommended I only add aggressive freshwater fish to the tank, i.e., African or South American cichlids."

What follows *i.e.* should be equal to what it's clarifying, meaning you should be able to replace one with the other without changing the meaning of the sentence. Try it out:

"The fish expert recommended I only add African or South American cichlids to the tank, i.e., aggressive freshwater fish." I'm sure there are other aggressive freshwater fish, but for this example, we'll assume there aren't.

Sometimes the situation would allow you to use either *e.g.* or *i.e.*; however, the meaning of the sentence may be affected. Let's take a look at the above sentence.

I said, "The fish expert recommended I only add aggressive freshwater fish to the tank." I then used *i.e.* to indicate that South

American and African cichlids were what he was referring to. If there were many choices, though, I could have use *e.g.* instead and still listed South American and African cichlids as examples. The difference is that by using *i.e.,* I'm indicating they are the only ones to use. By using *e.g.,* I'm indicating they are but a few examples, that there are others that would work. So *e.g.,* is used to provide an example and *i.e.,* to explain an example.

ergo

Ergo is the Latin abbreviation for *therefore* and, as such, is frequently preceded by a semicolon. It can also be separated by a comma or an em dash, depending upon usage.

I see no need to use *ergo*, but if you do, use it properly. This is from a blog I wrote, where I jokingly used *ergo*:

"Perhaps they think that by capitalizing words, those words, or the functions they represent, become more important; ergo, the person becomes more important. (Did I just use the word *ergo*? I did, didn't I? Smack me if I ever do that again.)"

Et al.

Et al. is an abbreviation of the Latin phrase *et alii* (male), *et aliae* (female), and *et alia* (neutral), meaning "and others." The term references groups of people (not things). *Et al.* is useful for citations and for referring to a group by a few of its members, as in "The world was protected by mutants: Professor Xavier, Cyclops, Wolverine, et al."

Et al. is only capitalized at the beginning of a sentence, and it always takes a period after *al* as it is an abbreviation for *alia*. Commas are optional but typically used.

etc.

This is an abbreviation for *et cetera*, which means "and so forth."

It should never be used in the same sentence as *including* or *includes*, and it should be preceded by a comma and followed by a comma when it appears in the middle of a sentence. If it comes at the end of a sentence, the period (which is part of *etc.*) suffices as the final punctuation.

I've also seen people use "and etc." which is also wrong as *etc.* means "and so forth," so the *and* is extraneous.

Some people may think the use of *ergo, et al., i.e.,* and *e.g.,* is pretentious, but the terms are perfectly fine, and they are common practice, especially in the legal and insurance professions. One other thing—*etc.* is used only for things. Use *et al.* when referring to people. (*Et al* means "and others," so it is appropriate.)

Also, *etc.* is used at the end of a list to indicate that there are more elements to the list being left out so that the list doesn't become too long: "All the objects in our solar system (planets, comets, etc.) orbit the sun."

When you use *etc.*, be sure all the items that follow it are similar. For example, you wouldn't say "My passions are reading, writing, taking care of animals, etc."

If you did, no one would know what the *etc.* stands for as you have listed items of different kinds.

Sic

I know you've seen this (usually in newspapers), where the author cites a quote that contains an error in the original, then follows it with the word *sic* in italics and enclosed within brackets.

Sic is a Latin term and means "thus." It means "This is exactly what the original quote or writing says," and it is used to let people know that an error was made and that the error was kept as it was by the writer.

Often it's a date, as in "America was discovered by Columbus in 1592 [*sic*]." The *sic* is needed as the date should have been 1492, but the writer wanted you to know that the person who originally wrote the article or made the statement did so erroneously. *Sic* is always enclosed in brackets [ ] (one of the few times brackets are used) and is always italicized.

So why use *sic* at all? Because a lot of statements, especially written ones, need to be copied word for word. It's not used to make the other person look bad.

Versus

Versus may be one of the most-used Latin words and yet most people don't know its origin. *Versus* means "against" or "as opposed to" and is often seen written as *vs.* or simply *v.*

You've probably seen in the newspapers something similar to "Samuels *v.* the State of Texas" or (and I know you've seen something like this) "Patriots *vs.* Falcons." In each of these instances, you could have substituted *versus* for the *v.* or *vs.* without changing the meaning.

Versus is used primarily when pitting one thing against another. In each case above, it signifies a fight or contest.

It can also be used as a comparison, as in "pounds versus kilograms" when comparing the weight differences, or "yards versus meters," or "ounces versus liters."

Circa

Circa is another one of those Latin words I'm sure you've seen. It is often used in newspaper or magazine articles when an exact date is unknown, such as in the construction or completion of an ancient project; for instance, "The completion of the Sphinx was circa 2500 BC." Another way to write it would be to say, "The Sphinx was built about 4,500 years ago (circa 2500 BC)." In each case, it means the Sphinx was built (about, around, or approximately) in the year 2500 BC.

Quid Pro Quo

Most people understand what *quid pro quo* means, but they may not know that the meaning is literal (exact). *Quid pro quo* means "one thing in return for another." You often hear it referred to in talk of politics where one politician will do a favor for someone who has done something for them, although the spread of the word has far outreached politics now and has become pervasive in almost all aspects of life. "A person's rise in politics is often the result of one *quid pro quo* after another." Many politicians rely on *quid pro quo* to get anything done.

Ad Nauseam

Most of you are familiar with the phrase "ad nauseam." It means "to the point of sickness" and is used (mostly figuratively) that way. "We argued the point ad nauseam but accomplished nothing."

Per Se

Many people use this expression having picked it up through osmosis but never really knowing its true meaning. *Per se* (not "per say") means that something is being considered by itself, not with other things lumped into it: "The ex-alcoholic felt there was nothing wrong with drinking, *per se*, but that it must be done in moderation."

Alibi

This is a word I never expected to find on the list; however, it was there. Anyone who has ever watched a police show or read a mystery book is probably familiar with the meaning, but did you know it's Latin for "elsewhere," as in "He has an *alibi*," meaning he was *elsewhere* when the crime was committed?

We've covered a lot of ground, but we haven't even scratched the surface. There are hundreds, if not thousands, of Latin expressions/words we could talk about. I'll bet you didn't know you knew so much Latin. Anyway, below is a brief list of a few of the more common terms.

- *caveat emptor*—"Let the buyer beware." It's a warning to prospective buyers that they may be taken advantage of.
- *ipso facto*—"by the fact itself"
- *veni, vidi, vici*—"I came. I saw. I conquered."
- BC and AD—"before Christ" and "anno Domini" (in the year of our Lord)
- *ad hoc*—"formed or used for a special purpose"
- *ad infinitum*—"without end or limit"
- *addendum*—a section of additional material added to a document or a book, etc. (plural is *addenda*)
- *affidavit*—a sworn statement
- *alma mater*—institution where one attended school
- *alter ego*—technically, it is a different version of yourself.
- *alumnus* or *alumni*—single and plural versions of graduates of a particular school or university: "He was a Princeton alumnus."

- *ante bellum*—"before the war" (especially the American Civil War)
- *aurora borealis*—Northern Lights
- *carpe diem*—"Seize the day."—a saying often used to urge someone to have fun while they can.
- *Cogito ergo sum*—"I think, therefore I am"
- *e pluribus unum*—I know you've seen this. It's on every dollar bill, written on the ribbon held by the eagle. It means "out of many, one" and is the motto of the United States.
- *fac simile*—means "to make alike" or "render a similar copy." As you may guess from the spelling, it is where the word *facsimile* comes from.
- *persona non grata*—an unacceptable or unwelcome person

Latin phrases are a part of the language, and they're not likely to change anytime soon, so it's better to learn the particulars while you can.

Chapter Fifty-Six

LINKING VERBS

*L*inking verbs are important because they often affect the way the remainder of the sentence reads.

The following verbs are linking verbs as are all forms of the verb be:

- am
- is
- are
- was
- were
- has been
- are being
- might have been
- become
- seem

If you can substitute *am*, *is*, or *are* and the sentence still sounds logical, the word is likely functioning as a linking verb.

Unlike action verbs, linking verbs show a relationship between the subject of the sentence and a noun or adjective being linked to it.

My dog *is* an Australian Shepherd. (*Dog* and *Australian shepherd* are linked because they are the same thing.)

My cat *is* furry. (*Cat* and *furry* are linked because furry describes the cat; the cat *is* furry.)

The most common linking verbs are forms of the verb to be: *am, is, are, was, were, being, been.*

Other common linking verbs include:

- appear
- become
- feel
- grow
- look
- remain
- seem
- smell
- sound
- stay
- taste
- turn

Examples follow:

- The noise I hear *sounds* like bells.
- I *feel* refreshed after resting.

To check if these are being used as linking verbs, try replacing them with the correct form of "to be." If they make sense and have the same or, almost the same, meaning, they are linking verbs.

- Laurie *appears* tired.
- Laurie *is* tired.
- You *seem* more relaxed now.

- You *are* more relaxed now.
- That cantaloupe *smells* rotten.
- That cantaloupe *is* rotten.
- The dog's fur *feels* soft.
- That dog's fur *is* soft.
- I have the flu, and I *feel* miserable.
- I have the flu, and I *am* miserable.
- These oranges look sweet and *taste* even better.
- These oranges look sweet and *are* even better.
- The milk *turned* sour.
- The milk *is* sour.

The Linking Verb

Recognize a linking verb when you see one.

Linking verbs are not used for action—they connect the subject of the verb to more information about the subject:

- Bob *is* a hit man.

Is is not an action verb. It isn't something Bob can do. *Is* connects the subject *Bob* to more information about him, that he kills people for a living.

- On cold nights, our cats *are* on the bed and under the covers.

Are is not an action verb. It isn't something the cats do. *Are* is connecting *cats* to a statement made about them—that they sleep on the bed.

- After eating bad meat, Nancy *became* sick.

Became connects the subject *Nancy* to something said about her, that she was sick. Try what we mentioned earlier; see if we can use *am, is, or are,* in the sentence instead of the verb that's there. "After eating bad meat, Nancy *is* sick." It isn't perfect, but it does work.

"A 300-mile drive seems long after getting no sleep." Try it here. "A 300-mile drive seems long after getting no sleep." It works much better in that sentence.

Seems connects the subject, a 300-mile drive with something said about it, that it *is* long if driven after not sleeping.

- Sandi always *feels* groggy after drinking wine.
- Sandi always *is* groggy after drinking wine.

Feels connects the subject Sandi to her state of being, grogginess.

Below you have a list of verbs with potential active meanings:

- appear
- feel
- grow
- look
- prove
- remain
- smell
- sound
- taste
- turn

Sometimes these verbs are linking verbs; sometimes they function as action verbs. *Become* and *seem* are always linking verbs.

The way to tell if a word is functioning as an action verb or a linking verb is by substituting *am, is,* or *are*. After doing that, see if sentence still sounds logical. If it does, it's probably a linking verb.

If, after the substitution, the sentence makes no sense, you are dealing with an action verb instead. Here are a few examples:

- Mollie *tasted* the heavily spiced sauce.

When you substitute, you get "Mollie *is* the heavily spiced sauce."

I don't think Mollie is the sauce! *Tasted*, therefore, is an action verb in this sentence, something Mollie is *doing*.

- The tomato soup *tasted* good.
- The tomato soup *is* good.

It works in the above sentence.

- I *smell* the lasagña.
- I *am* the lasagña.

Doesn't work. *Smell*, in this sentence, is an action verb, something I *am* doing.

- The lasagña *smells* great.
- The lasagña *is* great.

Substitution works in the above sentence.

- When Mollie *felt* the wet grass, she turned around and went back into the house.
- Mollie *is* the wet grass?

Since *is* doesn't work, then *felt* is an action verb, something Mollie is doing.

- Mollie *feels* sad from having to stay inside.
- Mollie *is* sad?

Absolutely. She likes going outside. Here's the list again so you don't have to look for it.

- appear

- feel
- grow
- look
- prove
- remain
- smell
- sound
- taste
- turn

This substitution will not always work for some of the words, such as *appear, turn,* etc. You have to understand how the words are being used. Look at the following sentence:

- The ghost *appeared* from nowhere.

In this example, *appeared* means the ghost suddenly showed up. We're not saying "The ghost looked like something" or "Seemed like something." We're saying "It *appeared* from nowhere"; in other words, it suddenly came into view.

If you try the substitution using *is*, you can see it doesn't work.

- The ghost *is* from nowhere.

The ghost has to be from somewhere; we just don't know where.

Now check this one out.

- The hawk *appeared* on the fencepost.

If you make the substitution, it works, but it's not the same meaning.

- The hawk *is* on the fencepost.

The meaning is not the same for both sentences. *Appear* is not a linking verb in this case but an action verb. The hawk appearing is a result of action.

What we're looking for is *appear* in the sense of *seem,* as in:

- The horse *appeared* lame.
- The hawk that appeared on the fencepost *appears* tired.

- The horse *is* lame.
- The hawk that appeared on the fencepost *is* tired.

You can usually substitue *seem* or a version of it, to see if the sentence works. Sometimes, *seem* provides better results. Look at the examples above.

- The horse *seems* lame.
- The hawk that appeared on the fencepost *seems* tired.

Now try it with the previous example where we used *hawk.*

- The hawk *appeared* on the fencepost.
- The hawk *seemed* on the fencepost.

It definitely didn't work. It showed us much better than using *is* did.

Below are some linking verbs to try. Use the substitutions and see if they work. In each sentence, I've placed a substitute in parentheses to see if it works.

- ☑ People *grow* (are) one year older every birthday.
- ☑ The puppy *remains* (is) happy during its bath.
- ☑ The lasagna *smells* (is) delicious.
- ☑ Bosses can be (are) demanding.
- ☑ The horses *appear* (seem) well-groomed.
- ☑ The Grand Canyon *looks* (is) amazing.
- ☑ He *seems* (is) afraid of the dog.

☑ His assignment proves (is) difficult for him.

☑ Classical music *sounds* (is) uplifting.

☑ Traffic *becomes* (is) congested after work.

☑ The doctor *seems* (is) confident about my recovery.

☑ Some leaves *turn* (are) yellow in the fall.

☑ The two instruments *look* (are) similar in size and color.

And here are a few examples when we have more than one word describing the subject.

☑ Apples *taste* (are) sweet and delicious.

☑ After exercising, I *feel* (am) stronger and energized.

☑ The beer *tastes* (is) cool and refreshing.

☑ The climate in San Diego *appears* (seems) pleasant and temperate.

☑ You *look* (are) healthy and fit.

☑ The air in the Grand Canyon *smells* (is) piney and clean.

☑ My wife *stayed* (was) relaxed and calm all evening.

A quick reminder: the above is the main reason why, when people ask "How are you?" you should say "good" not "well."

"How are you?" and "How are you feeling?" deal with linking verbs, so they take an adjective, not an adverb.

One more thing about linking verbs. I discussed them briefly in *More Misused Words, No Mistakes Grammar, Volume III.* But that chapter dealt more with flat adverbs. Here I'll mention how you *should not* use an adverb with a sense verb. So if any of the sense verbs are used in a linking-verb sense (which they usually are) then you use an adjective instead. As always, examples will probably explain it better, so I've provided a few below.

✗ He looks well. (Well can be used, but it's because *well* is an adjective as well as an adverb.)

☑ He looks good.

☑ I feel good.

✗ I feel well.

☑ Those burgers smell good.

✗ Those burgers smell well.

☑ The steak tastes good.

✗ The steak tastes well.
☑ That dress looks good on you.
✗ That dress looks well on you.
☑ That dress fits you well.
✗ That dress fits you good.

Analyses

In the first example, we said, "He looks well." The only way for that to work is if we meant he *sees* well, because what we're really saying is that he *appears* to be good.

We mentioned that you follow a sense verb with an adjective, but the reason may not have been clear. We use an adjective because we are describing the subject. So in the sentence "Those burgers smell good" we use *good* because it's describing the burgers or the aroma they are putting off. We couldn't use *well* or we'd be describing *smell* (the verb), and since burgers can't smell, it doesn't work.

Take the sentence "That dress looks good on you." We use *good* because it is describing how you *appear* in the dress. It is not describing *look,* because the dress is not looking. In the last sentence of the examples before the analyses, though, we use *well* because it is describing how the dress fits.

The following sentence provides examples of both.

- She feels bad because she sings so badly.

Chapter Fifty-Seven

MASS NOUNS AND COUNT NOUNS

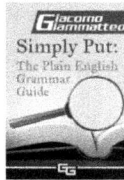

Mass (noncount) nouns are things that you can't count; therefore, they take a singular verb. In the following examples, *advice, air,* and *aluminum* are mass nouns.

- "His advice *was* adhered to," not "His advice *were* adhered to."
- "The air *is* warm" (not "The air *are* warm")
- "Aluminum *is* a durable metal," not "Aluminum *are* a durable metal."

- advice
- air
- aluminum
- applause
- beer
- biology
- boating
- cake
- cheese
- cloth

- dancing
- dust
- economics
- electricity
- equipment
- experience
- flour
- furniture
- glass
- hair
- harm
- heat
- history
- hockey
- homework
- ice
- leather
- luggage
- mathematics
- meat
- metal
- milk
- oxygen
- photography
- plastic
- poetry
- porcelain
- publicity
- reading
- rice
- smoking
- soccer
- steel
- sugar
- sunshine

- traffic
- water
- weather
- wine
- wood
- wool

Count nouns you can make plural, such as apples, pears, inches, cars, etc.

Mass nouns (noncount nouns) you can't: water, butter, milk, smoke, etc.

Chapter Fifty-Eight

ONLY, AND HOW TO USE IT

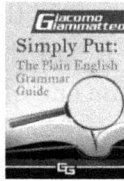

*T*he proper placement of adverbs in a sentence seems to be lost on a lot of people. I understand because I've done it numerous times. Fortunately, my editor was there to set me straight.

Of all the adverbs, one seems to be the top offending culprit: *only*.

Only may be placed in several parts of a sentence, but placement decisions can also affect the meaning of the sentence. Let's take a look.

✅ *Only* you may eat meat on Fridays.

✅ You may *only* eat meat on Fridays.

✅ You may eat *only* meat on Fridays.

✅ You may eat meat on Fridays *only*.

As you can see by the green checks, all four sentences are considered correct. But *correct* doesn't mean it's what you want. Let's look at each sentence and what is meant.

✅ *Only you* may eat meat on Fridays.

In this sentence, you're saying that *you* and *you alone* are allowed to eat meat on Fridays. No one else may eat meat.

✅ You may *only eat* meat on Fridays.

In this sentence, you're saying you may only *eat* meat on Fridays. You can't cure it, trim it, marinate it, or anything else.

☑ You may eat *only meat* on Fridays.

In the third sentence, you're saying you may eat meat on Fridays, but only meat; in other words, you can't eat any other food.

☑ You may eat meat on *Fridays only*.

By placing *only* at the end of the sentence, the emphasis falls on *Fridays*; in other words, it's saying you may eat meat on Fridays, but only on Fridays. You could have said the same thing by placing *only* before *on*, but I didn't think it had the same effect; the emphasis seemed stronger with *only* at the end of the sentence.

Let's look at a few different examples and look closely. When you place *only* in front of the subject (the person or thing doing the action), you are placing the emphasis there. The following example shows that.

- *Only I* like swimming at the beach.

In this sentence, you are saying that *you* are the *only* person who likes to swim at the beach. (It must be nice to have it all to yourself.)

When you place *only* before the verb, it emphasizes it more.

- I *only like* swimming at the beach.

This is an odd construction, but technically it means that you only *like* swimming at the beach; in other words, you don't *hate* swimming or even *dislike* it. You only *like* it.

When the adverb *only* is before the noun used as an object (after the verb), it once again changes the meaning of the sentence.

- I like *only swimming* at the beach.

In this example, we're saying you like swimming at the beach, but you like *only* swimming, not volley ball, or surfing, or even playing games at the arcades.

When *only* is placed at the end of the sentence (after the phrase "at the beach"), it changes again.

- I like swimming *at the beach only*.

With *only* in this position, you're saying you like swimming but at the beach only. You could have had the same meaning by saying "I like swimming only at the beach."

I HOPE THIS HAS SHOWN THE IMPORTANCE OF CAREFULLY positioning your adverbs. Not all adverbs have the effect *only* does, but there are others: *just*, *merely*, and *simply* are a few of them.

Chapter Fifty-Nine

OXYMORONS

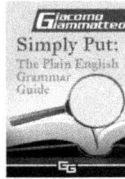

*O*xymorons are fun. They give you a chuckle, at least an inside chuckle. The name *oxymoron* is like an inside joke itself. When analyzed, it is an oxymoron.

The word 'Oxymoron' is originally derived from the Greek elements: oxy = sharp and moros (moron) = dull (foolish). Thus the word oxymoron is itself an oxymoron.

Let's look closer. According to the Cambridge Dictionary, an oxymoron is:

---

two words used together that have, or <u>seem</u> to have, <u>opposite</u> *meanings*

— CAMBRIDGE DICTIONARY

I want to take a moment to say that the definition used above came from the *Cambridge Dictionary* because *Merriam-Webster's* as well as Dictionary.com had explanations that were much less clear. Here's the one from Dictionary.com.

---

a figure of speech by which a locution produces an incongruous, seemingly self-contradictory effect, as in "cruel kindness" or "to make haste slowly."

— DICTIONARY.COM

And here's *Merriam-Webster's*.

---

a combination of contradictory or incongruous words (such as cruel kindness); broadly: something (such as a concept) that is made up of contradictory or incongruous elements.

— MERRIAM-WEBSTER'S

Both can be understood, but it may take a moment to digest what they're saying. In my opinion, the definition provided by Cambridge is far superior. Anyway, on with the show, so to speak. I borrowed a few of the examples below from the Search List, which has a huge list of oxymorons.

Oxymorons

- almost exactly
- alone together
- awfully pretty
- clearly confused
- deafening silence

- exact estimate
- found missing
- freezer burn
- jumbo shrimp
- larger half
- minor crisis
- only choice
- open secret
- pretty ugly
- same difference
- seriously funny

As you can see, each word is close to the opposite of the other. And yet I'd be willing to bet you've not only heard them used, you understand them. You may have even used them yourself.

Using Oxymorons on Purpose

There's nothing wrong with an oxymoron. At times, they are nothing more than humorous slip-ups, something you say without thinking. But there are times when oxymorons are used intentionally to draw attention to something or to encourage others to think in a particular mindset.

Look at the following examples from literature:

- a damned saint, an honourable villain!
- parting is Such Sweet Sorrow
- he is the only honest thief

Each of the above was taken from well-recognized literature: Romeo and Juliet and an essay by Charles Lamb.

"Painfully beautiful" was used as an explanation by YourDictionary to show how an oxymoron might be used to effectively describe a painting, and how that description might make people think.

One used frequently by writers of mystery (and by writers of horror) is "deafening silence," as in "She walked into the dimly lit house and was immediately struck by the *deafening silence*." When a reader sees something like that, they typically go on alert, waiting for something to happen.

Movies use it also, but without even having to say it. They just show the person entering the dark and eliminate sounds so it is silent.

The bottom line is oxymorons are fun. You can use them to your advantage when writing, and you can find humor in the inadvertent ones you hear.

Chapter Sixty

PARALLELISMS

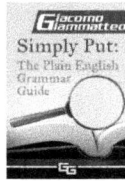

*P*arallelism involves the structure of sentences and much like the structure of anything—bridges, high-rises, etc. —the structure is important. A bridge must be supported equally by all its piers and a sentence requires no less.

Parallelism involves the practice of using similar parts of speech and similar phrases or clauses to balance a sentence. Imagine a sentence as if it were the *scales of justice*. Like the scales, a sentence has to be balanced.

The scales-of-justice image is below and following it are a few examples of parallelism done correctly as well as a few examples of parallelism done incorrectly.

One of the better-known examples of parallelism is the message sent to the Roman Senate by Julius Caesar after his victory at the Battle of Zela in 47 BC.

- I came, I saw, I conquered.

Notice how each part of that sentence consists of a subject followed by a verb in the simple past-tense form. Sentences don't have to be as simple as that, but it's a good example of parallelism in three parts.

I'm going to go on a tangent for a moment to discuss Caesar's saying. Notice it is not technically correct from a grammatical standpoint as it uses commas after *came* and *saw* instead of periods or semicolons.

When separating short clauses such as this, using commas amounts to a style choice by the writer. Even *The Chicago Manual of Style*, long a defender of the purity of the language, acknowledges this practice is okay.

And it *does* make a difference. Look at the same sentence expressed differently.

- I came, I saw, I conquered.
- I came. I saw. I conquered.
- I came; I saw; I conquered.

The second and third examples, despite being grammatically correct, don't have the impact the original does.

As a side note, the original Latin saying looks even better when viewed in its native language: "*Veni, vidi, vici.*"

Back to Parallelisms

From YourDictionary.com

>Parallelism uses similar words, phrases, or clauses to show that ideas have the same level of importance. This structure improves readability by giving a natural flow to a written work.

For native speakers of English, parallelism is often instinctive. We say, "I like reading, writing, and painting" instead of "I like to read, writing, and painting."

>However, one common mistake novice writers make involves failing to keep items in a list after a colon in a parallel form. "Writers can use an online dictionary to find help with these issues: word meanings, pronunciations, and finding correct spellings" does not use a parallel construction. Changing the text to read, "Writers can use an online dictionary to find help with these issues: word meanings,

pronunciations, and correct spellings" gives it a parallel construction and improves readability.

— YOURDICTIONARY.COM

Two areas where people often get into trouble follow. The first involves mixing gerunds and infinitives:

- I love to eat pasta and pastries and drinking coffee goes without saying.

That sentence could have been written several other ways:

☑ I love to eat pasta, pastries and drink coffee—the coffee goes without saying.

☑ I love to eat pasta and pastries, and to drink coffee goes without saying.

You could reword that sentence to make it work numerous ways; these are but two.

The second area people tend to get into trouble is when dealing with lists following colons.

✗ Pack your stuff for the beach: bathing suits, sunglasses, shovels, sand buckets, and you need to bring a book to read.

There are several things wrong with that sentence. The first is that the final part of the list states: "and you need to bring a book to read."

That doesn't fit with "bathing suits, sunglasses, shovels, and sand buckets." They are all mentioned as items to bring, but the final item is a whole sentence: "and you need to bring a book to read."

It would have worked if you had simply said, "Pack your stuff for the beach: bathing suits, sunglasses, shovels, sand buckets, and a book to read" (or some books to read).

Some people may even argue there's a problem with the sentence as it is because all the other items are plural, and "a book to read" is singular, but I feel that's nitpicking. If you want to write it correctly though, the example that follows shows how.

✅ Pack your stuff for the beach: bathing suits, sunglasses, shovels, sand buckets, and books to read.

When using infinitives (to eat, to be, etc.), it's fine to use the word *to* for the first example and not use *to* for the rest as long as you keep what follows in the same structure.

❌ We went to Vegas for Father's Day. I love to play poker, to play craps, and *playing* roulette.

✅ We went to Vegas for Father's Day. I love to play poker, craps, and roulette. (In the last sentence, the *to play* is understood, so there is no need to repeat it.)

❌ I love to play poker, to shoot dice, and gambling in general.

✅ I love to play poker, shoot dice, and gamble in general.

or

✅ I love playing poker, shooting dice, and gambling in general.

MAKING SURE YOUR SENTENCES ARE BALANCED ISN'T DIFFICULT; you simply need to be aware of the potential problems and look for issues.

Chapter Sixty-One

SUBJECT-VERB AGREEMENT

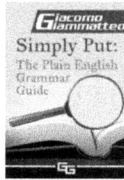

Giacomo Giammatteo
Simply Put:
The Plain English Grammar Guide

A frequently seen error, especially found in books or pieces of writing that haven't been professionally edited, is the misuse of subject-verb agreement. It doesn't seem to be such a grievous error, but it is one of the cornerstones of good grammar and should be adhered to.

On the surface, the rule appears easy to follow.

The subject and verb must agree with each other in number. In other words, if you use a singular subject, you need to use a singular verb. A plural subject requires a plural verb.

- A greyhound runs fast.
- Greyhounds run fast.
- Mary and Tom have coffee every morning.
- Mary has coffee every morning.
- Coffee is necessary in the morning.
- Many cups of coffee are necessary in the morning.

Two things to note: First, in case you weren't aware, a singular subject takes (what appears) to be a plural verb because it ends in *s*.

The reverse is true for plural subjects. (Remember that with plural nouns as well as *I* and *you*, you don't add an *s* to the verb.)

Examples follow.

- The greyhound (he or she) *runs* fast.
- The greyhounds (they) *run* fast
- Mary and Tom *have* coffee every morning.
- Mary *has* coffee every morning.
- I *skate* faster than she does.
- She *skates* faster than I do.
- They *skate* faster than both of us.
- You *skate* better than I thought.

As you can see, the pronoun *I* takes a plural verb, as does *you*, as well as *they*.

You use the singular verb (the one with the *s*) when the subject is in the third person present tense.

- He *plays* . . .
- She *sings* . . .
- It *bites* . . .
- Tom *drives* fast.
- Sheila *drinks* too much.

Don't let the substitution of *Tom* and *Sheila* fool you; using their names is just another way of saying *he* or *she*.

- Tom drives fast. = He drives fast.
- Sheila drinks too much. = She drinks too much.

This misuse of subject-verb agreement has led to one of the more prevalent grammar mistakes in all of writing. You won't see it much in books—at least not the ones that have been professionally edited—but you will see it frequently in casual writing, social media, and many blogs.

The misuse I'm speaking of is using the singular verb *is* with *there* or *here* or *where* when a plural subject is involved. A few examples may help. This happens more often when the words are used as contractions: *there's, here's, where's.*

❌ *There's* a lot of reasons why I did that.

❌ *Where's* the reports I asked for?

❌ Don't get all worked up, boss. *Here's* the papers.

✅ *There's* an issue we haven't spoken about.

Sentences one through three needed plural verbs (*are* not *is*). They should have been written as shown below.

- *There are* a lot of reasons why I did that.
- *Where are* the reports I asked for?
- Don't get all worked up, boss. *Here are* the papers.

The short answer for this is because when you use *there* or *here*, etc., the subject comes after the verb, so in the sentences above, *reasons*, *reports*, and *papers* are the subject, and since they are plural, the verb must be plural.

Sentence four, however, requires a singular verb because the subject is *issue*, which is singular. That makes *there's* ("there is") the correct form.

- *There's* an issue we haven't spoken about.

In sentences that begin with "there is" or "there are," the subject follows the verb and needs to agree with that in number. Let's look at the sentences above again with that in mind. All we need to do is turn them around. I put the subjects in italics.

- The *reasons* I did that are . . .
- The *reports* you asked for are . . .
- Don't get all worked up, boss. The *papers* are here.

This type of occurrence is not limited to those three words either. Quite often, it happens when a question is introduced by *what*. Consider the following:

- What are ten more minutes?

The reason this takes a plural verb is because "ten more minutes" is functioning as the subject. "Ten more minutes are what."

But questions beginning with *what* aren't the only additional culprits.

- Up *go* the blinds when the sun comes out.
- Down *go* the windows when it rains.

In both instances, we used the plural verb *go* because the true subject follows the verb and is plural (blinds and windows). The sentences would have read differently if structured with the subject first.

- The **blinds** *go* up when the sun comes out.
- The **windows** *go* down when it rains.

Another area that seems to confuse many people, writers included, is when dependent clauses fall between the subject and verb. Just remember they *don't* affect subject-verb agreement despite how it may sound.

- Sheila, who drives many different cars, is coming over tonight.

Sheila is the one who is coming over, not the cars, so the verb needs to agree with "Sheila."

You need to think about *who* or *what* is doing the action. *Who* is coming over?

Prepositional phrases are another minefield, but they're easy to navigate. If a prepositional phrase comes between the subject and verb, it *usually* does not affect agreement.

If you felt the hair on the back of your neck bristle, you have good sensations. I said *"usually* does not affect agreement," which almost always means *there are exceptions*. Here is the exception.

There can be times when the preposition or—more importantly —the object of a preposition, can affect verb agreement. I'll give you a few examples.

When *some, none, half, more,* and *all* are followed by a prepositional phrase, the object of the preposition determines the verb agreement.

- All of the *pizza is* gone.
- All of the *pieces are* gone.
- None of the *horses ran* a good race.
- Half of the *apples are* rotten.
- That half of the *apple has* a worm in it.
- More of the *ice cream is* left.
- More of the frozen *bananas are* left.

As you can see, when the objects of the prepositions are singular (pizza, apple, ice cream), the verb agrees with that in number, but when the objects are plural (pieces, horses, apples, bananas), the verb changes to plural.

To rehash a point made earlier, subjects do not always come before the verbs. This frequently happens (as noted) with *there*, *here*, and *where*. Let's look at a few sentences using *where*.

- Where *are* the grapes you bought?
- Where *is* that delicious-looking orange?
- Where *are* the test results?

An easy way to determine which verb form to use is to turn the sentence around.

- The grapes are where.
- The orange is where.
- The results (not test) are where.

When you refer to time or units of measurement, a singular verb is called for.

- Fifty miles *was* the recorded distance.
- Ten feet *was* the height of the fence.
- Eleven o'clock *is* her bedtime.
- Seven days *is* the planned vacation time.

And it doesn't matter how much distance or how much time is referred to:

- Three days is a long time to wait.
- Three hundred years is a long time to wait.
- Three feet is a long way for an ant to travel.
- Three thousand miles is a long way for anyone to travel.

It doesn't matter what the distance or time involved is because you're referring to it as one measurement. "Fifty miles" or "Five hundred miles" are both a single measurement. But things change if you speak about them as individual units:

- Three hundred miles are between Houston and Dallas?
- Five thousand two hundred and eighty feet are in a mile?
- Sixty seconds are in a minute?

WHEN TWO SUBJECTS ARE CONNECTED WITH "AND" TO FORM A compound subject, the verb is plural.

- The little pig and the horse *are* friends (two things: pig and horse).
- She and her husband (two things: she and husband) *attend* mass on Sunday.
- The viewing and the funeral *were* on successive days (two things: viewing and funeral).

You have to be careful the word *and* is forming a compound subject though and not just referring to a single subject made up of two nouns.

- Peanut butter and jelly *is* my favorite sandwich (one thing: a sandwich).
- Rich and creamy cake *is* my favorite dessert (one thing: a rich, creamy cake).
- Sweet and sour chicken *is* my favorite entrée (one thing: chicken that is both sweet and sour).

When an indefinite pronoun precedes the subject, new rules apply. Before you get worked up at my use of grammar terminology, let me state that an indefinite pronoun is nothing more than a word like *he, I she, they, we, etc.*, which can refer to *one* thing or *many*, and it can refer to either gender. Below is the list of the words I'm speaking of.

- anybody
- anyone
- anything
- each
- either
- everybody
- everyone
- everything
- neither
- nobody

- nothing
- one
- somebody
- someone
- something

While this may seem a daunting task, it isn't, thanks to Dr. Kip Wheeler, who has a marvelous website dedicated to the English language. It was while browsing this website that I found the following *rule*. I'll cite it as he did:

The words ending in "-one, -ing," and "-body" must use a singular form, even though these words might seem to be plural when we think of "everybody in a crowd" or "everybody in Texas."

Don't think of the word that way. Instead, think of it as being equivalent to "every single individual." For example, "Every single student took **his** book to class with **him**" is equivalent to "everyone took **his** book to class with **him**." Just as *each single student* is singular, *everyone* is also considered singular.

— DR. KIP WHEELER

Using Dr. Wheeler's rule of thumb, you only need to remember the rule plus three other words: *each, either,* and *neither*.

These indefinite pronouns use singular verbs. You would write, "Everyone is here." You wouldn't say "Everyone are here." A few more examples follow.

- Nobody *goes* to work today; it's Sunday.
- Something *is* wrong with Bob.
- Anyone who *wants* to come, get in the car.

- Neither of them *moves* very quickly.
- One of us *is* going to fail.
- Each person *decides* their own fate.

A note about the last sentence: It has been accepted for a while to refer to a singular person by using the plural *their*. Some still object to this, but it's changing, and it's changing quickly. In previous times, that sentence may have been written, "Each person *decides **his or her** own fate.*"

I think it's long past time to worry about issues such as those.

To coincide with the above, there are a few pronouns that always take plural verbs.

- all
- both
- few
- many
- several
- some

Let's look at a few sentences.

- Both of the girls *are* spending the night with Sally.
- Several *are* not enough to form a majority.
- Few *were* alive after the flood.
- All of the planets *revolve* around the sun.
- All of the pizza *is* gone.

Wait a minute. The last sentence shows a singular verb.

Yes, it does, and it's right. This is one of those exceptions that always seem to crop up just when you think you've learned things.

Remember earlier, when we said, "When *some, none, half, more,* and *all* are followed by a prepositional phrase, the object of the preposition determines the verb agreement"?

This is one of those cases. In the last sentence, the phrase ". . . of the pizza" determines the verb form, and since *pizza* takes a singular form, the verb is singular. In the sentence prior to that, the phrase following *all* was ". . . of the planets," containing a plural noun, hence the plural form of the verb.

If we wanted to use a plural verb in the last sentence, we could have changed it to read, "All of the pizzas are gone."

In that case, you would be referring to "pizza pies" in the plural sense.

Let's look at a couple other sentences.

✖ Each of the patients were treated with identical medicine.

✓ Each of the patients was treated with identical medicine.

Remember, *each* is one of the words that is always singular and not affected by the prepositional phrase that follows, so when you analyze it to determine the subject-verb agreement, the way to read the sentence is "Each was treated with identical medicine." You ignore the phrase that separates the subject and verb.

Each is tricky because it's often followed by a prepositional phrase with a plural object (each of the kids), and that tends to confuse many people regarding which verb form to use.

Remember that *some* is also one of the words affected by the prepositional phrase following it. But without the influence of the phrase, *some* is always plural. Look at a few more sentences:

- All of the pizza *is* gone.
- Some of the beer *is* left.
- Some of the beers *are* left.
- None of the cheese *is* left.

On to the next rule.

When you use the phrase "one of the *things* that" or "one of those who" preceding the subject, the verb following it will be plural. (This negates the previous rule of "indefinite pronouns" and singular verbs.)

I'll give you a few examples.

☑ He is *one of the dogs that love* to bite.

✗ He is *one of the dogs that loves* to bite.

✗ She is *one of those people* who always *chooses* chocolate.

☑ She is *one of those people* who always *choose* chocolate.

If you try to decide which verb form to use *without* the rule, you may have to think some. If you use the rule though, the choice is easy.

☑ It is one of the dogs that *love* to bite.

✗ It is one of the dogs that *loves* to bite.

✗ She is one of those people who always *chooses* chocolate.

☑ She is one of those people who always *choose* chocolate.

Now we're going to introduce a twist to this rule.

When *only* precedes either of the "one of . . ." statements, the verb following it is singular.

☑ It is *only* one of the dogs that loves to bite.

☑ She is *only* one of the people who always chooses chocolate.

Going back to the first rule dealing with indefinite pronouns, we can look at the following sentences:

- One of my favorite actors *is* Denzel Washington.
- One of the movies I love *is* The *Godfather*.

Essentially what you're saying is:

- Denzel Washington *is* one of my favorite actors.
- The Godfather *is* one of the movies I love.

Now it's time for another twist. We've already stated that if you use "one of the things that" or "one of those who," you follow it with plural verbs. Now let's look at a similar rule, but this rule deals with the word number.

When you use the phrase "the number of," it take a singular verb, but if you use "a number of," it takes a plural verb:

- *The number* of casualties *was* staggering.
- A *number* of casualties *were* documented erroneously.
- *The number* of Academy Awards *continues* to increase.
- *A number* of awards *aren't* necessary.

NOW FOR A CONFUSING RULE. SOME NOUNS ARE ALWAYS USED IN the plural sense, even though they appear to be singular. These nouns always take plural verbs. It will be easier to explain with examples.

- The *cattle love* grazing in the meadow.
- The *poultry have been* restless lately.
- Her *offspring were* plotting to kill her to get the inheritance.

The opposite of that rule entails the nouns that are always singular and are followed by singular verbs.

- Her *hair was* silky smooth after she conditioned it.
- The *scenery* in Ireland *was* breathtaking.
- The *furniture is* brand new.
- My *luggage has* not shown up yet.

Gerunds (*ing* verbs that function as nouns), act the same as nouns regarding agreement in number.

- *Swimming is* fun.
- *Crying* always *makes* my nose run.
- *Playing poker is* my favorite pastime.

And if they are joined by the word *and*, they take a plural noun (the same as a normal subject).

- *Playing poker and shooting dice are* my favorite things to do at the casino.
- *Swimming and surfing are* a blast.
- *Crying and laughing take* a lot out of you.

Here's another tricky one. When a sentence has a positive *and* a negative subject, the verb agrees with the positive subject.

I realize that sounds confusing, so let's look at a few examples.

- *Quality*, not low prices, *determines* what books sell.
- *Good health*, not material items, *determines* happiness.

As you can see above, the verb is singular to agree with the positive statement. It makes no difference if you turn the sentences around.

- Low prices, not quality, *determine* what books sell.
- Material items, not good health, *determine* happiness.

When two plural subjects are connected by or, nor, neither/nor, either/or, or "not only/but also, the verb following is plural.

- *Not only* Great Danes *but also* German shepherds, are considered working dogs.
- *Neither* horses *nor* cows are considered dangerous, but they kill more people than snakes.

Now to add complexity to that rule. If one of the subjects is plural but the other is singular, and they are connected by those same words, the subject closest to the verb determines the number:

- *Either* the jewels *or* the **cash** *was* taken first.

- *Neither* the cash *nor* the **jewels** *were* taken.
- *Not only* dope *but also* **guns** *are* in high demand on the black market.
- Guns or **dope**, *either* one *is* in constant demand.

The subject in **bold** determines the verb agreement. The verb is in *italics*.

If you join two infinitives (verbs beginning with *to* that can function as subjects) with *and*, the verb following them is plural.

- *To swim* and *to play* volleyball *require* a lot of coordination.
- *To eat* and *to drink* in excess *are* not recommended.

Titles of movies, books, poems, songs, etc., take singular verbs.

- *The Lost Boys was* one of my son's favorite movies.
- *Who Let the Dogs Out? was* a big hit with my kids.

Even if the subject seems to be plural, it takes a singular verb:

- *The Adventures of Wyatt Earp and Doc Holliday is* a good book.

When using "as well as" after the subject, it shouldn't affect the agreement. This also applies when using "with," "together with," "along with," "accompanied by," or "in addition to."

- Jim, *in addition to* John, *is* going to the prom.
- Sandy, *together with* Barbara, *is* riding to the beach with us.
- The feral cat, *as well as* its sister, *does* not like the dog.
- Skip, *along with* his brother, *is* on duty tonight.

Don't be fooled by the nouns that are always plural. They *do* take plural verbs—unless preceded by the phrase "a pair of"—in which case a singular verb is required.

- *A pair of glasses has* gotten expensive.
- My *glasses were* broken when I fell.
- Where *are* my *pants?*
- A new pair of *pants is* what he needs.
- *Scissors are* not to be run with.
- A *pair of pliers is* needed to remove that.

On the other hand, if "a pair of" refers to a plural subject, it takes a plural verb:

- *A pair of eyes* are watching you.
- *A pair of shoes* are required to enter.

On the opposite side of this are the words that may appear to be plural but require singular verbs.

- *Physics is* a difficult subject.
- *Measles is* a disease you normally get as a child.
- The *news seems* dreadful.

Going further, sometimes a word refers to a singular item but takes a plural verb.

- During the downturn, his **assets** *were* depleted.
- Our **thanks** *go* to the first responders on that fateful day in September.

In the first example, *assets* is referring to his total assets (net worth), not the items that make it up.

Using *either* or *neither* (without *or*). *Either* is used before the first of two alternatives (the other being introduced by *or*). It can sometimes refer to more than two, but in either case, you are referring to one person or thing when you use *either*.

Likewise, *neither* refers to "not one or the other of two people or things." *Oxford English Dictionary* gives these examples:

'neither side of the brain is dominant over the other'
    as pronoun 'neither of us believes it'

— OED

Again, if you look at the examples, *neither* refers to one thing: one side of the brain or one or the other people. As such, it should take a singular verb, but issues arise when *either* or *neither* is followed by *of* and a plural noun.

- Neither of the boys *curse*, but they do smoke.
- Do either of his parents *care* about him?

In the sentences above, notice that the verbs are plural. Some purists insist the verb should remain singular, but usage is moving in the other direction.

When you use *either/or* and *neither/nor*, you sometimes use a singular verb and sometimes plural. Let's look.

- The role of Doc Holliday was one of the best characters that **either** Val Kilmer **or** anyone else *has* portrayed.
- **Neither** the coal miners **nor** the union reps *were* able to negotiate increased wages.

In the first sentence, we're referring to *one* thing: Val Kilmer, but in the second, we're talking about the coal miners.

And finally, there are occasions when you will have a singular and plural noun mixed.

- Either the votes or the **voting machine** *was* rigged.
- Neither the student nor his **advisors** *were* aware of the problem.

When this occurs, I follow the rule already mentioned dealing with making the verb agree in number to the noun nearest it. If the noun closest is singular, as is the case above with "voting machine," the verb is singular (*was*). When the closest noun is plural as it was with "advisors," then the verb is plural.

Don't forget about contractions and what words they represent. *Doesn't* is a contraction for "does not" and takes a singular verb constuction. And *don't* is a contraction for "do not" and takes a plural verb construction.

You wouldn't say "He don't do that" or "She don't sing well." It would be "He doesn't do that" and "She doesn't sing well."

Chapter Sixty-Two

THEMSELF AND THEMSELVES

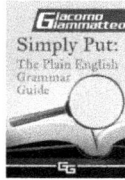

*L*anguage is evolving, as it always does, and some of the words and rules that were once considered substandard are now finding acceptance, primarily due to common usage. One example is the use of *themself* instead of *themselves*.

The accepted rule for ages has been to use *themselves* even when referring to a single person. Examples follow.

- The first person to draw the number *seven* can come to the stage and claim the prize *themselves*.

Last year, at the American Copy Editor's convention, CMOS announced that in their new edition, it would be acceptable to use *themself* for the singular instead of *themselves*. This is a long-overdue correction, and it follows the earlier approval of the use of *they*, *their*, and *them* for use when referring to someone of unspecified gender in the singular.

Themself or Themselves

If you look at the Google Ngram screenshot below, you'll see that *themselves* is still used far more often, but that's understandable because Google's Ngram only reflects the results of writing that's been published, and that writing would have more than likely been looked over by editors or, at the very least, spellcheckers, and both would have flagged *themself* as wrong.

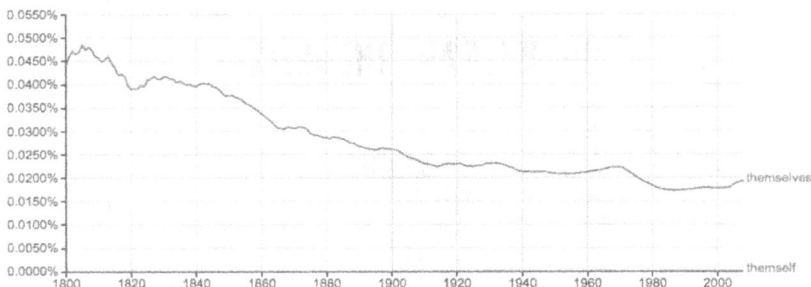

Is it Okay to Use *Themself?*

If you pay close attention to other writing like emails, blogs, and social media, I think you'll see the use of *themself* is far more prevalent.

I'm a firm believer in the sanctity of grammar. Maybe *preservation* would be a better word, but I'm also a staunch supporter of change when necessary, and I feel this change *is* necessary.

You can get a lot more clarification on specific words or phrases in my No Mistakes Grammar Bites books. There are twenty-five, and they're all only ninety-nine cents. You can't beat the price.

Plus the proceeds go to feeding and caring for the animals on our sanctuary. So pick out a book that deals with a word or words you need help with and spring for ninety-nine cents. You'll be learning something and helping animals at the same time.

Note:

Before sending this off to the editor, I decided to run it through a grammar checker or two. The checkers flagged the word *themself* five times as being wrong, offering *themselves* as an alternative. I guess they need to update.

According to CMOS:

CMOS 17 will state that *themself* (like *yourself*) may be used to signal the singular antecedent (though some people will prefer *themselves*).

And in three of the dictionaries I checked, *themself* wasn't even listed. In one dictionary, it was listed but as informal usage.

Chapter Sixty-Three

WHEN IS "CURRENTLY" NEEDED?

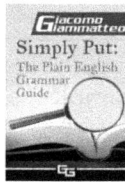

*W*hen is *currently* needed—almost never, and yet I hear it used frequently. Some of the worst misuses are found on answering machines and voicemails.

- I'm *currently* away from my desk.

Or even worse:

- I'm *currently* away from my desk right now.

The business world is rife with the misuse.

- He's *currently* working on . . .

- The company is *currently* developing a new device.

Even the dictionaries use what I think of as bad examples. Here is the definition from *Merriam-Webster's*:

: at the present time; currently engaged in scientific research, the movie currently running at the local theater. She currently lives in Texas. a product that is not currently available

Similar legislation is currently working successfully in 17 other states as well as in the nation's capital. —Tom Bourdon

Currently, only three such drugs are approved for use in the U.S. ... . —Michael Waldholz

Analyze a few of the examples above, then look at the one below by Dictionary.com.

- She is *currently* working as a lab technician.

And from *Merriam-Webster's* (above).

- She *currently* lives in Texas.

Wouldn't "She lives in Texas" suffice? If she lives in Texas, it *is* current; she's living there *now*.

And if she's working as a lab technician, it is current; otherwise we'd say "She used to work as a lab technician" or "She worked as a lab technician."

Many people—writers included—go through life without ever having to use the word *currently*. Look at a few examples below

- I'm *currently* away from my desk.
- They are *currently* on the way to Detroit.
- He is *currently* on vacation.

Now look at them without *currently*:

- I'm away from my desk.
- They are on the way to Detroit.

- He is on vacation.

The only difference in those sentences is you saved words, which is a good thing.

When you use *currently*, you're likely using a present-tense verb like *am* or *are*. And if you're using a present-tense verb, that verb is already signaling to us that the action is taking place *now*, or *currently*; therefore, *currently* is redundant.

Is Currently Ever Needed?

If you are mentioning a different time frame in the same sentence, it is still often not needed but acceptable. A few examples follow:

- I *used to* live in New York, but I *currently* live in Chicago.
- I *currently* live in New York, but I'll be moving to Chicago *next month*.

As you can see, in both instances, another time frame is mentioned. In the first example, it's a general time: *used to*. In the second it's specific: *next month*. You could still easily avoid using *currently*, but it sounds okay to use it as is or to substitute the word *now*.

- I used to live in New York, but I *now* live in Chicago (using *now*).
- I live in New York, but I'll be moving to Chicago next month (without *now*).

In the second sentence, you could use *now* or *currently*, or you could choose to not use either.

In the first sentence, you could use *currently* or *now*, but the sentence structure calls for something. You could also rearrange the sentence:

- Before I moved to Chicago, I lived in New York.

I don't want it to seem as if I have a vendetta against *currently*. I don't. I simply want to show that it's seldom needed. There are a few instances when you could use *currently* or *now,* but there are other options as well.

Summary

- You wouldn't say "I was doing laundry in the past." (*Was* indicates that it was in the past.)
- Just like you shouldn't say "I am currently doing laundry." (*Am* indicates it is in the present.)

Let the verb speak for itself. It doesn't need clarifying.

There are many other words that aren't needed or most of the time, they're not needed. A few of these are *presently, personal,* and *own.*

Chapter Sixty-Four

QUIZ 9

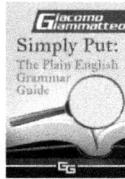

*Q*uiz 9
  Match the following with the correct sentence below.

1. You can't eat meat any day but Friday.
2. No one may eat meat on Fridays but you.
3. You can't eat anything but meat on Fridays.

A. ✅ Only you may eat meat on Fridays.
B. ✅ You may eat only meat on Fridays.
C. ✅ You may eat meat on Fridays only.

Part Five

PLURALS

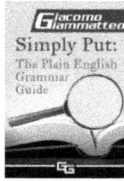

Plurals

We all know that English is a difficult language. Part of what makes it difficult is the confusion surrounding how to pronounce and pluralize words. Let's take a closer look at a few of the problems.

Chapter Sixty-Five

PLURALS

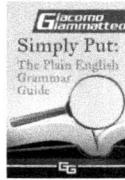

Plurals

We all know that English is a difficult language. Part of what makes it difficult is the confusion surrounding how to pronounce and pluralize words. Let's take a closer look at a few of the problems.

Learning how to make plurals is both simple—and difficult. It's simple with most words because all you need to do is add an *s* or an *es* and the word becomes plural.

In the examples below, the slash mark is to show which letters are being used to make the word plural.

- elephant/s
- rich/es
- lion/s
- weasel/s
- snitch/es
- wish/es
- ash/es

Problems arise when the plurals don't conform to the normal rules.

- tomato/es
- potato/es
- volcano/s
- tornado/s or tornado/es
- hero/es
- taco/s
- zoo/s
- echo/es
- torpedo/es

In the examples above, why do some of the words end in an *s* and some in *es* in order to make a plural?

We're not done with the confusion yet. Take a look at some of the words that end in *f* or *fe*.

- knife = knives
- life = lives
- shelf = shelves
- hoof = hooves, but hoofs is acceptable

Some *f* words do it differently.

- chief = chiefs
- roof = roofs
- proof = proofs

If that isn't enough, there are exceptions beyond those. Consider the following:

- scarf = scarves or scarfs
- dwarf = dwarves or dwarfs

The problems with plurals don't stop there. We haven't run out of issues. The following list contains a few of the words that are singular *and* plural.

- bison
- deer
- elk
- moose
- sheep

Then there are a lot of words derived mainly from Latin that really confuse the issue. In the list below, the singular version is listed first, followed by the plural.

- candelabrum = candelabra
- datum = data
- addendum = addenda (addendums is now acceptable also)

And from the *Oxford English Dictionary*, the following (the image is on the next page).

Here are a few more to further confuse things.

- diagnosis = diagnoses
- ellipsis = ellipses
- focus = foci
- fungus = fungi
- nucleus = nuclei
- ox = oxen
- radius = radii

There are also words that are always plural.

- amends
- pliers
- scissors

- shorts

The best advice for novices and experts alike is when a question arises, consult your favorite dictionary.

Inherited Plurals

What do I mean by inherited plurals?

They are those words everyone loves to hate. Like when people say "The media *are* reporting on that now" or "The data you requested *are* ready."

- "The media *is* reporting on that now."
- "The data you requested *is* ready."

Why would someone even say such a thing as "The data are ready"? It doesn't sound right.

While it's true that it doesn't sound right, the people using it that way probably think they're right. Perhaps they learned it that way when they went to school. But depending on the context, they *may* be right. And if we spoke Latin, they would be right. But we don't speak Latin. Not anymore.

Nowadays, Latin plurals and many others are quickly going out of style. Words like *data* and *media* are acceptable either singularly or as mass nouns, whichever is appropriate.

To analyze this, look at the following:

Data has long been treated as a count noun, in other words, a noun that would take a plural verb. Remember, if it's a count noun, it takes a plural verb; if it's not a count noun, it takes a singular verb.

So, "I bought ten bananas yesterday, and they were expensive." As you see, bananas is a count noun; we counted it. You bought ten of them.

But, "I sprinkled the yard with water yesterday; the water was hot." As you can see, you sprinkled it with water. You couldn't count the drops; it's a mass noun, an uncountable one.

Definition of *Data*

1: factual information (such as measurements or statistics) used as a basis for reasoning, discussion, or calculation.

The data is plentiful and easily available

— —H. A. GLEASON, JR.

Comprehensive data on economic growth have been published

— —N. H. JACOBY

2: information output by a sensing device or organ that includes both useful and irrelevant or redundant information and must be processed to be meaningful.

Data (with facts/plural. With information/singular)

Data is often written erroneously. The key is knowing what "kind" of data.

When *data* is a count noun (it refers to items that can be counted), the plural verb makes sense. In that type of sentence, you could replace *data* with another count noun, such as *facts*. However, when *data* is treated as a noncount noun (items cannot be counted), the singular verb makes sense. In those cases, you could substitute the word *information*.

Examples: If you are submitting sales reports to your boss, you might say "The data (facts) are ready."

But if you were referring to marketing information, you could say "The data (information) is ready."

Both would be correct.

🖐 Remember to substitute the words *facts* or *information* for the word *data*. If *facts* works, use the plural verb tense (*are, have, were,* etc.), but if *information* works, use the singular verb (*is, has, was,* etc.).

Using *data* either way is now accepted by all but the stodgiest of people, and most dictionaries will support you. Don't let anyone tell you differently.

By the way, the singular form of *data* is *datum*. I don't know if I've ever heard of anyone use *datum*, but it's there, waiting to be used. It has been for a long time.

Media

Media is another of those pesky Latin words that have unusual plurals. And, as usual, it has sparked controversy ever since it appeared.

Medium is the singular.

Media is the plural.

I understand if you're puzzled. The use of *media* meaning "mass communications" has confused people since it entered the English language in the 1920s. That's why you'll hear people say "The media are here" instead of "The media is here."

I believe it's only a temporary dilemma. Usage is changing, and it's changing fast. I doubt it will be more than a generation or two before *media* joins *data* as being acceptable either way. And before you go moaning about how you don't want to wait that long, take comfort that in the meantime, probably no one will notice how you use it; in fact, you'll likely get more questionable looks and raised eyebrows when you use it correctly.

As a side note, I believe most sources agree that *media* is counted as singular when it refers to the group of mass communications. But it is counted as plural when referring to the many people who work in the industry.

Examples are as follows:

• The media *were* swarming the new celebrity (meaning a lot of people/reporters).

• The media *is* concerned about the verdict (meaning numerous companies).

In the first instance, media is referring to the vast number of reporters shoving microphones into the celebrity's face.

In the second instance, media is referring to the collection of communications companies that make up the media, such as TV, newspapers, radio, etc.

If that didn't work, think of it this way. Imagine the media as Congress. When you're thinking of media in the sense of the people who work in that field, picture the members of Congress. There are a lot of them. Some would say too many.

And when you think of media in the sense of the companies that make up the communications industries, think of them as Congress.

On the one hand you would say "The members of Congress are passing the bill today."

But you would say "Congress is sure to veto his proposal."

Most sources acknowledge that *media* can be treated as either singular or plural. The problem is with the people who don't realize this yet, and many of those people are members of the media.

It won't be long before it changes, though. Most of the words we imported from Latin have become accepted over the years. Consider the following: *agenda, candelabra, data, ephemera, erotica, insignia, stamina, trivia,* and others.

And here are screenshots of the results of searches comparing the number of instances of using "media is" versus "media are," and "data is" versus "data are." (The images may appear on different pages.)

Data is and data are

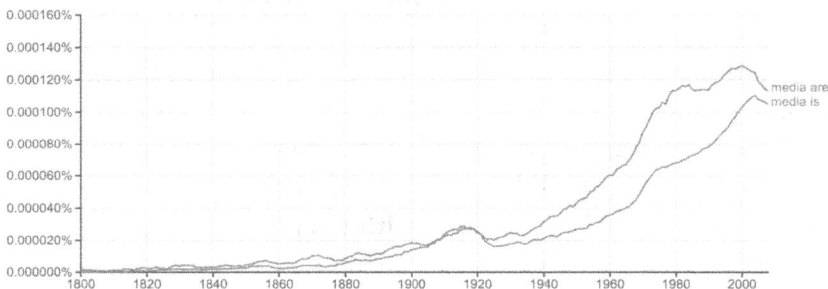

Media is and media are

As you can see, "data are" hit a peak during the 1980s, but it has since been on a decline. It's now about the same as "data is." On the other hand, *media* has remained reasonably consistent, though "media is" has caught up to "media are" in recent years.

As always, when in doubt, look it up in your preferred source. And if you still have questions, or if that source doesn't explain it well enough, find another.

Words from Other Languages

We've covered the big one—Latin—in a separate chapter, but there are plenty of other languages we have borrowed from. Here are a few:

French

- attaché

- blonde
- bon vivant?
- brunette
- cache
- cigarette
- cinema
- confidante
- embassy
- envoy
- helicopter
- niche
- parachute
- passport
- sorbet
- treaty

Italian

I'm sure you'll recognize a lot of these words, especially the words associated with foods and possibly music. Many of these words came from Wikipedia, as did the chart below the list showing what other languages contributed words.

- al dente
- al fresco
- America after Amerigo Vespucci
- antipasto
- arsenal
- artichoke
- assassin
- assassination (from Italian: assassinio. The first to use this Italian word was William Shakespeare in Macbeth. Shakespeare introduced a lot of Italian or Latin words into the English language.
- baguette
- bandit

- bank
- bankrupt
- banquet
- barista
- belladonna
- bergamot
- bimbo
- biscuit
- bologna
- bordello
- brigade
- brigand
- British Columbia after Christopher Columbus
- broccoli
- bruschetta
- candy
- cannelloni
- cannon
- cantaloupe
- capitalism
- cappuccino
- carat
- cartel
- casanova
- cascade
- cash
- casino
- catapult
- cauliflower
- cavalier
- cavalry
- charlatan
- chipolata
- ciabatta
- citadel

- coffee
- Colombia after Christopher Columbus
- colonel
- credit
- crime
- dildo (from Italian diletto, meaning "pleasure")
- discrimination
- embassy
- espresso
- fascism
- fascist
- finance
- flu
- ghetto
- gnocchi
- gorgonzola
- grappa
- gusto
- inamorata
- infantry
- influenza
- lasagne
- latte (or "Caffè latte")
- latte macchiato (Italian latte macchiato, "stained milk")
- lava
- macaroni
- macchiato (or Caffè macchiato)
- Machiavellian and Machiavellianism after Niccolò Machiavelli
- Mafia and Mafioso
- malaria
- management
- manifesto
- maraschino
- marinate

- martini
- merchandise
- military
- minestrone
- money
- mozzarella
- orange
- panini
- Parmesan
- pasta
- pepperoni
- pesto
- pistachio
- pizza
- politics
- post
- propaganda
- provolone
- quarantine
- radicchio
- ravioli
- risotto
- ruffian
- salami
- salvo
- scampi
- scimitar
- segregation
- sfogliatelle
- sociology
- spaghetti
- spumoni
- stiletto
- stratagem
- tarantula

- tortellini
- trattoria
- tutti frutti
- venture
- vermicelli
- vino
- volcano
- zebra
- zero
- zucchini

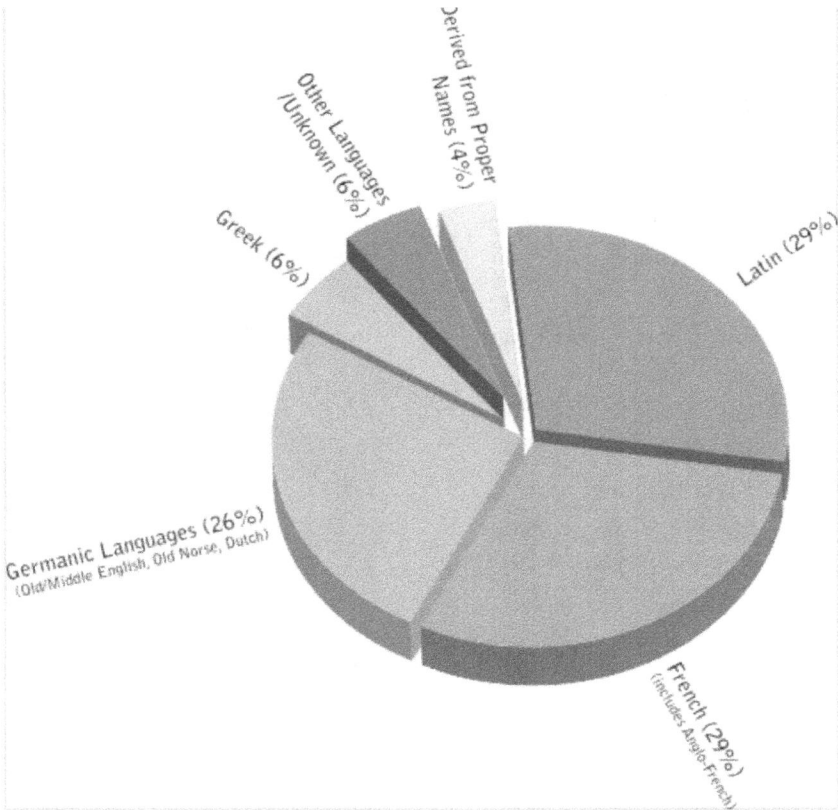

Spanish
We've managed to "borrow" more than a few words from

Spanish over the past one hundred years, though it's no surprise given that they are a neighbor, and that millions of Mexicans have emigrated to the United States. It's important to mention that some of these words made their way to us from the Spanish but they originated from the Arabic. Remember, the Moors occupied Spain for more than five hundred years—long enough to influence the language.

- albatross
- alcatraz
- alligator (the lizard)
- amigo
- apache
- armadillo (little armored one)
- banana
- burro (small horse)
- cafeteria (coffee store)
- California
- canyon
- Caribbean (got its name from the Carib Indians who lived there)
- coyote
- Florida
- guerrilla (small war)
- hacienda (meant estate)
- hola (hello)
- hombre
- hurricane
- Montana
- mosquito (little fly)
- pinto
- plaza
- potato
- rodeo
- salsa

- Spanish
- tomato
- tornado
- vigilante

Irish

We didn't acquire as many recognizable words from the Irish, but we did get a few.

- boycott (Abstaining from using, buying, or dealing with a person, organization, or country as an expression of protest—from Captain Charles Boycott, a 19th-century British land agent.)
- galore (plenty)
- hooligan (one who takes part in rowdy behavior or vandalism)
- kibosh, kybosh (to finish, to put an end to: "That's put the kibosh on it." Several sources say this word may have Yiddish origins.)
- slogan
- whiskey (water of life)

German

German is one of the languages that contributed the most words, although not as many are recognizable. Below are a few, but there are many more.

- Budweiser (popular brand of beer)
- delicatessen
- doppelgänger
- Doberman pinscher (dog breed)
- frankfurter (hot dog)
- gesundheit (substitute for "God bless you")
- hamburger
- kindergarten

- noodle
- poodle (dog breed)
- Rottweiler (dog breed)
- sauerkraut
- wiener (hot dog)

Greek

Along with Latin, Greek is probably the language that most influenced other languages around the world. Many English words derive directly from the Greek and knowing their origin and meaning is important. Here are a few you might like to know about:

- acme: The highest point of something. One could say that Rome reached the acme of its power in the year 117 AD, under the rule of Trajan.
- acropolis: *Acro* means "edge" or "extremity," while *polis* means "city." *Acropolis*, therefore, refers to cities built with security purposes in mind. The word *acropolis* is commonly associated with Greece's capital, Athens, although it can refer to any citadel, including in Rome and Jerusalem.
- agora: The agora was an open marketplace present in most cities of ancient Greece. Today the term can be used to express any type of open assembly or congregation.
- anathema: *Anathema* is a noun and means "a formal ban, curse or excommunication." It can also refer to someone or something extremely negative, disliked, or damned.
- anemia: *Anemia* refers to a condition characterized by a deficiency of red blood cells. Over the years, however, the term started to appear in other contexts, referring to any deficiency that lies at the core of a system or organization.
- dogma: *Dogma* refers to the established belief or set of

principles held by a religion, ideology, or by any
organization.

- eureka: The exclamation "Eureka!" is used to celebrate a
discovery and can be translated to "I have found!" It is
attributed to the famous Greek mathematician
Archimedes. While taking a bath, he suddenly realized
that the water displaced must be equal to the volume of
the portion of his body he had submerged. He was so
excited with the discovery that he left his home and
started to run through the streets of Syracuse shouting
"Eureka!"
- genesis: *Genesis* means "birth" or "origin." There are
many synonyms for this word, including *beginning, onset,
start, spring, dawn,* and *commencement.* Genesis is also the
first book of the Bible.
- kudos: *Kudos* means "fame or glory usually resulting from
an important act or achievement." (*Kudos* is always used
in plural form.)
- phobia: Many people wrongly think that a phobia is a
fear. In reality it is more than that. Phobia is an irrational
and exaggerated fear of something. The fear can be
associated with certain activities, situations, things, or
people.
- plethora: You have a plethora when you go beyond what
is needed or appropriate. It represents an excess or
undesired abundance.

Latin	≈29%
French	≈29%
Germanic	≈26%
Greek	≈6%
Others	≈10%

How to Form Plurals with Compound Words

There seems to be a lot of confusion regarding how to pluralize certain words, and we've already looked at more than a few. Standard words like *moth* and *tiger* are easy; these plurals are made by adding an *s* to the end of the word so they become *moths* and *tigers*.

But what do you do with words like *mother-in-law*, or *attorney-at-law*, or *major general?*

Some style guides say to pluralize the word that changes in number. In other words, using the examples above—and presuming you remarried—you could have several mothers-in-law, or if there were a convention for attorneys-at-law, you would have a hotel full of attorneys-at-law. The same applies for major general, though it would be major generals, as there would be a number of generals with the rank of major preceding their name.

The same logic applies to words like *sons-in-law* or *fathers-in-law*.

The number trick can fall apart when we have a word like *attorney general* as both *attorney* and *general* can be nouns and pluralized. So think of it this way: Imagine a room full of people and who they are. (Which are the nouns and which are the adjectives?)

Are the people in the room generals who happen to be attorneys? If they are, the word should be *attorney generals*, but more likely they are attorneys who happen to all bear the title "attorney general," so collectively they would be referred to as "attorneys general."

Major generals would be the reverse, as they are generals who happen to have their title preceded by the term *major*. So for the same reason it's not "reds flower" but "red flowers," it's "major generals," not "majors general."

🐾 Remember, it's the one that can increase or decrease in number that gets pluralized. If that logic doesn't work, look for the important one, the noun.

Problems with Plurals

Many people have a difficult time knowing when to use plural verbs in their sentences. The use of "there's" (contraction for "there is") versus "there are" is one of the more common grammar mistakes. But the issues surrounding "there's" are easy enough to learn.

I wrote an article on this problem, and it's included in a chapter of this book in the "Miscellaneous" section.

Today, however, I want to address another issue, one that is more complex. We're going to talk about *pluralia tantum*. Don't get nervous.

Pluralia tantum is merely the Latin for "plural only," and it is used to refer to words that have a plural form only (at least for that meaning).

Pluralia tantrum has a counterpart—*singulare tantum*—which is meant to refer to words used only as singular nouns. An example would be *dirt*. Another would be *milk*; in fact, all of the uncountable nouns usually fall into this category.

- I like to play in the dirt.

You wouldn't say "I like playing with dirts."

There is a plural for *dirt,* but it is similar to the plural of *fishes* in that you would be referring to different kinds of dirt, as in "I like playing in dirts of all kinds: wet, dry, sandy, gritty, etc.

Some nouns that are plural in form but singular in meaning require a singular verb:

- billiards
- calculus
- diabetes
- dizziness
- economics
- electronics
- gymnastics
- mathematics
- measles
- mechanics
- mumps
- news
- oats
- rabies
- sleepiness (and other nouns ending in "ness")
- summons
- thanks

I'll list examples using some of the words above:

- The *news* was good: no more storms.
- *Mathematics* was my least favorite subject in school.

- *Gymnastics* is a physically challenging sport.
- *Diabetes* is a deadly disease.

However, there are words that appear to be like these that can confuse you.

- Statistics was not a friend of mine in college. (singular)
- The *statistics* on voting were surprising. (plural)
- Electronics has been a growth industry for decades. (singular)
- *Electronics* constitute the heart of all computers. (plural)

The above words, along with many others, can function as singular or plural depending on how they are used.

There are other nouns that are always plural but which take plural verbs.

- pliers
- trousers
- scissors
- sunglasses
- surroundings
- manners

The above represents just a few of the words; many more can be added to this list. Now let's look at a few examples:

- The *pliers* are in the barn.
- Your favorite *trousers* are being washed.
- *Scissors* are not meant to be run with.
- Her *sunglasses* were expensive.
- His *surroundings* were bleak.
- Good *manners* were never his forte.

To confuse matters further, there are a lot of words that have singular forms only. They're the ones I referred to earlier as *singulare tantum*, or "singular only." A few examples follow.

- scenery
- furniture
- wheat
- dust
- silverware
- information
- news
- luggage

As usual, there are plenty more examples, but I think you get the point.

- The *furniture* was expensive.
- The *silverware* is in the drawer.
- The *news* is always bad.
- Your *luggage* is in the trunk.

And then there are the nouns that have identical forms whether singular or plural. I'm sure you are familiar with a few of them. Sometimes these words take a singular verb and sometimes a plural depending on how they're used.

- sheep
- deer
- moose
- fish
- shrimp
- police

A few examples:

- The sheep *needs* shearing. (one)

- The sheep *need* shearing. (more than one)
- He*'s* the police. (one)
- The police *are* here. (multiple)
- The shrimp *are* plentiful today.
- That shrimp *is* delicious. (one)

You're probably tired of hearing this, but it needs to be said again. It's nearly impossible to cover all situations in one book unless you're writing a dictionary or style guide, so pick the resource you're going to follow and look up any questionable words.

Chapter Sixty-Six

MORE ON PLURALS

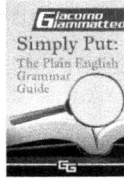

*M*ore on **Plurals**

Learning how to make plurals is both simple—and difficult. It's simple with most words because all you need to do is add an *s* or an *es* and the word becomes plural.

In the examples below, the slash mark is to show which letters are being used to make the word plural.

- elephant/s
- rich/es
- lion/s
- weasel/s
- snitch/es
- wish/es
- ash/es

Problems arise when the plurals don't conform to the normal rules.

- tomato/es
- potato/es

- volcano/s
- tornado/s or tornado/es
- hero/es
- taco/s
- zoo/s
- echo/es
- torpedo/es

In the examples above, why do some of the words end in an *s* and some in *es* in order to make a plural?

We're not done with the confusion yet. Take a look at some of the words that end in *f* or *fe*.

- knife = knives
- life = lives
- shelf = shelves
- hoof = hooves, but hoofs is acceptable

Some *f* words do it differently.

- chief = chiefs
- roof = roofs
- proof = proofs

If that isn't enough, there are exceptions beyond those. Consider the following:

- scarf = scarves or scarfs
- dwarf = dwarves or dwarfs

The problems with plurals don't stop there. We haven't run out of issues. The following list contains a few of the words that are singular *and* plural.

- bison

- deer
- elk
- moose
- sheep

Then there are a lot of words derived mainly from Latin that really confuse the issue. In the list below, the singular version is listed first, followed by the plural.

- candelabrum = candelabra
- datum = data
- addendum = addenda (addendums is now acceptable also)

And from the *Oxford English Dictionary*, the following (the image may be on the next page).

SINGULAR	PLURAL
addendum	addendums or addenda
aquarium	aquariums or aquaria
gymnasium	gymnasiums or gymnasia
maximum	maximums or maxima
memorandum	memorandums or memoranda
minimum	minimums or minima
moratorium	moratoriums or moratoria
referendum	referendums or referenda

SINGULAR	PLURAL
criterion	criteria
stratum	strata
phenomenon	phenomena

Here are a few more to further confuse things.

- diagnosis = diagnoses
- ellipsis = ellipses

- focus = foci
- fungus = fungi
- nucleus = nuclei
- ox = oxen
- radius = radii

There are also words that are always plural.

- amends
- pliers
- scissors
- shorts

The best advice for novices and experts alike is when a question arises, consult your favorite dictionary.

Part Six

REDUNDANCIES

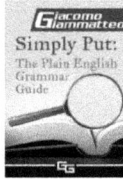

Redundancies are everywhere: TV, blogs, books, movies, and, of course, in everyday speech. If you are aware of what to look for (or listen for), you'll see and hear them everywhere.

One thing is certain: the more you recognize them, the more obvious their use—or should I say misuse—will become.

Chapter Sixty-Seven

REDUNDANCIES ARE ... REDUNDANT

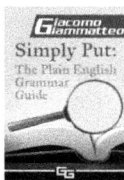

Giacomo Giammatteo
Simply Put:
The Plain English
Grammar
Guide

*W*e live in a complex world, but sometimes I think we make it more complex than it needs to be, mostly due to the way we communicate.

We communicate with each other by talking in person, through movies, and via the radio or phone. We also communicate in books, letters, emails, and on social media. But the one thing all these methods have in common is words.

Because words are the common denominator, we should strive to make sure we use them to our advantage. Part of that process is to ensure we don't use extra or confusing words.

Redundancies are a big part of that.

The world is full of confusion. We don't need to add to it. But add to it we do, and it's getting worse. All it takes is proximity to a workplace where more than a few people have gathered and a keen ear for the proper use of language.

Listen closely and you'll see what I mean. Put yourself in a situation like that and you're bound to hear plenty of words and phrases misused every day—hell, every hour. I've listed a few of the more obvious ones below.

The words inside the parentheses are the unnecessary ones.

Redundancies
(Absolutely) necessary

Necessary means "essential, indispensable, something you can't do without." An example: "Sand is a *necessary* ingredient for concrete."

(Actual) facts

Look at the definition for *fact*.

- Something known to exist or to have happened.

Now look at the definition for *actual*.

- existing in fact or reality; *actual* events.

Add (an additional)

- Add an electrical socket to that wall.
- Put an additional socket on that wall.

As you can see, we don't need to say "*Add an additional.*"

(Added) bonus

- I've added a few bucks to your paycheck this month.
- You got a bonus this month.

Adequate (enough)

Definition of enough from *Merriam-Webster's*:

: sufficient for a specific need or requirement

Definition of enough from Dictionary.com

adequate for the want or need

(Advance) warning
A warning *is* given in advance.
(Already) existing
If it *exists*, then it is *already in existence*.
(All-time) record

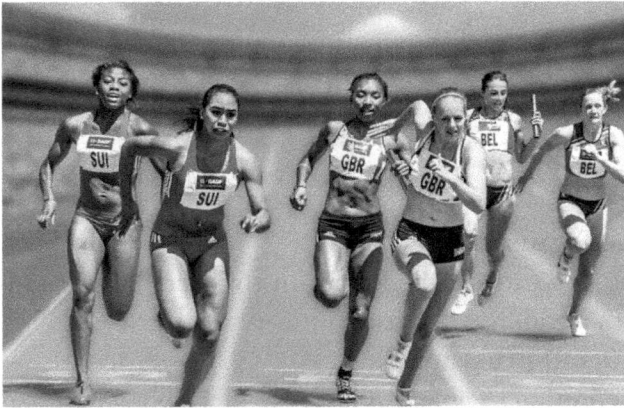

If someone's set a record, it is already "all-time," so no need to say it. "We've had *record* temperatures" means the temperatures were the highest (or lowest), regardless of which records were set. In a race, if someone sets a record for running a mile, it *is* an all-time record, otherwise it is mentioned as a school or an Olympic record.

Alternative (choice)
Choice is a synonym for *alternative*; in other words, it *is* an alternative, so no need to use it.

(And) etc.
This one is covered in the chapter for "Latin Expressions" under *etc.*, but I'll state it again. Since *etc.* means "and other things" or "and

so forth," there is no need to use *and*. It would be like saying "and and so forth."

(Armed) gunman

I think you can see the humor in this one. A *gunman* is already armed with a gun.

(Artificial) prosthesis

The definition of *prosthesis* is "an artificial body part," so there is no need to use the word *artificial* when describing it.

ATM (machine)

How many times have you said or heard someone say "I've got to stop at the ATM machine"? Or your spouse may say "Stop at the ATM machine on your way home and get some cash." An ATM is an automated-teller machine. The *m* stands for *machine*, so it's not necessary to use *machine*.

At the present time

: of, relating to, or constituting a verb tense that is expressive of present time or the time of speaking

— MERRIAM-WEBSTER'S

You could simply say "now" or "at present."

Autobiography (of his or her own life)

An autobiography *is* of your own life, told or written by you. Saying it's an autobiography is all that's necessary.

Bald (headed)

Bald refers to the head already. You can simply say someone is bald—you don't have to say baldheaded. Think of a bald eagle. It doesn't refer to its tail.

Balsa (wood)

Balsa is the name of the South American tree from which balsa comes. Since balsa is wood, there is no need to use *wood*. That's similar to saying the lumber was pine wood or oak wood.

(Basic) fundamentals

Fundamentals *are* basic.

Best (ever)

The best is the best. There is no sense in using *ever*. If it's the best, it's better than what came before it. (There is seldom reason to use *ever*.)

Biography (of his or her life)

A biography is an account of someone's life written by someone else. If someone has a book written about them—it is a biography. A biography already tells us that is about his or her life. An autobiography is written by the person in question, a biography by someone else.

(Blatantly) obvious

If you do or say something *blatantly*, it means you're not hiding it; in other words, you're being obvious.

Blend (together)

Blend means "to mix." No need for *together*. You don't blend something apart.

Bouquet (of flowers)

A bouquet is an arrangement of flowers; therefore, there is no need to say "He sent me a bouquet of flowers." "He sent me a bouquet will suffice."

(Brief) summary

A summary *is* brief.

Browse (through)

Browse, in this context, means to look through or glance at casually, as in "She *browsed* the bookshelves for a new mystery."

(Burning) embers

Ember by definition means "burning" (the remnants of a fire). "He stirred the embers to rekindle the fire."

Cancel (out)

I think this one is self-explanatory. You don't cancel out, and you don't cancel in. You simply cancel.

(Careful) scrutiny

Scrutiny by definition is "careful." It is the act of carefully examining something.

Cease (and desist)

I think detective shows are the culprit for spreading this misuse. *Desist* means "to cease." In fact, "to cease" is the first definition in many dictionaries.

Circle (around)

If you circle something (or someone), you are going around or surrounding it (or them). "Water circled the island."

(Close) proximity

Another cop-show misuse. *Proximity* means "close" or "nearby." Just say "He was in proximity to the crime." There is no need to say "close proximity." Saying "He was in close proximity to the hospital" is like saying "He was close close to the hospital."

(Closed) fist

To make a fist means "to close your hand."

Combine (together)

Combine means "to bring together."

Compete (with each other)

One of the definitions of *compete* is "to try to win something someone else is trying to win." In other words, you're competing for the prize.

(Completely) annihilate

Annihilate means "utterly destroy." Using *completely* is not necessary.

(Completely) destroyed

Destroyed means "in total." If something is damaged, simply say so. If it was destroyed, it was destroyed, so there is no need to use *completely*.

(Completely) eliminate

Eliminate means "to get rid of" or "wipe out." No need to use *completely*.

(Completely) engulfed

If something is engulfed, it is complete.

(Completely) filled

This one should be obvious. Think of a glass of water. Either it is or isn't filled.

(Completely) surround

Surround means "to be all around someone or something." You could *partially* surround something but not completely. *Surround* already means "all the way." "The island was surrounded by water." If you said, "The island was partially surrounded by water," it wouldn't be an island; it would be a peninsula.

Connect (together)

If you connect or join two or more items, you are bringing them together.

Consensus (of opinion)

Consensus means everyone is on the same page; they all agree. To arrive at a consensus, you need everyone's opinion.

(Constantly) maintained

Maintained means "to keep something (even your body) in good condition" or "to exist or continue without changing," so there is no need to use *constantly*.

Convicted felon

A few of the dictionaries I checked with provided wiggle room for this one, but Vocabulary.com states it plainly.

Technically, a felon is anyone who's been convicted of a serious crime, but you can use felon to describe anyone you think has done something terrible.

Here in the U.S. though, you're innocent until proven guilty, at which point people can call you a felon.

— VOCABULARY.COM

Could (possibly)

Consider this: "He could ride a bike when he was six." In other words, he was able to. There is no *possibly* about it. He either could or he couldn't. Or someone is lying.

Crisis (situation)

The definition of *crisis* is "a difficult or dangerous *situation* that needs serious attention." Please note the word *situation* in the definition.

(Critically) important

Important means it's critical.

(Current) trend

A trend *is* current.

Currently away (or unavailable)

This one is often made worse when heard on answering machines or voice mails.

- I'm currently away from my desk, right now.

If you're away from your desk, you are away right now or currently.

"I'm away from my desk" will suffice.

During (the course of)

"During the course of proceedings" and "During proceedings" are the same.

Each (and every)

You can pick *each* apple, or you can pick *every* apple, but not each and every apple.

Earlier (in time)

If you say "earlier," you are already referring to time. Consider this: "I saw her earlier today."

(Early) beginnings

Beginnings *are* the beginning; you can't get earlier.
Eliminate (altogether)
If you eliminate something, it is altogether.
Emergency (situation)
An emergency already is a situation, so no need to state it again. "We've got an emergency" not "We've got an emergency situation."

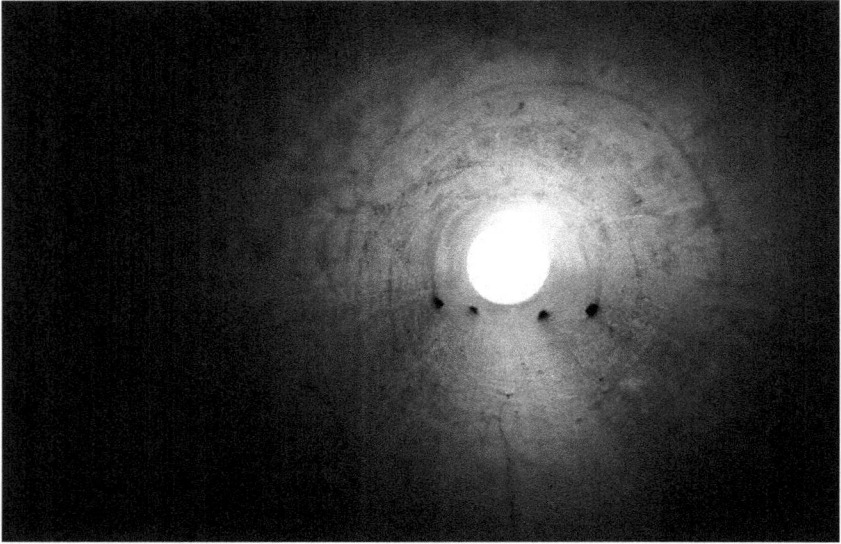

(Empty) hole
A hole is empty. Here's a dictionary definition: "A hole is a hollow space in something solid, with an opening on one side."
(Empty) space
A space is empty. Look at the definition: "You use space to refer to an area that is *empty* or available." So you could say "I have an *empty* spot in the closet." Or you could say "I have *space* in the closet." There is no need to use the words together.
Enclosed (herein)
Herein means "within a book or document," and *enclosed* means, well . . . enclosed. There's no need to use both.
(End) result

A result is the end.

Enter (in)

If you enter something, you are going in. If you enter a race or competition, you are taking part *in* it. If you *enter* a house, you go *in* it.

(Entirely) eliminate

Same thing as *completely*. If you eliminate something, it is in its entirety.

Eradicate (completely)

Same as *eliminate* and *engulfed*.

Evolve (over time)

Evolve implies a gradual change (meaning "over time"). Evolution doesn't happen instantaneously.

(Exact) same

Same means "identical, similar, or unchanged."

- She wore the exact same dress I did.
- She wore the same dress I did.

(Face) mask

A mask is worn on the face. You don't wear an arm mask or a leg mask. If you say someone wore a mask, it's obvious where they wore it. You wouldn't say "He wore a face mask" any more than you would say "He wore a hand glove" or a "foot shoe."

Fall (down)

Where else do you fall? If you say to someone "He fell," they'll know what you mean. They won't picture you falling up to the roof. They'll picture you falling down from somewhere, even if it's from an upright position.

(False) pretenses

---

an inadequate or insincere attempt to attain a certain condition or quality

— MERRIAM-WEBSTER'S

Pretense involves deceiving; it is always false.

(Favorable) approval

Approval implies a favorable response or action. Consider these:

- "He gave his approval."
- "He gave his favorable approval."

(Final) conclusion

A conclusion is final.

(Final) end

The end is final.

(Final) outcome

The outcome is final.

(First and) foremost

Foremost (as the name implies) means "most prominent," so no need to use first.

(First) conceived

Conceive, meaning "to think up" (not as in "to become pregnant").

First (of all)

- "First, let me say this."
- "First of all, let me say this."

Fly (through the air)

Where else would you fly?

(Foreign) imports

If they're not foreign, where are they coming from? Imports *are* foreign.

(Former) graduate

If you're a graduate, it *is* former—it is already in the past, therefore "former." You're not a former graduate, just a graduate.

(Free) gift

A gift is free; otherwise it's not a gift.

(From) whence

Whence means "from which" or "from where," so no need for *from*. It's similar to not using *and* with *etc.*

(Frozen) ice

I hope you see the humor in this one.

Full (to capacity)

Since capacity means "the maximum amount," there is no reason to say *full*.

(Future) plans

How many times has this question been asked in an interview? "What are your future plans?" A plan is always "ahead" of things, otherwise it wouldn't be a plan. You don't plan the past unless you own a time machine.

Gather (together)

To gather means to bring together.

(General) public

The easiest way to show this is to provide the definitions of both.

- Public—of, relating to, or affecting all or most of the people of a country, state, etc.
- General—of, relating to, or affecting all the people or things in a group, involving or including many or most people.

GOP (Party)

GOP stands for Grand Old *Party*.

Had done (previously)

If you already "had done" it, it *was* previously.

(Head) honcho

Honcho implies "top dog," "leader," or "person in charge."

HIV (virus)

HIV—the "v" stands for *virus*.

(Hollow) tube

A tube *is* hollow.

Hourly (or weekly, yearly, etc.) basis

If something is done at regular intervals, there is no need to say *basis*. "She did the laundry weekly" or "He did his taxes yearly" or "She did exercises hourly."

Hurry (up)

What is the difference between "hurry" and "hurry up?"

(Illustrated) drawing

Illustrated implies that a book or magazine, etc., contains drawings.

Incredible (to believe)

Incredible is not an intensifier, although it is quickly becoming one based on usage. It means "not credible" or "difficult to believe."

A "credible witness" is one who is believable, but something *incredible* means the opposite. If you say something is incredible to believe, it's like saying "It's difficult to believe to believe." Simply say it's incredible.

And please stop using it as an intensifier. Think about this: when someone tells you something, and you respond with "That's incredible," what you're really saying is "I don't believe you."

"Incredible, isn't it?"

🦣 Hint. It's the opposite of *credible* as in "The priest makes a credible witness."

That said, many dictionaries now recognize the use of *incredible* as acceptable when it is used to mean

"extraordinary" or "astonishing," so I wouldn't worry too much if you use it in that manner, especially in everyday speech or informal writing.

If you want to stick to the original intent, or if you're using the word in formal writing, I'd stay with "impossible to believe" for now, but I'm sure that will change soon.

Indicted (on a charge)

Indicted means "charged."

Interdependent (on each other)

Dictionary.com defines this word as:

---

mutually dependent; depending on each other

Introduced (anew)
Introduced means "to bring something to the attention of others for the first time," so, by definition, it would be new.
Introduced (for the first time)
Same as the previous example.
(Ir)regardless
Ir means "not," and *regardless* means "without regard." It defeats the purpose to combine them. Just use *regardless*.

Despite the fact that some dictionaries now recognize *irregardless* as a word, it is typically listed as nonstandard usage.

While I often say using a word that is *changing* is okay in everyday speech or informal writing, this is one I'd steer clear of. If there comes a time when it is more readily accepted, fine, but for now I wouldn't recommend its use.
ISBN (number)
We've been through similar situations before. The *N* in *ISBN* stands for *number*, so saying "ISBN number" is like saying, "number, number."

I've been harsh on the usage of initialisms like ISBN, VIN, etc., though I shouldn't be. There are still plenty of people who don't know what *ISBN* stands for, and for those people, using *number* afterward helps explain it.

If the person or audience you're addressing is familiar with the word, I'd say don't use *number* along with it, but if you think they may not be familiar, go ahead and use it. It's not the most grievous error.
Join (together)
We've been over this before as well. To join something is to bring it together.
(Joint) collaboration
Collaboration means "to work jointly with others."

- The engineer said, "Let's collaborate on this."
- The peace initiative was a collaboration of three countries.

Kneel (down)

How else would you kneel? Would you kneel up? Or sideways? You don't kneel on the ceiling; you kneel on the floor.

(Knowledgeable) experts

If they're experts, I would hope they're knowledgeable.

LCD (display)

LCD stands for "liquid crystal display." This is more of the same. Acronyms are rife with redundancy.

Later (time)

Later will suffice.

Lift (up)

Where else would you lift something? You wouldn't lift it down.

Made (out) of

There is no need to say "made out of." Simply say "made of," or "made from," or describe it differently—as in "He wore a pair of woolen pants," or "He wore pants made of wool," not "He wore a pair of pants made out of wool."

(Major) breakthrough

A breakthrough *is* major.

- We just had a breakthrough in the fight against cancer.
- We just had a major breakthrough in the fight against cancer.

Meet (with each other)

Meet implies there will be more than one person involved, whether for a lunch, a dinner date, a business meeting, or a chance occurrence. If you tell someone "Let's meet for lunch," there is no need to add "with each other."

(Mental) telepathy

Telepathy is mind reading; therefore it implies *mental*.

Merge (together)
To merge is "to bring together or join."
Might (possibly)
Might is used to express the possibility of.
(Number-one) leader in . . .
If you're the leader, you *are* number one.
(Native) habitat
Again, look at the two definitions:

- Native—the place or environment in which a person was born or a thing came into being.
- Habitat—the natural environment of an organism; the place that is natural for the life and growth of an organism.

(Natural) instinct
Instinct is what you do naturally. If you do something instinctively, you do it without having to give it thought—or *naturally*.
Never (before)
If it was never, then it wasn't before, either.

- I have never gone skydiving.
- I have never before gone skydiving.

(New) innovation
An innovation is new. The dictionary definition follows"

- An innovation is a *new* thing or a *new* method of doing something.

(New) invention
An invention is new. This is a definition from the dictionary:

- Invention is the act of inventing something that has never been made or used before.

In other words—*new*.

Nothing (at all)

If you have *nothing*, you have *nothing*. You don't need to say "at all."

(Number one) leader in . . .

If you're the leader, you are number one.

Off (of)

People say this frequently. "Get off of the couch." No need for *of*. "Get off the couch" will suffice.

(Old) adage

An adage is, by definition, old; in fact, some dictionaries refer to adages as *ancient*.

(Old) cliché

By inference, a cliché, like an adage, is old. It wouldn't be a cliché without having been around for a while.

(Old) custom

Same as *cliché*.

(Old) proverb

Same as *cliché*.

(Open) trench

A trench is a ditch. The word became famous during the trench warfare of WWI; regardless, a trench is open.

Outside (of)

The dog is "outside of" the fence. The cat is *outside* the fence. As you can see, it's the same.

(Over) exaggerate

Exaggerate means "to overstate" or "to stretch the truth." No need to say *over*.

(Overused) cliché

Cliché means *overused*.

(Pair of) twins

Twins are a pair.

According to the dictionary, a *pair* is:

a set of two similar things considered as a unit

And the definition for twins is:

Two people who were born at the same time from the same mother.

Unless you're using "pair of twins" to mean two sets of twins, or four of something, the saying is wrong.

Palm (of the hand)

Where else would the palm be?

(Passing) fad

A fad is short-lived, so it is always passing.

(Past) experience

Experience is in the past. So on your résumé, don't say "past experience." It makes you look foolish. It's simply *experience*.

(Past) history

Same reasoning as *experience*.

(Past) memories

Same reasoning as *experience*.

(Past) records (not as in feats but in record keeping)

Same reasoning as experience. A *record* is something that was recorded, so by definition it is in the past.

Period (of time)

A period is of time. If not, then a period of what?

Technically, a period could be referring to the punctuation mark, but I believe context would clarify that.

(Personal) friend

If they're not a personal friend, whose friend are they?

(Personal) opinion

If it's not a personal opinion, whose opinion is it?

Pick (and choose)

You can either pick something or choose something, but you can't do both.

PIN (number)

Same as ISBN, the *N* stands for *number*. You hear this one all the time. People say "I forgot my PIN number." If you do a Google search, you'll even see results from banks referring to it as a PIN number. They should know better.

Plan (ahead)

Same as "future plans"—plans *are* ahead.

Please RSVP

RSVP means "please respond," though it's of French origin, so I'll forgive you.

(Polar) opposites

You don't need to use *polar*. Saying *opposites* will suffice.

(Positive) identification

If you ID someone, you are positive who it is, as in a fingerprint or dental records or DNA.

Postpone (until later)

To postpone is to put off (until later).

Pouring (down) rain

Which way would it pour? A strong wind may carry it sideways for a while, but it *is* coming down sooner or later.

(Pre)board (as with an airplane)

To *board* (verb) is "to get into" or "get onto," so how can you get on before you get on? That would be like the airline announcing, "Passengers can now get on before they get on."

We know what is meant by *preboard*, but it doesn't make it right just because we know it.

(Pre)record

To record is to write something down or to save the digital (or taped) version of a voice/TV show/song, etc. You can't *pre* record something. That would be doing it before you did it. It would be like saying "Sue, record that song before you record it" or "Tim, write that down before you write it down."

This is the same as *preboard*. We know what is meant, but there is no need to use it.

Present (time)

The present *is* a part of time.

Proof (positive)

Proof means you're positive, as in "The detective had proof she committed the crime."

Protest (against)

A protest is an action or statement against something, like legislation. There is no need to protest *against* something; you simply protest it.

Raise (up)

Raise means "to move to a higher position," so if you don't raise *up*, where do you raise to?

RAM (memory)

Random access memory. The acronym already contains the word *memory*. It's similar to ATM, ISBN, PIN, etc.

Reason is (because)

A reason is "a cause or justification." He did it *because* he was angry. She couldn't go out *because* she felt bad.

Reason (why)

If you can tell me the difference between "What was the reason he did it?" and "Why he did it," I'll concede.

(Regular) routine

A routine is a sequence of actions performed regularly.

- Her routine consisted of stopping for coffee before work.

Revert (back)

If you revert to something, it means you go back.

Rise (up)

Duh.

(Safe) haven

A haven is a safe place. You've never heard of an *unsafe* haven, have you?

(Sand) dune

Dunes are made of sand. Look at the definition:

- A dune is a hill of sand near the ocean or in a desert.

(Serious) danger

Danger is serious.

(Sharp) point

A point is described as the sharp end of a tool, pencil, etc., so there is no need to mention sharp. The degree of sharpness may come into question, but *point* implies something sharp.

Sit (down) or stand (up)

I'm not going to chide people over this usage; however, it isn't needed as much as it's used.

- "Everyone should sit down," the teacher said. "And when class is over, you can stand up."
- "Everyone should sit," the teacher said. "And when class is over, you can stand."

Skipped (over)

You would say "We skipped the commercials," not "We skipped over the commercials." Likewise: "We skipped the boring parts," not "We skipped over the boring parts."

(Slight) edge

I'm not speaking of the edge of a cliff or a sharp edge; I'm referring to when *edge* is used to mean an advantage, and when used in that context, *edge* means *slight* or minor or small. It could even refer to insignificant.

Spell out (in detail)

"Spell out" means to provide detail, similar to the directions below.

- Turn right on Rodney Street, go four blocks, then turn left onto Tenth Street. Continue down Tenth until you intersect with Union Street.

Spliced (together)
Splice means "to join together," as in "He spliced the wires so they would work."

Start (off/out)
Consider the following: "The race started off with a bang" or "The race started with a bang."

(Steady) stream
A *stream* is a steady flow of something.

Sufficient (enough)
Sufficient is enough.

(Sum) total
To sum something is to total it.

Surrounded (on all sides)
Discussed this already.

(Sworn) affidavit
Another redundancy from law enforcement. An *affidavit* is sworn testimony.

(Temper) tantrum
A tantrum is "a fit of temper." It is an uncontrolled outburst.

Three a.m. (in the morning)
There is no need to say "in the morning" as a.m. is the morning.

(Three-way) love triangle
A triangle has three sides. There should be no reason to remind people of that. "Love triangle" says it all.

Time (period)
Talked about this.

(Total) destruction
See (completely) destroyed. Destruction is total.

(True) facts
By definition, facts are true—that's why they're called facts.

(Truly) sincere

Sincere is true.

(Two equal) halves

If a half weren't equal, it wouldn't be a half.

Tuna (fish)

A tuna is a fish. Is this to distinguish it from *tuna cow* or *tuna fowl.* We don't say *chicken fowl nuggets.*

Twelve noon or midnight

Noon and midnight mean at twelve o'clock: midnight and midday.

Ultimate goal

Some people claim a goal is your ultimate objective, but that's not always the case. You could have intermediate goals or goals occurring at any point of progress.

(Underground) subway

A subway is underground. The ones above ground are called *els*, or "surface trains." Here's the definition:

- A subway is an underground railroad.

(Unexpected) emergency

I think it's apparent an emergency would be unexpected. If you knew it was coming, you could prepare for it and it wouldn't be an emergency.

(Unexpected) surprise

Same reasoning as the previous example.

UPC (code)

Same as before. *Code* is included in the initialism.

(Usual) custom

A custom is usual.

(Very) pregnant

Don't make me laugh.

(Very) unique

Don't make me cry.

Visible (to the eye)

I prefer things that are visible to the ear or nose.

(Wall) mural

Since the definition of *mural* indicates location, what else would it be?

Warn (in advance)

If you warn someone, it is in advance of it happening.

A NOTE ON *PRE*

I have my preferences on *pre* and when to use it. I tend not to use it with verbs—words that denote action, such as: *preorder*, *preboard*, *prerecord*, etc. I do, however, use it with nouns or events and points in time: *presale*, *prewar*, *pre-Caesar*, etc.

Redundancies that may not be redundancies

I've seen some people list redundancies that may not qualify, depending on the circumstances. I'll give a few examples.

- boiling hot
- freezing cold

Explanations I've seen are "If it's boiling, it's hot," and "If it's freezing, it's cold."

But *boiling* and *freezing* can just as easily be adjectives explaining to what degree something is hot or cold; in other words, it's not just cold, it's freezing cold—so cold things can freeze. Or it's not just hot, it's boiling hot—hot enough to boil water.

Before you claim something is a redundancy, make certain it is.

On the other hand, if words like that are used simply to express that it's hot or cold, then they are, in fact, redundancies.

Arm's reach

A person's reach is how far their arm will go. *Reach* can mean other things though, so I don't consider this a severe redundancy because I see *arm* as defining the type of reach.

Reach can also mean communicate with, as in "The counselor was able to *reach* the teenager."

Reach can mean "the reach of the law."

Reach can also be interpreted as influence, as in "The crime lord has a long *reach*."

In the last example, you could be referring to the length of his reach, as in *arm's reach,* or you could mean his *influence* carries a long way.

MISUSED WORDS

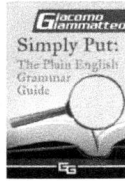

Read ten books and you're bound to find one or two with misused words. Read ten social media posts or blogs, and the number of misused words increases substantially.

English is a difficult language, and it's easy to mix things up, especially if you are in a hurry. That said, my hope is that this section will help prevent some of these issues.

This section deals with misused words. It doesn't cover everything, but it does include the most common offenders and even some of the lesser ones.

Chapter Sixty-Eight

MISUSED WORDS

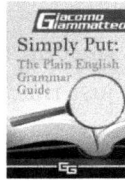

*M*isusing words when you speak may give others an impression you probably don't want to give.

Misusing words when you write is even worse because it's permanent. Someone might forget what you said, but if it's written, well . . . it's there to refer to forever. With that in mind, let's try to get it straight.

Don't get me wrong. I'm not here to tell you how to write. I have a difficult enough time myself.

When I send a manuscript to my editor, I get it back with more editing marks than you can imagine.

So what is my goal? To see if I can help even *one* person improve their writing or speech enough for them to be happy with it. If I sell a few books in the process, my animals will be happy. (All proceeds go to the animals on my sanctuary.)

The misused words section—which consists mostly of misused words you'd encounter in everyday life, covers more than two hundred everyday misused words, quite a few of them in business use.

Let's face it, the last thing you want anywhere—but especially in business writing—is to have the meaning of your words taken the wrong way. Whether you write cover letters, résumés, business proposals, or only emails to colleagues, you should learn to do it right.

It's a sin, but if you read enough blogs (and you know what you're looking for), you'll see hundreds—if not thousands—of mistakes every week. I have even caught grievous errors on grammar sites.

If you're going to write about grammar, you should make all efforts to get it right. I would never think of correcting someone's grammar in public, and yet one of the few TV shows I watch features a character who does just that. I wouldn't object, except he himself makes grammar mistakes—obvious ones.

My theory is that if you're going to have a character correct grammar, he'd better damn well be free of grammar mistakes.

Another note.

I thought about using definitions from dictionaries, but half of them I couldn't understand, so I've tried to make my own definitions. I hope that works out okay.

In some cases, quotes of famous people were used. I got these from Brainy Quote, which can be found here: http://www.brainyquote.com

Vocabulary

Depending upon which study you read, the average person has a vocabulary of somewhere between 8,000 and 20,000 words. The writing vocabulary would be slightly less. Let's assume for a minute that we're talking the lower end of this—say 7,500 words. That's still a lot of words to remember or to mix up. But this list constitutes the majority of the mixed-up and misused words in every day everyday usage.

By the way, I'm speaking of unique words, not plurals (like counting *sing* and *sings* as two words) or even other variants like *threw* and *thrown*.

Without further ado, let's get started.

Words:

A/an

A mistake I often see is the misuse of the indefinite articles *a* and *an*. The rules are simple, yet people often get them confused.

You use *a* in front of a word beginning with a consonant sound, regardless of spelling, so it would be a fox, a dog, a university (the *u* makes a *y* sound), and yes, it would be *a* historic event. (historic is pronounced with an *h* sound, though with British English it's pronounced differently.)

You use *an* in front of words beginning with a vowel sound, regardless of spelling. It would be an elephant, an ostrich, an antelope, and an honor. (in the word honor, the *h* is not pronounced.) Words beginning with *h* and *u* are the ones that confuse most people.

Acronyms are treated the same way as regular words. Go with the initial *sound* not letter. Look at the following:

- He was *a* CIA agent.
- He worked as *an* FBI agent before that.
- She worked as *a* U.K. translator.
- He bought *an* LCD with his poker winnings.

A la mode/à la mode

In English, this means *with ice cream*, an apparent reference to a time when ice cream on pie was the fashionable way to eat it, but in its day it meant much more than ice cream. Now, you'd be looked at oddly if you tried to use it that way.

A lot/alot/allot

This is an easy one. *Alot* is *not* a word. It is *always a lot,* spelled as separate words.

Allot is a different word, a verb meaning "to distribute, to mete out." It is spelled with two *l*'s.

A while/awhile

This distinction is primarily a usage problem. When used as a noun phrase—*a while*—it typically follows a preposition.

Example: "I think I'll stay for *a while*."

When it is used as an adverb it takes the one-word format and follows verbs, *never a preposition.*

Example: "If it's all right with you, I'll stay *awhile.*"

🖐 If the word you're looking for follows a preposition, such as *after, for, in* . . . use the two-word format, *a while.* If it follows a verb, use *awhile.*

Abjure/adjure

Unless you write historical fiction or fantasy, I doubt you'll have much use for either of these words, but just in case . . .

Abjure: to renounce or give up under oath

- After the wizard lost his powers, he abjured all titles or claims to power, choosing to hide out in a remote mountain village.

Adjure: to command sincerely; to make a person swear an oath or threaten them with harm to do something

- During the Spanish Inquisition, the interrogators adjured the people to swear to the truth under penalty of death.

Accede/exceed

Accede: "to agree or approve of something." It can also mean "to assume an office or title."

Note*:* accede is usually followed by the word *to.*

Exceed: "to excel or be greater than." On a résumé, you may see this under the accomplishments section—sales *exceeded* quota for region by forty-five percent.

🖐 Try to think of *exceed* as excelling. They both begin with *ex.*

Accept/except

Accept: to receive a gift, to agree, accept an invitation, accept your responsibilities, accept a package

- I have *accepted* the fact that everyone is incompetent —*except* me.

- I *accepted* responsibility for doing the project; no one else was doing it right.

"We must accept finite disappointment, but never lose infinite hope."

— - MARTIN LUTHER KING, JR.

Except: exclusion (in most cases, you could substitute *but* for *except*.)

- All the soldiers, *except* one, died at the Alamo.
- I would go to Italy, *except* I have no money.

Try to remember that *accept* is associated with *agree*, like if your spouse tells you it was your fault and you wisely say "Okay, I *accept* that." *Agree* and *accept* both begin with *a*.

And *except* means exclusion. Both begin with *ex*, same as *exceed*.

Accidently/accidentally

This mix-up is simply a spelling error. *Accidently* is not a word, it's simply how many people mispronounce and misspell *accidentally*.

Accommodate

This is another spelling mix-up. Many people spell it with one *m*. The easy way to remember this is that both *c* and *m* are doubled.

Acute/chronic

Many people use *acute* and *chronic* interchangeably, but they have distinctly different meanings.

Acute means "sharp," but when used as in "an acute care center," it describes where you might take your child for an emergency.

- If you smash your finger with a hammer, it will cause acute pain.

Chronic, on the other hand, means "long-term," as in "He suffered from chronic fatigue (long-term fatigue)." Or chronic back pain or chronic indigestion.

🖐 You may start out with chronic bronchitis and have a chronic cough, but the cough may cause you to break a rib, which would bring acute pain.

Acute can also mean other things, such as "the measurement of an angle less than ninety degrees," or "keen intellectual perception" (especially of subtle distinctions), or acute hearing—"the ability to distinguish the slightest sounds."

Ad/add

An *ad* is an advertisement and to *add* is to increase in number or find the sum of—like adding a room to your house or adding items to the grocery list.

🖐 This one is simple to remember. The one with two *d's* is the one that means to increase in number—you've *added* a *d*.

Adapt/adept/adopt

I *adopted* a policy of flexibility long ago, and as a result, I am *adept* at *adapting* to almost any situation.

Adapt: to change things; to learn to live with changes in life

- My grandfather, who was from Italy, had to learn to *adapt* to the new lifestyle he *adopted*.

Adept: an expert, a skilled person.

- The guy with the silk suit was an *adept* card player. He was *adept* at manipulating cards.

Adopt: to choose or take on as your own.

- The newlyweds couldn't have children, so they *adopted* a baby. The baby was *adopted*.

🐾 This is also an easy one. Look at the middle vowels in the three words: "a, e, and o."

Adapt has an *a*, think of *adjust.*

Adept has an *e,* think of *expert.*

Adopt has an *o,* think of *orphan.*

"Intelligence is the ability to adapt to change."

— ˜ STEPHEN HAWKING

Adverse/averse

- I am *averse to adverse* reactions.

Aside from the pharmaceutical company ads, where they mention over and over and over again the *adverse* effects you might experience from taking their drugs, not many people use these words. And that is why it's even more important that you get them right. If there's anything worse than using two-dollar words when they're not needed, it's using two-dollar words the wrong way.

Adverse is an adjective meaning "unfavorable," like the above example of an adverse reactions to drugs. Or perhaps you went hiking and a storm moved in, presenting you with adverse conditions, as in "The storm presented us with adverse conditions on Mount Shasta."

Averse means opposed to or against. On a résumé, you may see someone say they are not *averse to* rolling up their sleeves or not *averse* to doing hands-on work.

🐾 Try to remember an *adverse* reaction to drugs, and that both drugs and *adverse* contain the letter *d.*

🐾 And in almost every case, *averse* is followed by the word *to.* I can't think of a case where *adverse* would be followed by *to.* Also, think of *averse* as having a similar meaning to *against,* as in I'm not *against* rolling up my sleeves.

"I'm not *averse* to helping Wall Street when it helps Main Street."

— - BEN NELSON

Adherence/adherents

Adherence: "the act of adhering or showing allegiance," as in adherence to a political party; or "stick to," as in "Adhere to the letter of the law."

Adherents: things that stick or people who uphold a faction.

- Glue is an *adherent.*
- The GOP has strong *adherents.*

Advice/advise

- I *advise* you to take my *advice.*

- The headhunter *advised* Jane to take the job offer, but she ignored his *advice* and stayed where she was. She regretted it.

Advice is a noun and normally reflects someone's opinion or suggestion. *Advice* is something you give (or take).

Advise is a verb and represents the giving of *advice.* You may find this in a résumé listed as "advised board on strategy for acquisition candidates."

Advise is something you *do.*

🐟 You give or take *advice* and you *advise* someone.

When your mother asks, "Do you want a piece of advice?" it is a mere formality. It doesn't matter if you answer yes or no. You're going to get it anyway.

— ~ ERMA BOMBECK

"I have found the best way to give *advice* to your children is to find out what they want and then *advise* them to do it."

— HARRY S. TRUMAN

Affect/effect These words are often confused because both of them can function as nouns and verbs.

Affect as a verb means to have an influence on or to stir or move.

- The company layoffs *affected* the morale of the employees.
- The president's speech on foreign policy *affected* the listeners, stirring emotions.

Affect is seldom used as a noun.

Effect as a noun means "the result of something" or "the consequence of some action." (The *effect* of the layoff was a drop in morale.)

Effect as a verb means "to bring about." The president's speech *effected* a change in policy.

Although these words can both function as nouns or verbs, and both share the *influence* meaning, there is a way to get it right *most* of the time.

Affect is almost always used in the verb form, so think of *action*, which also starts with an *A*.

Effect is typically used in the noun form. Think of the *end result*. (even though "end result" is redundant.)

'To *affect* the quality of the day, that is the highest of arts.'

— - HENRY DAVID THOREAU

Affluent/effluent

Affluent: wealthy, rich, materially successful

- The newly promoted vice president dropped his former friends; he now traveled in *affluent* circles.

Effluent: An outflow or discharge of liquid waste, as from a sewage system, factory, or nuclear plant.
From Dictionary.com:

- "Sludge is the dirt that remains when sewage is cleaned into effluent."

You may think *affluent* and *effluent* are the same—and sometimes they may be—but there *is* a difference.

When you think of *affluent*, think of an *abundance* of wealth, and when you think of *effluent*, think of *excrement*. It's a crude example, but it works.

"Unfortunately, our affluent society has also been an effluent society."

— - HUBERT H. HUMPHREY

Afterward/afterwards

This rule applies to *afterward*, *anyway*, *backward*, *forward*, *onward*, *toward*, *untoward*, and all the others. It is *afterward*—no *s*. Using the *s* is appropriate in the United Kingdom, but the U.S. preference is no *s*.

When you're writing, check it *afterward* and remove the trailing *s* on each of the words.

On a side note, so many people use *backwards, forwards, towards*, etc., that I imagine it won't be long before they're accepted as normal usage.

Aid/aide/ade

- The politician, along with his *aide, aided* the sick and injured, by giving them *ade*.

Aid means to provide help or assistance.
Aide is an assistant or a helper like *the general's aide*.
Ade is a fruity drink like a lemonade.

Try to remember that the difference between *aid* and *aide* is that the one with the *e* is an employee, a person. The confusion comes because the past tense of *aid* is aided. Also remember that *ade* is just like lemon*ade*.

Aline or align

I'm glad we got an easy one. *Aline* is not a recommended word; it is simply a variant of *align*, which means "to form a line," or "make a line," or "straighten objects into a line," as in "Align those pictures, please. They don't look good that way."

All together/altogether

Altogether is an adverb. It means "entirely" or "completely."

- The Wi-Fi service went out *altogether* (went out completely).

All together is a phrase that means "in a group."

- Mrs. Johnson's fifth-grade class sang all together.
- Mrs. Johnson's fifth-grade class all sang together.

🖐 If you can replace *altogether* with *completely* or *utterly* without losing any meaning, then you are probably using the right word. And note that *all together* can be separated in the sentence and not lose its meaning, as in the example above.

"If I play hard to get, soon the phone stops ringing *altogether*."

— - MASON COOLEY

Allude/elude

Allude means "to refer to indirectly" or "make an indirect reference."

Elude means "to avoid or escape by cleverness, trickery, speed."

- The psychiatrist *alluded* to the man's cleverness, but the detective didn't listen until the man *eluded* him.

🖐 Try to remember that *elude* and *escape* both begin with the letter *e*.

"If you want something, it will elude you. If you do not want something, you will get ten of it in the mail."

— - ANNA QUINDLEN

Note: Along with these two words, when they appear as *allusion/elusion*, we can also add the word *illusion* to the mix. An *illusion* is a false perception of reality.

- Magicians use *illusion* to their advantage; in fact, much of their act depends on *illusion*.

Aloud/allowed

- First he thought it, and then he said it *aloud:* "Smoking is not *allowed* on campus."

Aloud means "to speak out loud."
Allowed has many meanings, but the majority of usage deals with permission or making provisions for.

- We run an animal sanctuary, but we don't *allow* the animals in certain parts of our house.
- Monica's schedule was tight, but she *allowed* herself a half hour a day for reading.

🔊 The easiest way to remember this is that *aloud* contains the word *loud*.

"A child who is *allowed* to be disrespectful to his parents will not have true respect for anyone."

— - BILLY GRAHAM

Already/all ready

- Are you *all ready*? Because we're *already* late.

Already is an adverb. It means "prior to, or "previously," or "so soon." It almost always implies time.

- Bob got to the meeting five minutes early, but his boss

was *already* there.

All ready is a phrase that means you are prepared.

🔸 Remember that *all ready* consists of two words, and the phrase *all ready* often refers to more than one person. If it's just you, there's no need to say I'm *all ready* to go, you'd say I'm ready to go. (or you should say that.)

"There cannot be a crisis next week. My schedule is *already* full."

— - HENRY A. KISSINGER

Alright/all right

Some people still think that *alright* is *all right*, but the majority of grammarians think that using *alright* is similar to using *ain't*.

Others disagree, and *alright* is listed in most dictionaries as acceptable, but when consulting the *AP Stylebook*, its advice is, never use *alright*.

Even though it is becoming more accepted as a standard word, why bother? My suggestion is to use *all right*.

🔸 When you're thinking of which word to use, remember that *alright* ain't *all right*.

It is *all right* for the lion and the lamb to lie down together if they are both asleep, but if one of them begins to get active, it is dangerous.

— - CRYSTAL EASTMAN

Note: I have to say, when researching the quotes for this one, the majority of quotes were by people who used *alright* and not *all right*. (What a shame!)

That said, while I may agree that *alright* is not *all right*, it doesn't change the fact that more and more people are using it in everyday speech as well as informal writing.

Altar/alter

Altar is a noun, meaning "a table, structure, platform, etc., . . . used for religious rites."

- The groom got nervous and the bride was left at the *altar*.

Alter is a verb, meaning "to change or make different. To modify in some way."

- The tailor rushed to *alter* the groom's tuxedo.

- You can *alter* the document by clicking the Edit button.

The second vowel in the words are *e* and *a*. Remember that *altar* and aisle both have an *a* and that *alter* and *edit* both contain *e*'s.

"Human beings can *alter* their lives by *altering* their attitudes of mind."

— - WILLIAM JAMES

"I have sworn upon the *altar* of God, eternal hostility against every form of tyranny over the mind of man."

— - THOMAS JEFFERSON

Altercation

A quick note about the word *altercation*. I have seen many writers use it to mean a physical fight, but its definition is:

a heated or angry dispute; a noisy argument or controversy."

It has been misused so often it is in danger of becoming standard, and I blame the continual misuse of the word on TV shows more than anything.

Example:

- My wife and I have had many *altercations*, but we've never laid a hand on one another.*

* I know that some people may think the using "on another" instead of "each other" is wrong, but it's fine, and I preferred it that way in this circumstance. See the notes in "Part of Speech."

Alternate/alternative

Alternate can function as a verb, an adjective, or a noun.

- A person suffering from bipolar disease might *alternate* between highs and lows.
- A chessboard has *alternate* black and white squares.
- An understudy for a Broadway play might get their big break if they are the *alternate*, and they have to fill in for the star one night.

Alternative can function as a noun or adjective. The definition is "being one of a number of possible choices."

- If you don't like buying books from Amazon, you have plenty of *alternatives.*
- When diagnosed with cancer, my friend looked for *alternative* treatments.
- If the freeway has an accident on it, try *alternative* routes (not *alternate* routes).

Try to think of *alternate* as a back and forth between two things, as in the examples above: highs and lows, black and white, and understudy and star.

On the other hand, *alternative* deals with multiple options: all of Amazon's competitors, multiple choices for treatment, many options on which roads to take.

The way to remember it is that *alternate* usually deals with two, and it is a shorter word than *alternative*, which usually deals with multiple options.

"For every failure, there's an *alternative* course of action. You just have to find it. When you come to a roadblock, take a detour."

— - MARY KAY ASH

Amused/bemused

Amuse is a verb meaning to entertain, or cause laughter.

Bemuse is a verb meaning to bewilder or confuse someone.

- The king was *amused* when his court was *bemused.*

Remember that *bemuse* means to *bewilder* and both start with *be.*

You shouldn't have to worry too much about this as the word *bemused* is seldom used.

Among/between

- As he prepared to address the crowd, the politician leaned toward his aide and said, "*Between* you and me, there is a spy *among* our group."

The long-standing myth has been that *between* was to be used only for choices of two items or people, and *among* when there were more than two.

That's not the case. You can learn more about usage in "Grammar Myths" in the "Between and Among" chapter.

Note: And yes, for any of you wondering, the correct form is "between you and me," not "between you and I."

Amoral/immoral

Some people live normal lives but are still judged immoral, while others embrace religion to conceal their amoral philosophy. *Amoral* means "having no moral standards." An amoral person might be indifferent to the fact that his neighbor is a thief.

Immoral means not conforming to the norm. An *immoral* person might aspire to becoming a thief.

🐦 An *amoral* person has no standards, and an *immoral* one has bad standards.

"About morals, I know only that what is moral is what you feel good after and what is *immoral* is what you feel bad after."

— ~ ERNEST HEMINGWAY

Anticipate/expect

Anticipate and *expect* are often used interchangeably, but there is a subtle difference. *Anticipate* means almost the same thing as *expect* except that *anticipate* carries with it the notion of preparation, as in

"He anticipated the storm and had sandbags on hand in case of flooding."

If you do nothing to prepare for it, you might say "He expected the storm to strike by noon, but he didn't do a thing about it." Another example might be:

- She anticipated the car ahead of her swerving, so she switched lanes to avoid hitting it.

Anxious/eager Some people use anxious and eager as if they were the same word. It is becoming more acceptable in common usage (which is a damn shame), but there *are* differences, meaningful differences. See the full text under the "Usage" section in the "Anxious and Eager" chapter.

Any time/anytime

Anytime is an adverb.

Any time is used as two words and can be an adverbial phrase or an adjective—*any* modifying a noun *time*.

Example:

- I like restaurants that serve breakfast at *any time* of day.
- Considering the state of the economy, it's doubtful I'll be finding a job *anytime* soon.

Any one/anyone

Anyone is a term meaning any person.

Any one as the two-word form means one specific person.

Example:

- In this day and age, *anyone* might be a spy.
- *Any one* of your friends might be a traitor.

Any way/anyway/anyways

If you used to watch the TV show, *NYPD Blue*, you probably

thought *anyways* was a word. It isn't. The word is *anyway*—without the *s*.

Suppose you're interrupted in the middle of telling a story. In that case, you might continue by starting with the phrase, *anyway*, . . . as in "*A*nyway, as we were driving to Dallas . . ."

Any way means, "in any manner."

- "Get it done *any way* you can," the frustrated teacher told his students.
- We were late for the movie, but we bought the tickets *anyway*.

Appraise/apprise

Appraise is "to estimate the price or value of" or "to assess or make a judgment about." A real-estate appraiser estimates the value of your house. A jeweler might appraise your jewelry collection.

- Napoleon was renowned for being able to *appraise* his enemies' strength with little more than a glance.

Apprise is "to give notice or inform."

- When they arrested us, the police *apprised* us of our rights.

🔊 *Appraise* has the word *raise* in it. *Raise* can be closely associated with value or price.

Are/our/hour

Are and *our* (and even *hour*) are often mixed up—and not just by English-as-a-second-language learners. It may stem from the way many people pronounce the words, though if done properly, there is a distinct difference.

Anyway, to get into the differences, *are* is a present tense form of the verb "to be." I don't like using grammar to explain grammar, so let's try a few examples.

- We *are* going to the mall.
- You *are* her cousin.
- *Are* you coming with us? (It's pronounced similar to the letter *r.*)

Our is a possessive. It is used to indicate ownership:

- That is *our* car.
- We just purchased *our* first house.
- You are *our* friend.

Hour is a measurement of time equaling sixty minutes. It is pronounced the same as *our.*

The easy way to remember this is that *our*, the word beginning with *o* means ownership.

Ascent/assent

Ascent is to climb, go up, advance in status.

- Her *ascent* into high society was a foregone conclusion.

Assent: "agree to, concur."

- The bride's father *assented* to the marriage.

- Obama gave his *assent* to put more troops in the Middle East. (You could also say "Obama put more troops in the Middle East.")

"Do not despise the bottom rungs in the *ascent* to greatness."

— - PULILIUS SYRIUS

🐟 Remember that *ascent,* the word with the letter *c,* means to climb.

Assault and battery

Assault and battery is another entry similar to *altercation.* Movies and TV often give the wrong impression. *Assault* usually implies physical contact and the attempt to harm, but that's not necessarily so. *Assault* (in legal terms) means to *threaten* to harm or do violence. An example may be pointing a gun at someone. It's not considered *assault and battery* unless you physically touch the person.

Assume/presume

Assume: Means to take for granted or to take on a duty or a persona.

- He *assumed* they would finish the project on time (took for granted).
- He *assumed* the role as head of the family when his father passed away (took on as a duty).
- In mythological tales, the gods often *assumed* human forms (took on).

Presume (verb) means "to *assume* something is true."

- He *presumed* the project was completed because everyone went home early.
- A defendant is *presumed* innocent until proven guilty.

Note: *Assume* and *presume* are close in meaning, but *presume* comes with a stronger conviction.

"I shall *assume* that your silence gives consent."

— ‑ PLATO

🪶 Remember that *presume* is the stronger of the two, and that if you *assume*, you may make an ass of yourself. The old saying is: If you *assume*, you make an ass of *u* and *me*.

Assure/ensure/insure

These words are frequently found on résumés and in business writing. They have the general meaning of making the outcome of a particular circumstance certain; however, there *are* distinct differences.

Assure is typically used to *assure* someone/or some living thing of an outcome. An assurance is similar to a promise.

- He *assured* his boss the project would be done on time and under budget.

Ensure is used more for things than people.

- To *ensure* the project gets done on time, you hire more people and secure additional resources.

Insure, in its pure form, refers to money or insurance.

- I *insured* the project for $10 million in case of accidents.

🪶 *Assure* is used for people. (You can make an *ass* of yourself if you promise your boss something and don't deliver.)

Ensure is used for things.

Insure deals with money/insurance.

Attaché

Attaché means "someone who's attached"; it's a person assigned to a diplomatic post or a military attaché.

Attain/obtain

Obtain—"get something, an object, something physical."

Attain—"to reach a goal, to put effort into acquiring something abstract."

- He *attained* moral superiority.
- She *attained* her goal of becoming a vice president by age thirty.

I've seen disagreement on the finer definitions of these words. Some state that *obtain* means "to acquire through effort," but you can *obtain* anything in any manner. You might *obtain* a bottle of beer or a pack of cigarettes by buying it, yet it seems as if you must *attain* something (usually abstract) through hard work.

🍃 Remember that *obtain* usually refers to an object and that both begin with *ob*. On the other hand, *attain* usually refers to something abstract and both begin with *a*.

Attendance/attendants

The primary use of *attendant* is as a noun, meaning one who waits on another, or one who is present. The parking *attendants* were all females.

Attendance is also a noun, but it doesn't refer to a person. An example would be: "Class *attendance* was at a record level."

🍃 The best way to remember the difference is that *attendance* has the letter *c* in it. Remember "class attendance."

🍃: Also, an *attendant* almost always deals with a person. Try to remember *female* parking *attendants,* and it might help.

Attorney/lawyer

Again, although these words are often used interchangeabley, there are differences.

A *lawyer* is someone who is licensed to practice law in a courty system (usually licensed by a state).

An *attorney* while they may be a lawyer, its' not necessarily so. An attorney is simply somone who is empowered to act for another. An example may be if you give your accountant *power of attorney* to represenet you against the IRS. Or if you give your spouse *power of attorney* to make decisions regarding your well being in case of an emergency.

If you have a license to practice law, you may be referred to as an *attorney at law.*

Auger/augur

An *auger* is a tool used to drill or bore holes. It can also be used as a verb, meaning "to drill or bore."

- I have an *auger* on the back of my tractor. It's how I drill holes for fence posts.

Augur—as a noun, "a seer or prophet." As a verb, "to make predictions, usually from omens or signs."

- In ancient times, *augurs* were often consulted before important decisions were made.

Remember that an *augur* can be a person and that an *auger* is a tool. So, you consult an *augur* and use an *auger*.

Avenge/revenge

Avenge usually means "to inflict punishment" or "to mete out justice in retribution."

- He *avenged* his son's murder by getting the killer convicted and sentenced to death.

Revenge means "to take vengeance or retaliate for injuries or wrongs that were either real or that you thought were real."

- He committed murder to take *revenge* for his son's death.

Note: The best explanation for the distinction between the two is the quote by Samuel Johnson:

"Revenge is an act of passion; vengeance of justice. Injuries are revenged; crimes are avenged."

— - SAMUEL JOHNSON

Average/mean

You often see reports (especially when dealing with real estate) that talk about *average,* or *mean* selling price, and *median ranges,* etc., Quite often, I think they are worded that way to confuse people. When discussing mathematical terms, *average* and *mean* are the same.

If you have five or fifteen or ninety numbers in a group, add them up and divide by the number of items: 6 + 9 + 33 + 55 + 77 = 180, then divide by the number of items (5) and you get: 180/5=> 36. So the *average* or *mean* is 36.

Ax/axe

I don't think anyone will mistake what you mean whether you write *ax* or *axe*; however, the first choice in most dictionaries is *ax* (without the *e*), and though it used to be predominant in American usage, Google's Ngram search results (next page) show that *axe* with the *e* has been, and continues to be, more popular.

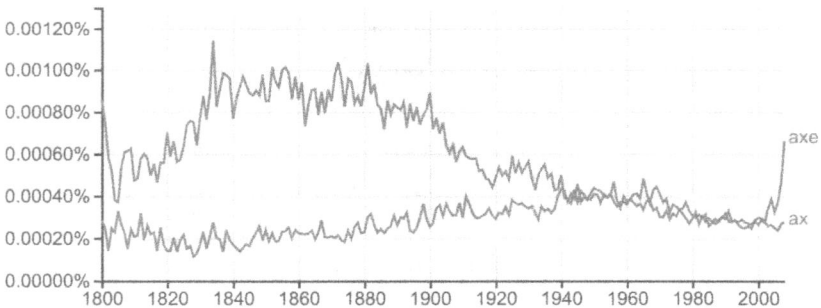

Backward/backwards

This is an easy one to remember. In the United States, you always use *backward*, without the *s*. In the United Kingdom, you use backwards. (It's like all the other *ard* words—*afterward, forward, inward, onward, toward,* etc.)

Bad/badly

Bad is almost always an adjective, but the confusion comes from people thinking it is sometimes used erroneously when combined with *feel*, as in "Ever since I got this cold, I've been feeling bad."

Most everyone thinks that sentence should read, ". . . feeling badly." The reason it is *bad* is because the word *feeling,* in that context, is a linking verb, which means the adjective—bad—is modifying the subject, not the verb. The same reasoning applies to "I feel good."

Baited/bated

Baited—you can bait a trap or a (fishing) hook, or you can bait a person into a fight or into doing something illegal (or anything a person wouldn't ordinarily do).

- She relentlessly *baited* him until he finally broke the law.

Bated—"to lessen the force or intensity of."

✅ He waited with *bated* breath

❌ He waited with *baited* breath.

🔊 Remember that *baited* has the word *bait* in it, and you use bait to catch an animal or set a trap.

Band/banned

This is easy.

Band is "a group of people or animals or things functioning together, like a musical group."

Banned means "to be barred or prohibited."

🔊 Remember that *banned* is similar to *canned* and in most cases if you're *canned* from a job, you're *banned* from the premises.

🔊 Also remember that if you enjoyed the performance, you would give the *band* a *hand*.

Bare/bear

Bare means "without clothing or naked." It can also refer to the *bare* walls, etc.

It also means "to reveal," as in "The woman *bared* her soul to the psychiatrist."

Bear

There are far too many definitions to list, but I've listed a few of the more common ones.

As a verb, it means "to stay firm," as in "He could not bear the financial burden." (He could not stand it, could not weather the storm.)

Or "to bring forth," as in to bear a child, as in "She would eventually come to bear three children. A tree bears fruit.

As a noun, a bear, as in a black bear or a polar bear.

- (The *bear* was huge; it weighed 1,500 lbs.

This is a crude way to remember it, but it works. With *bare*, the *a* comes before *e* and means naked. Think of your ass being exposed (*a* before *e*).

With *bear*, the *e* comes before the *a*. Think of a hungry bear eating your ass (*e* before *a*).

Teachers might not be able to use that tip for their students, but for the rest of us, it works.

Bazaar/bizarre

A *bazaar* is a place where goods are offered for sale (often outdoors).

- The church organized a *bazaar* to raise money for the homeless.

Bizarre means "unusual or not ordinary."

- Her lip piercings, combined with her red-and-blue hair, presented a *bizarre* sight.

Remember that *bazaar* has an *a* in it and so does *fair*. And *bizarre* has an *e* and an *i* and so does *weird*.

Berth/birth

Berth: a bunk or place to sleep on a ship or a train.

Birth: giving birth to something, a new baby or animal, even to something inanimate: "He gave birth to an idea."

Beside/besides

Beside: "alongside, next to," as in "She sat *beside* me on the bus" or "I sat *beside* her at the speech/movies/theater," etc.

Besides: "also, furthermore, in addition to," etc.

- We're going to the wedding because we accepted the invitation; *besides*, I'm the best man.
- *Besides* the towels, bring an umbrella.

Bit/bitten

I overheard a friend of mine say that his daughter was bit by a dog the other day. It's a shame that the dog bit her, but she wasn't *bit*; she was *bitten*.

Without getting too technical, *bit* is the simple past tense, and *bitten* is the past participle and is used with an auxiliary verb, i.e., a helping verb. (Note that my intentional use of *i.e.* was to demonstrate that an auxiliary verb and helping verb are the same.) Examples might better serve the point.

- The dog *bit* her.

But . . .

- She *was bitten* by the dog.

If there is a helping verb in the sentence, the word you are probably looking for is *bitten*. You can get a full list of helping verbs at Wikipedia.com or in the "Parts of Speech" section under "Verbs."

Blond/blonde

Blonde: "A golden, or yellowish-brown color"

As an adjective, it is used to describe a person, as in the often seen and heard phrase—"The blonde bombshell."

As a noun, it refers to a person who has such color hair, such as the sexist phrase, the "dumb blonde."

Since English doesn't use word-endings to distinguish the male/female attributes of a word—as in blond/blonde or brunet/brunette—the distinction between the versions soon got lost.

It is generally preferred to use *blonde* as a female noun, and *blond* as its male counterpart; however, *blond,* when used as an adjective, is often found used for both genders (especially in the United States.), and no one seems to make a fuss about it.

- He has *blond* hair, or he is a *blond.*
- She has *blonde* hair, or she is a *blonde.*

Some people refuse to give up the *e* when using blonde as a female noun or adjective. For the time being, I don't think it matters.

🖐 Remember the word with the *e* refers to *her,* which also has an *e.*

Board/bored

A piece of lumber used for many purposes, such as building a house, deck, or tree fort. Board can also refer to something used for display purposes, as in "The teacher wrote lessons on the (black)board."

Bored:

Bored can mean different things that aren't closely related. In one sense, it means "to drill a hole through something," as in "The carpenter bored a hole through the 4 x 4 post."

It can also mean to become *disinterested*, as in "We went to the movie, but it bored us."

🖐 Try to remember that *board* contains the word *oar* and both are made from wood.

🖐 *Bored* contains the word *ore*, and you *bore* through the ground to get *ore.*

Boarder/border

Boarder: "a person who rents a room or a place to stay (with or without meals)."

- *Boarders* were more popular years ago, and people liked it as it helped to pay the bills.

Border: "the edge of something, the outer rim."

- The *border* between the United States and Canada is not well protected.
- It is a *borderless* TV.
- The Rio Grande forms the *border* between Texas and Mexico.

🐗 Try to remember that *boarders* organize things and *border* contains the word *order*.

Bore/boar/boor

Bore: as a noun it means "a person that is dull or tedious." As a verb it means "to drill through." It can also be the past tense of *bear,* as in "She *bore* three children."

Boar: a wild boar; also refers to adult males of several mammals.

- My buddy Dennis is a wild *boar*.
- I use a wild *boar* image for tips.

Boor: a crass person with no manners.

🐗 Remember that you drill through *ore* and that *ore* is contained in *bore* (which means to drill).

Born/borne

Born: "to be birthed or brought into existence."

- The baby was *born* out of wedlock.

Borne: "transmitted by," as in "Malaria is a mosquito-borne disease." (Used in this sense, *borne* is part of a hyphenated word.)

Borrow/lend/loan

Borrow: Means "to ask for something with the understanding that you will return *it* (or something of equal value), as in "Let me *borrow* your car for the day. I'll bring it back tomorrow.""

It can also mean to *borrow* or *use* something abstract, as in "I *borrowed* your idea for remodeling the kitchen."

Lend: Lend is the opposite of *borrow*. You borrow *from* and lend *to*. An example might be:

- I'm going to *lend* him five hundred dollars.
- I *lent* (past tense) him my car.

Loan: Loan should not be used as a verb. You don't *loan* someone money. You may provide a *loan,* but that's a different story (and usually a bad idea).

👈 Remember that *loan* is not a verb. You don't *loan* someone money, but if they *lend* it to you, or if you *borrow* it from them, that constitutes a *loan.*

👈 Remember that you *lend to* and *borrow from*. You can't *borrow to* a neighbor or *lend from* a friend.

Both/either

These are words that are overused—similar to had and that but in a different respect. It is especially true when the conjunctions *and* and *or* are present. One way to know if *both* is needed is to remove it and see if the meaning of the sentence changes.

- Jim *both* robbed *and* killed the foreigner.

Wouldn't it be the same if you said, "Jim robbed and killed the foreigner?" It would, so why use *both*?

The same holds true for use of the word *either*. Look at this sentence: "The hostess was going to serve *either* shrimp *or* lobster." How does that differ from "The hostess was going to serve shrimp or lobster?"

🔊 Remember, remove the words from the sentence and see if the meaning changes. If it doesn't, leave them out.

This is not a huge error, but if you read it and think you can do without it while not sacrificing clarity, I would leave it out.

Breach/breech

Breach: "an opening or break in something," as in a "breach in the castle wall." Or "to breach something," as in "He breached the wall."

Breeches, on the other hand, represents a pair of trousers, as in "He put on his *breeches*."

🔊 The easy way to remember it is *breach* is spelled like *break* and means "a break in something."

🔊 Another thing to remember is that *breeches* is always seen in the plural form. You can't tell someone to put on their *breech*.

Break/brake

Break means "to separate into pieces," as in "I dropped the glass and broke (past tense) it," or it can mean "escape plan," as in "The prisoner made a break for it."

Brake means to slow down or stop action, or it can mean something that does this for you, like a brake pedal on a car.

- He used the *brake* to stop.

Breath/breathe

You take a deep *breath*, but you *breathe* deeply. Or it's rapid *breath*, but you *breathe* slowly.

🔊 Remember that *breath* is a noun and *breathe* is a verb. There is no extra *e* in breath, and there is no *e* in noun. But there *is* an extra *e* in breathe and there is an *e* in verb.

Bring and Take/Come and Go

The basics of *bring* and *take* are simple. It all depends on location. You bring things *here*, and you take things *there*. So if you're at a location and you want something brought to you, you would say "Please bring me some food." But if you wanted to send food somewhere, you might say "Please take some food to Margie."

There are a few subtleties you may have to learn, but if you master this, you'll be right ninety-nine percent of the time.

🔈 You bring things *here* and take things *there*. You come *here* and go *there*. Remember that *take* and *there* both start with a *t*.

Brunet/brunette—see blond/blonde

Callous/callus

Callous: "being indifferent or not sensitive; a person who shows no feelings toward others."

- He was a *callous* sort and didn't care about his wife's misery.

Callus: a hardened patch of skin (usually on the palm of the hand). Calluses are often the result of hard work.

- The bitter and *callous* farmer had *calluses* on his hands from plowing the fields.

Canon/cannon

Canon: "a secular law or rule."

- It is against the *canons* of the church for priests to marry.

Canon is also the name of a large company that makes cameras, copiers, printers, and more.

Cannon: a piece of artillery (usually using gunpowder) that fires heavy projectiles. Examples of effective weapons are mortars and howitzers, which were used extensively during WWII.

Can't/cannot

Can't is a contraction for *cannot*, as in "I can't pick Joey up because I have a doctor's appointment." As you can see, it is easy to substitute *cannot* for *can't*; the meaning is the same.

There is one circumstance where *cannot* is awkward, and that is when you use a word that begins with *wh*, as in "Why can't I go to the movies?"

Try the substitution and see.

- Why *cannot* I go to the movies? It doesn't sound right.
- What *can't* you do? What *cannot* you do?
- Where *can't* you go? Where *cannot* you go?

See what I mean? Aside from the *wh* examples, the words are interchangeable.

🔊 Remember that you shouldn't use *cannot* when you have word beginning with *wh*.

Canvas/canvass

Canvas is a heavy fabric typically used for sails on ships, tents, backpacks, etc. It may also be used by painters and artists, stretched across wooden frames, and painted, as in an artist's canvas.

Canvass: to *canvass* is "to conduct a survey or ask questions of a group of people."

- Detectives usually *canvass* the area after a homicide.

You also may see it expressed as shown in the example below.

- They canvassed politician x's supporters to see what they liked.

🔊 Remember that *canvas* (one *s*) can refer to one, as in "the artist's canvas," but *canvass* (two *s*'s) means talking to many people.

"If you're not prepared to accept the results, don't *canvass* the voters."

Capital/capitol

Capital: a capital is a town or city that is the official seat of a government, as in "Austin is the capital of Texas" or "Sacramento is the capital of California."

Capital might also mean "the center of an industry," as in "Silicon Valley is the semiconductor capital of the world" or "New York City is the financial capital of the United States."

It may also mean "financial assets," as in "The start-up company went public to raise more capital."

Capital may also mean "nonfinancial assets," as in "The republican candidate has the political capital to earn the nomination."

It may also mean extreme, as in "He committed a capital crime."

Capitol is a building (or several buildings) where a state legislature meets, or the building in Washington, D.C., where Congress meets.

🪶 Remember that unless you're referring to a building, you want *capital*.

- He committed a *capital* offense in front of the *capitol* and was convicted of *capital* murder.

Carat/caret/carrot/karat

Carat: a measurement (weight) for diamonds and other precious stones. It is typically thought of as being equal to two hundred milligrams.

Caret: a proofreading symbol (ˆ) used primarily to show where to place more text or pictures, etc.

Carrot: a carrot is a long, orange vegetable often found in salads. It is a member of the parsley family.

It is often referred to as an enticement for something performed well. A well-known method of motivation or training is the "carrot-and-stick" method. Entice them with the carrot and punish them with the stick.

Karat: a karat is a unit of measurement for gold. If something is sold as eighteen-karat gold, it is three-fourths gold. It is a variant spelling of *carat*.

Catalog/catalogue

This is one of the easy ones. *Catalog* is the U.S. usage, while *catalogue* is used primarily in the United Kingdom.

🖐 If you can't remember it any other way, try to remember that the *e* at the end of *catalogue* stands for *England*.

Cave/cavern

Definition of *cave from Merriam-Webster's*

1: a natural chamber or series of chambers in the earth or in the side of a hill or cliff.

Cave is technically a noun, but it has recently come to be used as a verb also, as in to "cave in" which means to fall down or inward. Or "We need to keep the walls from caving in."

In an informal sense: "to stop trying to resist or oppose something: to give in or submit to pressure."

- He *caved* in to pressure from his wife and kids.

While *cave* has other uses, such as those listed above, I don't know of any for *cavern*. You don't *cavern in* and the walls don't *cavern in*.

When used as nouns, many people use them interchangeably, but according to *Cavern Geology*, there is a difference:

"A cave is any cavity in the ground that is large enough that some portion of it will not receive direct sunlight. There are many types of caves.

A cavern is a specific type of cave, naturally formed in soluble rock with the ability to grow speleothems (stalagmites and stalactites).

🖐 The bottom line is that all caverns are caves but not all caves are caverns.

Cement/concrete

Many people use these words interchangeably but there is a large difference. *Concrete* is the final product: the sidewalk you use to go to and from places, many of the roads you travel on, the foundation support for most of the buildings, and even many of the floors of houses and commercial structures. All of those items represent *concrete.*

Cement, on the other hand, is the powdered material that goes into the making of concrete. It usually consists of crushed limestone, and it's mixed with sand, gravel, and water to make concrete.

Cement has come to mean anything used to stick things together, and even the act of doing so (gluing), as in "Your father needs to *cement* that so it will stick."

Censure/censor

Censor: a person who bans a book, a film, a musical piece or parts thereof.

Censure: the act of criticizing strongly or banning books, film, music, etc.

Cent/scent/sent:

Cent: a cent in the United States is a penny, but it is also 1/100 of a dollar. It represents that for the euro (€) as well.

Scent: an identifiable odor, as in "I love the scent of honeysuckle in the spring."

It can also mean "the scent of an animal," as in "The skunk left a distinct scent while passing by."

It can also identify the ability or degree of smell, as in "The pig's scent was remarkable; it could find truffles three feet under the ground." (I can testify to the remarkable scent of pigs, as I have seen them in action at our animal sanctuary.)

Sent: is the past tense of *send*, as in "My mother sent me to the store" or "He sent me a package/email/text, etc."

- President Obama *sent* more troops to Iraq.

🐗 Remember that the one with the *c* and no *s* is for currency.

Of the other two, *sent* is more like *send*, and *sent* is the past tense of *send*.

Cereal/serial

Cereal: an edible grain, like oats; a breakfast food made from grains.

Serial: happening in a series, such as a series of movies or books or a television series.

Chord/cord

Chord: a group of musical notes.

Cord: a length of string or piece of rope. Can also refer to a cord-like body part.

Cite/sight/site:

Cite: means to refer to an authority, or quote an authority. Lawyers are well-known for *citing* case law when they defend a case.

- Police might also *cite* you for violating a law.
- You might also be *cited* for bravery in the military.

Sight: sight is "the ability to see."

- If something is "out of sight" then you can't see it.

It's also an aim, or a device used to aim, as in "The sniper *sighted* the target through his *sights*."

It can also mean "The foreseeable future," as in "The shipwrecked sailor lost *sight* of rescue as there was no land in *sight*."

Site: the location where a building or structure has been or will be constructed, as in "The new office was built on the building's former site" or "The construction site was littered with nails."

- A common name for a URL, and short for *website*, as in the reference material can be found on my *site* (website).

Examples:

- To *cite* Sandra Day O'Connor became commonplace after her appointment to the supreme court.
- The *sight* of the tall ships in the harbor was amazing.
- The *site* for the new county morgue was approved by the city council.

Remember that you need *light* (spelled like sight) to see, and *sight* is like see.

Coarse/course

Coarse: "without refinement, vulgar, rough, gritty."

- My wild boar, Dennis, has *coarse* fur.
- The sailor had *coarse* manners, perhaps due to his extended time at sea.
- The street punk had *coarse* language.

Course: This word has so many meanings it's difficult to list them all. It might be better to provide a few examples.

- They bought a new house on the second hole of the golf *course*.
- The ship's captain set a southerly *course*.
- The *course* of the stock market continues its upward trend.
- The *course* of the river takes it right through the city.
- He listened, then took his own *course* of action.

There are many other examples, but I hope these suffice. Here's one with both:

- During the *course* of the day, we came across several *coarse* individuals, especially at the golf *course*.

🖐 The one spelled with *ou* can sometimes mean route.

Complement/compliment

Complement: there are two kinds of compliments, the flattery kind, and the *complement* that is associated with completion.

Flattery would be: "She was *complimented* by everyone on the look of her new earrings."

Completion would be: "Her new earrings *complemented* her lovely blue eyes."

She *complimented* him on how well the tie *complemented* his suit.

🖐 Try to remember that the *e* in *complement* stands for *extra*. That's close enough to help you get it right. (Ketchup and mustard are complements for your food.)

Comprise/compose/constitute/includes

Comprise: "consist, contain, include."

- The nursing staff *comprises* two males and five females.
- The nursing staff is *composed* of seven people.

The difference between *comprise* and *compose* is subtle but distinct. The whole is *comprised* of the parts, but the parts *compose* the whole.

You put something together, or compose it, as in "He composed a musical piece."

Compose might also mean "to settle or calm yourself," as in "It took a while for her to compose herself after learning of her mother's death."

🖐 You'd say "The United States is *composed* of fifty states," but "The United States *comprises* fifty states."

Sometimes *constitute* may be the better word to use, as in "These thirty books *constitute* my library." Or "Fifty states constitute the United States."

If you make a statement that is only a partial list, use *includes* instead of any of the others. "The nursing staff *includes* three minorities." Or "Of the states that compose the United States, eight of them begin with the letter *m*.

Confident/confidant/confidante

Confident is an adjective. To be confident is to be self-assured, or sure of an outcome.

Confidant, on the other hand, is a noun and means "someone to be trusted or confided in," as in "He was a trusted confidant of the CEO."

Confidante is the same as *confidant* and can be used interchangeably; however, some people still cling to the French origin and use it as a form of gender classification, meaning the word ending in *e* should be reserved for females and the one without the *e* for males. Much like *blond/blonde* and *brunet/brunette.*

I think either way is fine, but if you know that the person you're speaking of is male, then use *confidant*. And if you know the person is female, use *confidante*. It surely can't hurt.

Conscience/conscious

Conscience: "an idea of what is right and wrong," as in "After cheating on her boyfriend, she had a guilty conscience."

Conscious: "alert or awake; not in a coma or sleep-like state." It also means "thought out," as in "He made a conscious effort to visit his estranged son."

- He was *conscious* that he had a *conscience.*

🦐 Remember that the *n* in *conscience* stands for *noun. Conscience* is a noun.

Note: *Conscious* can also be a noun; however, unless you're studying to be a psychiatrist or often speak to them, I'd probably forget it.

Contingent/contingency

Contingent is something that depends on another event, as in "The chance of a flood was contingent on the dam breaking" or "The possibility of snow was contingent on the unlikely drop in temperature."

Contingency is a secondary plan, as in "We had a contingency escape plan in case the first one failed.

- The primary evacuation route was *contingent* on fair weather. Since that didn't happen, we opted for the *contingency* plan.

🐾 Think of the *y* in *contingency* and ask yourself why you're following the contingency plan.

Continual/continuous

continuous flow

These words have similar meanings. *Continual* means "regular but with the possibility of interruption," whereas *continuous* means "with no interruption."

dry creek bed

- Some people claim electronics technology has made *continuous* improvement, while others claim it has only been *continual*.

- *Continual* noise often makes for a *continuous* headache.

🐾 A swift-flowing river might be said to have *continuous* motion, while a small creek might only be *continual*, such as when it occasionally dries up.

Convince/persuade

Convince: to cause someone to believe that something is true.

- The drugs he found in his son's room *convinced* the father the boy had a problem.

- He *persuaded* his son to go into rehab after the boy's second incident.

Persuade: "to make someone decide to do something, especially by giving them reasons why they should do it, or asking them many times to do it."

A person may be persuaded to do something any number of ways: persistent requests, threats, intimation, etc., but a person it usually takes evidence to convince someone.

🔏 Remember that you *persuade* someone to do something, and you *convince* that person *of* something. *Persuade* is for action; *convince* is only to make up their minds.

- He might be *persuaded* to do that, but he will have to be *convinced* first.

Note: This word distinction is quickly falling by the wayside. Most people don't know the difference, and of those who do know, most don't care. If you're interested, learn it and stick with it. If you're not, I wouldn't worry about it.

🔏 Remember, you *convince* with facts and you *persuade* people. (Another one I use is "Scientists *convince* and salesmen *persuade*."

Could not **care less/Couldn't care less/**Could **care less**

You hear people say this both ways, but only one way is correct. The proper way is:

- You *could not* (or couldn't) care less, not you *could* care less.

If you *could not* care less, it means you *could not* think any lower of someone, therefore, you despise them.

If you *could* care less it may mean anything from "you love them" to "you hate them," but still not as much as you could. So if you really want to say the worst to, or about, someone, say "I *could not* (or couldn't)* care less."

Note. Some people use "I could care less" when speaking, but they say it with a sarcastic tone. If people pick up on the sarcasm, that works; however, it is difficult to convey sarcasm when writing, so I would stick to the proper way to ensure clarification.

Other sayings that are be similar:

- Can't hardly/can hardly
- Can't barely/can barely

You may hear someone say something like "Can hardly wait," as in, "I'm going to Europe for the summer, and I can hardly wait."

That would be using it the correct way, meaning the person is very excited about the upcoming trip. If they had said, "can't hardly wait . . . ," it would mean they were having no trouble remaining cool and calm about the trip.

"Can barely" is similar. You may hear someone say "I can barely lift that chair; it's heavy," which means you're having a difficult time lifting it. If you said "I can't barely lift it," it would imply that lifting the chair presents no problem.

Counsel/council:

Counsel: advice or expert opinion, as in legal *counsel*.

- If you are charged with a crime, you might seek legal *counsel*.

Council: a group of (usually) respected people brought together to offer *counsel* or advice on problems and/or strategy.

- The lawyer gave *counsel* to the church *council*.

If you can *give* counsel, it's *counsel, not council.* You cannot *give council.* The priest *counseled* the parishioner. He *gave counsel*, not *council*.

Creak/creek:

Creak: "to make a squeaking sound," as in how floorboards creak when walked on.

Creek: a small stream (usually shallow) that often feeds a larger creek or river.

It can also mean a member of the Creek Indian tribe.

🐦 Remember that both the stream *creek* and the person *Creek* contain the word *reek* in the spelling. And they are the only ones who can technically *reek*, or *smell*.

A *creak*—or a sound—cannot emit an odor.

Cue/queue:

Cue: most people think of a cue as a cue stick, a long, approximately four-foot tapered piece of wood with a leather tip used to strike the cue ball in the game of pool or billiards.

Queue: a line (often lengthy) of people or cars or vehicles. Think of the long lines at a popular movie or what you may endure at the DMV.

A queue might also refer to a series of commands waiting to be processed on a computer.

🐦 Remember that a *cue* is shorter than a *line* and the word *cue* is shorter than the word *queue*.

🐦 Or remember that the word *cue* means a stick and that both cue and stick both have the letter *c* in them.

Currant/current

Currant: a dried grape

Current: happening now, currently; a flow of water, usually referred to as a swift current or an air current or an electrical current.

Data (with facts=plural; with information=singular)

Data is covered elsewhere in this book, but I believe it's worth repeating; besides, not many people will read the book in its entirety, which means they may miss it.

Data is often written erroneously. The key is knowing what kind of data you're talking about.

When *data* is a count noun (items that can be counted), the plural makes sense. In that type of sentence, you could replace *data* with another count noun such as *facts*. However, when *data* is treated as a noncount noun (items cannot be counted), the singular makes sense. In those cases, you could substitute the word *information*.

If you are submitting sales reports to your boss, you might say "The *data* (facts) *are* ready."

But if you're referring to marketing information, you could say "The *data* (information) *is* ready."

Both would be correct.

🖐 Remember to substitute *facts* or *information* for *data*. If *facts* works, use *are* (plural), but if *information* works, use *is* (singular).

Decimate

This is another word people seem to be confused about. There are sides for and against the use of the word.

Many modern linguists support its meaning of "to destroy or kill a large portion of something." Other, more strict linguists continue to use it only in the sense of "to kill one in ten," citing etymological reasons (the Latin root of *decimate*).

Supposedly, an old punishment in Rome was to *decimate* a legion for a wrongdoing; in other words, to kill one in ten of them.

You are less likely to draw ire if you stick with the more classical meaning; however, there are enough reputable resources to support either position.

Decry/descry

Decry: to criticize or condemn; to rail against something.

- He wrote an opinion piece railing against (decrying) the new immigration policy.

Descry: to detect something by looking or listening closely.

- He *descried* a hidden agenda in the proposed bill, something he *decried*.

🖐 Remember that the *s* in *descry* stands for *see*.

Note: This is not a set of words most people will confuse, simply because most people don't use them; however, if you're tempted to use either of these words, make certain you use them correctly.

Defuse/diffuse

Defuse: "to take out or remove the fuse from a bomb or explosive device" or "to render a situation less dangerous," as in "Obama *defused* the tense situation in Iran."

Diffuse: "to thin out or spread out," as in "The thick smoke from the fire in the plastic factory gagged me at first, but then it *diffused*."

- He *defused* the bomb, and then the smoke *diffused* throughout the room.

Demur/demure

Demur is primarily a verb meaning:

- to object or take exception to.
- to hesitate because of doubt.

In this form, it is often used with *to* or *at*.

Some dictionaries also list it as a noun referring to the act of demurring, but the word usually gives way to demurral for this sense.

Demure means . . .

- modest and reserved
- affectedly shy.

It is only an adjective, as in "a *demure* young lady."

Desert/dessert

Desert: a dry patch of earth that receives little rainfall and normally experiences extreme temperatures.

Most people think of a *desert* as a hot, barren, sandy region, but there are *deserts* in Antarctica as well. A *desert* is defined more by the amount of annual rainfall (less than 10 inches) than temperature.

- Because of the lack of rainfall, *deserts* (hot or cold) have little vegetation.

Dessert: a dessert is a dish (usually sweet) served at the completion of a meal. It may be fruit, a sweet, a pastry, or ice cream. Originally, this custom may have started as a means to clear the palate. Now it is thought of more as a *treat*.

- Whenever I go out to eat, I usually opt for tiramisu as the *dessert*.

Remember that a *dessert* is something you might want two of, and there are two *s*'s in *dessert* and only one *s* in *desert*.

Device/devise

Device: "an object made to do one or more functions," as in "A glucose monitoring device is made to test the level of a person's blood sugar."

A device might also refer to a writer's *tool* used to advance a plot or introduce new characters, etc.

Devise: "to plan or come up with a new idea," as in "He devised a new medical device."

Think of *devise* as coming up with a strategy and how both *strategy* and *devise* have the letter *s*.

Different than or different from

There are some stodgy grammarians who consider it an error, or not proper usage, to use *different than* instead of *different from,* but an analysis of common usage shows us otherwise. No one is going to be confused when you say different than instead of different from.

In the United Kingdom, it's common to say different to.

As a side note, I often use *different than.*

Dilemma

Dilemma: "a circumstance where a person is put into a situation and must decide between what seems to be equally unfavorable choices." For example, in several old movies and comics, the protagonist was forced into a dilemma: he had to decide who would die—his wife or his daughter (or a similar choice).

Note: In the traditional sense, *dilemma* meant a problem of choices between two alternatives, but if you look at definition two from the *American Heritage Dictionary*, you will notice it refers to "a decision that defies a satisfactory solution."

That definition seems to be gaining support from both the public and from professional linguists.

Disburse/disperse

Disburse: "to pay out," as in "Every month they disbursed his trust-fund check."

Disperse: "to scatter or drive off," as in "The National Guard dispersed the rioters using tear gas."

🔹 Remember that you wouldn't "disperse" funds (scatter them), but you might "disburse" them from a *briefcase*, and both of those words contain a *b*.

Disconcerting/disconcerning

This is another easy one to recognize, as *disconcerning* is not a word. Despite that, I hear people use it frequently. What they really mean (I'm sure) is *disconcerting*, which means "upsetting, disturbing, or confusing."

I don't know how this confusion came about, but it is *disconcerting*.

Discreet/discrete

Discreet: "showing self-restraint," as in "The office coworkers were having an affair but had to be *discreet* as it was against office policy."

Discrete means "distinct, unconnected parts."

🔹 Try to remember that *discrete* means a distinct or separate thing, just like the *t* separates the two *e*'s.

Disinterested/uninterested

Disinterested: *disinterested* and *uninterested* are closely related but markedly different.

Disinterested means "not favoring one side or the other; showing no bias," as in "He had no stake in the argument; he was disinterested."

Uninterested means "not interested," as in not caring who won or lost.

- He was *uninterested* in the football game, so the outcome held no interest for him.

- An *uninterested* British historian might not be interested in writing about Napoleon, but a *disinterested* British historian would report the good and bad of each situation.

Dragged/drug

Dragged: *dragged* is the past tense of drag and means "to pull something" (usually thought of as heavy), as in "He *dragged* the crate out of the way so the truck could park."

On a computer, you can also *drag* an icon to another position using a mouse or trackpad.

Drug: a *drug* is a pharmaceutical product used to treat or diagnose a disease. It is also used in disease prevention.

A *drug* can also be an illegal product used for a person's pleasure although it is normally referred to in the plural, as in "He's on *drugs*."

A *drug* is a pharmaceutical.

Some people use *drug* as the past tense of *drag*. It seems to fit, so the usage seldom raises eyebrows, but if you research it, you'll see that *dragged* is the preferred use.

You shouldn't say "I drug him into the alley" but rather, "I dragged him into the alley." Although—unless there's a damn good reason—you shouldn't be *dragging* anyone into an alley.

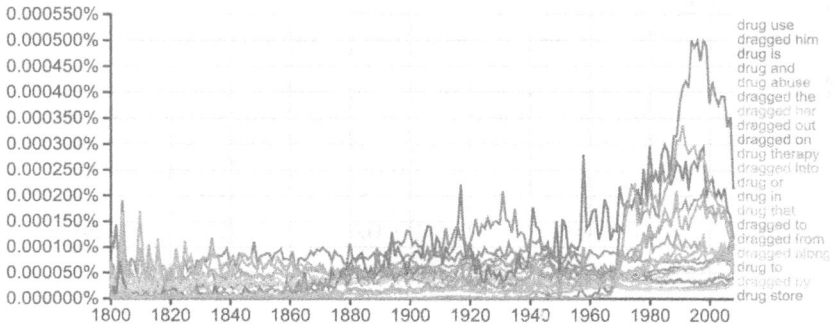

Dragged plus words, and drug plus words

As the N-gram above shows, the use of *dragged* is more prevalent than the use of *drug* when combined with words that may ordinarily follow it.

If you listen to everyday speech, though, I believe you'll hear a different story. Many people use *drug* instead of *dragged* in normal usage.

Based on what I've seen, I doubt it will be considered a misuse for long.

Drank/drunk

Many people confuse the use of these two verbs, especially if they've been drinking a lot of liquor.

Drunk, which can also be a noun, is easily identified when used as a noun. The confusion arises when people search for the right past or future perfect tense of *drink*.

Drunk can be used as a verb, adjective, or noun. Few people confuse it when used as an adjective or noun, as in "He's a drunk," or "She associates with drunk people."

But confusion sets in when we attempt to use it as a verb: Both "I *drank* the wine" and "He *has drunk* too much" are correct. If you use the verb "to have" in any of its forms, use *drunk*. If it's the simple past tense of "to drink," use *drank*, as in "I drank beer after dinner" or "He drank all of the wine." But "I have drunk every drop."

🖐 The same holds true for many verbs including: *bit* and *bitten* and *got* and *gotten*. If you use *have*, *had*, etc., use *drunk*.

Dual/duel

Dual: "having two parts," as in "Some of the cars used for driver's education have dual brakes and even dual steering wheels."

Duel: in the past, a *duel* was a formal combat between opposing parties, usually over a point of honor. Before the common use of handguns, *duels* were fought with swords. Now a *duel* has come to mean any form of combat (though normally physical) between parties to decide the victor.

🖐 Remember that the *e* is for *engage*. To engage in a duel, both *engage* and *duel* have an *e*.

Eg/ie/ergo/etc.

This is also covered in the chapter on Latin expressions.

E.g., is the Latin abbreviation for *exempli gratia*. Most style guides say italics are not needed, but it should be followed by periods and written in lowercase letters. A comma should follow the abbreviation.

E.g., means "for example" and should be used for that, not for clarifying what you mean to say. Leave that job to *i.e.*

Remember that *e.g.,* and *example* both start with the letter *e*.

I.e., is the Latin abbreviation for "that is" and is used to clarify the meaning of something. It is written similarly to *e.g.,* and is followed by a comma as well. It should precede a clarification.

Ergo: a Latin abbreviation for *therefore* and "as such," is frequently preceded by a semicolon. It can also be separated by a comma or an em dash, depending upon usage.

Etc.: this is an abbreviation for *et cetera*, which means "and so forth."

It should never be used in the same sentence with *including* or *includes*, and it should be preceded by a comma.

Some may think the use of *ergo, et al, i.e.,* and *e.g.,* are pretentious, but they are perfectly fine, and their use is common practice in the legal and insurance professions, among others.

One other thing: *etc.,* is used only for things. Use *et al* when referring to people. (Et al means "and others," so it is appropriate.)
Elicit/illicit

Elicit means to extract an explanation, as in "The detective elicited a confession."

Illicit means something illegal, not allowed, or unacceptable; against the law.

* The suspect committed an *illicit* act, but the detective *elicited* his confession.

Remember that *illicit* and *illegal* both start with *ill*, and *elicit* and *extract* both begin with *e*.
Embarrass/embarrass

Another misspelling of a common word. Both the *r* and the *s* are doubled, like both the *c* and *m* are doubled in accommodate.

* It would be *embarrassing* to misspell either *accommodate* or *embarrass.*

Remember that *accommodate, embarrass,* and *misspell* all have double consonants. It will help keep them straight.
Emigrate/immigrate (emigrant/immigrant)

Emigrate: to *emigrate* is to leave a country or place of residence—think of *export*.

Immigrate: to *immigrate* is to come *into* a country—think of *import*.

* My grandparents *emigrated* from Italy and *immigrated* to the United States.

You use *from* with *emigrate*, so you *emigrate* from somewhere, and you *immigrate to* somewhere.

Emigrate   from/immigrate   to.   *emigrate=export.* *Immigrate=import.*

Eminent/immanent/imminent/preeminent

Eminent: used to describe a well-respected and renowned person, especially in a particular field of interest.

- The *eminent* Dr. Henry Wells, a renowned biologist, will be speaking tonight.

Immanent: restricted entirely to the mind; subjective. American Heritage Dictionary:

Imminent—something that will happen no matter what you do.

- The attack was *imminent*.

Preeminent: leading the field, ahead of the pack, superior.

- He is the *preeminent* candidate.

A way to remember: If someone is trying to appear *eminent* and uses the word *immanent*, you can rest assured it is *imminent* I will kick his *preeminent* ass. (this mnemonic device puts the words in alphabetical order.)

Enervate/energize

Enervate means "to sap or to weaken" and does not mean to energize.

- The trip on the crowded subway was an *enervating* experience (meaning it was tiring, exhausting).
- The only thing that helped was the *energizing* espresso (meaning it provided some spunk or energy).

Enormity

Originally, *enormity* meant "of great evil—something wicked and bad"; however, it has evolved and is now commonly used to describe something great in size or scope—such as "the *enormity* of the project."

Many grammarians find fault with this, but it is more and more frequently used in this manner, so they (the grammar nerds) probably need to learn to accept it, as language is ever changing.

Envelop/envelope

Envelop: to cover or surround

Envelope: a paper container for a letter

Every one/everyone

It is almost identical to the examples cited in *anyone* versus *any one*.

Every day/everyday:

Everyday is an adjective usually describing a daily ritual, as in *everyday* life is boring.

While "every day" is used to mean each single day, as in I drink coffee every (each) day.

🖐 The easy way to remember it is if you can use *each* day instead of *every* day, you're speaking of the "every day" that's two words. Try it with the example above: I drink coffee *each* day. See, it makes sense—the sentence *and* the coffee drinking.

Exacerbate/exasperate

There is a similarity yet a difference between the words.

Exasperate means "to irritate, to bother, to annoy."

- The two young brothers' constant bickering *exasperated* their mother.

Exacerbate means "to worsen."

- The blood thinner he was taking *exacerbated* his condition, and he developed internal bleeding.

🔊 The way I remember it is that the *c* in *exacerbate* stands for *condition*, as in "worsening the condition."

Fair/fare

The difference between *fair* and *fare* is simple. *Fair* is unbiased, on an even keel, not pro or con, as in "He's a fair person" and "It was a fair fight."

Whereas *fare*, when used as a noun, typically refers to the price you pay to ride a taxi, or a bus, or train, or plane, or ship. It might also refer to *you* as the *fare*, as in "the cabbie took his *fare* to Central Park."

As a verb, *fare* may mean "to experience," as in "He fared well, considering his handicap" or "She fared poorly."

🔊 I try to remember that *pair* is spelled like *fair*, and if you have two people to buy tickets for you'd buy a pair to be fair.

Yes, it's a stupid example, but it works for me.

Famous/infamous/notorious

Notorious: "widely and, usually, unfavorably known," as in "Johnny Ringo was a notorious gunfighter."

Lately, the definition has evolved to mean more of a notoriety for something not so evil, as in "The company was notorious for its ruthless reputation." (Perhaps that is a negative connotation, but not necessarily evil.) The person or thing being described does not have to be evil or even thought of in a negative light.

Infamous: this one is as it sounds. It means "being famous for something bad or evil," as in Charles Manson is infamous for the murders he committed, or "Richard Nixon is, arguably, the most infamous president." The word has a negative connotation, and is never used in a positive light.

Famous: This is the typical meaning. "Michael Jordan is famous for his basketball achievements" and "Michael Jackson is famous for his vocal/singing achievements."

The differences:

While Michael Jordan may be *famous* for his basketball achievements, he is *notorious* for his golf gambling.

While Michael Jackson may be *famous* for his singing, he is *infamous* for his alleged pedophilia.

Farther/further

Farther is for physical distance, and *further* is for the metaphorical.

- She ran *farther* than I did.

- *Further* thought on the matter will do no good.

🖐 Try to remember that the "far" in farther means distance. If you do that, you'll be right ninety-nine percent of the time.

Fateful/fatal

This one is easy. *Fatal* refers to death, while *fateful* is the inevitable. So if it was a fatal accident, the person was killed. If it was a fatal heart attack, the person died. But a fateful event means that it was determined by *fate*, or it was bound to happen. A *fateful* event doesn't have to be bad; it could mean that you won the lottery.

🖐 Remember that fateful contains the word fate.

Fervent/fervid

Though some grammarians say that there is a subtle difference, common usage doesn't bear that out. Both mean "with great passion" or "passionate" and are used interchangeably.

Neither word is used often, but when they are used, you will be hard-pressed to identify the difference. If you have an inclination to use one, go ahead and do it. Either will work.

Fewer/less

Traditionally, the rule has been to use *less* for nouns listed as plural nouns and *fewer* for others. Example, he ate *less* pizza than she did. Or he ate *fewer* pieces of pizza. The difference being *pizza* is a plural noun while *pieces* is not.

This is all wonderful, except that there are too many exceptions to the rule. And there are too many citations throughout the ages for the *rules* to carry much weight.

In everyday use, I wouldn't worry about which word you use as long as you feel it's clear what you mean. In formal writing, I'd stick to the accepted rules to avoid criticism (if you care).

Fiancé/fiancée

Fiancé is used to describe a man who is engaged, and fiancée to describe a woman who is engaged. This comes naturally from the origin of the words—which are French.

These words are seldom used properly. Only one word is normally used—*fiancé*—so it is only used correctly when it refers to the man. We've gotten so accustomed to it that it has become acceptable usage for the majority.

Flammable/inflammable

This is a tough one. Both *flammable* and *inflammable* mean the same thing. I can't think of another word where the *in* version (any word with *in* as the prefix) means the same thing. Take a look at a few:

- Sane/insane, ability/inability, capable/incapable, destructible/ indestructible, vulnerable/invulnerable . . .

The list goes on and on, but I think you get the point. The question arises though, why do words as important as flammable/inflammable have the same meaning?

So that no one mistakes the meaning.

Originally, *inflammable* meant it could easily catch fire. People got confused by the "in" prefix, so they made *flammable* mean *inflammable* as well.

It's confusing, but safe. Now they both mean the product may easily catch fire.

Flesh out/flush out

To "flesh out" is "to complete an idea" or "to add to something," as in "Let's flesh out that idea," but to "flush out" is to "clear the bushes," so to speak, as in "They flushed out the birds (or the tiger)."

Flout/flaunt

This is one a lot of people mix up. You *flaunt* the new car you purchased, but you *flout* the law by running a stop sign with that new car.

🔊 Even after you learn the difference, it's difficult to keep it straight. I try to remember by using the *aunt* in *flaunt*. I pretend it represents an aunt who left me her wealth which I'm now *flaunting*.

🔊 The other way to remember it is to think of the "lout" in *flout* as a person who might "flout" the law.

Forego/forgo

Forgo means "to do without," as in "To *forgo* lunch would make him ill."

Forego means "to go before," as in "It was a foregone conclusion that Napoleon would win the battle against the Austrians."

🔊 Remember that *forgo* means "to do without," and you have left *out* the *e*, whereas *forego* means "to go before," and the *fore* is the same as *before*.

Foreward/forward/foreword

First of all, *foreward* is not a word. Now that that's out of the way, let's focus on the other two.

Forward (with an *a*) means *direction*, as in "he was facing forward," or "move forward."

Foreword (containing *word*) means just what you might think. *Fore*—meaning before—and *word*. It is a section of a book that is *before* the main work. It is usually written by someone else, typically someone respected.

🔊 This is an easy one to remember. The *word* in foreword relates to words.

Forth/fourth

Forth means *forward* in time, as in "Go forth."

Fourth represents a number following third, as in "He came in fourth" or "He's the fourth one."

It should be easy to remember. Forth starts with *for*, as in *forward* and they both indicate movement. Fourth starts with *four*, as in the number *four*.

Fortuitous/fortunate

In its original form, *fortuitous* meant "accidental, by chance (whether good or bad)." It has now come to mean "a lucky chance or fortunate accident."

- Was it *fortuitous* that the medieval knight found a brand-new sword while on his way to slay a dragon?

Foul/fowl

This should be one of the easiest mix-ups to remember. *Fowl* is *only* used when referring to birds, such as chickens, turkeys, pheasants, guinea hens, and geese.

- There are two types of fowl—land fowl and water fowl.

Foul refers to something wrong or nasty, as in a foul ball or a foul odor.

The easiest way to remember this is to realize that *fowl* contains the word *owl*—a bird—and even though an owl isn't considered a fowl, it is a bird, so it should clue you in.

Good/well

See chapter titled "Feel Good or Well" for more details.

Got/gotten

This is a pair of little words that causes a a lot of big problems.

Got is the past tense of *get*, and *get* means so many things it's almost ridiculous. I've listed samples from Dictionary.com.

I selectively chose examples, which is why the numbering is odd.)

As a verb (used with object), *got* or (archaic) *gat*; *got* or *got·ten*; *get·ting.*

1. to receive or come to have possession, use, or enjoyment of: to get a birthday present; to get a pension.

2. to cause to be in one's possession or succeed in having available for one's use or enjoyment; obtain; acquire: to get a

good price after bargaining; to get oil by drilling; to get information.

3. to go after, take hold of, and bring (something) for one's own or for another's purposes; fetch: Would you get the milk from the refrigerator for me?

4. to cause or cause to become, to do, to move, etc., as specified; effect: to get one's hair cut; to get a person drunk; to get a fire to burn; to get a dog out of a room.

5. to communicate or establish communication with over a distance; reach: You can always get me by telephone.

6. to hear or hear clearly: I didn't get your last name.

7. to acquire a mental grasp or command of; learn: to get a lesson.

verb (used without object), *got* or (Archaic) *gat*; *got* or *got·ten*; *get·ting.*

20. to come to a specified place, arrive, reach, to get home late.

21. to succeed, become enabled, or be permitted: You get to meet a lot of interesting people.

22. to become or to cause oneself to become as specified, reach a certain condition, to get angry, to get sick.

23. (used as an auxiliary verb followed by a past participle to form the passive): to get married; to get elected; to get hit by a car.

24. to succeed in coming, going, arriving at, visiting, etc. (usually followed by away, in, into, out, etc.): I don't get into town very often.

25. to bear, endure, or survive (usually followed by through or over), Can he get through another bad winter?

26. to earn money, gain.

As a noun

29. an offspring or the total of the offspring, especially of a male animal, the get of a stallion.

30. a return of a ball, as in tennis, that would normally have resulted in a point for the opponent.

31. British Slang. (A) something earned, as salary, profits, etc.: What's your week's get? (B) a child born out of wedlock.

Verb phrases

32. get about, (A) to move about; be active: He gets about with difficulty since his illness. (B) to become known; spread: It was supposed to be a secret, but somehow it got about. (C) to be socially active: She's been getting about much more since her family moved to the city. Also, get around.

33. get across, (A) to make or become understandable; communicate: to get a lesson across to students. (B) to be convincing about; impress upon others: The fire chief got across forcefully the fact that turning in a false alarm is a serious offense.

34. get ahead, to be successful, as in business or society: She got ahead by sheer determination.

35. get ahead of, (A) to move forward of, as in traveling: The taxi got ahead of her after the light changed. (B) to surpass; outdo: He refused to let anyone get ahead of him in business.

36. get along, (A) to go away; leave. (B) get on.

37. get around, (A) to circumvent; outwit. (B) to ingratiate oneself with (someone) through flattery or cajolery. (C) to travel from place to place; circulate: I don't get around much anymore. (D) get about.

38. get at, (A) to reach; touch: to stretch in order to get at a top shelf. (B) to suggest, hint at, or imply; intimate: What are you getting at? (C) to discover; determine: to get at the root of a problem. (D) Informal. to influence by surreptitious or illegal means; bribe: The gangsters couldn't get at the mayor.

Idioms

50. get back, (A) to come back; return: When will you get back? (B) to recover; regain: He got back his investment with interest. (C) to be revenged: She waited for a chance to get back at her accuser.

51. get even

52. get going, (A) to begin; act: They wanted to get going on the construction of the house. (B) to increase one's speed; make haste: If we don't get going, we'll never arrive in time.

53. get it, Informal. (A) to be punished or reprimanded: You'll get it for breaking that vase! (B) to understand or grasp something: This is just between us, get it?

54. get it off, Slang: Vulgar. to experience orgasm.

55. get it on, (A) Informal. to work or perform with satisfying harmony or energy or develop a strong rapport, as in music: a rock group really getting it on with the audience. (B) Slang: Vulgar. to have sexual intercourse.

As you can see, there are more definitions for *get* than you can imagine. Well, not quite, but there are a hell of a lot, and that makes understanding the nuances of the past tense confusing.

To top it off, there are exceptions to the norm, as in "I have got." It's usually shortened to "I've got" as it doesn't sound right as it stands, but then you have the expression (the exception) "I have got to get out of here" (meaning "must," as in "I must get out of here").

To make matters worse, the U.K. version is different. In the United Kingdom they say "have got" and consider it proper, while in the United States we say "have gotten." All of this means if you do business on both sides of the ocean, you're bound to get confused more quickly.

Some people use "have got" to indicate ownership or possession, as in "I have got a lot of cousins," which means "I have a lot of cousins." So why not just say that? *Got* is not needed.

"I have *got* to go" (meaning "I must go"). You could also say "I have to go" instead and save yourself a word.

Gotten can mean many things. It can mean "to acquire or obtain," as in "I've gotten a new car." (You could also say "I've bought a new car.")

It can also mean "become," as in "I've gotten interested in art" (meaning "I've become interested in art"). Or "I've gotten confused by his politics." ("I've become confused by his politics.")

It can also mean "moved," as in "He's gotten out of the car" or "He's gotten off the sofa" (meaning he's moved off the sofa).

Much of the confusion can be cleared up simply by eliminating the words *got* or *gotten*. Examples follow.

Tim and his brother have got a snake. (What that means is that Tim and his brother own a snake.) You could just as easily say "Tim and his brother have a snake (or own a snake)."

An example using *gotten* would be "I'll watch TV later; I haven't gotten the dishes done yet." You could just as easily replace that with "I'll watch TV later; I haven't finished the dishes yet."

Not only did you get rid of the "gotten" problem, you saved a word while doing it.

Sometimes the easiest solution is the simplest, and in this case, I think the simplest is to substitute a word. Instead of saying "have gotten a dog," say "bought." Instead of "He got over his cold," say "He recovered." Instead of "She got caught," say "She was caught." If you do that, no one will misunderstand you, and no one can complain.

If you're going to use the words, though, try to do it right. If there is a helping verb, use *gotten*. If not, use *got* (same rule as *bit* and *bitten*).

Grateful/thankful

At first blush, there doesn't seem to be much difference between the two, but if you dig deeper, you'll see that *grateful* is more a state of being, as in "You can be grateful you are a good person," whereas *thankful* is more in response to something given. You can be thankful for a gift or even someone's love, but you're grateful for being the person you are.

With that said, there is enough disagreement, or lack of agreement, on the subject to make it more than hazy. I don't think anyone will confuse your meaning no matter which word you use, and you can be *grateful* or *thankful* for that.

Gray/grey

These are the same words, simply variations in the spelling, and it's easy to remember. The *a* stands for America and the *e* stands for England.

Grisly/grizzly

These words should be easy to distinguish. *Grisly* means horrible, ghastly, gruesome, terrible, while *grizzly* is usually referred to as an adjective for brown bear. *Grizzly* also means *gray* or grayish hair, though it is seldom used that way.

The easiest way I found to remember it is grizzly and zebra both contain the letter *z* and both are animals.

Guarantee/guaranty

There's a difference here, but one of the words is seldom used except in the legal and insurance professions.

Guarantee functions as both a verb and a noun and is used widely.

- I *guarantee* this will be done.
- I offered him a *guarantee* on the car.

Guaranty functions as a noun and is almost exclusively used in the legal or insurance professions to represent something that is offered as a *guarantee*.

To remember this, think of the letter *y*, and ask yourself *why* you should use this word.

Hail/hale

Hail as a noun, is ice that falls from the sky, as in "It almost always hails preceding a tornado." It can also be used as a verb, as in "Hail, Caesar." You may also *hail* a cab, or ask someone where they *hail* from.

Hale means *healthy*, as in "hale and hearty" and other such expressions. There is also an old, out-of-date use as a verb, meaning "to *hale* or to *haul* something," though I have never heard it used that way.

An easy way to remember it is that *hail* has *ail* in it—the opposite of hale—and if you *ail* you're probably not hale.

Hanged/hung

Hanged is the past tense of *hang* and is used when writing or talking about a person who was hanged.

Hung is the past participle of *hang* and is used when writing or talking about an inanimate object that was *hung*. You can't say "He was hung for his crimes." It should be "He was hanged for his crimes."

🐟 So, "The sheets were *hung* on the line to dry," but "The man was *hanged* for his crimes."

Hangar/hanger

A *hangar* is where you store or maintain an airplane.

A *hanger* is what you hang your clothes on.

🐟 It's easy to remember. The *a* in hangar stands for airplane.

Heroin/heroine

Heroin is a highly addictive narcotic that is a derivative of morphine.

- Possession of *heroin* or sale of *heroin* is a criminal offense punishable by a prison term.

- A *heroine* is a female character (usually the lead) in a play or movie who possesses admirable courage or bravery.

As you can see, *heroin* is a vile drug, while a *heroine* is a respected female hero. Not to say that a heroine couldn't use heroin, but she'd have a steep hill to climb if she wanted to continue being a heroine.

- The *heroine* of the play was arrested for using *heroin*.

Here's

Here is and here are and there is and there are. See the chapter marked "Here's and There's" under "Usage."

Hear/here

Here is used as an adverb and indicates location.

- *Here* is the pen.
- Come *here*.
- *Here* is the dinner you ordered.

Hear is primarily used as a verb, meaning "to listen" or "to indicate the act of listening."

- She *heard* the music.
- *Hear* me out.
- Did you *hear* the sound of the squirrel?

This is also an easy one to remember. The word that contains *ear* is the one that deals with listening.

Hoard/horde

Hoard is used as both a verb and a noun. As a verb it can mean "the act of hiding a treasure for future purposes," as in "The knight hoarded the treasure he found in the church." As a noun, it could mean the treasure itself, as in "the dragon's hoard."

A *horde* is a large or massive group, as in a *horde* of gnats or a *horde* of Mongols.

The way I remember it is a *hoard* is spelled like *board* and a hoard might be hidden under a board.

Home/hone (homed in or honed in)

I don't know of anyone who gets confused over home and hone, but "home in" and "hone in" are different. That comparison seems to be ripe for confusion, so let's try to set the record straight.

Home is a base of operations or a haven.

- Home base, a home to live in, a place to call home, etc.

To *hone* is to sharpen something, as in "He honed the edge of the sword."

A missile *homes in on* its target; in other words, it is guided to the target. And yet, I constantly hear people say "hone in on . . ." That misused variation is gaining wider acceptance, but it is obvious and painfully erroneous.

Perhaps no one will question your use of "hone in on," but if you use "home in on," you can substantiate it and be safe in knowing you're using it correctly.

🥢 Think of a missile homing in on a target (aiming for a house).

Hopefully

This poor word has been beaten up badly, and I don't know why. It has long been used (and accepted) by almost everyone; in fact, Dictionary.com had this to say:

"Although some strongly object to its use as a sentence modifier, *hopefully*—meaning "it is hoped (that)"—has been in use since the 1930s and is fully standard in all varieties of speech and writing." (I added the em dashes. Dictionary.com did not have them.)

An example follows.

- Hopefully, tensions between the two nations will ease.

This use of *hopefully* is parallel to that of *certainly*, *curiously*, *frankly*, *regrettably*, and other sentence modifiers.

Hunger pangs/hunger pains

Hunger pangs: these are traditionally referred to as "hunger pangs," but they have come to be known as "hunger pains." It's a good thing, as most people seem to refer to them as hunger pains, anyway. If you say "hunger pangs" someone will invariably give you a look as if to say "What the hell are you talking about?"

However, if you wish to use the phrase correctly, refer those people to the internet (or preferably here) to verify the usage.

Impassable/impassible/impassive

Impassable

Incapable of being passed, as in "The bridge is out. It's *impassable*."

Impassible

Seldom-used word that means "Incapable of suffering; inaccessible to harm or pain; not to be touched or moved to passion or sympathy; unfeeling, or not showing feeling; without sensation"

Impassive

"Despite his potential financial reward, he remained *impassive*, showing neither interest in nor concern for our plight."

Imply/infer

This is easy to decipher.

To *imply* is to suggest or hint at something.

To *infer* is to guess or deduce what the person who implied something means.

Remember that the person speaking is always the one who *implies,* and the listener is the one who *infers.*

In/into

- The bottled water is *in* the refrigerator.
- She walked *into* the house.

👎 A basic rule is that *into* is an *action* item, while *in* implies *within.* This isn't always the case, but most of the time it is. If you follow this guideline, you'll be correct most of the time.

Incidence/incidents

Both words sound alike. The mass noun, *incidence*—which is a plural noun—means the occurrence of something, as in "The incidence of malaria in Panama has decreased."

Incidents is the plural form of *incident* and means "multiple incidents," as in "There were five incidents at the mall today."

Incredible/incredulous

These two words are similar, yet they're not. *Incredible* means "difficult to believe even though it's true." It is not meant to be used as an intensifier, as in "That was an incredible apple"; however, a fourteen-inch downpour that appears from nowhere can be incredible—difficult to believe, yet it did happen.

Incredulous is different. It is something that is difficult to believe because it is a lie or wrong. If someone tells you he *accidentally* got caught with cocaine, he might be considered incredulous.

Inquire/enquire

This is yet another U.S./U.K. variation.

Inquire is predominantly the U.S. spelling.

Enquire is the U.K. spelling.

Some people ascribe a slight variation in meaning to the words, but I see no concrete evidence of that. What I've heard is that *enquire* is used more in informal settings while *inquire* is reserved for formalities, but usage doesn't bear that out.

🍃 Once again, the *e* in *enquire* is for England.

Instant

Although *instant* has come to mean "quickly," or "instantly," it didn't always mean that. It originally referred to a precise, or specific, moment in time, as in "at the instant he passed" (that exact second) or "The instant I saw her, I fell in love."

Now it has come to mean "immediate" as in "instant coffee," or "I'll be back in an instant," or a mother admonishing her child with "Do what I say this instant."

Inter/intra

Inter means "between." (Think of interstate. The freeways go between states.)

Intra means "within," as in an "intrastate" highway. (It stays within the state.)

🍃 Within a company, you may have interdepartmental struggles, like between engineering and operations. But if you had an intradepartmental memo, it might be for the marketing group only.

Irregardless

The definition of *irregardless*, is "regardless." Both mean the same thing, although *irregardless* is considered nonstandard by just about everybody.

Regardless means "without regard" and by definition, *irregardless* means "without without regard." Yes, it doesn't make sense.

Regardless of what you think, using *irregardless* is wrong.

🖐 My suggestion is to not use *irregardless*, but if you do, know that is not accepted English.

Isle/aisle

An *isle* is an island. Some people only use it to mean a *small* island, but I've seen it used for descriptions of much larger ones.

An *aisle* is a passageway, as in "The bride walked down the aisle." Or the aisle of a grocery store, where the stocker might say the tomato paste is on aisle four, when asked.

🖐 This is easy to remember, as *isle* starts out just like *island*.

Its/it's

Seldom do three letters stir such confusion. And yet it's easy to spot the differences.

It's (with apostrophe) is *always*, and *only*, a contraction—either for "it is" or "it has," as in "It's been raining" (it has been raining). Or "It's mine" (it is mine).

Its (no apostrophe) is used for all other instances. You'd say "The company had its annual picnic on Saturday" or, "The zoo displayed its panda bears last week."

Even though *its* shows possession, it's (it is) like *hers* or *ours* or *theirs*. It doesn't take an apostrophe.

🖐 Remember *it's* is either "it is" or "it has"—nothing else.

Jam/jamb

Jam is a preserve made from sugared fruit, and *jamb* is the side of a door or window, as in the door jamb or the window jamb.

🖐 Remember you can bump into a door jamb, and both have *b's* in the word.

Ladder/latter

Ladder is a device used to ascend or descend. It usually has wooden or metal construction (sometimes rope) and has a series of rungs spaced between.

Latter means the last choice offered, as in "the former or the latter."

🖐 I try to remember it by the letter *d*. Descend begins with *d* and matches the *d* in ladder.

Lie/lay/lain versus Lay/laid/laid

See the "Lie, Lay, Laid" chapter under "Usage."

Leach/leech

To *leach* means to percolate through something or to penetrate gradually.

A *leech* is something or someone who attaches themselves to another for personal gain. It can be an animal like a bloodsucking worm or a person who is a member of an entourage for personal gain.

🖐 Leech and *eel* (The first three letters of *leech* spelled backward) are both found in the water.

Lead/led

When I did research for my *No Mistakes Résumés* book, the mistake I saw most often was the misuse of *lead* and *led*. I did a search of my database, which contains almost twelve thousand résumés, and, from the search results, I pulled up all the résumés that used *lead*.

I randomly went through the first three hundred, and in an astonishing 27 percent, the person had used the present tense *lead* instead of the past tense *led*.

Here is an example from one résumé:

- Developed prototype for new product geared toward revolutionized testing for . . .
- *Lead* efforts of twenty-seven engineers and brought in product on schedule and under budget.

As you can see, the first accomplishment was fine, done properly in the past tense using the word developed. The second, however, uses *lead* in the present tense, instead of *led*, which is the past tense of the verb.

This *leads* (present tense) me to believe that people don't have a good command of the English language. I was *led* (past tense) to this belief by seeing so damn many résumés with this same error.

This is one of the more common mistakes on résumés, but there are plenty of others.

Lessen/lesson

A *lesson* is something taught or learned, as in "The student learned more of a lesson than the teacher intended."

Lessen means to make fewer or decrease or reduce. If you lessen the archers, you might lose the battle.

🖐 Lessen and fewer both have two occurrences of the letter *e*.

🖐 This *lesson* is probably more for the adult crowd, as I'd hope the students know their lessons on lesson versus lessen.

Levee/levy

A *levee* is similar to a dam. It is a structure built to hold back water and prevent the land from flooding.

A *levy* is a tax or surcharge imposed upon a people or governed area. It could be money, food, soldiers, or anything.

These two words are homophones, so they sound alike, and in normal speech it would be difficult, if not impossible, to distinguish the difference. In writing, however, it's easy.

🖐 Remember, *levees* are dams, and *levy* is a tax, and the *y* is next to the *x* in the alphabet.

Libel/liable/slander

Libel is the defamation of a person's name in writing or any form other than spoken words. Example:

- If you say something about a person in writing, including on the internet, then you are *liable* to be sued for *libel*.

Slander is the defamation of a person's name "not in writing." Imagine you're a guest on a radio or TV talk show and you say something unflattering about someone. In a case like that, you may be *liable* for *slander*.

Slander has another legal requirement. The injured party must prove that they suffered a loss of income as a result of your slander.

In other words, a rap star, or anyone else, can't have you say something bad about them, see record sales soar, then sue for slander.

Liable means "to be held accountable for," or "likely or susceptible to happen," as in "The obese man was liable to have a heart attack."

- As a result of the tell-all book she wrote, she was *liable* to be sued.
- Don't step on the grass, or he's *liable* to get angry.

A way to remember the differences is that the *s* in slander is for speaking, and the *a* in liable is for *apt*, as in "He's apt to get angry," or "He's apt to have a stroke."

Lightening/lightning

I see this frequently even among writer friends. *Lightning* (without the *e*) is what occurs naturally in nature, such as an electrical discharge. *Lightening* (with the *e*) means to lighten.

- The marketing department wanted a *lightening* of the ad background.

The word *lightning* doesn't need the *e* (for energy); it has enough.

Literally

A lot of people use *literally* wrong. Its original meaning was "accurate in the strictest sense," as in "He took her words literally and jumped off the bridge."

Today, the usage has changed. Many people use it, but not in the strict sense, as in "She literally died when she saw him dressed like that."

She may have been aghast, mortified, or appalled, but I doubt she died.

Loath/loathe

Loath means "unwilling or reluctant." It is an adjective and is almost always followed by *to*, as in "She was loath to admit her mistake" or "He was loath to accept the stolen money."

Loathe is a verb meaning "to detest, abhor, or to feel utter disgust for," as in "She loathed the manner in which he conducted himself at the dinner table" or "He loathed gangsters and street thugs, but he had good reason; his father had been killed by a thug."

◀ *Loathe* has an *e*, and the word *verb* has an *e*.

Loose/lose

This is an easy one to remember, and yet many people confuse it. I have even seen many writers confuse it, which makes you wonder what kind of editors they have.

Loose means "loose fitting, unbound, unattached," while *lose* is a verb that means you misplaced or lost something or someone in another manner.

An example might be "The panicked mother lost her child at the beach" or "He lost his keys." But "The young man's loose-fitting clothes showed too much of his backside" or "The knot was tied too loosely, and she escaped."

◀ An easy way to remember it is to think of the extra *o* as being *loose* or slack in a rope, as in "The noose was loose" or a runaway moose, as in "The moose was loose."

Luxuriant and luxurious

Luxuriant means abundant or florid, not *luxurious*.

- The writer used her *luxuriant* imagination to create a new world.
- The furniture delivered today was *luxurious*.

◀ Remember that *luxuriant* and abundant both end with *ant*.

Mantel/mantle

A *mantle* is a coat or a cloak. I haven't seen it used much of late, but the spelling and a few lingering sayings continue to confuse people.

A *mantel* is the shelf above a fireplace (where you might hang stockings for Santa).

🖐 There aren't many good ways to remember this one, but try to remember that a mantel is a shelf, and both contain the letters *el*, in that order.

Marshal/martial

Marshal is the name of many occupations, but they all deal with law enforcement of some kind. It wasn't always this way. Hundreds of years ago, a marshal was a person who took care of the horses (in old Germany). Later, the word was associated with the leader of cavalry, and still later, a military officer similar in rank to a general.

- Napoleon had some of the finest *marshals* ever.

Now we have U.S. marshals, fire marshals, air marshals, etc. Notice the spelling is with a single *l*. This is a word often misspelled with a double *l*.

Martial means "inclined toward war," but it is almost always used as an adjective, as in *martial arts*.

🖐 Try to think of the *t* in martial as representing "tai chi." If you can do that, you'll get this straight.

Mask/Masque

A *mask* can be a disguise or a cover for the face. Masks are a common sight at Mardi Gras; in fact, to be unmasked would be unusual.

Someone may also *mask* his/her efforts in order to hide them.

Mask may also mean "to alter a photo."

Masque refers to a form of entertainment that appeared mostly in the 1500s and 1600s. The actors wore masks during the performances.

🖐 Remember, there are always *masks* associated with a *masque*.

Meat/meet/mete

There aren't many triple homonyms in the English language, but they all seem to present problems and meat/meet/mete is one of them.

Meat is normally referred to as the flesh of an animal, like a steak or chicken. It can also mean the edible part of fruit or a nut.

Meet is to greet or be introduced to, as in "It's nice to meet you." It can also mean to wait for someone to show up, as in "I'll meet you at the bus stop" or "I'll meet you for lunch."

Mete is to distribute (usually evenly) or to "dish out" justice, as in "He meted out the punishment to the man who stole the horse."

🗨 Remember that *meat* contains the word *eat*, and you eat *meat*.

Minute (minit) and minute (mynoot)

Minute and *minute* are spelled exactly alike but mean different things. These are called homographs. The English language is full of them:

- He *read* (sounds like red) the book.
- *Read* (sounds like reed) the book.
- Listen to the *wind* (sounds like pinned) howl.
- *Wind* (sounds like find) the clock.
- *Lead* (sounds like reed) the horse to the stable.
- Superman can't see through *lead* (sounds like dead).

A *minute* (pronounced "minit") is a measurement of time—1/6oth of an hour.

- Give me a *minute*, and I'll be ready.

Something *minute* (pronounced "mynoot") is tiny or small.

- The watch consisted of many *minute* parts.

🗨 Try to think of the phonetic spelling of minute (mynoot). It has a *y* and *tiny* has a *y*.

Moral/morale

Moral and *morale* look similar, but the pronunciation is emphasized on different syllables. *Moral* rhymes with *plural*, and *morale* rhymes with *corral*.

Moral—as a noun—is used to indicate a lesson learned from an example or story, as in Aesop's Fables, where each story had a moral.

As a plural adjective, it means "virtuous," as in "His morals left a lot to be desired."

Morale, on the other hand, is a noun meant to indicate a person or group of people's spirits, as in "The human resource department felt morale was low after the board announced the merger."

◢ Since morale is associated with a person's emotional state, remember the word with the *e* means emotional.

Must of/must have and should of/should have and could of/could've

I hear this far more often than I should, and it's not always from uneducated people. The bottom line is this: "must of" and "should of" are simply the result of people mishearing the common contractions for *must have* (must've) and *should have* (should've) or *could have* (could've) or any of the other contractions that end in *'ve*.

◢ Remember, there is no *of* in must've or should've or could've.

Noisome

This is a strange word. Not that many words aren't strange, but this one almost always throws me off track. Perhaps it's the pronunciation.

It's pronounced as the combination of two common words —*noise* and *some*, so you might think it has something to do with noise, but it doesn't.

Noisome means "objectionable to the senses," especially smell.

◢ Remember that *noisome* has nothing to do with your hearing, but it does affect the senses.

Nonplussed

This word has been misused so often the wrong definition is in danger of replacing the real one, or at least being an alternative.

Nonplussed does *not* mean "not impressed." To be *nonplussed* means "to be confused, confounded, puzzled, etc." I doubt you'll ever have a reason to use the word, but if you do, rethink your word choice.

Novel: only used for fiction (when referring to a book)

Novel might refer to a work of fiction, or to a new thought, as in "that's a *novel* idea."

It is not used to refer to a book that is nonfiction.

Onto vs. On to

You wouldn't say "The dog jumped *on to* the sofa, but you would say "The dog jumped *onto* the sofa.

Onto is a preposition that means "on top of," and this makes a clever way to straighten out the two. If you can use the word *up*, you probably need *onto*, as in "The dog jumped *up on* the sofa." Since you can use *up* and still have it make sense, use *onto*.

But if two kids are talking after English class and one says "Let's move *on to* the next class," it wouldn't work to substitute *up*. Try it: "Let's move *up on* the next class." It doesn't sound right.

The other thing to remember is if the verbs *hold* or *move* are being used, there is a good chance it is *on to* and not *onto*, as in "He moved *on to* the next choice" or "She held *on to* the pen."

If you're old enough, you can think of the old soul song from the 1960s, "Hold On" by the Radiants.

Overdo/overdue

To *overdo* something is to overindulge, as in eating or drinking too much. It is a verb.

- Don't *overdo* the drinking.

By contrast, *overdue* is an adjective and means something is late or past due to be paid.

- The electric bill was *overdue*.

It's easy enough to remember the difference. *Overdo* ends with *do*, which is a verb, as is *overdo*.

And *overdue* ends with *due*, as in the bill was due.

Palate/palette/pallet

- A *pallet* typically holds forty bags of Portland cement.

- The painter's *palette* consisted of ninety-six colors.
- Her *palate* was extremely sensitive, which allowed her to distinguish subtle tastes.

These three words constitute another triple homophone—all three sound the same, but are spelled differently and have different definitions.

Passed/Past

This should be another easy one, but people frequently confuse it. *Passed* is the past tense of *pass* and should never be used in the sense of time.

You can say "In the *past* (place in time), he *passed* me by for a promotion." Or you could say "She *passed* me the pepper," or "The police car sped *past* me," or "The police car *passed* me on its way to the accident."

Remember, the *t* in past is for *time*.

Patience/patients

Patience: The ability to accept problems, frustrations, or delays without becoming anxious.

- He was losing his *patience* when trying to teach his daughter to drive.

Patient, on the other hand, is the adjective, as in "Be patient."

- She was a *patient* person.

A problem arises (as in the examples above) when we see the singular form of *patients*, which is *patient*.

A patient, besides being the adjective for patient, also defines "a person under a doctor's care," as in "He was a long-time patient of the cardiologist." And the plural form, *patients*, means more than one patient, as in "The waiting room was filled with the doctor's patients."

🔊 Remember that *patience* has a *c* in it, and you have to control your patience. *Control* and *patience* both have *c*'s.

Also remember that *patients* (with an *s*) always refers to people. If you see an *s*, someone is seeing a doctor.

Peace/piece

Peace is what you experience when you're not at war.

- The Pax Romana was one of the longest durations of *peace* the world has known.

Piece is a part of something larger, as in "Please cut me a *piece* of pie," or "I'll have a *piece* of cake, please."

The issues of confusion seem to arise more with associated sayings than the words:

✗ I'll give him a *peace* of my mind.

☑ It should be I'll give him a *piece* of my mind.

To give someone a *piece* of your mind is to let someone "share" your thoughts. Imagine you are reaching in and slicing off a *piece* of your mind.

The real confusion arises due to the other saying, "Peace of mind," as in "All she wanted was a little *peace* of mind." In this case, the person wished for her mind to be at rest, in other words, not to war with itself.

🔊 To remember this, think of slicing a piece of your mind and giving it to someone. In that case, it's going to represent "a piece of mind." If you want peace of mind (something good/desirable), you're talking about *peace*.

🔊 Remember, peace of mind is something you want. A piece of your mind is something you give.

Peak/peek/pique
Peeked/Peaked/Piqued

If you're going to use one of these words—especially on a résumé or another important document—make certain you use the right one.

Peeked is used for things like "He *peeked* around the corner to get a look at the new neighbor in her bikini."

- Electricity usage *peaked* during August, typically the hottest month in Texas. (I can vouch for that.)

This can also refer to the *peak* of a mountain.

- The mountain *peaked* at 19,000 feet.

Let's not forget *piqued*.

- Dear Gatekeeper: My interest was *piqued* by reading an article on the company's new product.

🖐 Remember that *peeked* is similar to *looked* and they both have repeated vowels and that *peaked* is like a mountain peak.

Pedal/peddle/petal

A *pedal* is something you control with your foot, as in "the pedal of a bike," or "the gas and brake pedals on your vehicle."

To *peddle* is to sell. In the old times, it meant door-to-door. In even older times it referred to peddlers in wagons. Now it has come to mean something different, as in "He peddled his drugs too close to the school."

A *petal* is one of the colorful parts of a flower.

🖐 Remember that a *pedal* is something you use. *Peddle* is something you may do. And a *petal* is something you may want.

Peer/pier

A *peer* is, in one sense, an equal, as in a jury of his peers. It also means to look or stare in order to obtain a clearer sight.

A *pier* is a shipping dock. It is usually built on legs and begins on land, stretching into the water so that ships can moor there and load or unload cargo.

🖐 Remember that "to peer" is to see or look, and *peer, see, and look* have repeated vowels at the beginning.

Penultimate/ultimate

Penultimate confuses many people. They think it means "the most" or "the ultimate," when actually it means "next to the last."

It stems from the word *penult*, which means "the next to the last syllable." The problem is that many people don't know its meaning, so when they see *-ultimate*, they assume (erroneously) that *penultimate* is even more than *ultimate*.

I don't see the public changing anytime soon, so my advice (not *advise*) would be to refrain from using the word—that is, if you're ever tempted to.

People/persons

Person refers to one. *People* to more than one, as in "There were a lot of people at the beach."

Persons used to be the plural of person, but common usage has substituted *people*.

"Missing persons" and "persons of interest" are a couple of examples where you still see persons used frequently. It seems to be used more in law enforcement situations than anything.

Perpetrator/suspect

As any loyal fan of crime shows can tell you, a *perpetrator* is the person who did the crime, and a *suspect* is a person suspected of being a perpetrator.

- The police arrested a *suspect* for the robbery, but he was not the *perpetrator*.

Remember that a suspect is suspected of a crime, but they didn't necessarily commit the crime.

Persecute/prosecute

Prosecute means *to start legal proceedings against*, as in "The assistant district attorney decided to prosecute him for murder."

Persecute means to harass or torment, especially if related to religion, race, or sexual orientation.

- The pilgrims were *persecuted* for their religious beliefs.

🖋 Remember that *prosecute* begins with pro and it is usually (or should be) good.

Peruse

Peruse means "to examine carefully, or at length," but it is often used in the opposite sense, as in "I perused the résumé" when they really mean, "I scanned the résumé." Some dictionaries offer alternate definitions of *peruse* now—"to read casually"—which is the opposite of thoroughly.

Common usage is such that you could use it either way, but for the sake of consistency and clarification, I'd stick with one or the other, and preferably the right one.

Per se/per say

Per se is Latin for "by itself."

Per say is not a saying.

Per se means "by itself" or "in itself," as in "Stealing a loaf of bread to feed your child does not, *per se*, mean you are a thief."

Why would you say this instead of just "by itself?" I don't know, but if you are inclined to use the saying, do it properly.

Per say is simply a common misspelling of *per se*, so it is not a grievous error.

🖋 Remember the *y* in per say, and think why would I use the one with *y*?

Plethora

Plethora does not mean "a lot." It means "too many, an overabundance." An example may be—"The pond had a plethora of fish," meaning there were too many fish to live comfortably (or even too many to live). But you wouldn't say Baskin Robbins has a plethora of ice cream flavors.

Poisonous/venomous

If you're ever on a quiz show and the question is "How many poisonous snakes are native to North America?" The answer is *none*. A snake is not poisonous, it's venomous.

Certain tree frogs are poisonous. Some plants are poisonous. But anything that needs to bite or sting you to make you sick is considered venomous; therefore all poisonous snakes are venomous snakes. (There is one exception that I know of. The Asian Tiger Snake is considered to be venomous *and* poisonous due to a diet of poisonous toads.)

🖐 It's simple to remember. Things that are poisonous need to be touched or drank, while venom needs to be injected.

Pore/pour

A pore is a small opening, as in "the pores of your skin," and in the verb form, it means "to read or study something intently," as in "He pored over the law book."

Note that pore, when used as a verb, is almost always coupled with "over" or "through."

Pour, on the other hand, is "to flow," as in "He poured the customer a beer" or "It's going to pour (rain)." It doesn't have to be liquid either. Think of "Pour the sand out of the bucket."

🖐 Remember that *pour* and *out* both have the letters *o* and u in them, and you often use *out* with *pour*, (as in pour out the sand) but you never use out with *pore*.

Precede/proceed

Precede means "to take place before something else," as in "The discovery of America preceded the Revolutionary War."

Proceed is a verb meaning "to move forward, continue what you were doing, keep at it, etc.," as in "Proceed to the counter, please."

🖐 It's easy to remember the difference, as *precede* begins with *pre*, which means "before."

Premise/premises

A premise is a proposition upon which an argument is based, as in "The premise of her argument was . . ."

Premises is a site, as in "The police searched the premises" (always used in plural form).

Note that even though *premises* is spelled in the plural form and there may be several buildings on the site, it refers to one location. And even though it refers to a singular site, it takes a plural verb, as in "The premises were thoroughly searched."

🖐 Think of the *s* at the end of premises as meaning *site*.

Presence/presents

Presence is the opposite of absence; in other words, presence means "the state of being present, in existence." It can also mean "a person's state of mind," as in "She had the presence of mind to remain calm."

Present can be a noun, meaning a gift, as in "He gave her a bracelet as a present." It can also be a response to "roll call," as when a teacher calls your name and you respond, *Present*," meaning you are there, you are in attendance.

Present might also be a verb meaning to introduce formally, as in "He was presented to the ambassador" or "Let me present you to the ambassador."

Presents is the plural of present, as in "He received many presents at Christmas."

Preventive/preventative

There have been heated arguments over the usage of these two words, and yet, common usage shows *preventative* gaining ground. It's not gaining ground by increased usage, but because *preventive* is declining quickly as the screenshot below shows.

preventive and preventative

Some people subscribe to the theory that *preventive* is an adjective, and *preventative* is a noun, but there is no basis for this argument. As far as I'm concerned, use preventive and save a few letters.

Principal/principle

Principle can only be used as a noun, as in "a person of moral principle." A *principle* is not a person, so it is never a school *principle*. It is a school *principal*.

Principal can be a noun or an adjective, so you may pay the principal on a loan, go see the principal, or be the principal (main) person in a movie or stage production.

🖎 Remember that a *pal* is a person, and principal ends with *pal*, so the school superintendent is the principal.

Prostate/prostrate

Prostrate means to lie facedown on the ground, usually in supplication, like they did for the old kings and queens. There is no prostrate gland or cancer of the prostate.

When referring to the gland near the bladder, it is *prostate*—no *r* after the *t*.

If you hear that someone has a prostate problem, it doesn't mean that they have a problem lying (not *laying*) in front of their monarch.

🖎 Remember that prostrate contains an extra *r* and the word recline also contains an *r*. Both mean to put yourself in a certain position, either reclining or lying down as opposed to prostate, which is a gland.

Raise/raze

Raise and *raze* can almost be opposites. To raise something up is to lift it. To give someone a raise means to increase their pay.

To raze something is to tear it down, as in "The Romans razed the city of Carthage after the Third Punic War."

🖎 Remember that *raise* is contained in the word praise, and that they are both something good.

Rapped/rapt/wrapped

This is another triple homophone—they sound the same but have different meanings.

Rapt means to be engrossed in thought or focused on another place. I believe the word *rapture* comes to us from the same root word.

Rapped is the past tense of *rap*, meaning to tap or knock on the door, as in the line from Edgar Allen Poe's, *The Raven*, ". . . rapping at my chamber door."

Wrapped is the past tense of *wrap* and means "to cover something on all sides," as in "She wrapped all the birthday presents in princess paper" or "He was cold, so he wrapped himself in a blanket."

🐾 Remember that *rapt* is similar to rapture, *rapped* is like a rap star, and *wrapped* is like wrap a Christmas present.

Redundant

Something *redundant* is not needed or in excess.

- Some computers have redundant parts that are only there to function in case their duplicate parts don't.

- The welder's job became redundant with the purchase of the new robot.

A redundant phrase means one of the words is unnecessary, usually because it is implied in the other word. An example might be "advance notice," as in "The landlord gave me advance notice that the exterminator would be there." Isn't that the same as, "The landlord gave me notice that the exterminator would be there"?

As you can see in the previous sentence, *advance* wasn't needed; it was *redundant*.

Reign/rain/rein

This is another triple homophone, and some of the words are often confused. First let's look at the differences, then we'll see how to distinguish them.

To *reign* is to rule, as in "The king was benevolent and his *reign* was good. He *reigned* for fifty-four years." As you can see in the preceding sentence, reign can be a noun or a verb.

Rain is a liquid that falls from the sky, as in "It's going to rain like hell." It has come to mean other things, as in the 1980s song by the Weathergirls, "It's Raining Men," meaning there was an abundance of men.

Reins are the leather straps you might use to control a horse. *Rein* is also the word used in the sayings "Give it free rein" or "Rein it in."

🖐 So how to tell the difference? Try thinking of the *g* in *reign* standing for gold, and a king or queen should have gold.

🖐 Or think of rain is a pain.

Regard/regards
In regard to/In regards to/or as regards
Regards/"with regards"/Regarding

You may see any combination of these terms, especially in business writing. They are used when referring to something, as in "in regards to the project . . ." Or to close out a letter, as in "With regards" or "Regarding the meeting . . ."

The definitions are a bit confusing as well. There are so many, you may end up scratching your head.

- To hold in high esteem, to look at, to consider, to show respect for, and more.

Most style guides consider "in regards to" or "with regards to" as nonstandard, preferring "in regard to" or "with regard to" or even "regarding."

🖐 I have a standard rule I try to follow. If I am going to use *to*, I never use the plural—*regards*—and always use the singular—*regard*.

I would write, "in regard to" or "with regard to," not "in regards to" or "with regards to." Of course, I usually abandon both choices and opt for the simpler *regarding*.

If you're looking for a way to refer to something or someone, try using *regarding*. If you want to close a letter, there are plenty of other ways to do that, casual and formal. Try *sincerely, warmly, thanks, thank you, etc.*

🖐 If you decide to stick with *regard* (singular), remember that you don't use *anyways, afterwards, onwards,* or *towards*, and you don't use *regards*.

Regime/regimen/regiment

A *regime*, by definition, is a system of rule or a government.

- Hitler's regime did not tolerate religious freedom.

A regimen is a guide for living, as in "She had a strict diet-and-exercise regimen." People often use *regime* to mean *regimen*, and it has become accepted. What is not accepted is using either one in place of *regiment* or vice versa.

A *regiment* is a military unit, so unless you are literally walking behind a cohort of Roman soldiers, so to speak, you would not say "I follow a strict regiment."

🐘 The *t* in regiment is for *troop*.

Reiterate

Reiterate means "to repeat again and again."

The problem comes in because *iterate* also means to repeat, so reiterate would mean to *re*-repeat.

I'm sure I'll catch hell for this, as this is one of those words that has gained widespread use and recognition, but if I were you, I'd steer clear of the saying "Let me reiterate."

Besides, you don't need permission. Why not just say what you need to? No one has to *let* you say something, so just say it.

Some people say that iterate is for an action that's repeated and reiterate is for words, but I don't buy it. As far as I'm concerned, say it once. If they don't understand it, shame on them. If they didn't hear you, speak louder next time.

Reluctant/reticent

Reticent means "inclined to be silent or uncommunicative in speech," as in "He was reticent and wouldn't speak his mind."

Reluctant means "not willing to or afraid to do something," as in "He was reluctant to jump from the high dive."

You wouldn't say someone was reticent to perform an act. They may be reluctant, but not reticent.

Resume/resumé/résumé

Resume means to start again, as in resume the position.

Résumé is a noun. It is a document that is a summary of your work history.

As a verb, you have no problem. *Resume* (pronounced re-zoom) cannot be confused with résumé. But the spelling can still be an issue.

Résumé is derived from French (meaning "to sum up"), and diacritical marks are used to distinguish the spelling. The problems arise because most people, myself included, are too lazy to type *résumé* the way it should be. They end up typing it as *resume*.

I was chided for this in my book—*No Mistakes Resumes*. That chiding did the intended job though, as I immediately made a typing shortcut for *résumé* so I wouldn't have such trouble in the future. (If you want to see more writing shortcuts, see the book I wrote about it.)

In most cases, you don't have to worry. I think the majority will be able to decide, based on context, which one you mean, but if you want to be safe, take the time to write *résumé* instead of *resume*.

Retch/wretch

To *retch* is to vomit, as in "The sight of the mutilated body was so grotesque even the veteran detective wanted to retch."

A *wretch* is a person of disgust, an undesirable character. We usually think of a wretch as being old, but that's not a necessity.

The stench of the *wretch* almost made him *retch*.

Revert

To *revert* is "to return to a former state," not "to reply or respond to someone." An example may serve best.

- He was loudmouthed and aggressive the night before, but this morning he *reverted* to his nondrunken, sober state.
- After the drugs wore off, she *reverted* to the pleasant girl she normally was.

Review/revue

A review (when used as a noun) can be a critique of a work of art, as in "The critic reviewed (verb) the play" or "The *NY Times* review (noun) of his book was not flattering."

As a verb, *review* means to reconsider, look over again, or critique something.

A revue is (usually) musical entertainment that constitutes a parody of current events or personalities, as in "The revue parodied President Obama."

👍 Remember that *review* contains the word *view* and that one of the definitions of *review* is "to look over or look at again."

Riffle/rifle

These are commonly confused words, in spelling and meaning. As a verb, *riffle* means to shuffle cards, or to flip through a book, or to skim a stack of papers. It can also be something that causes ripples or waves in the water.

To rifle something is "to search for something in a hurry," as in "The burglar rifled through the file cabinet."

It can also be used for the more common usage meaning weapon, as in "The rifle was actually a musket."

👍 The origin of the word *rifle* was to plunder, and it keeps that connotation when used as a verb, as in "He rifled through the cabinet looking for the files he wanted."

Riffle is more like shuffle, and they both have two *f*'s.

Right/rite/write/wright

This is one of the few quadruple homophones I know of, and the words are confusing to a lot of people. Let's try to work out the problems.

Right is the opposite of left. It also means correct. In addition, it can mean permission, as in "She has the right to do that."

Rite is a ceremonial act, as in a wedding rite.

Write is to place words on paper or a tablet, anything—even a computer screen. Write is the present tense of "to write."

Wright is an old word brought to us from the English. It meant "a worker," so *shipwright* is a derivative, as is a word you may be more familiar with—*playwright*.

🖋 Remember that you have the right to write anything. Who knows, you might even become a playwright.

Rights-of-way or right-of-ways

This falls under the same rules as you'll see in the chapter dealing with pluralizing compound words like daughter-in-law and mothers-in-law. It's *rights-of-way* not *right-of-ways*. Learn more about why in that chapter.

Role/roll

Role is the only one of the two that refers to a person, as in "The actress accepted the role" or "She was a great role model."

Roll refers to movement of some sort, as in "He rolled the ball," or "The plains of Kansas seemed to roll on forever," or "He responded to the roll call," or "rock n roll" or "The river rolled through the valley." As you can see, roll usually refers to movement of some sort. There are, however, exceptions: *roll* call, a *roll* that you eat, etc.

🖋 My suggestion is to think of the differences as mentioned —*role* refers to a person and *roll* to movement and all else.

Rung/wrung

A (usually round) piece of material that forms the steps of a ladder, as in "The ladder had sixteen *rungs*." The pieces between the legs of a chair that strengthen it, as in "He rested his feet on the rung of the chair."

As a verb, *rung* is the past perfect tense of the verb to ring.

- If you don't arrive before 1:00, I will have *rung* the bell for the waiter.
- The child knew she was late for church as the bells had already *rung*.

Wrung is the past tense of wring, as in "She wrung her mop dry" or "She wrung her hands dry while worrying about her son."

🖋 Remember that you can't climb a *wrung*, and the telephone can't be *wrung*.

Set/sit

Set and *sit* are often confused, yet it's easy to distinguish the difference. Set is a transitive verb. I know this is getting technical, but I listed it so you may understand that set requires an object and sit does not.

You need to *set something*, whereas you can *sit* by yourself. You can order your dog to sit, but you need somewhere to set your coffee cup. (It's similar to lie, lay, and laid and can be used to substitute for those words.)

🔊 A chair can *sit* on the patio, but it has to be *set* there first.

Sear/seer/sere/cere

Another quadruple homophone!

A *seer* is a person who says they possess the ability to "see" the future, as in "The seer swore he could see a war coming."

To *sear* is to burn, as in "He seared his arm while grilling the steaks."

Sere is an adjective meaning dried up or withered, as in "The desert consisted of sere vegetation."

Cere: you may go through your life and never hear this used. *Merriam-Webster's* defines it as:

A usually waxy protuberance or enlarged area at the base of the bill of a bird

---

🔊 Remember that a seer says he can *see* the future.

Shear/sheer

To cut a sheep's hair/wool, as in "He *sheared* the sheep."

- The farmer missed with the hammer and *sheared* the bolt.
- It was a *sheer* cliff—very steep.
- The woman wore a *sheer* blouse, but none of the men complained.
- What he said was *sheer* nonsense.

🖐 Remember that sheer has two *e*'s, and steep has two *e*'s. And shear contains the word ear, and you have to be careful when you shear a sheep's ear.

Shudder/shutter

A *shutter* is a louvered cover for windows. In the past, I think all, or most, houses had shutters on the windows.

To *shudder* is to shake or convulse because you are cold, or perhaps afraid. It was so cold his teeth were chattering and he was shuddering.

🖐 If it's cold, your body may shudder, and you must close the shutters to keep warm.

Silicon/silicone

Silicon is an element found almost anywhere on earth. It is a great conductor of electricity and is used as the basis for microchips. Silicon Valley is the area south of San Francisco so named because so many companies use silicon in the manufacture of their chips.

Silicone is a synthetic polymer that is used in many products including silicone breast implants.

🖐 Remember that silicone has an *e*, and it is made from a synthetic/fake substance, and both synthetic and fake also have an *e*.

Slay/sleigh

To *slay* is to kill someone or something, as in "The hero of a video game might have to slay a dragon and rescue a princess."

A *sleigh* is something used to ride on snow. It is typically made of wood and has metal rails. Some places (especially romantic getaways) offer horse-drawn sleigh rides.

🖐 Remember that *slay* is spelled similarly to pray. The princess had to pray that the knight would come to slay the dragon.

Sleight/slight

Sleight is derived from an old word meaning "cunning or sly." You seldom see it used now except in the saying "sleight of hand," referring to a magician's skill in manipulating something with his hands.

Slight (without the *e*) is a word meaning "small or insignificant," as in "He is slightly taller than his wife," or "The knife slipped, and he received a slight cut," or "The lack of an invitation was a slight she couldn't tolerate."

🐾 Remember that slight has the word light in it, and a *slight* and light cut are similar.

Sneaked/snuck

These words both mean the same thing. They are both the past tense of the verb "to sneak." *Sneaked* is the preferred usage, though *snuck* is gaining ground. This is an irregular verb, and as such, is one of those that has to be committed to memory, as it follows no rule.

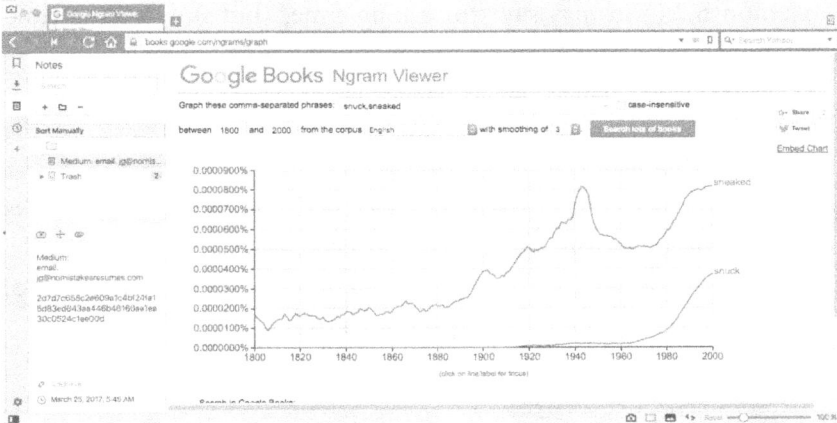

sneaked and snuck

While the usage of *snuck* is not as widespread as the verb *drug*, it is popular, as the Google Ngram results in the preceding screenshot indicate.

So to speak

"So to speak" is used to indicate that the preceding sentence or statement is not necessarily literally true but perhaps in a metaphorical way, as in "The dog was his baby, so to speak." It means that the dog wasn't really his baby, but he treated it as if it were.

Some time/sometime

This is another issue like *some one* and *someone* or *any where* and *anywhere,* etc.

Sometime means at an indeterminate point in time, as in "He is going to San Francisco sometime next month."

- It had been some time since he'd been to the book store.

🐟 Remember, if you can use "a long time" or "a short time" in place of the word, you're looking for *some time*, as in "It had been a long time (some time) since he'd been to the bookstore."

But you couldn't say "He is going to San Francisco a long time next month." (You may say "for a long time," but not "a long time next month.")

Spilled and spilt

While I don't see this as often in writing, I do frequently hear it used. The difference is primarily a U.S./U.K. issue, but it hasn't always been that way. I have provided two Ngrams—one shows usage in American English and the other in British English. Notice the shift of predominance in the United States around 1900, whereas it didn't happen in England until 1950.

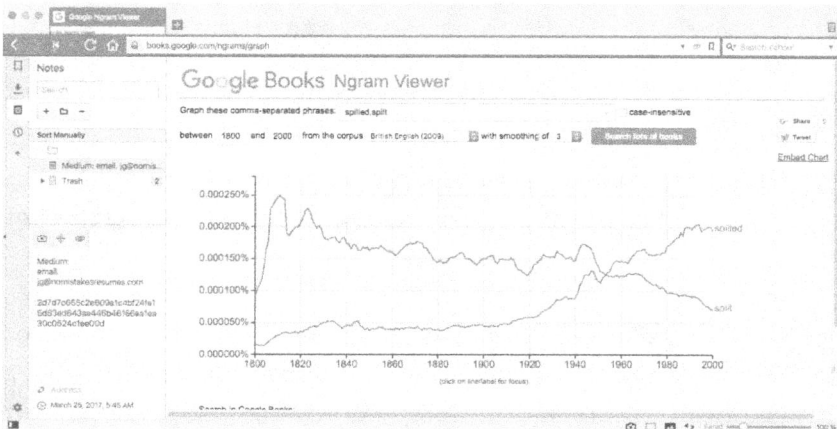

British usage

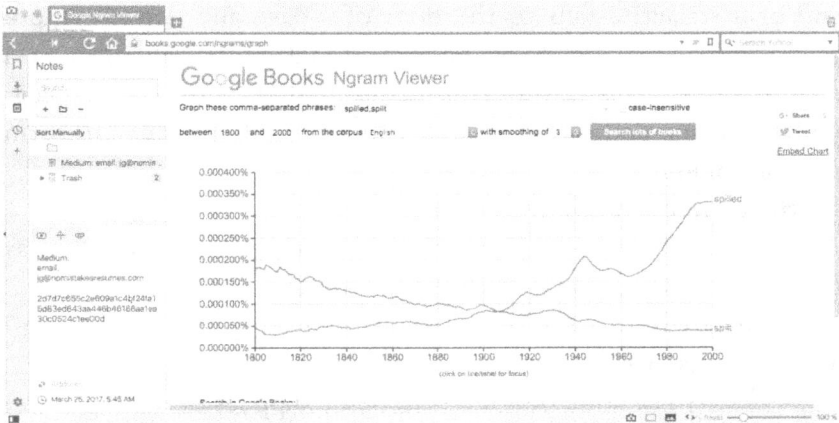

U.S. usage

Stair/stare

A *stair* or stairs (usually referred to in the plural form) is a platform or set of steps that exists between two floors of a home or building.

- He climbed the stairs to reach the second floor.

To *stare* at something or someone is to look at them (focus on them) without blinking, usually for an extended period of time. I know you've heard somebody's mother say:

- It's not nice to stare.

Remember that *stair* contains the word air, and a long set of stairs goes into the air. Also, *glare* and *stare* are spelled similarly.

Stalagmites and stalactites

Stalagmites are formed from the ground up, so water dripping onto the floor of a cave will make them over extended periods.

Stalactites are formed from the top down, so the water forms into stalactites as it slowly drips from the ceiling of the cavern.

According to How Stuff Works, the water dripping from the

end of a stalactite falls to the floor of a cave and deposits more calcite into a mound. Soon enough, a stalagmite will form in a conical shape. This is why you usually find stalactites and stalagmites in pairs, and sometimes they'll even grow together to form one big column.

Stationary/stationery

Stationary is an adjective meaning in a set place, not moving, as in "He was driving wildly and hit the stationary car."

Stationary is an adjective meaning "in a set place, not moving," as in "He was driving wildly and hit the stationary car."

Stationery is a noun that refers to office supplies or writing materials, as in "I need some pens and paper clips, so I'm going to the stationery store."

This is one of those words you may have to commit to memory. If you think of a tip for remembering the difference, let me know. The only one I can think of is that *stationery*, with an *e*, is the one that means office supplies, which would include a pen, which also has an *e*. (Weak, I know, but it's all I have for now.)

Steal/steel

Steal is a verb that means "to take from someone without paying." It can also be used as a noun (slang), meaning "a bargain," as in "The price on that TV is a steal."

Steel is a hard metal made from iron and carbon, as in "Superman is known as the man of steel."

Remember to think of Superman as the *man of steel* and you'll know which spelling to use. After all, Superman wouldn't steal.

Also, some wheels are made of steel and they are spelled in a similar fashion.

Story/storey

This is another one of those easy ones. *Storey*, with the "e," is not a word in the United States; however, it is in the United Kingdom. In the United Kingdom, *storey* is the level of a building, as in "His office is six storeys high." In the United States, you would say "His office is six stories high."

- *Storey*—a level of a building (United Kingdom)
- *Story*—a tale or account

Remember, like so many others, the one with the *e* is for England.

Straight/strait

A *strait* (without the *gh*) is a narrow body of water connecting two larger bodies, as in "The Bering Strait separates Alaska from the Soviet Union, and connects the Pacific Ocean with the Arctic Ocean."

Strait can also mean "bound tightly," as in *straitjacket* or *strait-laced*. (not straightjacket—although it is recognized—or straight-laced) Straight-laced has now come to be, not only a variant spelling, but a variant meaning.

Straight-laced describes a person rigid in their views, while *strait-laced* refers to the more traditional meaning of "narrowly bound," as in "The slim girl's movement was restricted by the strait-laced corset."

In the plural sense, *straits* means "in a difficult situation," as in "Having lost everything in the stock market, he is now in dire straits."

A *straight* is a hand in poker, not as good as a flush but better than three-of-a-kind.

It can also mean "without bending, no angle," as in "Can you draw a *straight* line?"

Or the shortest distance between two points is a straight line. It can also mean "honest and upright," as in "He'll make you a straight deal" or a sober person, free from drugs or alcohol, as in "He's straight now." Cops often ask you to walk a straight line as a means of testing for alcohol.

Swim/swam/swum

This trio, though often confused, is easy to remember and get right.

Swim is present tense, as in "I like to swim."

Swam is past tense, as in "I swam in the pond yesterday."

Swum is only used with helping verbs, as in "She hasn't swum in years."

🖐 Helping verbs. Need I say it again? If you use a helping verb, use *swum*.

Tack/tact

Tact is the ability to deal with, or have sensitivity toward, social or political situations, as in "The ambassador was hired due to his tact."

Tack is a less often used but quite often misused word that means "opting for a different course or a different approach," as in "to change tack" (not "change tact").

Tack can also mean "to add to" as in "The state tacked on a surcharge of $1.50 per pack on cigarettes.

Furthermore, it can mean a small nail, as in "He pricked his finger with the thumbtack," or "He used a tack to hang the calendar on the wall."

Isaac Newton said "Tact is the art of making a point without making an enemy."

— ISAAC NEWTON

Taught/taut

Taught is the past tense of *teach*, as in "He taught us Latin" or "The new Spanish teacher taught us the language of the streets."

Taut is "to pull tightly," as in "The continual use of steroids had pulled the skin tautly across his bones."

🖐 Remember, "He taught me how to catch a snake" and "He caught the snake." (*Caught*—the past tense of *catch* is spelled like *taught*.)

Tenet/tenant

A *tenet* is a belief, an opinion, or a principle usually held to be true.

A *tenant* is a person who rents an apartment, a house, land, an office—anything for a limited time.

🖎 Remember that tenant has the letter *n* as does *apartment*.

Than/then

Than and *then* are two of the more confused words ever, and yet there is a simple rule to follow to distinguish the difference.

Than is used for comparison.

Then is associated with time.

It's probably best to show you with examples.

- I would rather play golf *than* swim (comparison).
- Let's play golf, *then* go swimming (time).

In the first example, we are comparing the options, and in the second example, we are suggesting a time or sequence of doing things. Let's first do this, then we'll do that.

🖎 Since this is such a difficult choice for some people, I'll try to provide another tip. *Than* (which is used as a comparison) has no one-word substitute. In other words, you cannot use another single word that means the same thing. Try it. In the sentence "I would rather eat a pear than an apple," try to use another word.

You could say "I would rather eat a pear as opposed to an apple," but then it wouldn't be one word.

Then, on the other hand, can have many substitutions (synonyms). Try it. "Let's watch the movie, then we can eat." Now substitute *afterward*. "Let's watch the movie; afterward, we can eat."

You can also use subsequently, after, and any other synonym that fits. They don't all work in every instance, but in many cases they do.

Then can also refer to things other than time. Look at these definitions from *Merriam-Webster's*.

: in addition : BESIDES

  then there is the interest to be paid

: as a necessary consequence; if the angles are
equal, *then* the complements are equal

: in that case; take it, *then*, if you want it so much

: used after *but* to qualify or offset a preceding statement;
she lost the race, but *then* she never really expected to win

---

As you can see, *then* can have many uses, but *than* is only used for comparison.

Theater/theatre

Same as *catalogue*. It's another U.S. versus the U.K. situation.

Theater is United States, while *theatre* is United Kingdom

🖎 Remember it the same way as *catalogue*. The one that ends with the letter "e" stands for *England*.

Their/there/they're/there're

Their is a possessive, as in "Where is *their* house?" or "Which house is *theirs*?"

There is an adverb. In some cases it is the opposite of here, as in "Do you want to come here, or should we go *there*?"

It can also be a noun or a pronoun, as in "*There* is the golf course I want to play."

or, "*There* will be hell to pay when she finds out what you did."

They're is a contraction for "they are," as in "They're eating dinner now."

🖎 Remember, if the word you are looking to use is a possessive, use *their*. If the word is a contraction, and you can use "they are" instead, use *they're*. And in all other circumstances, use *there*.

There's/where's/here's

See explanation under *here's* in the "Miscellaneous" section

Threw/through/thru?

Threw is the past tense of *throw* and means "to propel, hurl, or cast." It usually means to hurl by hand, as in "The young boy threw a rock through the window." It can also mean to throw your voice (ventriloquism) or cast a shadow (throw a shadow).

Through means to go through something, as in "He went

through the traffic signal" or "Tarzan swung through the trees." It can also mean to be done with, as in "I'm through with that."

Thru is now listed as a variant spelling of through, though it is still not universally accepted. It's okay in informal settings, such as texting or emailing a friend, but I wouldn't suggest it for business usage.

Till/until

Till and *until* are interchangeable words. Take a look at these sentences:

- We ate till we were stuffed.
- We ate until we were stuffed.
- We watched movies till midnight.
- We watched movies until midnight.

Some people think that *until* is more formal, but *till* is the older word. When it goes wrong is when people use the contraction *til*.

If you want to use *till*, feel safe. If you want to use *until*, feel safe. But if you want to feel safer, use until, then no one will question you.

Time:

When writing a.m. and p.m., you may use lowercases letters with or without periods. You may also use uppercase letters with or without periods. Just remember to be consistent.

To/too/two

To is a preposition used to express or indicate a motion or direction:

- He went to the market.
- I'm sailing to Italy.
- Let's go to the mall.
- Give the ball to her.

Too means "in addition to" or "also." It can also function as an intensifier meaning "excessive," as in "The bathtub was too full, causing it to overflow when the boy got in." Or imagine several teenagers conversing. One may say "I'm going to the mall," and another says "I want to go too (also)."

Two is the way to write out the number two, as in "I'd like two bags of potato chips."

🐚 Despite this being one of the most confused homophones, it's fairly easy to remember. Two can be substituted with the number 2. If you can't use 2, then it's one of the others.

🐚 You have *to* and *too* left. Think of it this way: *too* has an extra *o*, so it's the word that means *also* or "in addition to," as in "I want one too." That leaves only one choice, so if your word isn't one of the first two, the only one left is *to*.

Tortuous/torturous

Something that is *tortuous* is twisting and winding, as in a *tortuous* climb up the side of the mountain, while something *torturous* is most likely painful.

🐚 *Torturous* is associated with torture. Remember they both have two "r's."

Toward/towards

Same as *backward/backwards*. In the United States, use the word without an *s*. If you're in the United Kingdom, use the *s*.

Other words that fall into this category are: afterward, backward, forward, inward, onward, outward and toward.

I'll include a few Google Ngram screenshots. One is United States and one is United Kingdom.

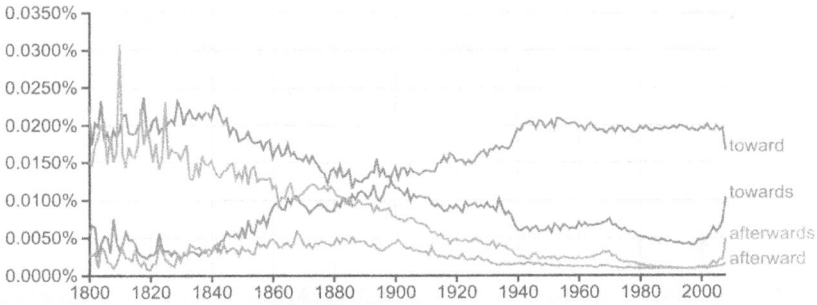

U.S. usage

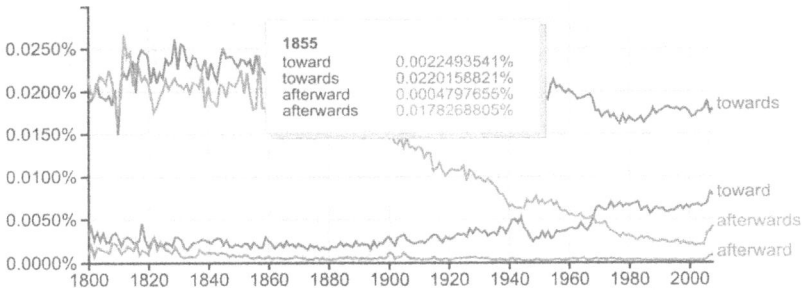

1855	
toward	0.0022493541%
towards	0.0220158821%
afterward	0.0004797655%
afterwards	0.0178268805%

U.K. usage

Trimester

A *trimester* is a period of three months. Some people think it means one-third (⅓) because the word *trimester* is typically used with things that last nine months, such as pregnancies or school years. But the word actually means "three months," which means a year has four trimesters. It just so happens that a pregnancy and a school term have nine months, so a trimester equals one-third, making a trimester a convenient way to divide them up.

Try to/try and

This is one of the most questioned usage issues in all of grammar. So which is correct?

It would be easy to say "try to" was correct, but almost all research points to "try and" as an informal usage that is acceptable.

I lean toward "try to" simply because it sounds better to me, and there are a few sentences where "try and" doesn't sound right.

As an example, imagine someone speaking to Bob, and they say "Bob, try to fix the kitchen sink." Now read it the other way. "Bob, try and fix the kitchen sink."

To me, the second example doesn't sound right.

🖐 If you want an answer, I don't have one, but unless you have a specific reason, I'd suggest using "try to," and you'll be safe. Remember the two *t's*.

Ultimate

This is a word used to mean the last in a list; however, it is almost never used that way. It has come to be defined as "the best," "the most," etc., and seldom will you hear it used as originally intended.

Oddly enough, a closely related word, *penultimate*, as mentioned previously, is also misused. *Penultimate* means "next to the last," as in "the penultimate chapter" or "the penultimate choice," but it has also been used as "beyond ultimate" or "better than the best."

I don't know how that's possible, but it has.

So don't fear if you misuse *ultimate* as an intensifier, Google will back you up. However, if you want to impress others, use it the right way.

🖐 An easy way to remember the two is that *ultimate* begins with a "u" and "u" comes after "p," just like *ultimate* comes after *penultimate*.

Note: I had planned on *ultimate* being the *ultimate* on this list, but unfortunately it will not even be the penultimate.

Very

Very is another intensifier that is seldom needed and very, very overused. Remove it from the sentences below and see if it makes a difference (or does it make a difference in your head only?). If it doesn't affect the sentence, take it out or use another word to describe what you're trying to say.

- It was a very hot day.

- It gets very cold in Minnesota.
- He can be a very mean boss.
- She's a very pretty lady.

Now look at them without *very*.

- It was a hot day.
- It gets cold in Minnesota.
- He can be a mean boss.
- She's a pretty lady.

Doesn't make any difference, does it? The best solution is to use a better choice of words:

- It was a scorcher.
- It's freezing in Minnesota eight months of the year.
- My boss can be a tyrant.
- She's gorgeous.

Vice versa

Vice versa is a saying from old Latin that means "the other way around," implying the reverse is true.

- My daughter-in-law loves her children and vice versa.

Vice versa implies that the reverse holds true also—that the children love her.

Want/won't/wont

Want, *won't*, and *wont* are often confused, especially with ESL students. The difference between "He won't go to the movies with his wife" and "He doesn't want to go to the movies with his wife," is subtle but significant.

In the first instance, he refuses to go, and in the second, he doesn't want to go, but he will.

Wont is a word that is almost never used. It means "accustomed to" or "usual (habit)." As an example, you might say "He was wont to run every morning."

🔊 Remember that *want* is one word, meaning "a desire or a need," and *won't* is a contraction of two words—"will not." You can almost forget about *wont* as it is unlikely you will encounter it.

Ware/wear/where

Ware and *wares*, represent products a merchant might sell, as in "The manufacturer sold his wares direct to the consumer."

To *wear* is to don a piece of clothing, as in "She wore a long skirt." It can also mean "to erode," (usually used with away) as in "The swift-moving river will soon *wear away* the banks that contain it."

Where is an adverb meaning place, as in "Where is he? We were expecting him by now?"

Weather/whether

There is an almost never-used word (wether) meaning male sheep or ram, but I doubt if you'll ever hear it, so for now we'll concentrate on the difference between *weather* and *whether*.

Weather is the condition of the atmosphere that tells you if it is snowing, raining, sunny, cloudy, etc. It may also refer to a future condition, as in "The weather forecast calls for rain tomorrow."

Whether is used to introduce a choice, as in whether you go or not, is up to you. Or it's going to rain whether you like it or not.

Whether (or not) Notes on usage

Courtesy of *Garner's Modern American Usage*: "Or not" is necessary when the phrase "whether or not" means "regardless of whether."

There are several complicated ways to determine whether to use "or not," but why be complicated? The simplest way to determine whether the "or not" can be omitted is to see if the sentence still makes sense without it. Here are a few examples:

- I don't know whether (or not) I'm going to the concert.
- If you use "or not," it makes no difference, so it's not needed. (You could also have used *if*.)

- I don't know if I'm going to the concert.
- I am going to the concert whether she goes or not.

Now, try the last sentence without the "or not," and you'll see it doesn't make sense. "I am going to the concert whether she goes" doesn't make sense, so the "or not" is needed.

Wheelbarrow/wheelbarrel

This surprised me that so many people misused this word. I had grown up around the word, so I learned it early, but apparently many did not. The short answer is that *wheelbarrow* is the correct way to say and spell it.

Wheelbarrow comes from *wheel* and *barrow* which is derived from the old English word *bearwe*, which was a device used for carrying loads.

There is no such word as a *wheelbarrel*.

🪨 I tell people to remember it by remembering barrels don't have wheels; in other words, there's no such word as *wheelbarel*.

Who/That

The general rule is to use *who* for people and *that* for inanimate objects (and animals with no name).

- The girl *who* you asked out is my sister.
- *That* rock is a ten-million-year-old fossil.
- Mollie (name) is the name of the dog *who* bit you.
- *That* dog is mean. (no name)

Which vs. That

See in-depth article under "Miscellaneous."

Who/whom

There's an easy way to know which word to use. Substitute *he* or *him* for *who* or *whom*. If *he* works, then use *who*, but if *him* works, use *whom*. Furthermore, you may need to turn the question into a statement to see if it works. So with the question "Who should I talk to?" You turn the question around and say "I should talk to him.

Since the answer was *him*, the proper way to phrase the sentence would be "Whom should I talk to?"

Note: most people don't use *whom* or even try to use it; in fact, if someone does use it, they are often looked at as if they were from another planet. The truth is the use of *whom* is quickly fading, and my guess is it's not long for this world.

👈 Remember to substitute he or him and that him ends with the letter *m*, the same as whom.

Who's/whose

This is another oft-confused word situation that is easy to rectify. *Who's* is a contraction for "who is" or "who has."

- *Who's* got the keys? (Who has the keys?)
- *Who's* going with us? (Who is going with us?)

Whose is a possessive form of who, as in "Whose car is this?" What you're asking is who owns the car.

👈 If you can substitute "who is" or "who has," then the word to use is *who's*. If you can't substitute those words, then the word is *whose*. There is never a case where you could substitute *who is* or *who has* for *whose*.

Widow/widower

There is a difference between the words—*widow* refers to a wife who has lost her husband, and *widower* refers to a husband who has lost his wife.

I'm not going to wonder how or why this distinction came about. I'm more concerned with remembering the difference.

👈 The way I remember it is by thinking of the black widow spider. It's the female whose bite is dangerous, and both a female who has lost her husband and the spider are widows.

With and withe

This example is for inadvertent mistakes, specifically the kind spellcheckers won't pick up on.

Suppose you're busily typing and while spelling the word *with*, you mistakenly type *withe*. *No problem*, you think, *the spellchecker will catch that*. It won't. Not if it's a good spellchecker. And that's because *withe* is a word, a real word. You may not have heard of it, but it's real, and it's pronounced the same way as *with*.

Now that you know it's a word, let's look at the similarities and differences.

The similarities are easy. Except for the first four letters, there are none. The differences follow.

With

With means accompanied by someone or something, as the following examples show.

- I often drink wine and eat cheese smothered with garlic.
- He often wears a red tie *with* his blue suit.
- She is never seen *without* her purse.

Now let's look at *withe*.

According to *Merriam-Webster's, withe* is:

: a slender flexible branch or twig

Etymology Online lists this as part of the word's history.

Old English wiðð e "twisted cord, tough, flexible twig used for binding, especially a willow twig," from PIE *withjon-, from PIE *wei- (1) "to turn, twist" (see withy).

One reputable source said it usually refers to branches of the current or preceding year.

Summary

I doubt if you will knowingly mix these words up, but mistakes happen, especially if you're not an accomplished typist. I hope if you make that mistake, you have a good proofreader because your spellchecker may not catch it.

Your/you're

I was going to add *yore* to this list, but it's seldom used, so I abandoned the idea.

Your is possessive, as in "Is that *your* car?"

You're is a contraction for "you are" and can easily be replaced by those words. An example would be "You're a superstar." (You are a superstar.)

There is a simple way to distinguish the difference. If you can substitute "you are," the word is *you're*. If you can substitute *my* and the sentence still makes sense, the word you're looking for is *your*: "Is that my (your) car?" or "Is that my (your) pencil?"

Chapter Sixty-Nine

FORMATTING AND STYLING OF WORDS

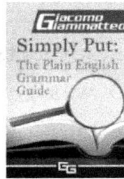

*T*he following words are not such grave errors, and often reflect a misinterpretation of what was understood (often from TV or the movies).

Assassin/killer/murderer

An *assassin* is considered someone who kills a prominent person (usually for money or a cause).

A *killer* is anyone who kills (the motive could be anything); in fact, *heart disease,* or *cancer* can be considered killers.

A *murderer* is anyone who is convicted of murder.

Burglary/larceny/robbery/theft

All the above words are related, but they carry different meanings.

Burglary (legal definition) means to enter a building and remaining (illegally) with the intent of stealing or committing a crime. Maybe you walked into a bank, then hid somewhere until after they were closed, with the intent of taking money.

Larceny is legalese for taking someone else's property or belongings.

Robbery occurs when violence or the threat of violence is involved: a stick-up on the street, or a car-jacking whether it involved a weapon or not, as long as a threat was implied. Stealing from an unoccupied house may also be considered *robbery*, as in the wider sense of the definition, it can mean "to plunder or rifle" which implies a person need not be home for *robbery* to take place.

Theft is the same as larceny that does not involve threat, violence, or plundering.

Claim/said

Claim and *said* are similar but they have slightly different connotations. *Claim* almost implies that what is being said is suspect, as in the store owner *claimed,* "The suspects were two, young Hispanic men," but the customer who was getting milk *said,* "They were Middle-Eastern men."

Days of the week

Spell out days of the week when writing, and all should be capitalized: Sunday, Tuesday, Friday, etc. Do not abbreviate them unless it's for inclusion in a table or a short list:

Sun. - hairdresser	Mon. -school	Tues. -nails
Weds. - grocery store	Thurs. - lunch w/Jean	Fri. - nothing

While we're on days of the week, we might as well cover months. Spell out months in running text, but if they must be abbreviated, such as when included with a table or when specific dates are used, follow these guidelines:

abbreviations

January = Jan.
February = Feb.
March = March
April = April
May = May
June = June
July = July
August = Aug.
September = Sept.

October = Oct.
November = Nov.
December = De.

- Jan. 14, 1957 is the year Humphrey Bogart died.
- The pool opened in May 2011.
- July 25th will be a good day.
- Dec. 25th will be a better day.
- Dec. 25, 2020 will be the best day.

Currency (money)
Dollars
A surefire way to be right is to spell it out:

- The candy cost eighty-three cents.
- He charge me seven dollars!

If spelling it out isn't an option, follow these rules:
Do not use $ along with the word *dollars*.

- He owes me $25.
- She bought a new car and it cost twenty-five thousand dollars.
- I heard the senator's house cost $4.12 million.

Cents
When writing cents there are only a few things to understand:
If it's a combination of dollars and cents, use the dollar sign and the decimal point placed in the right location. $7.56, $12.89.

- That milk was $5.69 per gallon!; I remember when it was less than a dollar.
- And those cigarettes you bought were $7.49 per pack; I remember when they were less than a quarter.

But if the amount is less than $1, no dollar sign is needed, though it may be used. 76c, 83c, and 13c is the preferred way, though $0.76, $0.83, and $0.13 is acceptable. Don't mix the styles up though. Pick one and stick to it.

Dimensions

Using numbers with measurements/dimensions. The first thing to know is in all but the most casual writing, spell out the words of the dimensions:

- He was a giant, 7 feet, 6 inches tall.
- The unexpected snowstorm brought 15 inches of snow.
- The worst rainfall I've seen was during Harvey. Houston got 53 inches of rain in three days.
- My barn is 40 x 60, that's 2,400 square feet.

In some situations, it's acceptable to substitute a *prime* mark for feet and inches. Examples below show.

- At 6' 8" he is a sure bet for the NBA draft.
- That fence is 5' 4" tall. He can't jump it.

If you go this route, make sure the marks you use are prime marks (not curly quotes). Below I show a measurement using curly quotes followed by one done properly.

- 5' 4" — 5' 4"

We've mentioned this before, but the easiest way to do this (on a Mac) is to type a regular quotation mark (single or double), then immediately press "⌘ z" (undo), and it will change the curly quotes to straight ones.

Ex

Ex is a little word, so it would be only right if there wasn't much fuss about it. *Ex* functions as a prefix, and there's not much to learn. When it is used with words meaning *out*, as in "He was *excommuni-*

cated (cast out) from the church, *excrete* (expel from the body), *execute* the process (carry it out)—use as one word.

When it is used in the sense of *former*, as in the *ex-president,* or the *ex-wife*, or the *ex-convict*, then the word requires a hyphen.

Homicide

Homicide is a legal term for slaying or killing.

Murder involves premeditated homicide. Some states define certain homicides as murder if the killing occurs in the course of armed robbery, rape, etc.

Generally speaking, *manslaughter* is homicide without malice or premeditation. To *execute* a person is to kill that person in compliance with a military order or judicial decision.

Military

The military and all its branches, rules, and regulations are too much to cover here, but we'll at least touch on it. The following table deals with the army only, ranks of officers and enlisted men.

army

Amry Officers: title	Army Officers: abbreviation
general	Gen.
lieutenant general	Lt. Gen.
major general	Maj. Gen.
brigadier general	Brig. Gen.
colonel	Col.
lieutenatn colonel	Lt. Col.
major	Maj.
captain	Caps.
first lieutenant	1st Lt.
second lieutenant	2nd Lt.

Officers

Enlisted Personnel: titles	Enlisted Personnel: abbreviation
sergeant major	Sgt. Maj.
command sergeant major	Command Sgt. Maj.
sergeant major	Sgt. Maj.
first sergeant	1st Sgt.
master sergeant	Master Sgt.
sergeant first class	Sgt. 1st Class
staff sergeant	Staff Sgt.
sergeant	Sgt.
corporal	Cpl.
specialist	Spc.
private first class	Pfc.
private	Pvt.

Enlisted men

This doesn't include Navy personnel or Air Force, or any other. The Marines would be similar.

Prison/jail

There is a difference between prison and jail, but if you listen to some people talk, there doesn't seem to be.

Jails are typically used to hold people (locally) on a temporary basis: if they're awaiting trial; people charged with misdemeanors/traffic tickets.

Prisons are typically used for long-term offenses (felonies and such), and the prisons are usually (but not always) situated away from the population.

- He spent two nights in *jail* for drunkenness.
- He was sent to *prison* for six months on the charge of drug possession with intent to sell.

That

There has been a big push to eliminate *that* from damn near all sentences, but some sentences do better when *that* is left alone. Let's take a look.

After the verb *said*, you can *usually* eliminate *that*.

- "His mother warned him. She said (that) 'It's going to be cold' "
- The CFO said (that) bonuses will be issued on Monday.

If you place a time element between *said* and *that*, it is usually needed.

- The CFO said *on Friday that* bonuses will be issued on Monday.
- The CEO announced *on the 22nd that* the offices would close until Jan. 2.

That is necessary after certain verbs:
advocate, assert, contend, declare, estimate, make clear, point out, propose, and *state.*

That is necessary before subordinate clauses beginning with the following conjunctions:
after, although, because, before, in addition to, until, and *while.*

- The actress said *that after* her latest performance, she was done.
- The gambler won a huge pot and said *that although* he was short of his goal, he was quitting.

Part Eight

USAGE

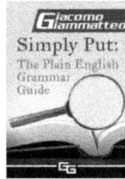

This section deals with some of the more common usage mistakes. In most cases (not all), the misuse is just that, the words being used in a manner which may not agree with recommended practice, but a few of the usage notations correct practices that are incorrect.

The "Misused Words" section covered the majority of items, but the ones that needed more discussion are covered here.

A few of the items covered here could have been placed in the "Grammar Myths" section, but I chose to put them here instead.

Chapter Seventy

LIE, LAY, LAID

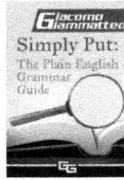

*T*here are more than enough misused words in the English language, and the proper use of *lie, lay, laid, lain* may be the worst.

Every explanation I ran across was rife with grammatical terms and difficult to understand. I did all I could to ensure the following has none of that.

The Easy Way to Use Lie, Lay, and Laid

Let's discuss two of the easier ways to remember how to use these words properly. Because not everyone learns in the same manner, one may suit you better than the other. Either one works, so pick which works best for you.

The Substitution Method

Never again struggle with how to properly use *lie, lay,* or *laid—* and even *lain*.

With this simple-to-understand chart, you'll immediately see whether you're using the words properly.

We'll be using a word-substitution process, and we'll be using commonly known words, so it should be simple.

By the way, the lesson includes *lain,* but almost nobody uses that word these days, so I don't mention it much.

Look at the chart, then look at the examples that follow.

Tense	Sit/sat/set	Lie/lay/laid
Present (meaning rest)	Sit	Lie
Past (meaning rest)	Sat	Lay
Present (meaning put down or place)	Set	Lay
Past (meaning put down or place)	Set	Laid
Present (meaning rest)	Sitting	Lying
Past (meaning put down or place)	Setting	Laying

Let's analyze the chart so that you understand it.

If you're confused about which version of *lie* or *lay* to use simply substitute *sit*, *sat*, or *set* to see which word sounds right, then refer to the chart to see which word to use.

Let's look at a simple example. If you were going to tell your dog to get down on the floor, would you say "Lie down" or "Lay down."?

Because you're telling your dog to do it *now,* you need to look at the chart next to *lie* and *lay* in the *present* tense. There are only two options—*sit* and *set.*

You wouldn't tell your dog to *set* down, you'd say, *sit* down, so looking at the chart, you'd see the answer is *lie.* You would tell your dog to *lie* down.

I could go on for pages, but I think that would only confuse things. If you use the chart, it's easy to determine which word to use by substituting the proper form of *sit* or *set.* Besides, *set* meant *put down* or *place* and those options didn't fit.

TENSES OF LIE/LAY/LAID AND SIT/SAT/SET

If you were going to write something like "I think I'm going to *lay* down." Before committing to the word *lay*, think of how you'd write the sentence if you were using either of the verbs *sit* or *set*.

If you are "going to *lie/lay* down," it is happening *now*, which means it's present tense. Looking at the chart, we see the only option for resting in the present tense is *lie*. So the correct way to write that sentence would be "I think I'm going to *lie* down."

When you want to use any of the verbs *lie, lay, laid, and lain*, think of what you'd say if you were talking about "sitting" or "setting" and use the appropriate word from the chart.

Let's look at a few sample sentences before moving on to the next lesson.

You may need to refer to the chart often when you first start. Afterward, using the words properly should come naturally.

To make it easier, I'll include the chart again (next page or next column, depending on which device you're using to read). I'll also list it further on so you'll have easy access to it.

Tense	Sit/sat/set	Lie/lay/laid
Present (meaning rest)	Sit	Lie
Past (meaning rest)	Sat	Lay
Present (meaning put down or place)	Set	Lay
Past (meaning put down or place)	Set	Laid
Present (meaning rest)	Sitting	Lying
Past (meaning put down or place)	Setting	Laying

See if you can get these right without looking at the answers.

GIACOMO GIAMMATTEO

- I was tired after working out, so I *laid* down for a nap.
- If you don't feel good, *lay* down for a while.
- The baby just woke. He must have been tired of *laying* down.
- You'd better *lie* down. You don't look so good.
- Shh. The baby's sleeping. My wife just *laid* him down to sleep.
- My wife is sleeping. She just *lay* down to sleep.

NOW, LET'S LOOK AT THE ANSWERS.

✕ I was tired after working out so I *laid* down for a nap.

    ✕ If you don't feel good, *lay* down for a while.

    ✕ The baby just woke. He must have been tired of *laying* down.

    ☑ You'd better *lie* down. You don't look so good.

    ☑ Shh. The baby's sleeping. My wife just *laid* him down to sleep.

    ☑ My wife is sleeping. She just *lay* down to sleep.

LET'S LOOK AT WHY THESE ARE RIGHT AND WRONG. IN SENTENCE number one, we said:

    ✕ I was tired after sleeping, so I *laid* down for a nap.

You said, "I *was* tired . . ." so it happened already, which means it is the *past* tense. When you look at the chart, you see that the only option for resting in the past tense is *lay*. Because that's the case, the sentence would read:

    ☑ I was tired after sleeping, so I *lay* down for a nap.

    🖒 *Laid* is *never* used to mean rest. It is *always* associated with setting or putting something down. Whenever you use *laid*, you should be able to ask "What?" as in "Laid what?"

Two More Examples

    ☑ I *laid* the flowers on the table (Laid *what* on the table? The flowers).

✖ I was tired, so I laid down for a nap. (Laid *what* down for a nap? See, it doesn't work.)

The next few sentences simply show the substitutions. And I've included another display of the chart.

Tense	Sit/sat/set	Lie/lay/laid
Present (meaning rest)	Sit	Lie
Past (meaning rest)	Sat	Lay
Present (meaning put down or place)	Set	Lay
Past (meaning put down or place)	Set	Laid
Present (meaning rest)	Sitting	Lying
Past (meaning put down or place)	Setting	Laying

✖ If you don't feel good, *lay* down for a while.

This is wrong because you're talking about the present tense—if you don't feel good, rest. Do it *now*. Because it's present tense, you'd use *lie*. What you should say is:

✅ "If you don't feel good, *lie* down for a while."

✖ The baby just woke. He must have been tired of *laying* down.

That's wrong because if you look at the chart, the continuous tense meaning "to rest" would be *lying*. What you should say is:

✅ "The baby just woke. He must have been tired of *lying* down."

✅ You better *lie* down. You don't look so good.

✅ Shh. The baby's sleeping. My wife just *laid* him down to sleep.

Here we use *laid* because your wife physically set/put him down. (As you can see, it answers the "What" question as well. My wife laid what down? She laid the baby down.)

But we're talking about sleep, you might say. We're really not. We're saying my wife *set* something down. That something happens to be the baby. So the baby is *lying* down, but he was just *laid* down.

✅ My wife is sleeping. She just *lay* down to sleep.

This sentence represents the instance many people have a problem with. But if you use the chart, you won't go wrong.

Also, you can't get it wrong if you adhere to the rule that *laid* is *never* used to mean sleeping or resting.

SUBSTITUTIONS WORK BEST

In the following exercises, try testing *sit, sat* or *set* as a temporary substitution for *lie, lay,* and *laid*, and I think you'll see it works nicely.

Tense	Sit/sat/ set	Lie/lay/ laid
Present (meaning rest)	Sit	Lie
Past (meaning rest)	Sat	Lay
Present (meaning put down or place)	Set	Lay
Past (meaning put down or place)	Set	Laid
Present (meaning rest)	Sitting	Lying
Past (meaning put down or place)	Setting	Laying

TRIAL EXERCISES

Choose the right word, then look at the next pages for the correct answers.

1. Where were you? I tried calling, but got no answer. Were you (laying/lying) down?
2. What time did you call? I was probably (laying/lying) down.
3. Please be quiet, I just (lay/laid) the baby down.
4. Now I (lay/lie) me down to sleep.
5. Now I (lay/lie) down to sleep.
6. I was tired yesterday afternoon, so I (lie/lay/laid) down for a nap.
7. If you don't feel well, you should (lay/lie) down.
8. Those groceries look heavy. (Lay/lie) them on the table.
9. When it's cold outside, I like to (lay/lie) in bed all day.
10. Bobby said he feels cold. (Lay/lie) him by the fire.
11. Bobby had a fever last night, so my wife (lay/laid) him by the fire.
12. Two hours after she put Bobby down, she felt bad, so she (lay/laid) down herself.

ANSWERS TO TRIAL EXERCISES

☑ 1. Where were you? I tried calling, were you *lying* down?

You use *lying* because you would have used *sitting* as a substitute.

☑ 2. What time did you call? I was probably *lying* down.

Same reason as above. You'd use *lying* because you would have used *sitting*. As a side note, you don't use *laying* if you're referring to rest, only for setting/putting something down. So it's the same as *laid* in that regard. Add that rule to your book. You don't use *laying* to refer to rest—**ever**.

☑ 3. Please be quiet, I just *laid* the baby down.

You'd use *laid* because you *set* something down—the baby.

☑ 4. Now I *lay* me down to sleep.

So, yes, as illogical as it sounds, this age-old saying is grammatically correct because it is talking about "laying" something down. The fact that it's talking about laying yourself down, which would not be easy to do, makes no difference from a grammatical standpoint.

It would be no different than saying "Now I lay the elephant down to sleep." We know you couldn't pick up an elephant and set it down, just as we know you couldn't pick up yourself and set yourself down, but from a grammatical standpoint, it's logical.

☑ 5. Now I *lie* down to sleep.

This one is different because you're not setting anything down, so it would be *lie*. In the previous example, we said, "Now I *lay me* down to sleep."

☑ 6. I was tired yesterday afternoon, so I *lay* down for a nap.

You're talking about rest, and you're referring to the past (yesterday), so according to the chart, you'd use *lay*.

☑ 7. If you don't feel *good*, you should *lie* down.

Again, look at the chart. It's speaking of resting, and it's present tense, so it's *lie*.

This was a double trick. Notice I changed the "feel well" to "feel good." We'll cover that in another section.

☑ 8. Those groceries look heavy. *Lay* them on the table.

This is the opposite of the two previous sentences. You're not speaking of rest, and it's present tense, so it's *lay*.

☑ 9. When it's cold outside, I like to *lie* in bed all day.

Try the substitutions for this one. "When it's cold outside, I like to (sat/set) in bed all day." As you can tell, they don't work, which means it's *sit*, and according to the chart, that means you should use *lie*.

☑ 10. Bobby said he feels cold. *Lay* him by the fire.

This one is similar to the children's prayer. You're laying something down—Bobby—so you would use *lay*.

☑ 11. Bobby had a fever last night, so my wife *laid* him by the fire.

This follows the same logic as the previous sentence. Because your wife is *laying* something down and not resting herself, the proper word is *laid*. Remember, if you run into trouble, use the chart. It clears things up immediately.

☑ 12. Two hours after she put Bobby down, she felt bad, so she *lay* down herself.

This one is different. She is no longer *laying* something down, she is resting. Looking at the chart, we see that because it concerns resting, and since it's past tense, the proper word would be *lay*.

🔊 **Remember, you don't use *laying* if you're talking about rest, and you don't use *laid* if you're talking about rest.**

If you can keep that in mind, you may be able to remember this: if you're talking about *rest*, you can only use the following:

- lie = present tense.
- lay = past tense.
- lying = any continuous use (present, past, or future) (I am lying. I was lying. I will be lying.)

I hope you now have a good grasp on when and where to use *lie*, *lay*, *laid*, or *lain*.

I don't want to leave you with the impression that all you just read was worthless, so consider this a great back-up. Learn the three rules below and you should be set, but if you forget the rules, you have the *substitutions* to fall back on.

🔊 The first rule is a simple reminder. **Never** use *laid* or *laying* to mean rest or sleep. If you remember that, all you need to work on are the words *lie* and *lay*.

🔊 If you are tempted to use the word *laid* associated with rest or sleep, use *lay* instead.

🔊 And if you are tempted to use *laying* associated with rest, use *lying*.

The rules that follow are easy, and there are only three of them. Learn them and you've mastered the use of *lie/lay/laid/lain*.

THE RULES

1. If you start to say "I was laying down when you called," you may realize that *laying* cannot be used with rest, so use *lying* instead. "I was lying down when you called."
2. If you start to say "I laid down," realize that *laid* cannot be used with rest so use *lay* instead. "I got tired last night and lay down."
3. Anytime you use *lie* or *lay* meaning "to rest," check the tense in your head. If you're talking about now, the word to use is lie. If you're talking about something that already happened, use *lay*.

That's it. You're done. You now are a master regarding the use of *lie*, *lay*, *laid*, and *lain*.

Chapter Seventy-One

MYSELF OR ME, AND ME OR I

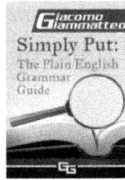

I often hear people overuse or misuse the word *myself*. It's not difficult to get right, so let's look at when to use *myself* and when to use *me*.

Myself or Me?

The use, or should I say *misuse,* of *myself,* usually occurs when there are multiple subjects. I don't like using grammatical terms, so I'll show you using a few examples.

- ✗ He went fishing with Jimmy, Missy, and *myself*.
- ✗ If you have questions, call Sean, Dante, or *myself*.

Both of those sentences are wrong. Think of how you would say the sentence without using the other people. You would likely say "He went fishing with me" or "If you have questions, call me."

Think of how you'd say a sentence without the other people, then add in whoever you want. In other words, if the sentence "If you have any questions, call me" is correct, so is "If you have any questions, call Sean, Dante, or me." The same holds true for "He went fishing with Jimmy, Missy, and me."

The use of *myself* as a subject is also considered wrong. In the examples above, turn them around to see. (I could have said, "to see for yourself," but that's a separate topic.)

- ❌ Jimmy, Missy, and *myself* went fishing.
- ✅ Jimmy, Missy, and *I* went fishing.
- ❌ Sean, Dante, and *myself* answered the calls.
- ✅ Sean, Dante, and *I* answered the calls.

If you're wondering when to use *myself* or *me*, remove the other people from the sentence and think of how you'd say it.

You wouldn't say.

- ❌ Myself went fishing
- ❌ Myself answered the calls.

You'd say.

- ✅ I went fishing
- ✅ I answered the calls.

When to Use Myself Correctly

One instance when you can correctly use *myself* is when you are the subject and object of a sentence. (I know I said I wouldn't resort to grammatical terms, but this isn't bad.) In the following sentences, the use of *myself* is correct.

- ✅ I can see *myself* parachuting. It would be fun.
- ✅ I'm going to treat *myself* to a new car with the extra money from the promotion.

There is another case where many people use *myself* for emphasis. It is accepted, if a bit dramatic. Examples are below:

- I witnessed the crime *myself*.
- I drew that *myself*.

While these are technically correct sentences, the use of *myself* is unnecessary. Look at the sentences without the word:

- I witnessed the crime.
- I drew that.

I understand why people use the word in instances like this; they use it to add emphasis. I simply don't agree with it.

Me or I?

The correct way to use *me* and *I* is easy; in fact, it's not much different than what you just learned. I think many people instinctively know it, but they have been corrected so often at an early age, they tend to overcorrect.

When you're young and first learning, teachers hammer in the basics to force you to learn. One of those basics is "You should use *I* when it's the subject, the one doing the action." A sentence like the following requires *I* to be grammatically correct, not *me*.

✅ Bob and I went to the movies.

❌ Bob and me went to the movies.

Most people had that example drummed into their heads so often that it not only stuck, it corrupted their instinct and made them hypersensitive to any construction using x and *me*.

That fear brings about sentences like the following:

❌ Mom gave Bob and *I* tickets to the movies.

✅ Mom gave Bob and *me* tickets to the movies.

Your instinct may have been to say, "Bob and me," but your tendency to overcorrect made you say "Bob and I."

Learn to trust your instinct; it was correct. And the reason it was correct was the same reason we discussed when speaking of "myself."

To see which word to use, remove the other parties from the sentence and determine which word you'd use.

✅ Mom gave *me* tickets to the movies.

❌ Mom gave *I* tickets to the movies.

It's definitely not *I*, so you use *me*.

Chapter Seventy-Two

COMPARE TO AND COMPARE WITH

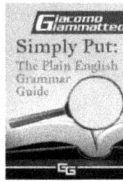

Compare to or Compare With
I was going to write something specific for these words, but then I thought it may be better just to copy a blog post I wrote about comparison using "compare to" and "compare with."

Some authors claim that "compare to" and "compare with" mean essentially the same thing, but this is not supported by actual data. The verb *compare* has several different meanings, some of which take the preposition "to," while the others take "with."

- Compare A *to* B to claim A and B are similar.
- Compare A *with* B to claim A and B are different.

To compare to is "to point out or imply resemblances between people or things." If you want to cite the similarities, use "compare to."

"To compare with" is mainly to point out differences between people or things. *If you want to point out differences use* "compare with."

The following examples will give you an idea of each (I hope).

The above (or previous page) picture shows the well-known apples-and-oranges comparison (with a few other fruits thrown in). While they are both fruits, and they are both round, and they both grow on trees, there are numerous differences, hence the saying that "You can't compare apples to oranges."

In fact, *Merriam-Webster's* likens it to comparing large trucks to compact cars.

Let's Look at another example

President A was passive, thoughtful, and an excellent orator. He is often compared to President Lincoln, who exhibited many of the same traits.

Or . . .

President A was passive, thoughtful, and an excellent orator. Compare that with *President B*, who is antagonistic, impulsive, and needs a lot of help with his speeches.

In the first example, we use President Lincoln to show how similar the two are. In the second example, we use *President B* to show how different the two are.

It's important to note, though, that the differences between "compare to" and "compare with" are largely ignored; in fact, common usage statistics show that in the United States., "compare to" is used almost as much as "compare with." There is not much difference in the U.K. usage either. The Google Ngram charts below demonstrate this.

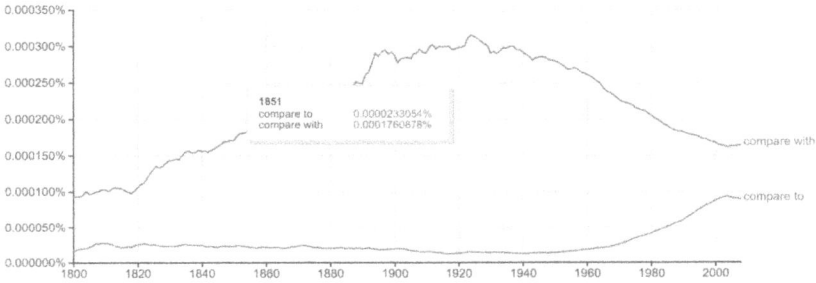

British usage

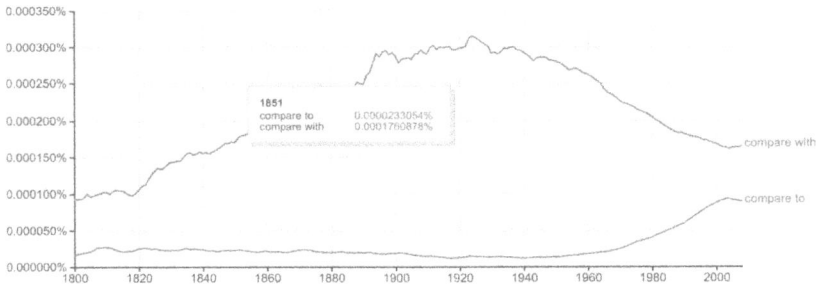

American usage

I admit I'm guilty of misusing this as much as anyone, but I'll work on getting it right.

Now that I've said all that, it's not uncommon to see *compare to* and *compare with* used interchangeably. And it's not such a grievous error. Regardless of usage, the readers will know what you mean, and that (clarity) is the goal of all writing—to make it clear what you're talking about.

Chapter Seventy-Three

HERE'S AND THERE'S

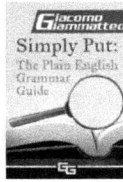

*I*s it *here's* or "here are?" *Here's* has crept up on my grammar list as the number-two mistake of all time, superseded only by *there's*. The way the language is changing, I'm sure it won't be categorized as a mistake much longer. But for the time being, let's look at why I list it as a mistake.

- "Here's ten things to put on your list."

Why is this wrong?

Because it should be "Here are ten things to put on your list."

Here's is a contraction for "here is." It is no different from the number-one error I see or hear, and that is *there's*.

Here's an article I wrote about the use of *"there's"* on résumés:

There's a Lot of Reasons ...

. . . why I'm writing this post, and the heading of this sentence is one of the primary ones. To a growing number of people, the phrase "There's a lot of reasons," and others like it are okay. They're acceptable. But to other people, in particular, résumé screeners and gatekeepers . . . let's just say it will make them cringe.

What's Rong wit Dat?

The correct way to write that phrase would be, "There are a lot of reasons ..." We use "are" because *reasons* is plural. You wouldn't say "We *is* going to the store" or "I *has* a reason for doing that."

The misuse of *there's* has grown to be one of the worse mistakes in language these days, followed closely by the misuse of *here's*, as in "Here's the reports you asked for." And even, *where's*, as in "Where's the reports I asked for?'

In all of the above cases the plural form should have been used. "Here are the reports you asked for." And "Where are the reports I asked for?'

Many of the problems stem from the use of "a lot." It can be singular or plural. Look at these examples:

- There is (there's) a lot to do.
- There are plenty of places to park

One trick is to substitute *much* or *many* in place of *a lot*. If *much* fits, use *there's*. If *many* fits, use "there are." In the sentences above, that would look like this: "There's much to do." (You certainly wouldn't say "There are many to do," would you?)

Or "There are many parking spaces." (Same thing—you wouldn't say "There are much parking spaces.")

If the sentence contains *a lot* and you can substitute *much,* use *there's* or "there is." But if you can substitute *many,* use "there are."

I even saw this mistake on a big site in a post about—are you ready for this—grammar mistakes.

In case you're wondering, "What's it gonna hurt?" Let me give you a little insight from someone on the other side of the desk. I'm a headhunter. I know. A not-so-noble profession by many standards. But some of us take our work seriously. If a client gives me an assignment, and that assignment calls for a candidate with "excellent communication skills," I take that requirement seriously.

So? You May Ask

So when I see a cover letter that starts out with "There's a lot of reasons why I fit this job . . ." there are two thoughts that cross my mind and only two:

- The candidate *doesn't know* they made a mistake using "there's" instead of "there are."

- The candidate *doesn't care* they made a mistake.

The problem is that no matter which of these thoughts is correct, it doesn't bode well for the candidate. If I think they don't know the proper way to say it, I'm forced to wonder why I'd hire them. And if I think they don't care, I definitely won't hire them.

Bottom Line

This advice is not restricted to cover letters or résumés. Anything you write is subject to scrutiny and judgment even your emails. And let's face it, you never know who will see them.

I'm sure the majority of you have heard the maxim, "Anything worth doing is worth doing right." And I'm sure you take that to heart in your job. But try to remember that rule applies to language as well.

Chapter Seventy-Four

I FEEL GOOD

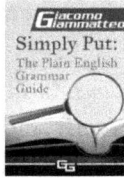

"*I* feel good" is wrong

There are a lot of phrases and words that are often misused. One of those phrases concerns the response to the oft-heard questions "How are you?" and "How are you feeling?"

This isn't the most difficult usage to grasp. That designation belongs to *lie* versus *lay*, but *good* versus *well* runs a close second.

I go to therapy twice a week. Invariably, I need to sit in the waiting room, and it's while I'm sitting there I often hear people's responses to the questions "How are you?" and "How are you feeling?"

A few people respond with "Good. How are you?" But most say "I'm doing well" or "Well, thank you." And they often emphasize the *well* as if to state, "That's how you say it."

Many of us grew up learning to respond that way, being taught that "well" was the preferred response because *well* is an adverb and *good* is an adjective. The problem is the questions "How are you?" and "How are you feeling?" do not require an adverb as a response.

I'm not going to get technical, as I don't like doing that. If you want technical reasons for why you need to use *good* or any adjective, for that matter, feel free to write to me. For our purposes, I'll make it easy to understand.

Any of the "to be" verbs, such as *am, is, are, was, were, been,* etc., as well as "sense" verbs, those verbs that describe the senses—*sight, feel, smell,* and *taste*—require adjectives (hearing does not apply, but the verbs *seem* and *appear* do).

Let's look closer at sense verbs

I'm going to list a few examples of statements or questions using sense verbs. And I'll list them with both adjectives and adverbs.

- ☑ That lasagna *smells delicious*. (adjective)
- ✕ That lasagna *smells deliciously*. (adverb)
- ☑ The apple pie *tastes wonderful*. (adjective)
- ✕ The apple pie *tastes* wonderfully. (adverb)
- ☑ That apple *seems crisp*. (adjective)
- ✕ That apple *seems crisply*. (adverb)
- ☑ She *looks amazing*. (adjective)
- ✕ She *looks amazingly*. (adverb)
- ☑ He said he *feels great*. (adjective)
- ✕ He said he *feels greatly*. (adverb)

As you can see, the sentences marked with the green check use adjectives, and they sound right. The ones marked with the red X use adverbs and do not sound natural.

So, yes, "How are you?" and "How are you feeling?" require an adjective, not an adverb, for an answer.

To Really Confuse You

I hope I don't confuse you with this, but *well* can be an adjective as well as an adverb. So for those of you who say "But I've seen *well* used as a response," this may be the reason why.

If someone says "How are you?" and you respond with "Well," know that you're using *well* as an adjective (meaning healthy) and not an adverb. What does that mean? It means you could have answered with *good, great, fine, wonderful, magnificent* or any other appropriate adjective.

Think of the reverse. If someone asks you, "How do you feel?" and you don't feel good, would you say "I feel bad" or "I feel badly?"

I am not going to go into a long discussion of action verbs, but they are at least worth mentioning. Action verbs are like they sound: they denote action. So with the sentences we just looked at —"How are you?" and "How do you feel?"—if they had been asked with an action verb, such as "How did you perform?" or "How did you dance?" it would change the way you respond.

In response to those questions, you'd say "I performed badly" or "I danced poorly." Take note that both answers included adverbs. Adjectives wouldn't have worked. Take a look: "I performed bad" or "I danced poor."

You may have heard that when referring to health, such as "How are you feeling?" You should respond with *well* all the time.

That is nonsense. It was (probably) instigated by the fact that since you can respond with *well* (using it as an adjective), people think it's an adverb (because *well* can be both).

But if you have questions, look at this statement from *Merriam-Webster's*:

An old notion that it is wrong to say "I feel good" in reference to health still occasionally appears in print. The origins of this notion are obscure, but they seem to combine someone's idea that good should be reserved to describe virtue and uncertainty about whether an adverb or an adjective should follow feel. Today nearly everyone agrees that both good and well can be predicate adjectives after feel. Both are used to express good health, but good may connote good spirits in addition to good health.

The next time someone asks you, "How you're feeling?" or "How are you?," feel free to say "I feel good," and know that it's a proper response.

And if you have a difficult time remembering which answer is right, think way back to the 1960s when the Godfather of Soul, James Brown, had a hit that was grammatically correct—"I Feel Good."

Chapter Seventy-Five

ANXIOUS AND EAGER

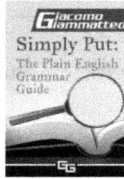

*A***nxious/eager** Some people use anxious and eager as if they were the same word. It is becoming more acceptable in common usage (which is a damn shame), but there *are* differences —meaningful differences.

Anxious stems from the word *anxiety*. The *Merriam-Webster's* dictionary defines anxiety as:

A: an abnormal and overwhelming sense of apprehension and of fear often marked by such physical symptoms as tension, tremor, sweating, palpitation, and increased pulse rate.

— MERRIAM-WEBSTER'S

Dictionary.com defines *anxious* as:

---

full of mental distress or uneasiness because of fear of danger or misfortune; greatly worried.

- I am *anxious about* meeting my fiancée's father, but I'm *eager to* meet her mother.

Dictionary.com defines *eager* as:

keen or ardent in desire or feeling; impatiently longing.

Notice that *eager* is usually coupled with *to*, and *anxious* goes with *about*.

You wouldn't tell the hiring manager that you are *anxious to* come for an interview.

You may be *anxious about* interviewing, but you should tell them you are *eager to* come for an interview. It will mean more to them.

"No one is more arrogant toward women, more aggressive or scornful, than the man who is *anxious* about his virility."

— - SIMONE DE BEAUVOIR

"When a man is willing and *eager* the gods join in."

— - AESCHYLUS

As with many words and phrases that break established rules, *anxious* and *eager* are no different.

While I stand by the traditional usage of *anxious* referring to anxiety or an anxious state, there is no denying that a significant portion of the people are using it to mean *eager*.

If you look at the Google Ngram below (or next page), you'll see that the use of "anxious to" has risen dramatically in the last few decades.

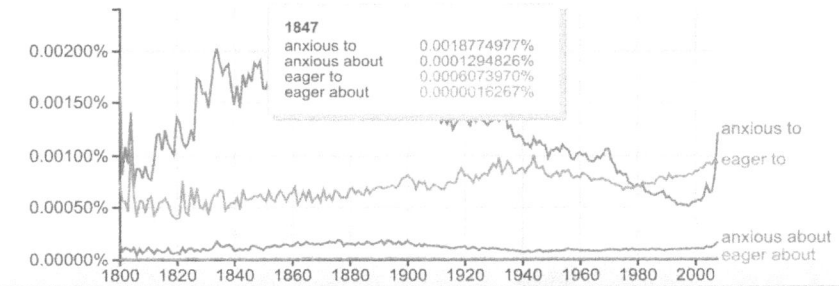

And despite not agreeing, I'm forced to admit there doesn't seem to be any stopping the transition. Look at this from the American Heritage Dictionary's usage note.

Anxious has a long history of use as a synonym for eager, but some prefer that anxious be used only to describe those who are worried or uneasy, as in the sentence He's anxious about his upcoming surgery. The acceptability of anxious to mean eager has been increasing, however. In our 1999 survey of the Usage Panel, 47 percent approved of the sentence We are anxious to see the new show of British sculpture at the museum, whereas in 2014, this sentence was acceptable to 57 percent of panelists. The acceptability was higher for this usage in a sentence about a situation with a tinge of uneasiness: After a four-hour bus ride, the children were anxious to get outside (acceptable to 69 percent of the Panel in 1999 and 78 percent in 2014). Although resistance to the use of anxious to mean eager is waning, writers should be aware that there are still those who frown upon using the word in situations where no anxiety is present.

— AMERICAN HERITAGE DICTIONARY

Chapter Seventy-Six

ANOTHER

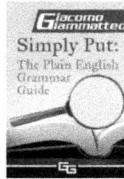

*A*nother is often used as a synonym for *additional,* and it can be used that way, but only under certain circumstances.

Another is used to refer to something previously mentioned, but only when it is duplicating the amount or number mentioned originally. Examples will show better.

Suppose you were at a retirement party and you ordered four beers for the people at the table. A few minutes later, you were joined by two more co-workers, and you called to the waitress and said, "I'll have another six beers." What you should have said is the following:

☑ I'll have six more beers.

Another is used to refer to the same amount previously mentioned; no more and no less.

If someone is on a diet and loses ten pounds, then the next week loses two more, you don't say "She lost another two pounds." You can say "She lost two more pounds," but not "another two."

ANSWERS TO QUIZZES

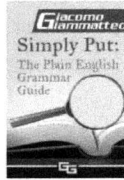

The quizzes dealt mainly with punctuation issues that were covered in the first section. One dealt with subject-verb agreement.

Chapter Twenty-Nine

ANSWERS TO QUIZ 1

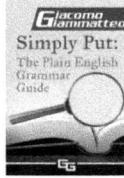

a **nswers To Quiz One**

    1. ✖ Sally went home for a nap then decided to stay awake (needs a comma before *then*).

    1. ☑ Sally went home for a nap, then decided to stay awake.

    2. ☑ When Sally went home, she took a nap before dinner (comma after introductory clause).

    3. ✖ Going home was not her first choice, but once she made the decision she took a nap. (Needs a comma before *but* because it's a coordinating conjunction joining two independent clauses, and it needs one after *but* to offset the nonessential phrase that follows.)

    3. ☑ Going home was not her first choice, but once she made the decision, she took a nap.

    4. ☑ Bob went to the store and bought some ice cream and cake. (No comma is necessary.)

    5. ☑ The dog that bit me, the German shepherd, is right over there. (Commas surround the nonessential phrase.)

Chapter Thirty

ANSWERS TO QUIZ 2

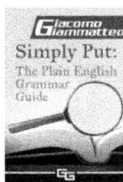

*a*nswers To Quiz Two

1. ✅ I went to the store and got some milk.

2. ✖ When I visited Italy I returned with limoncello. (It needs a comma after *Italy*.)

2. ✅ When I visited Italy, I returned with limoncello.

3. ✖ We vacationed in Europe, and bought a lot of clothes (no comma necessary).

3. ✅ We vacationed in Europe and bought a lot of clothes.

4. ✖ I went to Italy to see the sights, but also the people (no comma necessary).

4. ✅ I went to Italy to see the sights but also the people.

5. ✖ I took a train from Rome to Naples and while on the train, I saw Sofia Loren. (Comma is necessary after Naples because *and* is a coordinating conjunction connecting independent clauses, and commas enclose the nonessential phrase "while on the train.")

5. ✅ I took a train from Rome to Naples, and, while on the train, I saw Sofia Loren.

Chapter Thirty-One

ANSWERS TO QUIZ 3

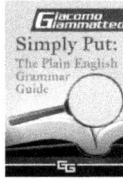

*a*nswers To Quiz Three

    1. ✖ I love Italian pastries such as, *cannoli*, *sfogliatelle*, and *pizzelle*. (The comma does *not* go after "such as"; it goes after *pasties*.)

    1. ☑ I love Italian pastries, such as *cannoli*, *sfogliatelle*, and *pizzelle*.

☑ I love Italian food, such as ravioli, lasagna, and gnocchi.

☑ I love Italian food, such as ravioli, lasagna, and gnocchi, but not dishes that include seafood.

Chapter Thirty-Two
ANSWERS TO QUIZ 4

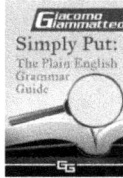

*A*nswers To Quiz 4

☑ The dog was panting because it had just chased the mailman.

☑ You'll go to the beach when I say you can, young man.

☑ You can't go to the beach, and it's because I said so.

☑ Cell phones, which were a rarity even in the '90s, are now everywhere.

☑ Barbara earned fifty dollars for babysitting, but she spent it all on eyeliner and makeup.

Chapter Thirty-Three

ANSWERS TO QUIZ 5

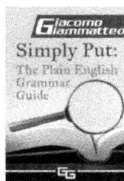

*A*nswers To Quiz 5

☑ Bill turned to Jean. "That's what she told me. She said, 'Do it, or else,' and so I did it."

☑ We should stop and visit Maggie; she lives in Washington D.C.

☑ My kids loved the song "Who Let the Dogs Out?"

☑ Is the traffic bad in D.C.?

☑ Traffic is bad in D.C.!

nswers To Quiz 6

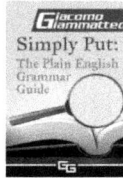

- The onset of the clinical trial showed patients' tolerance for the new drug as "unacceptable"; the conclusion was quite different.

First, *patients* is plural, and it ends in *s*, so the apostrophe goes after it. Second, the semicolon goes *outside* the quotation marks because that's where semicolons go.

- The third chart from the left (see figure two) is the correct one.

Remember, do not capitalize what's inside a parentheses if it's not a complete sentence. (And there are exceptions to that.)

Chapter Thirty-Five

ANSWERS TO QUIZ 7

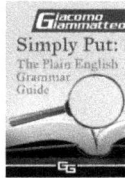

Glacoma Glammatteo
Simply Put:
The Plain English
Grammar
Guide

A **nswers To Quiz 7.**

☑ Bob and his dog *do* everything together. (Both of them do it—Bob *and* his dog.)

☑ My mom, as well as my dad, *is* going to the party. (It's my mom going to the party; she's just bringing Dad along with her.)

☑ *There's* a lot to do before we're done. (There *is a lot to do* . . .)

☑ He, my sister, and my dad *jog* every morning. (It's the three of them who *jog*, not just *he*.)

Chapter Thirty-Six

ANSWERS TO QUIZ 8

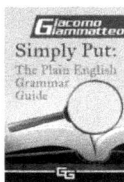

Answers To Quiz 8

☑ He said he'd go to the theater (Will he?).

☑ "She said (at least, I think she said), 'Let's go to the beach.' "

☑ We saw a koala bear (have you ever seen one?) when we went to the zoo.

Remember, for punctuating around parentheses, say the sentence without the parenthetical expression, then punctuate it. So the last sentence would be punctuated as if it had been written:

• We saw a koala bear when we went to the zoo.

Chapter Thirty-Seven

ANSWERS TO QUIZ 9

Q uiz 9

- **One goes with C.**
- **Two goes with A.**
- **Three goes with B.**

As you can see by the green checks, all the sentences are considered correct. But *correct* doesn't mean that's what you want.

Let's look closer at each sentence and what it means.

Only you may eat meat on Fridays.

In this sentence, you're saying that you and you alone are allowed to eat meat on Fridays. No one else may eat meat.

You may eat *only meat* on Fridays.

In the third sentence, you're saying you may eat meat on Fridays, but only meat; in other words, you can't eat any other food.

You may eat meat *on Fridays only*.

By placing *only* at the end of the sentence, we put more emphasis on *Fridays*; in other words, we are saying you may eat meat on Fridays, but only on Fridays.

Let's look closely at a few different examples. When you place *only* in front of the subject (the person or thing doing the action), you are placing the emphasis there. The following example shows that.

- Only *I* like swimming at the beach.

In this sentence, you are saying that *you* are the only person who likes to swim at the beach. (It must be nice to have it all to yourself.)

When you place *only* before the verb, it emphasizes the verb.

- I only *like* swimming at the beach.

This is an odd construction, but technically it means that you *only like* swimming at the beach; in other words, you don't *hate* swimming or even *dislike* it. You only *like* it.

When the adverb *only* is before the noun used as an object (after the verb), it once again changes the meaning of the sentence.

- I like only *swimming* at the beach.

In this example, we're saying you like *swimming* at the beach, but you like *only swimming*, not volleyball, or surfing, or even playing games at the arcades.

When *only* is placed at the end of the sentence (after the phrase "at the beach"), it changes the meaning yet again.

- I like swimming *at the beach* only.

With *only* in this position, you're saying that you like swimming, but *at the beach only*.

I HOPE THIS SHOWS YOU THE IMPORTANCE OF CAREFULLY positioning your adverbs. Not all adverbs have the effect that *only* does, but there are others: *just, merely,* and *simply* are a few of them.

Part Nine

HOW TO PUNCTUATE DIALOGUE

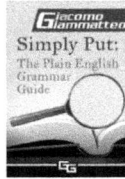

This is not advice on creating good dialogue. This section deals with the specifics of how to punctuate dialogue. A later chapter deals with how to capitalize dialogue.

Chapter Seventy-Seven

PUNCTUATING DIALOGUE

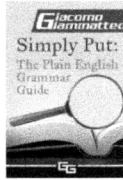

*H*ow to **Punctuate Dialogue**

I've written about dialogue several times: how to capitalize it and how to use dialogue tags. Today, we'll talk about how to properly punctuate it.

Many writers will tell you that writing realistic dialogue is one of the bigger challenges when putting together a novel. It's difficult to make the dialogue sound realistic without boring the readers. Part of the trick to doing it right is to ensure it is punctuated properly.

As I've said many times, punctuation is critical to a comfortable and enjoyable read.

Dialogue is critical to a good novel. It not only moves your plot along, it is one of the bigger factors in developing character, which, in my opinion, is key to a good novel.

How do you punctuate dialogue? It's both easier and more difficult than you may think.

Dialogue consists of the words that a character speaks, and those words are always enclosed in quotations. The words need to be spoken aloud, but even if they're whispered or mumbled, the quotations are needed.

- "You can't go to the party," Sean's father said.
- Sean's father said, "You can't go to the party."

If one of your characters is simply thinking something, use italics to designate that.

- *I shouldn't let him go to the party*, Sean's father thought.

If you want to get rid of the "Sean's father thought" part, try using a beat first to clue the reader as to who's speaking.

- Sean's father got up from the chair and paced. *I shouldn't let him go to the party.*

We'll discuss capitalizing dialogue in the chapter dealing with capitalization; instead, let's concentrate on the other punctuation.

Going back to the first example, notice the punctuation following "party" is *inside* the quotation marks. Remember, periods and commas *always* go inside the quotation marks in American English (with almost no exceptions).

Also note in the second sentence there is a comma following "said." That's because it introduces a direct quotation—Sean's father saying "You can't go to the party."

- Sean sulked for a moment, then said, "I don't care what you said. I'm going!"
- His father glared. "What did you say, young man?"

In the two examples above, the exclamation point and the question mark were also inside the quotation marks because they were part of the sentences.

Dialogue Interrupted, and Then Continued by the Same Speaker

- As Sean left the room, his father slammed his fist on the

table and said, "I'll tell you what I should have done . . ."
He took a few deep breaths and a sip of wine. "I should
have grounded his ass."

No matter if dialogue is continued by the same speaker (as
above) or by someone else, the quotation marks are used as they
always are.

Whenever you are addressing someone directly, use a comma
before their name even if it's a nickname (though not a term of
endearment).

- "Sean, you'll do *what* I say, and you'll do it *when* I say it."
- Sean mock-saluted his father, then went to his room. His
  brother was watching TV and looked over when Sean
  came in.
- "I heard you and Dad arguing. What did he say?"
- "He said, 'You'll do *what* I say, and you'll do it *when* I say
  it.' "

Let's analyze this exchange of dialogue and see why it was punctuated the way it was.

- "Sean, you'll do *what* I say, and you'll do it *when* I say it."

This one is easy, the entire quote is in quotations. "Sean" is
offset with a comma because he is being spoken to. There is a
comma after "say" because the punctuation is following the rules
for sentences using *connecting* words (and) when followed by independent clauses. (you'll do it when I say it.) And the period at the
end is *inside* the quotation marks because that's where periods go.

- Sean mock-saluted his father, then went to his room. His
  brother was watching TV and looked over when Sean
  came in.
- "I heard you and Dad arguing. What did he say?"

- "He said, 'You'll do *what* I say, and you'll do it *when* I say it.' "

Sentence two and three should be self-explanatory. In sentence three, "Dad" was capitalized. The chapter dealing with capitalization of dialogue will explain that.

Sentence four is full of things to analyze. The sentence is surrounded by quotation marks, and the comma after "He said" is there because it is introducing an indirect quote. (Sean is telling his brother what his father said, word for word.) "You'll" is preceded by a single quotation mark because that's what you do with a quote within a quote (at least in American English). The comma after "say" is the same as in sentence one, as is the period.

The single quotation mark after "it" closes out the indirect quote. There is a *half space* following the single quotation mark and before the double quotation mark.

That took up a lot of space, but I hope it was clear.

Nicknames

- "Mom, is there any cake left?"
- "You know what I said, young man. No cake until we get to Uncle Bob's."

In the sentences above, notice that a comma follows "Mom" even though it's not her true name. It also precedes "young man."

Dialogue That Continues for More Than One Paragraph

When you have a long passage of dialogue, and it continues for more than one paragraph, you do not use closing quotation marks on the first paragraph, but you do open the second with quotation marks. Below is an example.

Detective Cinalli paced, frustrated with his officer's action. "You can't pass judgment on someone because you *think* he's guilty.

"It's not right, and it's against the law. I don't want to hear of anything like this again. Understood?"

There are a few things that a writer can change and attribute it to a style choice, but it would be wise to conform to what are considered the accepted rules.

No matter what though, be consistent.

Summary

We covered the placement of semicolons, colons, and em dashes with quotation marks in an earlier chapter, so let's move on to punctuating dialogue tags.

Chapter Seventy-Eight

PUNCTUATING DIALOGUE TAGS

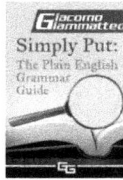

Good dialogue is key to an enjoyable book, and proper punctuation is key to good dialogue.

I've mentioned previously that I don't believe in writing rules. I view "writing rules" and even grammar rules as guidelines. The grammar ones I adhere to almost all the time, but that may be because I agree with them.

There is one grammar rule that I am not such a staunch supporter of though, and we'll discuss that now.

This is a rule we've already discussed in the chapter on commas. It is implied as part of "rule number two."

Use a comma before a coordinating conjunction that connects two independent clauses.

The flip side of this rule is that you *do not* use a comma if a coordinating conjunction (connecting word) is used to connect clauses other than independent ones. Following that rule, in the following sentences, the first *would not* require a comma and the second one would.

- She went to the bank and made a deposit.
- She went to the bank, and she made a deposit.

To me, commas imply a sequence of events:

- Honey, would you please stop at the hardware store, pick up our prescriptions, and get some milk.

That request indicates a sequence in the actions that need to be performed. She wants him to go to the hardware store, pick up the prescriptions, and *then* stop and get milk.

The example consists of three things in the list, so it needs commas; however, even if it had only two things, I feel it would be better with a comma.

- Honey, would you pick up a hammer while you're out, and get a gallon of milk, please.

When I read this, I can picture the husband stopping to get the hammer and then stopping to get the milk. And when things like this occur with dialogue, it seems like even more of a sequence. Look at the following.

- "I'm not staying here any longer!" she said and slammed the door.

This is the way the above sentence *should* be punctuated. But I view the sentence written that way as a woman standing with the door half open and shouting that she isn't staying there any longer.

I prefer to use a comma in cases like this, especially if I'm trying to convey a different sequence of events.

- "I'm not staying here any longer!" she said, and slammed the door.

When I read the same sentence *with* a comma, I picture her making the statement (possibly even in another room), and *then* slamming the door as she left.

I realize I could have easily said, "and then" or even "then," but there are times when I don't want to use that construction so often.

My solution to this is simple. I use a comma in cases where an example like that occurs within a dialogue tag, and I adhere to the rules when it doesn't, such as the example with the bank deposit. The main thing is I do it consistently.

Part Ten

CAPITALIZATION

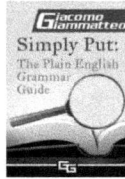

Overuse of capitalization has become a major issue, especially in business writing. I think people often capitalize in an effort to draw attention to the word or words they're using, regardless if it's correct.

Or maybe it's to draw attention to themselves?

Chapter Seventy-Nine

GENERAL CAPITALIZATION

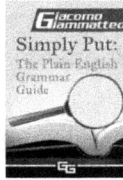

Knowing when to capitalize and when not to capitalize is an important part of writing. One thing that makes it difficult to master is the ever-changing rules, not to mention the disagreement between style guides and dictionaries. That's why it's important to select a style guide and a dictionary you like, and then stick with them. Don't begin a book using CMOS and switch to AP at the halfway point.

This chapter *is not* intended to be a comprehensive list of all capitalization rules, covering all circumstances. It is meant to address the more common problems. For everything else, you should consult your favorite dictionary or style guide.

Without further ado, let's move on to the general rules.

Rule Number One

The first rule is simple:

1. Start each sentence with a capital letter.

You wouldn't think so, but even this rule has exceptions. There are a few words (usually brand names) that the companies spell with the initial letters as lowercase letters. A few of them are: iPhone, iPad, iCloud, iMac, eBay, etc.

The suggested way to deal with this is to rewrite the sentence so those words do not begin it, but if it *does* begin the sentence, a writer may choose to either capitalize it anyway or stick to the company's suggested formatting and keep it lowercase. Examples follow.

- iPhones have become the best-selling phone of all time.
- According to Apple, iPhones have become the best-selling phones of all time.
- IPhones have become the best-selling phones of all time.

If it were me, I'd choose to rewrite (example two). I don't like the lowercase *i* to begin the sentence nor do I like the look of *IPhone*. The spelling of *iPhone* with a lowercase *i* is so recognizable that capitalizing the *I* looks out of place.

Rule Number Two

Capitalize names of family members, including nicknames.

- Uncle Ralph was one of my favorite uncles.

Note that both *uncle* and *Ralph* are capitalized (because *uncle* is part of Ralph's name in that circumstance, but *uncles* is not capitalized. A few more examples may help.

- "Mom, may I go to the mall?"
- "I went to the mall with Mom."
- "She's going to the mall with her mom."

In the first sentence, *Mom* is being addressed. In the second, *Mom* is a substitute for her name (whatever that may be), and in the third, neither of those situations apply. We're simply referring to *her* mom.

If you use a personal pronoun with a person's nickname, it

doesn't require capitalization unless that nickname is being used as part of the person's name. Examples follow.

- my mom.
- Mom
- her uncle.
- her Uncle Ralph.
- his aunt.
- his Aunt Sally.

Rule Number Three

1. Capitalize titles as a part of a name (preceding the name, not coming after it)

☑ Senator Ted Ingles did not attend the rally.

☑ Ted Ingles, senator from Texas, did not attend the rally.

✖ Ted Ingles, Senator from Texas, did not attend the rally.

Rule Number Four

Do not capitalize a title if it is used as a general reference without the name.

☑ The president will not be coming tonight.

✖ The President will not be coming tonight.

Some style guides make allowances if *president* is being used to refer to the U.S. President, but not others.

- The president of Google just retired.
- Zimbabwe's president lands at Dulles airport tomorrow.

Rule Number Five

1. Capitalize when used in direct address.

☑ It's nice to meet you, Congressman.

☑ Senator, how nice to meet you.

✗ May I see you privately, detective?
✓ May I see you privately, Detective?

Rule Number Six

1. Capitalize proper nouns as well as adjectives derived from proper nouns.

Examples:

- The Statue of Liberty
- The Brooklyn Bridge
- Italy
- San Francisco
- The King James Bible

The list of proper nouns is extensive, including names of people, specific places, companies, days of the week, months, manmade structures with names, specific geographic locations, cities, states, provinces, countries, islands, celestial bodies, works of art, museums, streets and roads, religions, names of deities, ethnicities, etc. Some examples follow.

- Washington Monument
- Mount Rushmore
- Mars (but not moon or sun)
- Venus (but not moon or sun)
- Baynard Boulevard
- Kansas
- Austin
- Africa
- Sicily
- East Coast
- the Hamptons (some people capitalize "the" before the name, but it should be lowercased.)
- the Atlantic Ocean

- the Amazon River
- Lake Superior
- The Hague (one of the few instances where *the* is capitalized)
- Apple
- Microsoft
- the Baltic Sea
- World War II
- the Constitution
- Napoleon
- Friday
- January
- Houston Chronicle
- Pittsburgh Penguins
- Texas Rangers
- Coca Cola
- Congress
- Hinduism
- Buddha
- Bible
- Caucasian
- Oriental

I listed "The Hamptons" and "the Atlantic Ocean" and many others preceded by *the*.

Even though *the* is frequently, if not always, preceding the proper noun, it is seldom capitalized. *The Hague* is one of the only examples I can think of when i *the* is capitalized related to a place name.

The list goes on and on. One exception to the rule mentioned earlier regarding names is this:

If a title is mentioned, and that title refers to a specific high-ranking executive of the government—and *only* to that person—you capitalize it.

- Secretary of State
- Speaker of the House
- The President of the United States

Rule Number Seven
When referring to animals capitalize the part of the breed that is a proper noun; otherwise use lowercase.

- German shepherd
- Irish wolfhound
- English bulldog
- boxer
- cocker spaniel
- Bengal tiger
- California Condor
- Maine coon
- Kodiak bear
- Texas longhorn

Great Dane, Great Pyrenees, Old English sheepdog, and Bracco Italiano are exceptions, along with a few others. Every source I checked had them listed as "Great Dane" or "Great Pyrenees," or "Bracco Italiano," all with capitalized first words, but I couldn't find a reason. The only reason I could think of is that the first names are considered part of the name, just like *general* in "General Patton" would be capitalized.

If you wanted to tell someone they had a *great* German shepherd, that would be okay, but it would look odd to say *great great Dane*. If it were capitalized though, as in *great Great Dane*, it wouldn't look out of place.

Following the theory that the capitalization follows the way a dog is named, I'm guessing "Miniature Australian Shepherd" would also be capitalized, although I couldn't find a resource to back that up.

In all the other breeds I checked, the word that required capitalization occurred first: Irish setter, German shepherd, Anatolian shepherd, etc.

One more exception I found goes against the rules the other way: *dalmatian* is often seen with no capital. Many dictionaries list is as lowercase, though there is typically a note that it is often seen capitalized. But why it's not capitalized is beyond me because it derives its name from Dalmatia, a region of Croatia, so by all accounts it should be capitalized.

The only possible explanation is that some people have suggested the origin of the breed was not Dalmatia, but ancient Egypt or another part of the Mediterranean Sea, which would seem to negate the capitalization based on a geographic region. However, I don't know if I agree. The rule says if a breed was named after a region to capitalize it. It doesn't say it had to have originated in the region.

There is a lot of contention regarding this capitalization of all breeds. Many people do not follow the suggestion, including most who are associated with the American Kennel Club. (They capitalize all recognized breeds.)

The results of two Google Ngram searches are below. One shows Great Dane, great Dane, German shepherd, and German Shepherd. The second shows English sheepdog, English Sheepdog, Great Pyrenees, great Pyrenees, Yorkshire Terrier, and Yorkshire terrier.

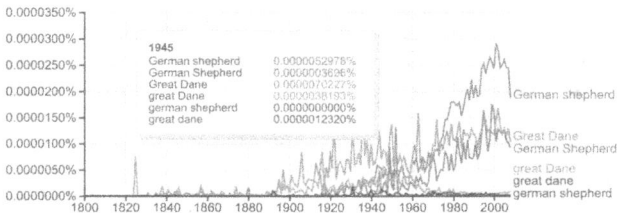

Great Dane, German shepherd

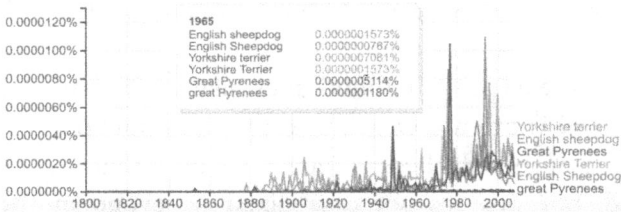

	1965	
	English sheepdog	0.0000001573%
	English Sheepdog	0.0000000787%
	Yorkshire terrier	0.0000007081%
	Yorkshire Terrier	0.0000001573%
	Great Pyrenees	0.0000005114%
	great Pyrenees	0.0000001180%

English sheepdog, Yorkshire terrier, Great Pyrenees

The Google Ngram searches reflect the style guide rules for the most part, however, when you analyze social media (Facebook posts and blogs) they paint a different picture, and the capitalization used is much closer to that supported by the AKC.

The capitalization of dog, cat, and horse breeds, etc., is so widespread that I don't see it presenting a problem—as long as you're consistent.

For a more comprehensive look at capitalization of all breeds of animals, see the animal breed section.

Rule Number Eight

Capitalize food names only when they contain a proper noun.

- Italian dressing
- Louisiana hot sauce
- Kentucky Fried Chicken (now KFC)

In some cases, there are exceptions to this also. Examples follow, and they are all from major dictionaries.

- Caesar salad
- Brussels sprouts
- Waldorf salad
- french fries
- Boston cream pie
- napoleon

A curious person might wonder why it isn't "French Fries." I looked this up in several dictionaries. Most of them had it listed as lowercase, although a few had it capitalized as an option. I found one dictionary that had the capitalized version listed first and the lowercase as the option.

As far as *napoleon* goes, I didn't understand why it wasn't capitalized either.

I continued researching, determined to uncover the truth. After much work, I finally found an explanation, and not only for the napoleon but french fries as well.

Napoleon

I had always known what a *napoleon* was, but I associated it with the emperor, Napoleon. Little did I realize the name came from my ancestral city of Naples.

The *napoleon,* for those of you who don't know, *is a* flaky pastry layered with custard and icing. The dessert's original name was a *napolitain*, referring to its origin (the city of Naples, Italy). Below or on the next page is a picture of a napoleon.

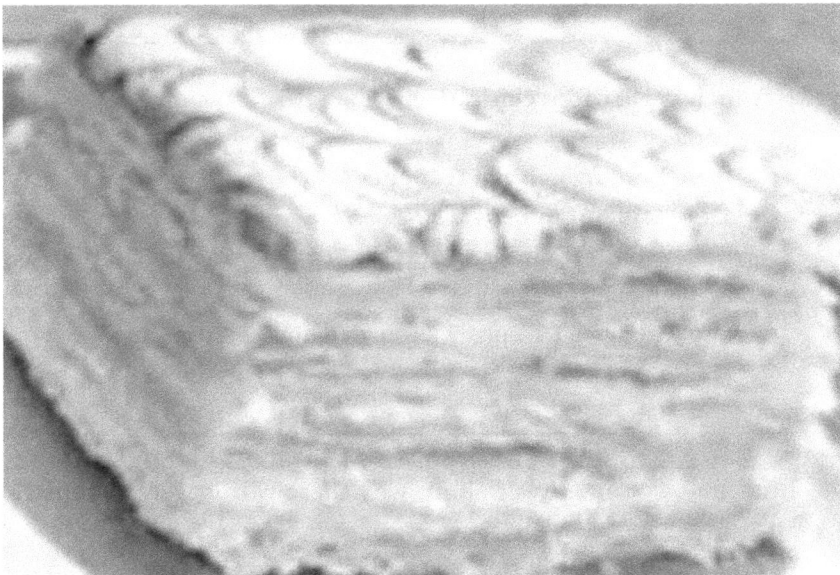

I found out the history of "napoleons," but I still don't understand why they're not capitalized if they were named after Naples—that is a proper noun.

Now to address the issue with "french fries." It wasn't until I looked for information regarding the napoleons and why they weren't capitalized, that I discovered the following about french fries.

There doesn't seem to be concrete evidence, but what I found persuaded me enough so that I included it.

One version states that "french fries" was a dish invented in Belgium and had been a popular food source for years. During WWI, American soldiers were introduced to these "fried potatoes," and since the people spoke French, the Americans named the dish "french fries."

Another version is that they are so named because the potatoes are *frenched,* not because they're a French invention. I hesitated when I read this because I was not familiar with the word *frenched.*

I looked it up in several dictionaries, finding it in *Merriam-Webster's.* Below is the definition.

---

french verb, often capitalized
\ 'french \
frenched; frenching; frenches
Definition of *french* *transitive verb*
: to trim the meat from the end of the bone of (something, such as a chop)
: to cut (green beans) in thin lengthwise strips before cooking

---

I not only got an answer about why these words weren't capitalized, I learned a lot as well.

Rule Number Nine

Capitalize the first word in a complete quotation, even if it occurs in mid-sentence.

- John Paul Jones is reputed to have said, "Give me liberty or give me death."

Rule Number Ten
Capitalizing academic degrees and job titles

The *Chicago Manual of Style* (CMOS) recommends writing academic degrees in lower case except when directly preceding or following a name. Proper nouns, of course, should still be capitalized.

Examples:

- Carlos is pursuing a bachelor of science in civil engineering.
- Carlos is pursuing a bachelor of arts in English.
- He introduced Jennifer Miller, Master of Fine Arts.
- He introduced Master of Fine Arts Jennifer Miller.

There is agreement, however, that *abbreviations* of academic degrees are to be capitalized. CMOS recommends omitting periods unless required for tradition or consistency (BA, BS, MA, MS, PhD), but AP prefers retaining the periods (B.A., B.S., M.A., M.S., Ph.D.).

Another exception to the rule is that CMOS makes allowances for degrees listed on business cards or used on résumés when cited as the degree achieved (and not in running text).

Capitalize degrees on business cards, on diplomas, or when displayed in a directory or resume. Lowercase them in running text, where they are almost always generic in nature. Some contexts—especially in an academic publication or in advertising—suggest that a specific degree is being named, and it's common to capitalize: "All applicants for the Master's in Cerebral Cosmetic Surgery should send $24,000 in unmarked bills to the Bob's Your Uncle Online University at the address below." But even then, a master's in cerebral cosmetic surgery is generic in that anyone with the cash can have one, so lowercasing it (per *Chicago* style) would also be fine.

— CMOS

Rule Number Eleven

Titles of works

There are several ways to approach this topic, and there are numerous rules associated with it. The easiest one I've found seems to suffice for almost all situations. The following list consists of the words *not* to capitalize in titles of books, songs, movies, and other works of art.

- *a, an, and, at, but, by, for, in, nor, of, on, or, out, so, the, to, up,* and *yet.*

All other words, you capitalize (as well as *any* word (even if in the above list) that is the first or last words in the title).
- Capitalize the title's first and last word.
- Capitalize all adjectives, adverbs, and nouns.
- Capitalize all pronouns (including *it*).
- Capitalize all verbs, including the verb *to be* in all forms (*is, are, was, has been*, etc.).
- Capitalize *no, not,* and the interjection *O* (e.g., *How Long Must I Wait, O Lord?*).
- Do not capitalize an article (*a, an, the*) unless it is first or last word in the title.

The following title would be capitalized like this.

✅ The Time for Peace Is Up.

not

❌ the Time for Peace Is up.

☑ Of Mice and Men
✗ of Mice and Men

• Do not capitalize a **coordinating conjunction** (a connecting word), such as *and, or, nor, but, for, yet, so,* unless it is first or last in the title.

• Do not capitalize the word *to,* with or without an infinitive, unless it is first or last in the title.

There are other rules governing how to cite works of art. Some should be in italics, some enclosed with quotation marks, and some should be underlined. For a comprehensive list, I suggest you refer to the style guide you use because they may differ.

Capitalization with geographical terms (compass points)

There are a lot of rules related to capitalizing geographical terms, but the ones mentioned below should suffice for most issues. We'll cover it in more detail later.

If you're using north, south, east, northeast, etc., to indicate a direction, use lowercase, however, if you're using those words to indicate a specific region, they should be capitalized. Examples follow.

- I gave my sister directions to come visit me: go south for about six hundred miles, and when you see a sign that says "Welcome to the South," turn right.
- To reach the beach, drive south for an hour, then go east for two hours.
- He lives on the Eastern Shore (a specific spot in MD).
- She moved to the West Coast, not the Ivory Coast.
- He was born in the Mid Atlantic, but he moved to the Midwest about two years ago.
- It was easy to tell who was speaking; he has a noticeable Southern accent.

Heavenly bodies

Earth is lowercase except when used as a proper noun.

☑ The third planet from the sun is the *Earth*.

☑ He loves the cool, moist feeling of digging through *earth* when he plants things.

☑ The *Earth* is one of eight planets in our solar system. (They used to say there were nine.)

✗ He's a down-to-Earth person.

✗ Mary? She's the salt of the Earth.

In both of the examples above, *earth* should be lowercase.

Capitalization when dealing with race

Capitalize the names of races, nationalities, tribes, etc.: Italian, German, Caucasian, Japanese, Chinese, Middle Eastern, Oriental, but you would use lowercase with terms like *black* or *white*.

Company names

Capitalize company names the same way you would individual names. Also abbreviate and capitalize *corporation (corp.), incorporated (inc.), limited (ltd.)*, etc., when those words are used following the name.

- 3M Company
- Abbott Laboratories
- American Express Company
- AT&T Corp.
- Bank of America Corporation

You keep the capitalization even if you don't use *Co., Corp., Inc., Ltd.*, etc., when following the names.

- Apple Inc.
- Apple
- General Motors Company
- General Motors
- Samsung Electronics Co., Ltd.
- Samsung

Capitalization of brand names

Capitalize company names as well as recognized brand names: Apple, Google, Coca Cola, Cadillac, etc., but also the following.

- Band-Aid
- Bubble Wrap
- Chapstick
- Crock-Pot
- eBay
- Frisbee
- iPhone
- iPad
- Jacuzzi
- Jeep
- Kevlar
- Kleenex
- Kool-Aid
- Memory Stick
- Onesies
- Popsicle
- Post-it
- Q-tip
- Rollerblade
- Scotch Tape
- Sharpie
- Styrofoam
- Teflon
- Tupperware

Note how three of the products are lowercase: *iPhone, iPad,* and *eBay.* That's because the companies want them formatted that way. It's part of their brand strategy.

There are many more words that require capitalization, but these are some of the more common ones. If you suspect an item may be a brand name, check with your dictionary or do an online search before committing to a course of action.

Capitalization with roads

Capitalize the names of specific roads, highways, turnpikes, etc.

- U.S. Route 66
- Interstate 95
- Pennsylvania Turnpike
- Baltimore Parkway

But you'd write the following examples in lowercase.

- I take the *turnpike* from Philadelphia to Pittsburgh.
- Is there an *interstate* that goes to Atlanta?
- I need to drive to California, but I'd like to go via U.S. *highways*, not *interstates*.

Government organizations, political parties, names of specific courts, etc., are all capitalized.

- Grand Old Party (GOP)
- The Supreme Court
- Yellowstone National Park
- Big Bend National Park
- Federal Bureau of Investigation
- Central Intelligence Agency

Political parties

You capitalize political organizations, such as the Republican Party, the Democratic Party, the Libertarian, etc. But you don't capitalize the words when used in the common sense.

- "He's a lifelong *democrat*"
- "She always votes *republican*."
- For the first time they both voted *democratic*.

- "She's a long-time member of the *Republican Party*."
- "He campaigns relentlessly for the *Democratic Party*."

If used jointly or in the plural sense though, the word *party* or *parties* would not be capitalized because it would no longer be a part of the name as it would not be connected. It is much like the reasoning why a word may lose its capitalization when a comma or other words come between it and the named party. Let's look at a few examples.

- The presidential candidates all come from the Democratic or Republican *parties*.
- The Potomac and Shenandoah *rivers*.
- The Budget and Finance *committees*.

AP Stylebook suggests lowercasing any title that is separated from a person's name.

- When Obama was president, there were kids in the White House for the first time in years.
- As the former chairman of Apple, Steve Jobs wielded his power mercilessly.

Names of Organizations or Institutions

- American Diabetes Association
- American Medical Association
- American Cancer Society
- The Mystery Writers Guild

But you'd say, "He's a member of a medical association or "She donates to various cancer societies."

Awards and medals

Capitalize named awards, medals, military decorations, etc.

- Heisman Trophy
- Academy Award
- Golden Globe
- Medal of Honor
- Purple Heart
- Pulitzer Prize

Room

Capitalize *room* only when used with the number of the room or if it is part of the name.

- The wedding was held in the *Green Room*.
- The reception will be held in the *Bridal Room*.
- The White House has had many famous guests stay in the *Lincoln Room*.
- Governor Adams is in *Room 477*.
- *Room 1212* is reserved for Ms. Marsano.

But if referring to multiple rooms, it isn't capitalized (when *rooms* follows the proper nouns):

- The ceremonies were held in the Green and Gold rooms.

But if that's reversed, *rooms* is capitalized.

- Remember to reserve Rooms #412, #615, and #1410 for the senators, according to their request.

Also to note, if a letter is joined to the room number, it isn't hyphenated.

- Room *A17* is available.
- He always requests Room *1010B*.

Chapter Eighty

CAPITALIZING DIALOGUE

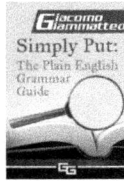

*D*ialogue Interrupted by a Dialogue Tag
Dialogue is often interrupted by a tag and then continues after the tag in the same sentence. You *do not* capitalize the dialogue when you start again if it is a continuation of the original dialogue.

- "Sean cared for you," she said, "but you didn't love him."

- "Sean cared for you," she said, biting her tongue, "but you didn't love him."

- "Sean cared for you," she said, biting her tongue. "Despite that, you threw his love away."

As you can see—in the first two sentences—the dialogue picked back up without capitalization. In the third sentence, however, "despite" was capitalized because it was the start of new dialogue, not a continuation of the previous dialogue.

Also note that the comma after "tongue" in the second sentence was changed to a period in the third to indicate the end of that sentence.

Do not capitalize the dialogue tag unless it starts a new sentence or if it's a proper noun.

- "Let him go," she said. "He didn't do anything."
- "Let him go." She should have known they'd blame him.

Note in the first sentence "she" is lowercase, but in the second sentence, "she" is capitalized. It is capitalized in the second example because it starts a new sentence.

Capitalization with dialogue is not much different from other writing, but there are a few areas to watch out for.

Capitalization in Dialogue

Dialogue is one of the areas that makes authors stumble, especially new authors. Don't let it. It's not that difficult. We briefly discussed dialogue tags earlier; now we'll talk a little about how to capitalize when using dialogue.

I know what you're thinking—my editor will catch that. And they probably will, but why make them? Why not get it right the first time? You wouldn't purposefully misspell words, would you? Then why misuse dialogue?

Now that you're convinced to do it properly, let's dig in.

Punctuating Dialogue

Dialogue is a great way to get inside your protagonist's and antagonist's heads. But some dialogue is done poorly. The wrong tags are used, the wrong punctuation, and the author either overuses a person's name or doesn't use the name enough. Then there's a problem I see all too often—how to capitalize when using dialogue.

What's different?

A lot.

Example one: You wouldn't ordinarily capitalize the word *captain*. If it began a sentence, yes, or if you referred to the person using captain as a title, such as "Captain Joseph Estelle was recently promoted," then yes.

But in dialogue, you would also capitalize it if you were addressing the person even without their full name.

- Connie walked up the stairs. "Hey, Captain. How's it going?"

The same thing goes for your parents or anyone else. If you can substitute the person's name for the term, it is capitalized. Here's another example:

- "Can I go to the mall, Mom?"

We capitalized *mom* because he could just as easily have said, "Can I go to the mall, Margaret?" He may have gotten slapped in the face, but he could have said it, and it would have made sense.

On the other hand, if you said,

- "I'm going to the mall with my mom," no capitalization is necessary.

You couldn't comfortably substitute a name for *mom*. Try it. "I'm going to the mall with my Margaret." See? It doesn't work.

That was easy, right? From now on, when writing dialogue, substitute the person's name and see if the sentence still sounds right. If it does, capitalize. If it doesn't, don't.

One more thing before we sign off.

Terms of Endearment—an Exception

There's always an exception.

Terms of endearment aren't capitalized. For example, let's say you call your husband *honey*. I know it's unlikely unless you're a newlywed, but it could happen.

You may come home from work, smell food cooking, and say,

- "Thanks for the dinner, honey."

But you wouldn't call your mother and say

- "When I got home, honey was already making dinner."

So you don't capitalize it in either case. Even though you could have substituted his name in the first instance, it has to work both ways.

Nicknames are different. They are substitutes for the real name to be used by anyone. For example, one of the characters in my book *Murder Takes Time* is named *Doggs*. That's not his real name, but when people address him, they use his nickname.

- "Give me a smoke, Doggs."
- "Hey, Doggs, you got a smoke?"

Let's assume his real name is Tony. Now, substitute *Tony* in each of the examples above.

- "Give me a smoke, Tony."
- "Hey, Tony, you got a smoke?"

As you can see, it works perfectly. No problem.

Learn this rule regarding capitalization and your editor will thank you for it.

J

O

Q

R

W

Y–Z

❀ Created with Vellum

ACKNOWLEDGMENTS

This book wouldn't have been as complete or as good without the help of Jeanne Haskin and JJ. Toner who provided a tremendous amount of feedback and valuable suggestions as well as correcting many mistakes.

I also need to thank my four grandkids, Joey, Dante, Adalina, and Carmine, who provide endless inspiration and undying support.

I also need to thank my editor, Michele Preisendorf, of Eschler Editing, for her undying patience and diligence in keeping me straight.

ABOUT THE AUTHOR

Giacomo Giammatteo is the author of gritty crime dramas about murder, mystery, and family. He also writes non-fiction books including the No Mistakes Careers series, No Mistakes Publishing, No Mistakes Grammar, and No Mistakes Writing.

When Giacomo isn't writing, he's helping his wife take care of the animals on their sanctuary. At last count, they had forty-five animals—eleven dogs, a horse, six cats, and twenty-six pigs.

Oh, and one crazy—and very large—wild boar, who takes walks with Giacomo every day and also happens to be his best buddy.

nomistakespublishing.com
gg@giacomog.com

ALSO BY GIACOMO GIAMMATTEO

You can see all of my books here.

And you can buy them on the platform of your choice.

This brings up a thought: with more than fifty books out now, it is becoming difficult to try to update the list in the back of all of them. If you want to know what books I have out, use the link above, which takes you to my website, or download the latest copy of my GG recommended reading list, which is free.

Nonfiction :

Careers:

No Mistakes Resumes, Book I of No Mistakes Careers

No Mistakes Interviews, Book II of No Mistakes Careers

Grammar:

Misused Words, No Mistakes Grammar, Volume I

Misused Words for Business, No Mistakes Grammar, Volume II

More Misused Words, No Mistakes Grammar, Volume III

Visual Grammar (this is a compilation of volumes I–III with a bit of new information added. It also includes pictures. The world's first visual grammar book)

Misused Words and Then Some, No Mistakes Grammar, Volume V

More Grammar:

No Mistakes Grammar Bites, Volume I, Lie, Lay, Laid, and It's and Its

Fiction:

Friendship & Honor Series:

Murder Takes Time

Murder Has Consequences

Murder Takes Patience

Murder Is Invisible

Murder Is a Promise

Murder Is Immaculate (coming soon)

Blood Flows South Series:

A Bullet For Carlos: A Connie Gianelli Mystery

Finding Family, a Novella

A Bullet From Dominic

The Good Book

The Ranger (coming soon)

Redemption Series:

Necessary Decisions: A Gino Cataldi Mystery

Old Wounds

Promises Kept, the Story of Number Two

Premeditated

The Ranger (coming soon)

Rules of Vengeance Series: (Fantasy)

Light of Lights (the beginning, a novella)

A Promise of Vengeance

Undeniable Vengeance

Consummate Vengeance

Vengeance Is Mine (2019)

Note. The Light of Lights is a novella. It's about 100 pages long and sets the stage for the series. The other books in the series are between 650 and 850 pages long.

∽

OTHER BOOKS

You can always see the current and coming-soon books on my website.

Fiction:

Memories for Sale (mystery/sf)

The Joshua Citadel (SF novella)

Children's Books:

No Mistakes Grammar for Kids, Volume I—Much and Many

No Mistakes Grammar for Kids, Volume II—Lie and Lay

No Mistakes Grammar for Kids, Volume III—Bring and Take

No Mistakes Grammar for Kids, Volume IV, "Would've, Should've" and "Your and You're"

No Mistakes Grammar for Kids, Volume V, "There, They're, and Their" and "To, Too, and Two"

Shinobi Goes to School—Life on the Farm for Kids, Volume I

Fiona Gets Caught, Life on the Farm for Kids, Volume II

Coco Gets a Donut, Life on the Farm for Kids, Volume III

Squeak Gets a Home, Life on the Farm for Kids, Volume IV

Biscotti Saves Punch, Life on the Farm for Kids, Volume V

The Adventures of Adalina, Volume I, Adalina and the Five Tiny Bears

Coming Soon:

The Adventures of Adalina, Volume II, Adalina and the Underwater Bears

Get on the mailing list, and you'll be sure to be notified of release dates and sales.

Mailing list

And don't forget to leave a review!